SOCIOLOGICAL THEORY

AN INTRODUCTION

SOCIOLOGICAL THEORY

AN INTRODUCTION

WALTER L. WALLACE

Editor

HEINEMANN

London

Heinemann Educational Books Ltd

LONDON EDINBURGH MELBOURNE TORONTO
AUCKLAND SINGAPORE JOHANNESBURG
HONGKONG NAIROBI IBADAN

Cased edition   SBN 435 82914 9
Paperback edition SBN 435 82915 7

First published 1969

Published by Heinemann Educational Books Ltd
48 Charles Street, London W1X 8AH
Printed in Great Britain by
Morrison and Gibb Ltd, London and Edinburgh

ACKNOWLEDGMENTS

For this book, I especially appreciate

- The Department of Sociology at Northwestern University, which made an essential contribution simply by being a vigorous and congenial band of colleagues (it helps, to say the very least, that some of my most enjoyable friends and most persuasive critics are in this department);
- Robert K. Merton, who graciously read Part I of this book and suggested valuable modifications in it;
- Carolyn Baecker, and also Lynn Rode, who expertly, interestedly, and cheerfully typed the manuscript through most of its revisions;
- Russell Sage Foundation, which provided the time and Virginia Glickstein's and Betty Bonta's thoughtful secretarial skills to carry out the final amendments; and
- My wife and daughter, who are merely indispensable.

Naturally, the above share all blame for this book's weaknesses; I alone am responsible for whatever strengths it may still contain.

PREFACE

THE USES OF THEORY

To the extent that sociology is a scientific discipline, it may be said to consist of five parts: methods, observations, empirical generalizations, hypotheses, and theories. In order to examine the uses of theory, or of any other single part, its interrelations with the others must be shown. This is the main objective of the following discussion.[1]

Before beginning, however, certain advance qualifications of the discussion (apart from its obvious brevity and lack of fine detail) seem to be in order. First, note that although the five principal components of scientific sociology can be named separately and distinctively, actually they shade into each other—though methods may be more distinct than the rest. Even with the strictest arbitrary definitions, it is difficult or impossible to tell exactly when observations become empirical generalizations, when these become theories, when theories become hypo-theses, and when hypotheses become observations. (This continuity is reflected in the minimal, and therefore broadly inclusive, definition of "theory" that is offered early in the first part of this book.)

Second, despite these overlaps in meaning among the components, to the extent that they *can* be distinguished from one another, each component may vary internally to a large degree, and independently of the others in its form—especially in its degree of formalization. Thus, in a given study, the hypotheses or the theories may be only hinted at, while the methods, observations and generalizations may be quite clearly specified. This variability in the degree of formalization differentiates between studies that "explore" some area of social life and studies that "test" specific hypotheses, but it also emphasizes differences of degree rather than all-or-nothing differences. In other words, it does not seem to be the case that some sociological studies thoroughly implicate theory, while others are "atheoretical" and do not implicate theory at all; rather, all studies implicate theory, only some pay more deliberate, explicit, and formal attention to it while others pay more casual, implicit, informal attention. Theory, indeed, seems inescapable in sociology, as in every science.

Third, I am not concerned in this book with all sociological theories that anyone might ever have dreamed of (for example, supernatural theories of social life are left out), but only with those that have achieved a relatively high degree of formalization and explicit expression in "the sociological literature"—and indeed, only with the most widely and currently influential of these theories. On the one hand, this focus means that other theories that may still be unpublished or even deliberately "underground" are discriminated against here. But on the other hand, it follows from the inevitability of theory in sociology that to say that this book is concerned only with explicit theories in sociology is not to say that the relevance of its argument ends with those studies that make an explicit avowal of theoretic position. Even though a particular theory may have already been published, many studies that adopt its viewpoint may do so only implicitly. Therefore, although this book focuses on theories having a relatively high degree of formalization, its relevance is meant to extend to sociological studies in which such formalized theories play a highly informal role.

Now let us turn to a direct examination of relations existing among the five components of scientific sociology. Consider the diagram on page ix, which is intended to be nothing more than a skeletal outline—too idealized to convey the full intricacy, art, vitality, and intuitiveness of scientific work. In this diagram, scientific sociology is represented as a succession of manipulations of information (generally moving clockwise in the diagram), each of which is con-

trolled by a particular kind of method. One class of such methods (scaling-and-measurement) governs the manipulations involved in transforming observations into empirical generalizations; another (logical induction) governs the transformation of empirical generalizations into theories; still another (logical deduction) governs the transformation of theories into hypotheses; and the last (operationalization-and-instrumentation) governs the transformation of hypotheses into observations. (The things sociologists usually mean when we talk about "methods" are most likely to be recipes for operationalization-and-instrumentation, and for scaling-and-measurement. They are least likely to be recipes for logical induction and deduction. We generally rely on logicians—or our "common sense"—to supply these latter.)

I shall not here attempt formal definitions of all the information manipulations and methods shown in the diagram, since they are not all essential to the primary concern of this book. Instead, I shall rather loosely suggest their meaning and relations by using an illustration of the sociological process as a whole, taking Durkheim's classic study of suicide as a model.

Suppose we became interested in trying to explain suicide (a phenomenon that might seem at first glance to be individualistic in the extreme) sociologically. The first step might be to make direct observations on several persons who have committed suicide, and these observations might then (through counting and computing rates for various subcategories of such persons) be transformed into an empirical generalization like "Protestants have a higher suicide rate than Catholics." The next information transformation depends on answering two parallel questions: (1) What other distinctive characteristics do persons have in common because they are Protestants or Catholics, and that can explain the

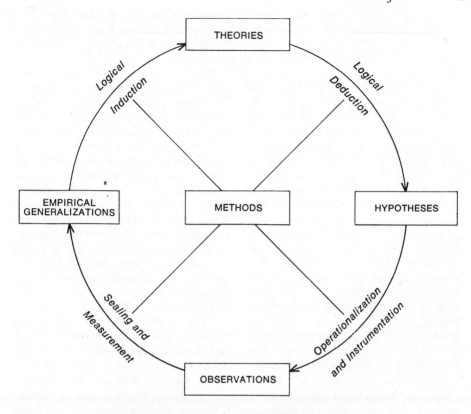

The Components and Process of Scientific Sociology.

difference in their suicide rates? In other words, *of what factor is religious affiliation a special case* when one is concerned with accounting for the suicide rate differential? (2) *Of what can the suicide rate differential itself be taken as a special case?* The two questions together ask whether the phenomenon-that-explains and the phenomenon-to-be-explained can be inductively generalized beyond their original formulation, and whether, therefore, the amount of available scientific information can be further increased. The transformation yielded by answers to these questions may be expressed in theoretic statements like "suicide rates vary inversely with degree of *social integration*" (in which only religious affiliation—the phenomenon-that-

explains—is generalized) and "acts of *personal disorganization* vary inversely with degree of *social integration*" (in which both suicide—the phenomenon-to-be-explained—and the phenomenon-that-explains are generalized). In the next three manipulations of information, hypotheses are logically deduced from theory (*e.g.*, if the theory is true, and it is assumed that unmarried persons experience less social integration than married persons, the former should have a higher suicide rate than the latter), observations and empirical generalizations to test the truth of the hypotheses are generated by operationalization-and-instrumentation and by scaling-and-measurement and then incorporated into the theory by logical induction. And so on, through one spiraling cycle around the diagram after another, as each component is improved in its turn.

But if methods serve as the principal *controls* over the way in which sociology is pursued, theories are the most powerful informational *products* of this pursuit. By this I mean that individual observations can contain only very small amounts of information about given phenomena, and empirical generalizations and hypotheses are limited to moderate amounts of information, but theories (insofar as each theory is synthesized from several different generalizations, and each empirical generalization is synthesized from several different observations) can contain the maximum amount of information. This is not to say that all theories can contain the *same* high amount of information, since, all other things being equal, a theory that is induced from two empirical generalization will contain less information than a theory induced from three such generalizations, and so on. Further, the notion that theories can be informationally very powerful does not contradict the fact that some theories are informationally very weak, either because they are based upon erroneous generalizations or because the generalizations are based on erroneous observations. In short, to say that theory *can* be the most powerful product of a scientific enterprise is to say that it has this *potential*, even though it may fall short of this potential in any actual instance. One aspect of theory's informational power is its role as information storehouse for the discipline. This implies that, although there are always "lags" between what has previously been incorporated into theory and what is being hypothesized, observed, and generalized in the discipline at any given moment, theory—insofar as it incorporates propositions having great empirical confirmation (i.e., scientific "laws") as well as propositions having relatively little confirmation—is probably

more representative of a discipline's basic store of information than are its current hypotheses, observations, or empirical generalizations.

But the scientific uses of theory extend beyond being a passive storehouse of large amounts of information; indeed, the above diagram suggests that theory itself actively performs two crucial roles in generating the information that is stored within it: (1) theory specifies the factors one should be able to measure *before* doing research (i.e., before formulating hypotheses and making observations), and (2) theory serves, *after* the research is done, as a common language into which the results (i.e., the empirical generalizations) may be translated for purposes of comparison and logical integration with the results of other researches.

These appear to be the two closely related functions of theory that Merton and Homans, respectively, have in mind. Merton writes: "It is only when ... concepts are interrelated in the form of a scheme that a theory begins to emerge. Concepts, then, constitute *the definitions (or prescriptions) of what is to be observed*; they are the variables between which empirical relationships are to be sought."[2] And Homans quotes Willard Gibbs' statement that "it is the office of theoretical investigation to give *the form in which the results of experiment may be expressed.*"[3]

One can hardly imagine uses that are more important to the Scientific Enterprise in general and to the Sociological Enterprise in particular, than these.

THE USES OF THIS BOOK

This book is an introduction to eleven (plus one "missing link") current, influential, and explicitly formulated theoretic viewpoints in sociology. It therefore describes current thinking regarding "what is to be observed" in any given future sociological investigation and regarding "the form in which the results" of such an investigation may be expressed.

In Part I of this book, I have tried to produce an accurate but highly compressed survey of the theoretic viewpoints in question, and, as a result, only their most distinctive and essential features are discussed. (The reader is directed to the footnotes for some important details that do not meet these criteria for inclusion in the text itself.) In Part II, fifteen selections from the work of major modern theorists have been assembled to illustrate or comment on the viewpoints discussed in Part I.

The aim of Part I is not merely to summarize but to systematize. The "Overview of Contemporary Sociological Theory" (1) offers a "language," or "frame of reference," or "conceptual apparatus," that can be useful in more detailed and advanced studies of sociological theory *per se*, and (2) states, as briefly, exactly and systematically as I can, the kinds of factors that sociological theory asks sociological research to address. Part I is thus intended to be a kind of "foundation" on which two competences can be built: a detailed

knowledge of sociological theory itself, and a theoretically-oriented mastery of research.

Instead of a large number of short excerpts from many authors and their works, the reader will find that Part II contains fairly long selections (with only two exceptions they are complete articles or complete chapters). In this way, the reader is encouraged to follow particular arguments in detail, acquire an appreciation of authors' styles, and, hopefully, become sufficiently intrigued to examine the rest of their work.

The readings in Part II have short editorial prefaces and are "keyed" to the basic taxonomy of varieties of sociological theory (shown in Figure 2 of Part I) so as to insure both flexibility and coherence in their use. That is, the two parts of this book may be read in sequence, or the reader may work back and forth between them, or he may focus on a particular theoretic viewpoint as it is differently treated in Part I and Part II. The keying of Part II readings to the Part I overview is thus meant to help retain the desired correspondence between them, no matter which approach the reader finds most useful at a given moment.

NOTES

1. For a similar discussion of the role of theory in sociology, see Robert K. Merton, "The Bearing of Sociological Theory on Research," and "The Bearing of Empirical Research on Sociological Theory," in *Social Theory and Social Structure* (rev. and enl.), Glencoe, Ill.: Free Press, 1957, pp. 85–117. In my view, the discussion to be presented here encapsulates Merton's essential points—some of which are left more implicit than explicit by him. For example, in the "Bearing of Theory" essay, Merton does not explicitly distinguish between empirical generalizations (which yield theories through induction) and hypotheses (which are yielded by theories through deduction), and in the "Bearing of Research" essay he does not explicitly distinguish between empirical research (hypotheses, observations, and empirical generalizations) and research findings (empirical generalizations). Arthur L. Stinchcombe, in his *Constructing Social Theories*,

New York: Harcourt, Brace and World, 1968, pp. 15–18, offers a view that is also closely related to the present one, and that also does not make some of the distinctions (e.g., between observations and empirical generalizations) that I find useful. Merton's "Notes on Problem-Finding in Sociology" in Robert K. Merton, Leonard Broom and Leonard S. Cottrell, Jr. (Eds.), *Sociology Today*, (New York: Basic Books, 1959), pp. ix–xxxiv, supplements his two "Bearing" essays and examines certain questions (e.g., the nature of scientific "problems" and rationales for addressing them) that are not explicitly dealt with in the present discussion.

2. Robert K. Merton, *op. cit.*, p. 89 (emphasis added).

3. George C. Homans, *The Human Group*, New York: Harcourt, Brace and Co., 1950, p. 441 (emphasis added).

CONTENTS

SOCIOLOGICAL THEORY
AN INTRODUCTION

PART I

OVERVIEW OF CONTEMPORARY SOCIOLOGICAL THEORY

This essay systematically introduces the reader to eleven (plus one) theoretic viewpoints from which human social phenomena are currently being investigated. The introduction is systematic in the sense that it depends on a single, multidimensional, framework for differentiating as well as integrating all eleven viewpoints.

In developing this framework, my aim has been to discover useful ways in which different types of theory complement each other, rather than ways in which they contradict each other. There are two reasons for choosing this emphasis. First are the impressions that no single current viewpoint adequately represents the full range of sociological interest; that none is wholly "right" about all aspects of social life; that each is "right" about some of these aspects;[1] and that when it comes to doing a particular research, sociological analysts often draw on several different viewpoints for hypotheses

---

[1]. Pitirim Sorokin took the more extreme view that "existing theories are mutually exclusive or contradictory only where they are wrong" ("Sociology of Yesterday, Today, and Tomorrow." *American Sociological Review* [December, 1965], 30:842).

and interpretations. These apprehensions suggest that it may not be necessary, after all, to be unswervingly loyal to one particular theory; that one may be eclectic and be neither renegade nor indecisive; that a systematic assessment of complementarities among theories may be useful in understanding the theories themselves and in applying them to empirical research. In other words, one may reasonably prefer "the Jain logic of ancient India, with its doctrine of *syadvada*: that every proposition is true only up to a point, in a manner of speaking, in certain respects, . . . [as] in the Jain legend of the seven blind men and the elephant."[2]

The second reason for emphasizing complementarities among different viewpoints rests on the rule of parsimony: when a scientific discipline has developed several theories bearing on the same problem, their number should be reduced by rejecting some and/or integrating some or all of them into a single theory expressing their common and complementary features.[3] Although emphasis on contradictions (especially contradictory predictions) between theories is required when deciding which theories to reject and which to retain, when one seeks, instead, to integrate several theories that seem equally acceptable, it is more useful to focus on their complementarities. It has been said that sociology has "too much theory." If this is so, it may be due not only to the fact that "competing conceptual systems and theories have not been adjudicated,"[4] but also to the fact that the identities and complementarities among them have not been sought out. In principle at least, the reduction of theory can proceed by condensation as

well as by elimination. Obviously, the result of any theoretic synthesis must incorporate at least its predecessors' identities and complementarities, although it need not incorporate nor seek to resolve their incompatibilities. "In an important sense, new scientific theories do not 'refute' the old ones but somehow remake them; even scientific revolutions preserve some continuity with the old order of things."[5]

Having thus chosen to concentrate on a synthetic integration of theories, my discussion is not intended to be another "summary" or "review"; still less is it intended to be a "critical essay." I shall not deal with any particular theory in full detail, and I shall not attempt systematically to evalutate or to proselytize for any theory. My aim here is severely limited: to expose and integrate the distinctive features of several current theoretic viewpoints. And it should be noted in passing that the *distinctive* features of a particular viewpoint need not be either its most *emphasized* features or its most *persuasive* features.

But granting this, there remains the problem of selecting among the undoubtedly large number of possible dimensions according to which the viewpoints in question might be classified. In the present case, I have tried to select dimensions that refer directly to the sociological subjectmatter as such, and have avoided dimensions that refer, instead, to non-sociological thought systems. That is, I have rejected philosophy of science descriptions like "positivistic," "phenomenological," "nominalistic," and "systemic," and I have also rejected discipline descriptions like "ecological," "biological," and "psy-

2. Abraham Kaplan, *The Conduct of Inquiry* (San Francisco: Chandler, 1964), p. 310. Whitehead wrote to the same effect: "All general truths condition each other" (*Process and Reality* [New York: Macmillan, 1929], p. 15).

3. For discussion of the alternation of analyzing and synthesizing periods in science, including the

speculation that sociology is about to enter a new synthesizing period, see Sorokin, *op. cit.*, pp. 833–843.

4. Wilbert E. Moore, "Sociology and Demography," in Philip M. Hauser and Otis Dudley Duncan (Eds.), *The Study of Population* (Chicago: University of Chicago Press, 1959), p. 845.

5. Kaplan, *op. cit.*, p. 304.

chological." Needless to say, I have also avoided the relatively uninformative practice of simply listing theoretic viewpoints according to the chronological order of their publication or according to the names or nationalities of their principal authors. Although several sorts of terms (including some just mentioned) will be used here to describe specific theoretic viewpoints, the terms that will be used to describe the classification of such viewpoints are of a more primitive order, more intimately tied to possible observations and less intimately tied to existing conceptual systems. I have asked, in short, What kind of direct observations does each theory imply?—rather than asking, What kind of non-sociological conceptual framework does each theory resemble?

This stress on the *observations* (and the empirical generalizations based on them) that theories indicate, of course, allows the scheme to suggest conclusions not only about theories, but also about the

design and interpretation of empirical *research*—a possibility that will be made more explicit in the "Conclusions" of this discussion.

The term "theory," in its most minimal and unqualified sense, will be taken to mean any set of symbols that is claimed verifiably to represent and make intelligible specified classes of phenomena and one or more of their relationships.[6] In one very important qualification, however, a theory is said to be "of" a particular class of phenomena when the theory is constructed in such a way as to offer an explanation of phenomena in that class (i.e., when the latter is treated as explanandum or dependent variable, regardless of what the explanans or independent variable may be.)[7] Thus, all theories of the class of phenomena called "social" treat phenomena in that class either as causal results of antecedent phenomena, or as logical deductions from higher order abstractions, or as both.[8] Through such theories of the

6. This definition can be viewed largely as a merger and condensation of Braithwaite's and Kaplan's definitions. Braithwaite says, "a scientific theory is a deductive system in which observable consequences logically follow from the conjunction of observed facts with the set of the fundamental hypotheses of the system" (p. 22). (Query: What are hypotheses?) "Scientific hypotheses, which, if true, are scientific laws, will then, for the purpose of my exposition, be taken as equivalent to generalizations of unrestricted range in space and time" (p. 12). (Query: What are generalizations?) "A generalization is a proposition asserting a universal connection between properties.... The generalization may assert a concomitance of properties in the same thing or event ... or it may assert that, of every two events or things of which the first has the property *A* and stands in the relation *R* to the second, the second has the property *B*.... Or it may make more complicated but similar assertions about three or four or more things. The relationship between the things may be a relationship holding between simultaneous events in the things, or it may hold between events in the same thing or in two or more things which are not simultaneous" (p. 9). (Richard Bevan Braithwaite, *Scientific Explanation* [New York: Harper Torchbooks, 1960].) Kaplan says, "the term 'theory' ... stands for the symbolic dimension of experience, as opposed to the apprehension of brute fact" (p. 294), and "a theory is a symbolic construction" (p. 296). (Query: Why symbolic?) "Theory puts things known into a

system.... [It makes] sense of what would otherwise be inscrutable or unmeaning empirical findings. A theory is more than a synopsis of the moves that have been played in the game of nature, it also sets forth some idea of the rules of the game by which the moves become intelligible" (p. 302). (Kaplan, *op. cit.*) Note also that although Stinchcombe does not offer a definition of "theory," his definition of a "theoretical statement" closely approximates my own. To Stinchcombe, a theoretical statement "says that one class of phenomena will be connected in a certain way with another class of phenomena" (Arthur L. Stinchcombe, *Constructing Social Theories* [New York: Harcourt, Brace & World, 1968], p. 15).

7. George C. Homans says: "A theory of a phenomenon is an explanation of it, showing how it follows as a general conclusion from general propositions in a deductive system" ("Bringing Men Back In," *American Sociological Review* [December, 1964], 29:809).

8. Strictly speaking, theoretical explanation involves deducing a lower from a higher order abstraction—whether the abstractions contain references to causation or not (see Braithwaite, *op. cit.*, esp. pp. 293–368; and Israel Scheffler, "Explanation, Prediction, and Abstraction," in Arthur Danto and Sidney Morgenbesser (Ed.), *Philosophy of Science* [Cleveland: World Publishing Co., 1960], esp. p. 285). However, it seems useful, or at least intuitively appealing, to think of logical deduction as an answer to "why" the phenomenon in question exists (i.e.,

social we are informed about why or how social phenomena occur—what brings social systems, societies, social actions and interactions, into existence, and what keeps them working. It is exclusively with this variety of social theory that I am concerned here.

There is, however, a second variety of such theory, which, despite the fact that it will not figure in the following discussion, should be mentioned for the sake of contrast. This second variety treats the social class of phenomena either as causes of postcedent phenomena, or as higher order abstractions from which other deductions are made, or as both.[9] Through such theories we are informed about the role of social phenomena in other phenomena—for example, in individual perception, individual personality formation, individual decision-making, and in physically changing the atmosphere and general face of the earth and other planets, etc. In brief, this second variety of theory treats the social as a class of phenomena-that-explain while the first variety treats the social as a class of phenomena-to-be-explained. For denotative clarity, the term "sociological" will be applied here to the first variety only. In this terminology there can be social, but not sociological, theories of individual personality or behavior.

It is obviously possible to have an extremely large number of sociological theories so defined—extending to all possible classes of all possible explanatory phenomena in all their possible relationships.[10] Even if one pays attention only to variability in the classes of possible explanatory phenomena and leaves aside variability in their relationships, a huge list can readily be imagined, with places for theories that explain the social with psychological, physiological, geographical, and technological phenomena; with electromagnetic, chemical, and gravitational phenomena; and so on and on. Of course, somewhere in this gigantic array, one would also find *social* theories of social phenomena wherein one subclass of social phenomena would be offered as the principal explanation of another.[11] Obviously, therefore, when all the theories under consideration are presumed to define a common class of phenomena-to-be-explained (in this instance the social), one major source of variation among them lies in the differences in the classes of phenomena that they propose as principal explaining phenomena.[12] The discussion below will take this variation as one of its

---

it "must" exist) and of causal production as an answer to "how" it exists (i.e., it "results").

9. In this paper, these will be considered social theories of the phenomena in question, rather than theories of social phenomena. Duncan and Schnore may be referring to this variety of theory when they speak of the "behavioral perspective" as being "centrally concerned with how the individual participates in social life" (Otis Dudley Duncan and Leo F. Schnore, "Cultural, Behavioral, and Ecological Perspectives in the Study of Social Organization," *American Journal of Sociology* [September, 1959], 65:137) [p. 72, this volume].

10. Of course, other sources of variation are the kind of symbols employed by the theories (e.g., words, mathematical notation), the kind of relationship that they propose between the dependent and independent events (e.g., causal or classificational), their degree of known correspondence to observation (i.e., their empirical confirmation), etc.

11. This, of course, is the kind of sociological theory advocated by Durkheim: "The determining

cause of a social fact should be sought among the social facts preceding it . . ." (*The Rules of Sociological Method* [Glencoe, Ill.: Free Press, 1950], p. 110). The rest of Durkheim's sentence—"and not among the states of the individual consciousness"—however, bears upon two other questions discussed below. One of these involves the explanation of social phenomena by factors that operate on social participants' environments versus factors that operate on the social participants themselves (see Figure 2 and accompanying discussion). Durkheim, in eschewing "the states of the individual *consciousness*" as explanations of social facts, gave emphasis to factors operating from without (i.e., environing "constraints"), rather than from within, social participants. Secondly, in eschewing "the states of the *individual* consciousness," Durkheim emphasized cell (d) of Figure 8, below. That is, Durkheim was urging that the sociological explanandum and the sociological explanans should be conceptualized at the same "macro" level.

12. Other aspects of explanation (for example

two central foci. My aim in this connection, then, is to construct reasonable categories for analyzing differences in the kinds of things that sociological theories take as phenomena-that-explain.

The second central focus of discusssion arises from the unfortunate and often confusing observation that sociological theories purporting to share the same class of phenomena-to-be-explained do not always do so. I refer, of course, not to the plain fact that some are theories of stratification and some are theories of socialization (for example), but to something more essential: there exist different ways of defining "the social"—fundamentally different opinions of what qualities are required before a given phenomenon can be called social.[13] The second focus of this paper, then, is on variation in the sort of phenomena thought to be eligible objects of explanation for sociological theories.

To put both foci succinctly, the discussion that follows seeks to discover the answers provided by sociological theories to two questions: (1) How is the social *defined*? (2) How is the social *explained* (i.e., by what classes of phenomena)? *Both questions are required, and joint answers to them will be sought here*, because it seems wholly inadequate to differentiate theories in terms of the

single, loose, and indefinite question of what they are "interested in," or what their "approach" is, or what they "deal with," although this is often done. The question is indefinite because, given that all scientific theories require both an explanandum and an explanans, it is apparent that two quite different theories may be equally "interested" in the same class of phenomena. That is, one theory may be interested in it as explanandum, while the other theory may be interested in it as explanans. The distinction between *kinds* of theoretic interest is therefore crucial. It is chiefly on the basis of an effort to maintain this distinction between how the social explanandum is defined and how it is explained that the present discussion is formally distinguishable from most earlier ones at classifying sociological theories.[14]

DEFINITIONS OF THE SOCIAL

All definitions of the social seem to have in common at least one statement clearly setting it apart from other phenomena: a social phenomenon is always defined in terms of interorganism behavior relations. That is, it seems generally agreed that a social phenomenon is constituted by the regular accompaniment of one organism's behavior by at least one other organism's behavior.[15]

---

the kind of relationship that is proposed as existing between explanans and explanandum) will not be considered here.

13. Thus attention is here being directed to the features that all "levels" and subtypes of the social have in common by virtue of their socialness. Distinction between, say, "social interactions', and "societies" will not be pursued until the micro-macro distinction is discussed below.

14. See, for examples, Helmut R. Wagner, "Types of Sociological Theory: Toward a System of Classification," *American Sociological Review* (October, 1963), 28:735–742; George C. Homans, "Contemporary Theory in Sociology," in Robert E. L. Faris (Ed.), *Handbook of Modern Sociology* (Chicago: Rand McNally, 1964), pp. 951–977; and Pitirim Sorokin, *Sociological Theories of Today* (New York: Harper and Row, 1966).

15. "Like an organism, a society is a system of

relations, but relations between organisms themselves rather than between cells" (Kingsley Davis, *Human Society* [New York: Macmillan, 1949], p. 26). Franz Adler, in "A Unit Concept for Sociology," *American Journal of Sociology* (January, 1960), 65, notes that "sociologists, lacking interest in behavior as such, deal with social behavior, that is, behavior items and clusters whose meaning contains the probability of their being preceded, accompanied, or followed by behavior items or clusters of other organisms. . . . Sociology may be defined as the study of this social behavior" (p. 360). This stress on interorganism behavior regularities also seems to be the basis for Sorokin's distinction between "social systems" and "social congeries" (see "Sociology of Yesterday, Today, and Tomorrow," p. 839, and *Sociological Theories of Today*, pp. 26–30). Note that the definition's mention merely of "regularities" and "accompaniment" deliberately leaves open the

But granting this as part of the boundary of common definition distinguishing sociological theory as a whole from other theory, there remain several dimensions of possible variation within that boundary. For example, the "organisms" in question may be defined as humans, termites, bees, bats, monkeys, wolves, wild dogs, gorillas, geese, fish, etc., or any of a great variety of interspecies combinations. The criterion of "regularity" may be defined in relatively simple or complex terms (analogous to the varieties of musical rhythm), with more or less statistical rigor (e.g., deliberate scaling and counting versus casual gathering of impressions), and may be set at a high or low level (i.e., the coincidence of behaviors may be "common" or "rare"). Further, the "accompaniment" of one organism's behavior by that of others may be required to be simultaneous, temporally ordered one way or another, or sequence may be irrelevant; it may be demanded that the accompaniment occur at a fast tempo, or at a slow tempo; and so on.

Of special interest here, however, is the further possibility that the kind of "behavior" that theories specify as essential to the social, and whose explanation is therefore the objective of the theories, may also vary. Again, I do not refer to the obvious fact that different "middle-range" theories, all taking homo

sapiens as the subject organism, may seek to explain voting behavior, suicidal behavior, child-rearing behavior, religious behavior, or whatever. Attention is called instead to the more abstract observation that in all such theories, and in more general or "grand" theories as well, definitions of the social fall into two types: one stresses *objective*, or overt, or motor, behavior relations, while the other stresses *subjective*, or covert, or dispositional, behavior relations. Ideally, an objective behavior definition argues that the social is to be identified according to whether the *overt* walking, waving, talking, praying, singing, eating, fighting, writing, breathing, etc. of one participant is related to some similarly objective behavior of another participant, even when such relations are not accompanied by covert or subjective behavior relations. In contrast, an equally idealized subjective behavior definition identifies the social with the *covert* perceptions, goals, sentiments, opinions, habits, desires, needs, etc. that participants hold in common, in complementarity or in conflict, even when this sharing remains latent so far as objective activity relations are concerned.[16]

In passing, it may be suggested that the difference between these definitions of the social corresponds to the difference between the Newtonian and the Weberian definitions of "action." Newton's definition of mechanical action was

question of "causation." The causes, or, more generally, explanations, of the social are thus expressly reserved for theoretical proposition and empirical test rather than pre-empted by conceptual definition.

16. Note that one other, mixed objective-subjective behavior relations, definition of the social is logically possible. Such a definition would identify the social according to whether the objective behavior of one participant is related to the subjective behavior of another participant (or vice-versa). Such a definition does not seem to have gained currency in sociology to date and therefore will not be discussed here. Of course, objective behavior relations are often explained theoretically by subjective behavior relations (e.g., social values are often said to cause social structure), and vice-versa, but this is explanation of the social, rather

than definition of the social. It may also be briefly noted that my distinction between objective and subjective definitions of the social clearly differs from that expressed in Marion J. Levy, Jr., and Talcott Parsons, "Culture and Social System: An Exchange, *American Sociological Review* (April, 1959), 24:247–250. Levy and Parsons argue that the distinction between what they term "social system" and "culture," and I term objective and subjective behavior relations is an "analytical" rather than "concrete" one. My own argument is the reverse: that each is a concretely different phenomenon, rather than a different analytic dimension of a single phenomenon. The ultimate significance of this difference may be summed up by noting that concrete phenomena can physically *influence* one another, while analytical dimensions can only *covary*.

entirely in terms of external observables. In fact, his first law (inertia) went so far as to propose that bodies' changes in motion could be explained without *any* reference to their internal states. Weber took exactly the opposite view by asserting that bodies' social action is so far distinguishable from mechanical action as to be definable *only* in terms of their internal states. "Action is social . . ." Weber said, "by virtue of the subjective meaning attached to it by the acting individual. . . ."

In actuality, of course, most sociological theories define the social partly in terms of objective behavior relations and partly in terms of subjective behavior relations. The analytic question to be answered for each theory, however, is how much stress it places on each relation compared to the other. The operational insistence to be made in the present analysis, that every theory be classified according to its single prime emphasis, is likely to fit most theories, but obviously it will not accommodate those conferring exactly equal emphasis on both objective and subjective relations. (As a result, this rule will be reexamined later on in this essay.)

But no matter what degree of overlap between the two sorts of definitions of the social may be found to exist empirically, the logical distinction between them remains. An important consequence of blurring this distinction is that sociologists who in reality have quite different explanatory goals are wrongly encouraged to think that they have the same explanatory goals. Theorists may therefore vigorously and wastefully debate their differences regarding the means of *explaining* the social, unaware of the fact that they may differ also in their manner of *defining* the social and that the former difference may only echo the latter.

One likely reason for the lack of clarity between the two alternative definitional emphases lies in a persistent (but in principle not inevitable) technical shortcoming: until recently, no subjective behavior has been directly observable.[17] But what is today not directly observable may be so tomorrow, and claims about the literal and permanent inobservability of this or that phenomenon are likely to prove short-lived. Nevertheless, technical inabilities so far have made arguments about the existence of "values," "norms," "sentiments," "knowledge" and other such subjective behavior and relations across individuals entirely inferential. In other words: Each investigator has been able to claim only (1) direct evidence of his own, and no other's, subjective behavior; (2) direct evidence in his own case, and in no other, of the connection between subjective behavior and objective behavior; but (3) direct evidence of others', as well as his own, objective behavior. Claims to the effect that others besides himself engage in subjective behavior and that this unobserved behavior is connected to observed behavior on their part, are therefore only inferences. But they lead one to the further and sociologically pivotal claim that there exist *subjective*

---

17. As Durkheim said, "it is necessary . . . to substitute for the internal fact which escapes us an external fact that symbolizes it and to study the former through the latter" (*Division of Labor in Society* [New York: Macmillan, 1933], p. 33). See also George C. Homans, *The Human Group* (New York: Harcourt, Brace, 1950), pp. 38–40. For some of the recent developments I have in mind, see Ekhard H. Hess, "Attitude and Pupil Size," *Scientific American* (April, 1965), 212:46–54 and John P. Clark and Larry L. Tifft, "Polygraph and Interview Validation of Self-reported Deviant Behavior," *American Sociological Review* (August,

1966), 31:516–523. Whatever remains of *technical* inability to observe subjective behavior directly should not be mistaken for *logically* defined identity of that behavior with the indirect, objective, and crude indicators that we have so far been forced to use. Thus, the operationalist opinion that "values as such can be equated with overt behavior probabilities" (Adler, *op. cit.*, p. 361) would destroy the crucial analytical distinction between events that occur outside and inside an organism, and prematurely abandon the technical search for ways to observe each sort of event independently of the other.

behavior relations (e.g., "social values"), as well as objective behavior relations (e.g., "social interaction"), among individuals. The essential point to note is that the empirical supports of the former claim have not been (and still are not) equal to those of the latter, and that in fact the former has depended on the latter. Perhaps as a result, it is often not immediately clear whether the objective behavior relations referred to by a given theory are viewed as directly definitive of the social or as presumably indicative of subjective behavior relations which are themselves the direct definition of the social. In short, when we examine actual sociological theories, the distinction between definitions of the social is not at all so clear-cut as a description of the idealized difference would suggest.

The problem, then, is to devise a reasonable operational distinction. In pursuing a solution, note that because of the dependence to date of claims regarding subjective relations on observations of objective relations, many objective relations theories ignore, or even specify the definitional irrelevance of, subjective relations. But for the same reason, it is not likely that any theory so far devised can either ignore, or specify the irrelevance of, objective behavior and such relations. Therefore, theories here classified as giving prime emphasis to subjective relations almost always involve objective relations, but their distinguishing mark is in the *way* such relations are involved: such theories imply or explicitly claim that the social exists only when subjective behavior relations are inferable from, and accompany, objective behavior relations.

A classical example of a subjective behavior emphasis is Max Weber's famous definition that "action is social insofar as, by virtue of the subjective meaning attached to it by the acting individual (or individuals), it takes account of the behavior of others and is thereby oriented in its course."[18] Or again, "an organization is a system of continuous purposive activity of a specified kind."[19] An equally famous classical example of an objective behavior emphasis is Engels': "The production of the means to support human life—and, next to production, the exchange of things produced—is the basis for all social structure."[20] And also Marx's statement: "In the social production which men carry on they enter into definite relations that are indispensable and independent of their will.... The sum total of these relations of production constitutes the economic structure of society—the real foundation on which rise legal and political superstructures and to which correspond definite forms of social consciousness."[21]

In our time, Merton emphasizes the primacy of objective behavior relations in defining the social: "The sociological concept of group refers to a number of people who interact with one another in accord with established patterns.... This [is] one objective criterion of the group."[22] Merton also declares that "social function refers to observable objective consequences, and not to subjective dispositions (aims, motives, purposes)."[23]

Homans also stresses objective behavior relations and quite unambiguously declares, in *The Human Group*, that "a group is defined by the interactions of its

18. Max Weber, *Theory of Social and Economic Organization* (Glencoe, Ill.: Free Press, 1947), p. 88.
19. *Ibid.*, p. 151.
20. Friedrich Engels, *Socialism: Utopian and Scientific*, quoted in Lewis S. Feuer (Ed.), *Marx and Engels, Basic Writings on Politics and Philosophy* (Garden City, N.Y.: Doubleday Anchor, 1959), p. 90.
21. Karl Marx, *A Contribution to the Critique of Political Economy*, quoted in Feuer, *op. cit.*, p. 43.
22. Robert K. Merton, *Social Theory and Social Structure*, revised and enlarged (Glencoe, Ill.: Free Press, 1957), pp. 385–386. There are further complexities in Merton's discussion of "social formations" of different kinds. Some of these will be discussed in connection with Figure 5 below.
23. *Ibid.*, p. 24.

members,"[24] while warning that "saying a group is defined by interaction is not the same thing as saying that interaction is the whole of group life."[25] In his later work, *Social Behavior: Its Elementary Forms*, Homans is somewhat more ambiguous. Here he says that in order for behavior to be social, "when a person acts in a certain way he is at least rewarded or punished by the behavior of another person, though he may be also rewarded or punished by the non-human environment."[26] One may argue that although the idea of persons acting in certain ways implies overt, objective behavior relations, the experience of *reward* implies that subjective evaluations are involved.[27] But Homans' insistence that "the exchange [of person's action for alter's reaction] is direct rather than indirect; and it is actual behavior and not just a norm specifying what behavior ought to be,"[28] seem to justify placing the later as well as the earlier Homans among the objective behavior theorists.

Blau, in his more recent book, regrets that "preoccupation with value orientations has diverted theoretical attention from the study of the actual associations between people and the structures of their associations."[29] And, although when he speaks of associations between people as involving "their associating together in work and in play, in love and in war, *to* trade or *to* worship, *to* help or *to* hinder,"[30] value orientations insinuate themselves back into "the study of the actual associations between people," it

seems clear that his intended definitional emphasis is on objective behavior relations. In an earlier work, Blau cited Homans' definition of a group in terms of its members' interactions and added that "common expectations and orientations arise or crystallize in the course of interaction and subsequently influence it. While these are elements of the group structure, its core is an observable pattern of interaction."[31]

Finally, on the objective behavior side, ecologists are often the least ambivalent of all. Duncan and Schnore assert that "the ecologist is interested in the pattern of observable physical activity itself rather than the subjective expectations that individuals may entertain of their roles."[32] They argue that "it is ... premature to proclaim that any and all study of social organization must be couched in terms of the goals that men supposedly seek."[33] For their part, Gibbs and Martin scorn those human ecologists who "spend their research hours assaying their data hopefully for values, sentiments, motivations, and other elusive psychological elements" and argue that "by placing its emphasis on societal organization human ecology is potentially capable of stemming the current trend which threatens to reduce sociology to social psychology."[34] They propose that "the problem of human ecology ... is to develop generalizations about sustenance organization at a level that does not include individual motivations and attitudes."[35]

24. Homans, *The Human Group*, p. 84 [p. 108, this volume].

25. *Ibid.*, p. 86 [p. 109, this volume].

26. George C. Homans, *Social Behavior: Its Elementary Forms* (New York: Harcourt, Brace and World, 1961), p. 2.

27. *Ibid.*, p. 380 [p. 125, this volume].

28. *Ibid.*, p. 378 [p. 124, this volume].

29. Peter M. Blau, *Exchange and Power in Social Life* (New York: John Wiley, 1964), p. 13 [p. 187, this volume].

30. *Ibid.*, p. 12. Emphasis added [p. 186, this volume].

31. Peter M. Blau, *The Dynamics of Bureaucracy* (Chicago: University of Chicago Press, 1955), p. 117.

32. Duncan and Schnore, *op. cit.*, p. 137 [p. 74, this volume]. John H. Kunkel, in "Some Behavioral Aspects of the Ecological Approach to Social Organization," *American Journal of Sociology* (July, 1967), 73: 12–29, also suggests that the ecological model of man "emphasizes observable activities ... and makes a minimum of inferences concerning man's internal state" (p. 17). See also Otis Dudley Duncan, "From Social System to Ecosystem," *Sociological Inquiry* (1961), 31(2) esp. p. 142.

33. Otis Dudley Duncan and Leo F. Schnore, "Rejoinder," *American Journal of Sociology* (September, 1959), 65:150.

34. Jack P. Gibbs and Walter T. Martin, "Toward a Theoretical System of Human Ecology," *Pacific Sociological Review* (Spring, 1959), 2:29.

35. *Ibid.*, n. 13 on p. 33.

On the other side—the side of contemporary subjective behavior definitions of the social—Sorokin said: "The component of 'meaning' is decisive in determining whether a phenomenon is sociocultural (superorganic). Without it there are no sociocultural phenomena...."[36] Caplow is equally explicit and Weberian in declaring that "human interaction is social if it involves symbolic communication."[37] And Moore expressly limits the term "revolution" to "fundamental change in the normative order, including notably the forms of legality and, crucially, the basis of legitimacy for the state itself."[38]

One of the most prolific modern proponents of a subjective behavior definition is Talcott Parsons (and his several collaborators). In an early statement, he argues that the action frame of reference implies "a normative orientation of action, a teleological character. Action must always be thought of as involving a state of tension between two different orders of events, the normative and the conditional. As process, action is, in fact, the process of alteration of the conditional elements in the direction of conformity with norms.... [and] the normative elements can be conceived of as 'existing' only in the mind of the actor."[39] His illustration is quite clear: "In dealing with a case of suicide by jumping off a bridge, the social scientist will describe it as an 'act'; the physical scientist as an 'event.' For the social scientist it has a 'concrete' end, death by drowning—the actor anticipates 'himself, dead in the water.'"[40]

This subjective relations definition of the social persists throughout Parsons' writings. In one 1951 publication, Shils and he define "a social system [as] a system of interaction of a plurality of actors in which the action is oriented by rules which are complexes of complementary expectations concerning roles and sanctions."[41] And in another publication of the same year, Parsons defines sociological theory as "concerned with the phenomena of the institutionalization of patterns of value-orientation in the social system."[42] In 1960, Parsons declares that "the structure of systems of action is conceived as consisting in patterns of normative culture."[43] And in a 1966 publication, he says: "We treat the social system as one of the primary subsystems of the human action system.... Action consists of the structures and processes by which human beings form meaningful intentions and, more or less successfully, implement them in concrete situations. The word 'meaningful' implies the symbolic or cultural level of representation and reference."[44]

The distinction that has just been discussed—between objective behavior relations and subjective behavior relations—will be the principal one used here in differentiating the explananda of theo-

36. Sorokin, *Sociological Theories of Today*, p. 13. For discussion of several definitions of the social that rely on similar imputations of subjective behavior relations, see also Edward A. Tiryakian, "Existential Phenomenology and the Sociological Tradition," *American Sociological Review* (October, 1965), 30:674–688.

37. Theodore Caplow, *Principles of Organization* (New York: Harcourt, Brace and World, 1964), p. 75.

38. Wilbert E. Moore, "The MacIver Lecture: Predicting Discontinuities in Social Change," *American Sociological Review* (June, 1964), 29:337.

39. Talcott Parsons, *The Structure of Social Action* (Glencoe, Ill.: Free Press, 1949), pp. 732–733.

40. *Ibid.*, p. 734. Note that defining the social in terms of subjective relations (a conceptualization

decision) is not equivalent to taking the actor's point of view (a methodological decision). Subjective relations can be, and often are, observed from the investigator's point of view and described in his terms rather than in the actor's terms.

41. Talcott Parsons and Edward A. Shils, "Values, Motives and Systems of Action," in Talcott Parsons and Edward A. Shils (Eds.), *Toward a General Theory of Action* (New York: Harper Torchbooks, 1951), p. 195.

42. Talcott Parsons, *The Social System* (Glencoe, Ill.: Free Press, 1951), p. 552.

43. Talcott Parsons, "Pattern Variables Revisited: A Response to Robert Dubin," *American Sociological Review* (August, 1960), 25: 481 [p. 286, this volume].

44. Talcott Parsons, *Societies* (Englewood Cliffs N.J.: Prentice-Hall, 1966), p. 5.

retic viewpoints. This focus, however, should not be taken to mean that no other distinctions are important. Indeed, a later section of this overview examines three others: between macro and micro levels of the social, between its genesis and maintenance, and between its stability and change. Still other dimensions of variability in the sociological explanandum can be brought to mind, including the *complexity* of the behavioral relations that define it (i.e., the degree to which each participant's behavior is different from every other participant's behavior), the *persistence* and *periodicity* of these relations (i.e., how long given social phenomena last and how often they recur), and the *number of participants* in them (i.e., the "size" of given social phenomena). And of course one must recognize the importance of distinctions in the *content* of social relations (considered from the observer's standpoint and separately from the participant's intention). For example, the content of objective behavior relations may be judged chiefly competitive or cooperative, chiefly economic, political, military, educational, etc. Similarly, the content of subjective behavior relations may be judged primarily expressive, evaluative, cognitive, or technical, and so forth. The importance of such distinctions is not to be denied, since they justify specialities in sociology such as those of face-to-face interactions and complex organizations, of nations, social strata and families, of cities, factories, prisons and schools, of values and norms, conformity and deviance. The present discussion, however—because it is concerned exclusively with analyzing the general theoretic viewpoints that inform (and are informed by) all of the more specific, "middle range" and "institutional," sociological interests—will treat these distinctions as secondary to the primary

"objective-subjective" one, and will not attend to them except in passing.

EXPLANATIONS OF THE SOCIAL

The elements that are proposed by various sociological theories to explain social phenomena may also be grouped into two broad types. The first type of explaining element stresses conditions that are *imposed on* the social by the given nature of the participants or by the nature of the universe that environs them. From this point of view, the social is rather more "controlled" and "determined" by these temporally prior and/or logically more primitive conditions. The second type of explaining element emphasizes conditions that are *generated by* the social itself in affecting the participants or the universe that environs them. From this point of view, the social is rather more "free" and "self-determining."

An example of a theoretic viewpoint that stresses the imposed type of explaining element is what may be called "functional imperativism." The essential feature of theories proposing functional imperatives or "requisites," of course, is that certain classes of events are put forward as universal and inevitable conditions of social phenomena. The social phenomena themselves are then explained as adaptations to these imposed conditions. Thus, Aberle *et al.* argue that "functional prerequisites refer broadly to the things that must get done in any society if it is to continue as a going concern. . . . the definition of the functional prerequisites in a society logically precedes the development of a scheme of structural prerequisites."[45] So also, Parsons and Shils argue that "every social system has certain tasks imposed on it by the fact that its members are mortal physiological organisms, with physiological and social

45. D. F. Aberle, A. K. Cohen, A. K. Davis, M. J. Levy, Jr., and F. X. Sutton, "The Functional Prerequisites of a Society," *Ethics* (January, 1950), 60:100.

needs, existing in a physical environment together with other like organisms."[46] More recently, Parsons observes that "a fundamental principle about the organization of living systems is that their structures are differentiated in regard to the various exigencies imposed upon them by their environments."[47]

Levy proposes structural as well as functional requisites: "In seeking to discover the structural requisites of a unit one seeks the answer to the question, 'In a given unit what patterns must be present such that operation in terms of these patterns will result in the functional requisites of the unit?'" Levy thus arrives at the explanatory variable status of functional requisites or imperatives: "The concept of functional requisites is not, generally, a focus of interest in and of itself. The end of analysis is generally the patterns of action and not the necessary conditions of action."[48] Moore makes the same point: "requisite functions provide the steppingstone to a consideration of the structural characteristics of human societies."[49]

In this same general tradition of imposed explanantes of the social, Wrong refers to "man's animal nature" and asks:

Can we really dispense with the venerable notion of material "interests" and invariably replace it with the blander, more integrative "social values"? . . . That material interests, sexual drives, and the quest for power have often been overestimated as human motives is no reason to deny their reality. . . .

The view that man is invariably pushed by internalized norms or pulled by the lure of self-validation by others ignores—to speak archaically for the moment—both the highest and the lowest, both beast and angel in his nature.[50]

In contrast to such emphases on imposed factors that are held to explain the social is an emphasis on socially generated factors. One example here is symbolic interactionism, where an essential idea is that social phenomena are continuously emerging from the present interaction of symbols generated in past interaction, and that this emergence is not predictable from imposed conditions. Thus Blumer claims that

with the mechanism of self-interaction the human being ceases to be a responding organism whose behavior is a product of what plays upon him from the outside, the inside, or both. Instead, he acts toward his world, interpreting what confronts him and organizing his action on the basis of the interpretation. . . . Symbolic interaction involves interpretation or ascertaining the meaning of the actions or remarks of the other person, and definition, or conveying indications to another person as to how he is to act. Human association consists of a process of such interpretation and definition.[51]

A second example of the socially generated type of explaining element is found in Ogburn's technologism. Ogburn notes that "the interrelationship of sociology and technology is of two kinds. One is in the sociological situation that gives rise to invention and discovery and to their uses by society. The other is in the effects upon society of the uses of invention and discovery."[52] Ogburn's emphasis, of course, is on the latter relationship:

How technological changes cause social changes depends on an understanding of the nature of causation, and is seen to be a process. Basic to the process is the fact that a technological influence does not always stop at its

46. Parsons and Shils, op. cit., p. 198.
47. Parsons, Societies, p. 8. See also Kingsley Davis, op. cit., pp. 28–29.
48. Marion J. Levy, Jr., The Structure of Society (Princeton: Princeton University Press, 1952), pp. 63–64.
49. Moore, "Sociology and Demography," p. 836.
50. Dennis H. Wrong, "The Oversocialized Conception of Man," American Sociological Review (April, 1961), 26:190–191.
51. Herbert Blumer, "Sociological Implications of the Thought of George Herbert Mead," American Journal of Sociology (March, 1966), 71:537 [pp. 235 and 237, this volume].
52. William Fielding Ogburn, "The Meaning of Technology," in Francis R. Allen et al. (Eds.), Technology and Social Change (New York: Appleton-Century-Crofts, 1957), p. 9.

first direct effect upon users and producers, but often has a succession of derivative effects which follow one another like the links of a chain. These are not often recognized, because an effect is generally not the result of one cause alone but of several converging causes. Also, since the impact of an invention may have several effects dispersed in different directions, the process is more like a network than a chain.[53]

THE BASIC TAXONOMY

The definitional and explanatory dimensions just set forth yield the simple property-space[54] for classifying sociological theories that is shown in Figure 1. Before attempting to use it in the analysis of specific sociological theories,

**The Principal Behavioral Relations
that *Define* the Social are:**

	Objective *(Materialist)*	Subjective *(Idealist)*
Imposed on the Social *(Determined)*		
Generated by the Social *(Free-willed)*		

The Principal Phenomena that *Explain* the Social are:

Figure 1. *Basic Property-Space for Classifying Viewpoints in Contemporary Sociological Theory.*

53. William Fielding Ogburn, "How Technology Causes Social Change," in Allen *et al.*, *op. cit.*, p. 25.

54. See Allen H. Barton, "The Concept of Property-Space in Social Research," in Paul F. Lazarsfeld and Morris Rosenberg (Eds.), *The Language of Social Research* (Glencoe, Ill.: Free Press, 1955), pp. 40–62.

however, two further preliminaries will be helpful.

First, some attention should be paid to certain broadly philosophical implications of the property-space itself. Although the dimensions of that space were inductively derived from inspecting the data (i.e., current sociological theories), on reflection it appears that these dimensions are closely related to two central and long-lived philosophical problems (indicative terms for them are given in parentheses in Figure 1). Thus, the question of whether the social is to be defined in terms of subjective or objective behavior relations seems to reflect philosophical problems long expressed in the antinomies of idealism and materialism, mind and matter, thought and deed, contemplation and action, good intentions and paving-stones. Similarly, the question of whether the fundamental explaining conditions are imposed on, or generated by, the social seems to echo the still more resounding philosophical questions of whether man is to be considered primarily a determined consequence of prior and/or higher events, or as primarily a free-willed maker of his own constitution and history.

Therefore, it seems reasonable to hope that the stated dimensions of Figure 1 may not only cast some light on the scientific status of the theories to be located there, but that a translation of these dimensions into the implied philosophical dimensions just mentioned may also illuminate their philosophical status. In other words, if the scheme proves successful, one should be able to describe a given sociological theory as being, for example, of the "imposed-objective-relations" sociological variety, and also of the "determined-materialist" philosophical variety. Or a given theorist's career may be described as having shifted sociologically from, say, "socially-generated-subjective-relations" theory to "imposed-subjective-relations," and philosophically from "free-willed-idealism" to "determined-idealism."[55] Inasmuch as the broadly philosophical differences I have mentioned are at least as tenaciously contested as are the more narrow scientific differences, the connections between the two may help account for an occasional vigor in arguments regarding sociological theory, since what may ultimately be at stake in such debates are world-views and not merely society-views.

In the second preliminary, somewhat more detail may usefully be added to one dimension of Figure 1. This consists in adding "medium of operation" sub-dimensions to that of "explaining phenomena." Thus, imposed explanations of social phenomena may be classifiable as, on the one hand, emphasizing conditions that operate on the social through the nature of the participants themselves. These conditions may be further specified by dichotomizing them into "nervous system" conditions (e.g., humans can perceive, think, imagine, desire, recognize, despise, etc.) and "not-nervous system" conditions (e.g., humans can reproduce sexually, require food, shelter, and clothing, pass through childhood and adulthood phases, etc.). But on the other hand, imposed explanations of social phenomena may emphasize conditions that operate on the social through characteristics of the participants' environments.[56] These latter may also be

55. Cf. John Finley Scott, "The Changing Foundations of the Parsonian Action Scheme," *American Sociological Review* (October, 1963), 28:716–735 [pp. 246–267, this volume].

56. It should be noted that environmental variables can only affect a participant if he has some receptor or disposition that is capable of transmitting the environmental variable to the appropriate responding mechanisms inside the participant. In principle, this seems no less true of an atomic explosion in the immediate vicinity of a participant than of the rising moon. Such necessary transmission seems to be the significance of Stinchcombe's references to "mapping variables" that "map the environmental variables onto the individual" (*op. cit.*, pp. 204–207).

further specified as primarily implicating the number and/or kind of other people in participants' environments (e.g., social phenomena occur in dyads, triads, crowds, "masses," in densely populated cities, in sparsely populated villages, etc.), or as primarily implicating the "not-people" objects in participants' environments (e.g., social phenomena occur in deserts and fertile river valleys, under diurnal, seasonal, and climatic variations in light, temperature, food and shelter availability, etc.). Similarly, the self-generated factors that can explain social phenomena may refer primarily to socially induced modifications in participants' own "nervous system" or "not-nervous system" characteristics (e.g., socialization, the physiological consequences of training and diet, etc.), or primarily to socially induced modifications in participants' "people" or "not-people" environments (e.g., formally structured organizations, steam engines, etc.). Figures 2 makes use of these elaborations.

Every classification has its dysfunctions. First, of course, every scheme, by being only itself and not others as well, magnifies certain differences, ignores others, and so may trick us into believing the former more "real" than the latter. Second, the requirement that every observation must be placed on one or the other side of a classificatory line, and that no observation may be placed on the line itself, deliberately ignores the subtlety of actual observation and so may trick us into mutilating observations to fit the classification. And third, of course, the posited dimensions of classification may be simply erroneous insofar as they may rest on unfruitful premises or unreliable observations.

With respect to the first of these dysfunctions, perhaps it is mitigated in the present book by noting that I do not claim that the distinctions that will be drawn below are any more real than others; I claim only that they are not less real—not grossly contradicted by the data (i.e., the cited writings of sociological theorists)—and that they are useful for understanding theory and doing research. Perhaps the second dysfunction is also somewhat mitigated here by noting that Figure 2 classifies "*isms*" rather than theories and rather than the works of particular theorists. For example, Figure 2 refers to ecologism instead of ecological theory and instead of Duncan's or others' publications. This terminology is meant to convey the idea that the objects of attention are *idealized* types of sociological theory, and thus theoretical *viewpoints*, rather than concrete theories or concrete works. As a general rule, concrete theories and works are carefully moderated rather than extreme in their arguments (or become so moderated in successive restatements), in the sense that each theory usually includes some reference to the same elements that every other theory includes. The differences among such theories are therefore mainly differences of emphasis. It is as though the theories were teams, all coming to bat in the same baseball game, and all touching the same bases on the same playing field. But what is home plate for one team seems to be only first base for another, second base for another, and so on. Although I shall cite evidences of moderation and attempted universality in every theory discussed below, my chief concern will not be with these similarities but rather with highlighting the differences in conceptual emphasis among theories that this analogy is meant to suggest.

The third dysfunction, or rather danger, of classification—i.e., possible reliance on erroneous premises or observations—must also be acknowledged as a threat here. For example, the "nervous system" vs. "not-nervous system" distinction is not an altogether easy one to maintain in the face of the strong

The Principal Behavioral Relations that *Define* the Social are:

Objective   Subjective

Objective	Subjective
ECOLOGISM	(adaptive)
DEMOGRAPHISM	(integrative)
MATERIALISM	FUNCTIONAL IMPERATIVISM (goal attainment)
PSYCHOLOGISM	(pattern-maintenance)
TECHNOLOGISM	(nonsocial objects)
THE SOCIAL STRUCTURALISMS: FUNCTIONAL, EXCHANGE, AND CONFLICT	(social objects)
	SOCIAL ACTIONISM (actor)
SYMBOLIC INTERACTIONISM	(orientation)

The Principal Phenomena that *Explain* the Social are:

Imposed on the Social, via

Characteristics of the Participants' Environments, which are principally → Not-People
Characteristics of the Participants' Environments, which are principally → People

Characteristics of the Participants Themselves, which are principally → Not-Nervous System
Characteristics of the Participants Themselves, which are principally → Nervous System

Generated by the Social, via

Characteristics of the Participants' Environments, which are principally → Not-People
Characteristics of the Participants' Environments, which are principally → People

Characteristics of the Participants Themselves, which are principally → Not-Nervous System
Characteristics of the Participants Themselves, which are principally → Nervous System

Figure 2. *Eleven Viewpoints in Contemporary Sociological Theory.*

interdependence between psychological and physiological facts that the term "neuroendocrine" seems to epitomize. Similarly, to distinguish between explanantes that are "imposed on" the social vs. "generated by" the social risks overlooking the role of each in the other. For example, the number of participants involved in a given social phenomenon (see the discussion below of demographism) is never wholly imposed on the social, since mating or some other social recruitment procedure always generates that number (excepting only parthenogenesis). The only protections I can offer against this danger are first, the warning itself, and second, my intentions to abstract the main emphases in sociological theory, rather than to set forth the detailed moderations there, and within these limitations of factual accuracy, to produce a taxonomy that is useful for comprehending theory and for doing research. Of course, the road that these presumably good intentions actually pave is for the reader to decide on arrival.

ELEVEN VIEWPOINTS IN CONTEMPORARY SOCIOLOGICAL THEORY

Ecologism

Duncan and Schnore's, and Gibbs and Martin's, statements of the ecologistic definition of social phenomena have already been quoted, and it is clearly objective behavior relations that are central there. Just as clearly, ecologism's principal class of explanatory events is imposed on the social, rather than generated by the social, and operates via those characteristics of participants' environments that are primarily nonhuman. For example, Hawley says: "The com-

munity . . . is in the nature of a collective response to the habitat; it constitutes the adjustment of organism to environment. . . ."[57] "Culture is nothing more than a way of referring to the prevailing techniques by which a population maintains itself in its habitat."[58] And again:

The distinctive feature of the study [of human ecology] lies in the conception of the adjustment of man to habitat as a process of community development. Whereas this may be an implicit assumption in most social science disciplines, it is for human ecology the principal working hypothesis.[59]

In much the same tradition, Quinn defines human ecology as the "study [of] the relations of man to man as influenced by limited supplies of environmental resources. . . . No sociological study can be called truly ecological unless it uses certain aspects of environmental influence as principles of interpretation."[60]

More recently, Duncan notes that "ecology has exploited most systematically the assumption that ways of life are a function of conditions of life," and asserts that "social institutions . . . do not themselves evolve, but rather adjust to new conditions, originating either from environmental change or from technological development."[61]

At the same time that they emphasize imposed factors as explanantes, ecologists usually argue for socially generated factors as well (for example, the "technological development" in Duncan's last sentence above). Along these lines, Hawley says:

human ecology . . . deals with the central problem of sociology, that is, the development and organization of the community. Human ecology, however, does not pretend to exhaust that problem. The human community is more than just an organization of functional

57. Amos H. Hawley, *Human Ecology* (New York: Ronald Press, 1950), p. 37.

58. Amos H. Hawley. "Ecology and Human Ecology," *Social Forces* (May, 1944), 22:404.

59. *Ibid.*, p. 405.

60. James A. Quinn, "The Nature of Human Ecology: Reexamination and Redefinition," *Social Forces* (December, 1939), 18:163.

61. Otis Dudley Duncan, "Social Organization and the Ecosystem," in Faris, *op. cit.*, p. 36, and p. 50.

relationships and to that extent there are limitations to the scope of human ecology. Man's collective life involves, in greater or lesser degree, a psychological and a moral as well as a functional integration. . . .[62]

Also, the "ecological complex" that Duncan proposes includes (apart from social organization itself) population and technology as well as natural environment.[63] Moreover, Duncan warns that

you cannot throw away what is most distinctively human—communication with symbols, custom, and the artificial or cultural transformations man makes in his environment—and treat the residue as the ecology of the species. There is no need to adopt such a strategy.[64]

Despite these disclaimers, however, ecologism seems typically to accord such factors secondary theoretical status. Thus Park argued that the ecological, economic, political, and moral orders "seem to arrange themselves in a kind of hierarchy. In fact they may be said to form a pyramid of which the ecological order constitutes the base and the moral order the apex."[65] Similarly, Gibbs and Martin claim that

while it is possible to construct a very plausible explanation of the extraordinary standard of living in the United States by linking it to cultural values and the American character, such an explanation merely takes for granted the complex structure of sustenance organization which makes possible such an abundance of material things.[66]

And Schnore says of Durkheim's *Division of Labor* that:

In order to provide maximum utility in ecological analysis, Durkheim's theory needs certain modifications, particularly along the lines of bringing the environment into the schema as a factor worthy of recognition. As a result of its conceptual heritage from biology, human ecology has a rather full appreciation of the role of the physical environment as it affects social structure. This is not to say, however, that the ecologist is an environmental determinist; rather he points to the relevance of the environment as it is modified and redefined by the organized use of technology.[67]

Note that even in the qualifying last sentence, Schnore emphasizes the *natural environment* as modified by technology, rather than *technology* as modified by the natural environment. The latter emphasis is more characteristic of technologism—to be discussed below.[68]

Demographism

Hauser and Duncan distinguish between two meanings of the term "demography":

Demographic analysis is confined to the study of components of population variation and change. Population studies are concerned not only with population variables but also with relationships between population changes and other variables—social, economic, political, biological, genetic, geographical, and the like. . . .

62. Hawley, *Human Ecology*, pp. 73–74 [p. 68, this volume].

63. Otis Dudley Duncan, "Human Ecology and Population Studies," in Hauser and Duncan, *op. cit.*, pp. 678–716. Duncan's "ecological complex" (POET) may be viewed as an attempt to integrate some central propositions from what are here termed demographism (P), the social structuralisms (O), ecologism (E), and technologism (T). For a nearly identical enumeration of concepts (the whole being called "the universe of inquiry for human ecology" instead of "the ecological complex"), see Gibbs and Martin, *op. cit.*, p. 33. An older, but similar list is in Robert E. Park, "Human Ecology," *American Journal of Sociology* (July, 1936), 42:1–15.

64. Duncan, "Social Organization and the Ecosystem," p. 77.

65. Park, *op. cit.*, p. 14.

66. Gibbs and Martin, *op. cit.*, p. 30.

67. Leo F. Schnore, "Social Morphology and Human Ecology," *American Journal of Sociology* (May, 1958), 63:631.

68. As ecologists have moved away from an adaptation model (wherein social phenomena are seen as mainly determined by temporally antecedent habitat-imposed environmental conditions) and toward a systems model consisting of simultaneous and mutually determining variables (as manifest in Duncan's discussions of the "ecosystem" and the "ecological complex"), they have shifted their attention from the genesis of the social to the maintenance of the social. These two theoretical problems are discussed later in this essay.

Thus, "demography" may be conceived in a narrow sense as synonymous with "demographic analysis" or in a broad sense as encompassing both "demographic analysis" and "population studies."[69]

The present discussion clearly rests upon the second, broad, definition of demography,[70] and it is this definition that is meant by the unfortunately awkward term "demographism."[71]

As a theoretic viewpoint in sociology, demographism contributes two distinctive and related explanations of the social in claiming that social phenomena are influenced, and therefore explained, (1) by the number of participants in them, and (2) by the extent to which dead or emigrated participants are replaced in them. The "numbers" proposition builds upon the definitional statement that all social phenomena involve at least two participants by adding the theoretic prediction that these phenomena will vary in systematic ways according to the exact number that are involved, whatever that number may be.[72] The "replacement" proposition builds upon the conventional assumption that social phenomena must involve living-and-dying things by adding the theoretic prediction that the persistence of a given social phenomenon beyond the life-spans of its initiators depends on participant replacement, and that the social phenomenon itself will vary with the nature and extent of such replacement.[73]

The proposition that the number of participants affects the nature of social phenomena has an important tradition in sociology. For example, Malthus held that the number of social participants tends to increase more rapidly than food supply and therefore to prevent any but temporary rises in level of living.[74] Simmel argued that social phenomena involving three participants differ radically from social phenomena involving two participants.[75] Durkheim, too, developed a theory of the bearing of numbers of participants on social phenomena, as Moore has pointed out:

In Durkheim's famous work on "Division of Labor," organic solidarity, based on specialization, is related to "moral" density, which in turn is linked to demographic density and growth. . . . In a simplified way,

---

69. Philip M. Hauser and Otis Dudley Duncan, "Overview and Conclusions," in Hauser and Duncan, *op. cit.*, p. 3. Kingsley Davis draws a similar distinction between "formal demography" and "population theory." ("The Sociology of Demographic Behavior," in Robert K. Merton, Leonard Broom, and Leonard S. Cottrell, Jr., (Eds.), *Sociology Today* [New York: Basic Books, 1959], p. 311).

70. Moore even identifies " 'the' population problem" as "the interrelation between demographic phenomena and their social settings" ("Sociology and Demography," p. 845).

71. Davis has remarked on some other terminological difficulties: "[The term] 'demography' . . . implies that the purpose is highly descriptive, whereas the science of population is highly analytical. The best term would be *demology*, but this is too close to *demonology*" ("Sociology of Demographic Behavior," n. 3 on p. 311).

72. A variant of the demographic proposition regarding the bearing of over-all numbers on social phenomena is the proposition that social phenomena are influenced by the number of specific *kinds* of participants such as is represented in a "population pyramid". Thus, Stinchcombe goes so far as to identify all demographic causal explanation as "one in which a causal force is assumed to be proportional to the number of people of a certain kind" (*op. cit.*, p. 60).

73. Both propositions entail the characteristic demographic variables of "natality, mortality, territorial movement and social mobility (change of status)." (Philip M. Hauser and Otis Dudley Duncan, "The Nature of Demography," in Hauser and Duncan, *op. cit.*, p. 31.) The bearing of natality and mortality is self-evident: they readily yield statements about total as well as group-specific number and replacement rates. The bearing of territorial movement and social mobility becomes clear when these concepts are viewed as special cases of replacement, wherein recruits come and go between societies, strata, or other social phenomena (rather than between the womb and the grave), thus changing the numbers of participants in the social phenomena from which they come and to which they go.

74. See D. V. Glass (Ed.), *Introduction to Malthus* (London: Watts and Company, 1953).

75. See Georg Simmel, "The Number of Persons as Determining the Form of the Group," in Edgar F. Borgatta and Henry J. Meyer (Eds.), *Sociological Theory: Present-Day Sociology from the Past* (New York: Knopf, 1956), pp. 126–158.

therefore, this may be viewed as a *"demographic"* theory of social change.[76]

Contemporary writers have dealt with the same general question, as is evident in the following statement by Spengler:

Increases in population density operate within limits to produce mechanical effects making for increasing returns. They often are accompanied by improvements in communication, by fuller use of economic and social overhead capital, by improvements in inter-industry fits, by reduction in transport and distributive costs, and, above all, by intensification of specialization and division of labor.[77]

The second distinctively demographic proposition (i.e., replacement) also has a classical forebear—in Weber's analysis of leadership succession. Ryder presents a modern view of the succession or replacement problem in general:

Any organization experiences social metabolism: since its individual components are exposed to "mortality," the survival of the organization requires a process of "fertility." The problem of replacement is posed not only for the total organization but also for every one of its differentiated components. The ineluctability of social metabolism is from one view a problem that any organization must solve in the interests of continuity and from another view a continual opportunity for adaptation and change.[78]

Considering Ryder's reference here to "ineluctability" and considering also Moore's linking of demographic variables to the "requisite functions" of societies,[79] it seems clear that demographism views the requirements of number

and replacement as imposed upon the social by logical definition and by the reproductive and mortal nature of organisms.[80]

Regarding the classification in Figure 2 of demographism as a viewpoint whose explanans operates via participants' environments insofar as these environments consist of other people, note that the necessary and operative implication of the "number" proposition is that interparticipant behavior regularities will be different under circumstances in which each participant has few fellow participants in his environment and circumstances in which he has many fellow participants in that environment. The "replacement" proposition implies the same claim with respect to variations in participant replacement. These implications seem to underlie Durkheim's propositions that the transition from mechanical solidarity to organic solidarity was directly occasioned by a change in moral *density*, i.e., in the socially controlling population of each participant's environing life-space.[81]

Further, the classification in Figure 2 of demographism as a theoretic viewpoint which defines the social in terms of objective behavior relations recognizes the fact that most demographic explanations of social phenomena seek to account for such objective relations as are represented in urbanization, economic productivity, political systems, educational systems, etc., although some, of course, are also concerned with accounting for subjective behavior regularities such as cultural values.[82]

76. Moore, "Sociology and Demography," p. 844. Parsons makes the same point in *The Structure of Social Action*, p. 322.

77. Joseph J. Spengler, "Population as a Factor in Economic Development," in Philip M. Hauser (Ed.), *Population and World Politics* (Glencoe, Ill.: Free Press, 1958), p. 174.

78. N. B. Ryder, "Notes on the Concept of a Population," *American Journal of Sociology* (March, 1964), 69:461 [p. 101, this volume].

79. Moore, "Sociology and Demography," p. 838.

80. It should also be noted that the extent to which these imposed necessities are actually met was treated as socially generated by Malthus himself, in stressing the six socially generated "positive and preventive checks" on numerical growth. See also *ibid.*, p. 836.

81. See note 176 below on Durkheim's use of the same idea in his "egoism-altruism" explanation of suicide rates.

82. See, for example, Spengler, *op. cit.*, p. 184.

Materialism

Marx and Engels have already been quoted regarding their definition of the social. With respect to explaining the social, they had this to say:

The social structure and the state are continually evolving out of the life process of definite individuals, but of individuals not as they may appear in either their own or other people's imagination, but as they really are, i.e., as they are effective, produce materially, and are active under definite material limits, presuppositions, and conditions independent of their will.... We must begin by stating the first premise, namely, that men must be in a position to live in order to be able to "make history". But life involves, before everything else, eating and drinking, a habitation, clothing, and many other things. The first historical act is thus the production of the means to satisfy these needs, the production of material life itself.[83]

Note that although ecologism, demographism, and materialism define the social in objective relational terms, these statements of Marx and Engels emphasize the physiological nature and needs of the individual man in their explanation of social phenomena, whereas ecologism emphasizes man's nonhuman environment, and demographism emphasizes man's human environment.

The earlier quotation from *A Contribution to the Critique of Political Economy* and the one immediately above from *The German Ideology* have indicated the primacy given by Marx and Engels to the economic structure of society insofar as it (1) satisfies man's physiological needs for food, drink, shelter, clothing, etc., and (2) also creates new physiological and non-physiological needs which are then satisfied by the legal and political superstructure that rises on this base. In later

years, however, Engels modified this one-way causal image:

The economic situation is the basis, but the various elements of the superstructure—political forms of the class struggle and its results ... also exercise their influence upon the course of the historical struggles and in many cases preponderate in determining their *form*. There is an interaction of all these elements in which ... the economic movement finally asserts itself as necessary.[84]

Now consider the closely parallel view in Homans' statement that:

Assuming that there is established between the members of a group any set of relations satisfying the condition that the group survives for a time in its particular environment, physical and social, we can show that on the foundation of these relations the group will develop new ones, that the latter will modify or even create the relations we assumed at the beginning, and that, finally, the behavior of the group, besides being determined by the environment, will itself change the environment.[85]

Such common emphases on satisfying material "needs" (Marx and Engels) or "conditions" (Homans) of survival as social "base" (Marx and Engels) or as "foundation" (Homans), and on the interaction of "base and superstructure" (Marx and Engels) or of "external system and internal system" (Homans), are not all that Homans' viewpoint shares with Marxian materialism. Both explain the social by referring to the presumed nature of man rather than to the nature of his habitat. Indeed, the chief factor that developed, especially in Homans' later work, to distinguish the two orientations is Homans' emphasis on the *psychological* nature of man, and Marx' and Engels' emphasis (in the "materialism" aspect of their theory, as distinct from its "dialectical" aspect) on the physiological nature of man.[86] Homans' recent view

---

83. Karl Marx and Friedrich Engels, *The German Ideology*, quoted in Feuer, *op. cit.*, pp. 246–249.

84. Friedrich Engels, "Letter to Joseph Bloch," in Feuer, *op. cit.*, p. 398.

85. Homans, *The Human Group*, p. 91 [p. 112, this volume].

86. The reader will have noticed that the term "materialism" is used in two senses in this essay. The

seems the more exclusive, since he has written that "the only general propositions of sociology are in fact psychological."[87] One can hardly imagine Marx or Engels (or, for that matter, the more materialistic Homans of *The Human Group*) arguing that the *only* general propositions of sociology are physiological.

Psychologism

Perhaps the clearest single expression in *The Human Group* of the central explanatory role of imposed psychological motives (i.e., sentiments that "come into the external system," rather than being "generated within the group we are concerned with at the moment")[88] is the following passage. Here Homans not only again indicates his strong affinity at that time for the materialist viewpoint, but also distinctly forecasts the psychologistic theme which *Social Behavior* is to develop more fully.

To set it going, so to speak, a group needs motives for cooperation, a set of activities it is to carry out, and a scheme of interaction among its members. So far we have studied groups that were part of a complex society, and we have considered the sentiments entering into the external system to be those that the members bring to the group in question from other groups in the larger society. The desire for wages to support a family is a typical example of such a sentiment. But Tikopia is an isolated island; it is not part of a larger society, and its members cannot bring sentiment to the group from other groups outside. Nevertheless there are sentiments that can be treated as parts of the external system of the Tikopia family, and these are the biological drives of men . . . the drives for sex, food, and child care are quite enough to set the system going. A warning is

badly needed here. On the plea that this is not a psychology textbook, we are going to dodge the great debate on instinct. All of these drives are, at one and the same time, biological and social, inherited and acquired. . . . Only so far as they have a biological component do they come into the external system, as we use the term. . . . The biological drives are satisfied by the co-operative activities of men and women, the form of the activities being determined, in greater or lesser degree, by the environment and the available tools and techniques.[89]

Social Behavior, Homans' next major work, may be viewed as an elaboration of the above passage. In other words, *Social Behavior* appears to be an effort to show exactly how imposed psychological motives come to be the prime explanations of the group and of all other variables in the external and internal social systems, including activity, interaction, norms, and sentiments generated by the social. Thus, Homans here focuses attention on forms of social behavior that are conceived as invariant from one society and culture to another and so must be considered as imposed on the latter, rather than generated by them. And since Homans defines elementary social behavior in terms of the exchange of rewarding and/or punishing acts, the crucial question is how different acts come to be experienced as rewarding or punishing. Although his argument is inconclusive in this regard,[90] Homans proposes that although "contrived" rewards and "roundabout" exchanges are involved in normatively controlled institutional social behavior, "natural" or "primary" rewards and "direct" exchanges are involved in elementary or "substitutional" social behavior.[91] Although they are never

---

first (see Figure 1) refers to a general philosophical outlook, and the second (see Figure 2) refers to a more specific sociological viewpoint. The distinction corresponds roughly to the Marxian one between dialectical materialism as a world-view and historical materialism as a society-view.

87. Homans, *Social Behavior*, p. 817.

88. Homans, *The Human Group*, p. 96 [p. 115, this volume].

89. *Ibid.*, pp. 232, 233, and 234.

90. James A. Davis, in his review of Homans' book (*American Journal of Sociology* [January, 1962], 67:458) makes a similar point.

91. A similar distinction was made by Karl Marx between "two types of human drives and appetites: the constant or fixed ones . . . and the 'relative' appetites." (Erich Fromm, *Marx's Concept of Man* [New York: Frederick Ungar, 1961], p. 25).

declared outright to be innate, "natural or primary" rewards have this clear implication. For Homans, these characteristics not only give rise to complex social phenomena ("probably there is no institution that was not in its germ elementary social behavior"),[92] but they also continue to sustain complex social phenomena after they have been formed ("the people following the norms may cease to be conscious of the primary reward, which continues to do its work, but out of sight").[93]

Technologism

Ogburn, author of the "cultural lag" theory, takes a viewpoint that focuses chiefly on technology or "material culture." He argues that

. . . material culture accumulates. The use of bone is added to the use of stone. The use of bronze is added to the use of copper and the use of iron is added to the use of bronze. So that the stream of material culture grows bigger. . . .[94] These material culture changes force changes in other parts of culture such as social organization and customs, but these latter parts of culture do not change as quickly. They lag behind the material culture changes. . . .[95]

Ogburn notes that socially created material culture is to be distinguished from the *natural* material conditions of life that so occupy the ecologistic attention: "Material culture is replacing in significance to a certain extent the geographic environment of old. But there is this distinction, the material culture today changes frequently whereas the changes in geographical conditions are slow."[96] Therefore, for example, "the introduction of steam makes changes in

home production, the growth of cities, changes in the position of women, new causes of war."[97] And lest the main causal direction be mistaken, Ogburn adds that "there is no reason to think that steam was adopted in order to make an adjustment to some part of the non-material culture."[98]

In an article published 34 years after his first major statement of "the hypothesis of cultural lag," Ogburn sought to qualify his presentation in three ways. First, he declared that "I do not consider all delays in taking up a new idea as being a lag,"[99] and centered attention on the "maladjustments" that arise from delays, rather than on the delays as such. Second, he generalized his hypothesis to cover the relationship between any two social parts—not only the "material culture" part and the "adaptive culture" part: "A cultural lag is independent of the nature of the initiating part or the lagging part, provided that they are interconnected. The independent [initiating] part may be technological, economic, political, ideological, or anything else."[100] But third, against this vast moderation of the theory, he posed an empirical limitation that returned technological inventions to their original primacy for many present sociological purposes. Thus Ogburn said, although "it is quite probable that religion and not technology was the cause of most social changes in India 2,500 years ago at about the time of Buddha . . . , in our own times in the Western world, technology and science are the great prime movers of social change."[101]

A second illustration of technologism in sociological theory comes from Cottrell. He argues that technology determines the energy that is available to man,

92. Homans, *Social Behavior*, p. 6.
93. *Ibid.*, p. 382 [p. 126, this volume].
94. William Fielding Ogburn, *Social Change* (New York: Viking Press, 1933), p. 73.
95. *Ibid.*, p. 196.
96. *Ibid.*, p. 277.
97. *Ibid.*, p. 270.
98. *Ibid.*, p. 271.
99. William Fielding Ogburn, "Cultural Lag as Theory," *Sociology and Social Research* (January–February, 1957), 41:169.
100. *Ibid.*, p. 171.
101. *Ibid.*, p. 171.

and "the energy available to man limits what he *can* do and influences what he *will* do."[102] Cottrell clearly eschews the premises of both psychologism and materialism:

There are and have been many kinds of labels used in explaining why man persists in or modifies his behavior. He has been variously classified as primarily a power-seeking or political animal, a money-seeking or economic being, a being endowed by blood and soil with racial instincts which guide his choices, the helpless puppet of physical or biological forces which move him, an anarchistic element in time and space guided only by his will, and many other kinds of creatures. The makers of these labels, having endowed man with a basic nature, then proceed to infer how such a creature should act and predict how in fact he will act. Here we provide no such grand scheme. We are trying to discover the relations between the energy converters and fuel men use and the kind of societies they build.[103]

Cottrell's book is, therefore, largely concerned with describing the social and cultural impact of the historical invention of particular energy converters other than man himself—such as domesticated animals and the steam engine. He says, "the series, then, runs something like this: Increase in the use of high energy converters leads to the creation of large production units. This in turn requires concentration of control. The use of high-energy technology also requires a tremendous increase in the specialization of labor, with increased development of specialized codes governing specific areas of performance."[104]

It seems clear from these quotations that Ogburn's and Cottrell's technologistic theories share a common definition of the social (i.e., primarily objective behavior relations) with materialism and psychologism, but differ from them insofar as technological theories explain the social through reference to socially generated nonhuman phenomena (i.e., "machines") that operate on participants' external environments.

The Social Structuralisms: Functional, Exchange, and Conflict

The next three theoretic viewpoints are intimately related by their common effort to explain the social (defined as objective behavior relations) mainly through reference to the socially generated, established (i.e., "structured"), statuses of participants.[105] The social structuralist viewpoints are distinguished from technologism inasmuch as the former are concerned with the things that *social participants* do to one another (no matter what material instruments they use), whereas the latter is concerned with the things that material *inventions* do to participants (no matter who originates or operates these inventions). In other words, the assumption that the socially generated environment in question is augmented by the physical inventions of man is essential to technologism, but irrelevant to the social structuralisms. Similarly, the assumption that the socially generated environment in question is differentiable according to participants of more or less fixed positions is essential to the social structuralisms, but irrelevant to technologism.

There are at least three social structuralist viewpoints, each of which will be an object of separate discussion below. One of these is represented by Kingsley Davis, Robert K. Merton and others, and may be called "functional structuralism." The second is represented by Thibaut and Kelley, Blau, and others, and may be called "exchange structuralism." The third is represented by Coser, Dahrendorf,

102. Fred Cottrell, *Energy and Society* (New York: McGraw-Hill, 1955), p. 2.
103. *Ibid.*, p. 3.
104. *Ibid.*, p. 227.

105. Merton defines a structural description of social behavior as inhering in the practise of "locating . . . people in their inter-connected social statuses" (*op. cit.*, p. 56).

and others, and may be called "conflict structuralism."

Functional Structuralism

Although exchange structuralism will be described in the following analysis as the most general and inclusive of all three structuralist viewpoints, my exposition of them will begin with functional structuralism. This seems advisable because the term "functional structuralism" suggests two linkages: one, of course, to the other structuralist viewpoints, but also a linkage to the other functionalist viewpoint (functional imperativism) that is discussed later in this essay. An examination of functional structuralism therefore seems especially strategic for an understanding of all these theoretic viewpoints in sociology.

Let us start by attending to the link between functional structuralism and functional imperativism. It should be made clear that these two terms are meant to distinguish between types of what is more usually called "structural-functionalism,"[106] and that the distinction rests essentially on the observation that one type stresses the explanatory power of socially generated *structure* as just defined (I call this "functional structuralism"), whereas the other stresses the explanatory power of imposed *imperatives* as defined earlier (I call this "functional imperativism"). At the same time, it is to be emphasized that the two types of structural functionalism have in common their view of the *consequences* of one pheno-

menon as the causes of other, subsequent, phenomena—i.e. their "functionalism."[107] Let us focus on this commonality first, since it is the typically functionalist (and sometimes confusing) view of a consequence at time$_1$ as a cause at time$_2$ that makes it possible to say of a single phenomenon that it is both "a function *of*" (i.e., a consequence of), and/or "functional *for*" (i.e., a cause of) other phenomena.

Although Merton, and Davis, refer somewhat indiscriminately to functional "analysis," "theory," "method," and still more vaguely to "an interpretational scheme [that] depends upon a triple alliance between theory, method and data,"[108] the strictly theoretic aspect seems isolable from the rest. It is this theoretic viewpoint, of course, that is meant by the term "functional structuralism." In general, the viewpoint holds that in order to explain the existence of a given social phenomenon (call it A), we must find out its function for—i.e., its consequences for —the larger social system of which it is a part (call this larger social system B). But clearly, more of an explanation than this is required, since the consequences of A *for* B may explain B, but they certainly cannot, by themselves, explain A. As Gouldner has pointed out,[109] functionalism addresses this problem by implying the hypothesis that B responds to the influence of A by producing commensurate functions or consequences for A (i.e., by "reciprocating" or "repaying" A), and thus by sustaining A when it has positive influence on B and eliminating A

---

106. See Walter Buckley, "Structural-Functional Analysis in Modern Sociology," in Howard Becker and Alvin Boskoff (Eds.), *Modern Sociological Theory in Continuity and Change* (New York: Holt, Rinehart and Winston, 1957), pp. 236–259. In a private communication, Merton notes that the distinction proposed above between aspects of structural-functionalism also appears in Filippo Barbano, "Social Structures and Social Functions: The Emancipation of Structural Analysis in Sociology," *Inquiry* (1968), 11:40–84.

107. Stinchcombe defines a "functional explanation" as "one in which the *consequences* of some

behavior or social arrangement are essential elements of the *causes* of that behavior." (*op. cit.*, p. 80). This definition, as well as his full discussion of functional explanation (pp. 80–101), gives exclusive emphasis to the self-maintenance ("homeostatic") element in functionalism. This element, though undoubtedly present in much functionalist analysis, does not seem to me to be indispensable to it.

108. Merton, *op. cit.*, p. 19.

109. Alvin W. Gouldner, "The Norm of Reciprocity: A Preliminary Statement," *American Sociological Review* (April, 1960), 25:161–178.

when it has negative influence on B. (Of course, B may respond to the *anticipation* —perhaps based on past experience—of A's influence, but even so, the explanation of A still rests in B's consequences for A.) Note that in functional structuralism such reciprocation is an *implied* hypothesis, but, as will be pointed out below, in exchange structuralism and conflict structuralism it is made explicit.

In the last analysis, then, functionalism does not literally view a social phenomenon's consequences for larger social structures as the most direct explanations of that phenomenon, but rather as intermediate indicators of the true direct explanations, i.e., as indicators of the larger social structure's consequences for the phenomenon in question. This seems to be the detailed argument that best interprets Merton's statement that "the central orientation of functionalism [is] expressed in the practise of interpreting data by establishing their consequences for larger structures in which they are implicated,"[110] as well as Davis' somewhat less restrictive statement that functional analysis is "the interpretation of phenomena in terms of their interconnections with societies as going concerns."[111] Of course, the above argument can also account for the frequency with which functionalists (including Merton himself, especially in his theory regarding

social structure and anomie) pursue just the reverse of the analytical sequence described by Merton—i.e., functionalists often seek to interpret data by establishing them as consequences of larger social structures in which they are implicated.

It is important to note, however, that in both the Merton and the Davis quotations, while the emphasis is explicitly on the consequences of smaller social phenomena for larger social phenomena, no *a priori* specifications are offered with respect to what these consequences are likely to be—much less what they *must* be. Merton, for example, carefully elaborates the point that the consequences, both of given social phenomena and of their totality, are apt to vary widely; that some may sustain and regenerate the original social phenomenon ("functions") while others may transform or eliminate it ("dysfunctions"); and that the latter type of consequence is at least equal in importance to the first type.[112]

Thus, in tracing the consequences of specific social phenomena, the functional structuralist does not *have* to make assumptions about their net result—he may allow this to be freely determined by empirical investigation.[113] But when he observes that some larger social organization of which the specific phenomena seem to be parts persists longer than they

110. Merton, *op. cit.*, pp. 46–47. See also Gouldner, *op. cit.*, esp. p. 161, for discussion of the polemical context of this statement.

111. Kingsley Davis, "The Myth of Functional Analysis as a Special Method in Sociology and Anthropology," *American Sociological Review* (December, 1959), 24:760. Davis' statement is less restrictive because "inter-connections" can operate in *both* directions between social phenomena and entire societies. Davis' and Merton's (see n. 110 above) statements share a definition of functionalism as seeking to explicate *the dependence of the whole on its parts*. Merton seems to add to this a second and quite different definition stressing *the dependence of parts on each other*: "It is this connotation [of 'interdependence,' 'reciprocal relation,' or 'mutually dependent variations'] which is central to functional analysis as this has been practised in sociology and social anthropology" (Merton, *op. cit.*, p. 21). Reflecting the same concerns, Blau also distinguishes

two kinds of (functional) interdependence: "First, substructures are dependent on each other, which means that changes in one lead to changes in the others.... The second kind of interdependence ... involves the dependence of the substructures, not on each other, but on the larger social structure, because a centralized authority in the larger collectivity coordinates and directs the major courses of action in its subgroups" (*Exchange and Power in Social Life*, pp. 302–303).

112. See Merton, *op. cit.*, pp. 19–84.

113. As Moore says, "the functional approach is not limited to the search for universal structural features of human societies" (Moore, "Sociology and Demography," p. 838); and, in his discussion of functional explanations, Stinchcombe *mentions* neither functional nor structural imperatives (*op. cit.*, pp. 80–101), although he alludes to them favorably in a different context (pp. 234–235).

do, and that that whole may originate after its several parts do, he *can* be led to assume that the net result or function of the parts must be to generate and/or maintain the whole. The analytic problem then becomes one of devising a classification of the minimum functions that can possibly yield such results. Lists of functional imperatives are such typologies; they seek to classify all the possible social phenomenal consequences that can lead to the genesis and/or maintenance of any social phenomenon that may be treated as having parts. To repeat, functionalism in sociology, when it rests on such assumptions and classifications, is here termed functional imperativism; but when it does not rest on them, it is here termed functional structuralism.

Now, particularly because Merton is being cited here as a leading functional structuralist, rather than as a functional imperativist, Merton's own apparent denial of this classification must be acknowledged. Merton refers to the assumption "that there are certain functions which are indispensable in the sense that unless they are performed, the society (or group, or individual) will not persist," as being an element common to all functionalism in social science.[114] Perhaps even more explicitly he declares that "embedded in every functional analysis is some conception, tacit or expressed, of the functional requirements of the system under observation."[115] Merton thus seems to suggest that no distinction, such as is

here being urged, is possible between functional structuralism and functional imperativism; that, in other words, every functional structuralist analysis is also a functional imperativist analysis.[116]

Two arguments, however, can be mustered against this suggestion—arguments that rely on Merton's own work. First, when one compares the avowedly functionalist writings of Parsons (here classified as a functional imperativist in the more recent stages of his career) with those of Merton, it is quite evident that the latter has made little or no use (at least no express use) of the very conceptions of requirements that he himself holds are common to all functionalist analyses, whereas Parsons has made very great and explicit use of such conceptions. Second, and more important than this, are the implications of one of Merton's most distinctive theoretic contributions, namely his insistence that "functional alternative" must be included among the essential concepts of sociological functionalism. The term might more aptly have been "*structural* alternative,"[117] since Merton means by it that there is more than one *way* of accomplishing a given constant function. In other words, he means that there is more than one way to skin a cat; alternative *structures* are capable of performing a given function.[118] But seen in the oblique light cast by the term "structural alternative," Merton's own term—"functional alternative"—has the unintended consequence of

114. Merton, *op. cit.*, p. 33.
115. *Ibid.*, p. 52.
116. Of course, there are two probably only semantic loopholes in Merton's statement, through which the distinction being advocated here may creep: First, to claim that every functional analysis *does* contain some conception of functional requirements (i.e., imperatives) is not the same as claiming that they *must* contain such a conception. And second, to claim that a certain conception may be "*tacitly*" present, without specifying the criteria to be used in judging such presence, invites free speculation regarding what these criteria might be. One can then, of course, easily imagine criteria whereby at least some functional analyses that do not "expressly" use conceptions of functional

requirements would be judged not to include them "tacitly" either.
117. Moore refers to "structural substitutability," thus implying the term "structural substitute"—which may be viewed as a (superior) functional alternative to "functional alternative" ("Sociology and Demography," p. 838).
118. Merton says: "Once we abandon the gratuitous assumption of the functional indispensability of particular social structures, we immediately require some concept of functional alternatives, equivalents, or substitutes. This focuses attention on the range of possible variation in the items which can, in the case under observation, subserve a functional requirement" (*op. cit.*, p. 52).

suggesting something that, at first glance, seems quite far from its original meaning. The suggestion is that not only can there be *more than one structure* serving a given function, but there can also be *more than one set of functions* serving the persistence of a given constant social system. Once this latter possibility is considered, the ultimate reduction is easily reached: there can be only one sure requirement or imperative for persistent social systems, and that is simply persistence itself. All other conditions and contingencies are ways or structures through which this persistence may or may not be accomplished —and as such, apt to have alternative rather than unique or imperative states.

Thus Merton's own highly influential contributions to functionalist theory in sociology seem to question the need for imperativism in all functionalism, and to place him more securely among those taking a functional structuralist viewpoint than among those taking a functional imperativist viewpoint.

Exchange Structuralism

The relationship between functional structuralism and exchange structuralism may be summed up in the following manner: whereas functional structuralism typically focuses on one side of a given social transaction, exchange structuralism attends to both sides. This means that, in accounting for social phenomenon A, functional structuralism pays most attention to the consequences of A for social phenomenon B and implies that the sustaining consequences of B for A are automatic and therefore theoretically nonproblematic. Exchange structuralism, however, rejects the latter assumption and explicitly treats both sides of each social transaction as problematic. On this point, Gouldner says:

It seems evident . . . that simply to establish its consequences for other social structures provides no answer to the question of the persistence of [the structure in question]. . . . To state the issue generally: the demonstration that A is functional for B can help to account for A's persistence only if the functional theorist tacitly assumes some principle of reciprocity.[119]

Gouldner defines reciprocity itself as cooperative, i.e., as "a mutually gratifying pattern of exchanging goods and services,"[120] but he also briefly acknowledges the existence of "negative norms of reciprocity, that is, . . . sentiments of retaliation where the emphasis is placed not on the return of benefits but on the return of injuries."[121] In accordance with his emphasis on the exchange of benefits rather than of injuries and rather than any mixed benefit-injury exchange, however, Gouldner suggests that the norm of reciprocity "defines certain actions and obligations as payments for *benefits* received,"[122] and "in its universal form, makes two interrelated, minimal demands: (1) people should *help* those who have helped them, and (2) people should *not injure* those who have helped them."[123] (The theoretic viewpoint that best takes account of the exchange of injuries, or of injuries for benefits, or of benefits for injuries, will be discussed below, as "conflict structuralism.")

Gouldner emphasizes that two special characteristics of the norm of reciprocity make it a powerful explanation of social behavior. The first characteristic is that the norm integrates both past events and future events with present behavior. Thus, on the one hand, the norm of reciprocity involves "duties that people owe one another . . . because of their prior actions. . . . We owe others certain things because of what they have previously done for us."[124] In this, its orientation to

119. Gouldner, *op. cit.*, p. 163.
120. *Ibid.*, p. 170.
121. *Ibid.*, p. 172.

122. *Ibid.*, p. 170. Emphasis added.
123. *Ibid.*, p. 171. Emphasis added.
124. *Ibid.*, pp. 170–171.

the past, the norm of reciprocity "engenders motives for returning benefits even when power differences might invite exploitation. The norm thus safeguards powerful people against the temptations of their own status; it motivates and regulates reciprocity as an exchange pattern, serving to inhibit the emergence of exploitative relations which would undermine the social system."[125]

But in its orientation to the future, the norm "actually mobilize(s) egoistic motivations and channel(s) them into the maintenance of social systems . . . if you want to be helped by others [in the future] you must help them [in the present]."[126] Thus, Gouldner argues that the norm of reciprocity's future orientation can serve as a genetic or "starting mechanism" for social interaction insofar as it "provides some realistic grounds for confidence, in the one who first parts with his valuables, that he will be repaid,"[127] while its past orientation serves as a maintenance mechanism for social interaction insofar as it insures that a past act will be repaid in the present, and that this latter act will also be repaid, and so on.[128]

A second special characteristic of the norm of reciprocity is

its comparative indeterminancy. Unlike specific status duties . . . this norm does not require highly specific and uniform performances from people whose behavior it regulates. . . . This indeterminancy enables the norm of reciprocity to perform some of its most important system-stabilizing functions. Being indeterminate, the norm can be applied to countless *ad hoc* transactions. . . . The norm, in this respect, is a kind of plastic filler capable of being poured into the shifting crevices of social structures, and serving as a kind of all-purpose moral cement.[129]

Gouldner argues, therefore, that the "plastic," status-nonspecific, norm of

reciprocity differs from the more rigidly structured rights and duties that characterize complementarities between roles that are associated with specific social statuses (e.g., between customer and clerk). In this "indeterminate," "plastic filler," quality, the norm of reciprocity seems very much like Homans' "elementary social behavior" that grows "in the gaps between institutions [and] clings to institutions as to a trellis."[130]

In some contrast with this emphasis, Goode has discussed complementarities, transactions, or exchanges between specific statuses from the point of view of one of the participants in such an exchange, and concludes that

social structures are made up of role relationships, which in turn are made up of role transactions. . . . Consequently, the sum of role decisions [by each participant] determines what degree of integration exists among various elements of the social structure. . . . [And] the total efforts of individuals to reduce their role strain within structural limitations directly determines the profile, structure, or pattern of the social system.[131]

Goode therefore sees exchange between occupants of different social statuses as a fundamental explanation of social systems. But he also sees the exchange itself as depending on the individual's management of the sum of all his role obligations (a sum which is inevitably "overdemanding") and therefore on the strain-reducing mechanisms provided him by his culture and society, such as "compartmentalization," "delegation," the family as a "role budget center," etc.

It should be noted that Goode stresses the social origin of such mechanisms that control exchange processes between specific social roles. Gouldner seems to hold the same view, but he does not

125. *Ibid.*, p. 174.
126. *Ibid.*, p. 173.   127. *Ibid.*, p. 177.
128. See discussion of genesis and maintenance of social phenomena below.
129. Gouldner, *op. cit.*, p. 175.
130. Homans, *Social Behavior: Its Elementary Forms*, p. 391 [p. 132, this volume].
131. William J. Goode, "A Theory of Role Strain," *American Sociological Review* (August, 1960), 25:194. Cf. Robert K. Merton, "The Role-Set: Problems in Sociological Theory," *The British Journal of Sociology* (June, 1957), pp. 106–120.

explicitly discuss the origin of the norm of reciprocity, and therefore of social exchange—i.e., he does not explicitly indicate whether the norm is to be viewed as biologically inherited by all social participants or in some other way imposed on the social, or as generated by the social itself. Blau, however, clearly argues that the origins of the norm of reciprocity and other such controlling mechanisms lie not in the social itself but elsewhere, in an imposed "necessity" that Blau leaves unexplicated. He says:

In contrast to Gouldner . . . it is held here that the norm of reciprocity merely reinforces and stabilizes tendencies inherent in the character of social exchange itself and that the fundamental starting mechanism of patterned social intercourse is found in the existential conditions of exchange, not in the norm of reciprocity. It is a necessary condition of exchange that individuals, in the interest of continuing to receive needed services, discharge their obligations for having received them in the past.[132]

Surely Simmel would have noted no "necessity" in such discharge so long as appropriation by robbery or gift remain alternative methods of acquiring needed services. As will be pointed out in greater detail below, Simmel would undoubtedly have attributed the selection of the exchange alternative over the robbery or gift alternatives to the social invention of abstract value concepts, rather than to any non-normative "existential conditions" such as Blau suggests.

In a similar vein, Coser notes that in discussing contractual relations (which may be viewed as formalized exchange relations) Durkheim wrote that " 'a contract is not sufficient unto itself but is possible only thanks to a regulation of the contract which is originally social.' " Coser goes on:

Contractual relations are actually established in a context of norms that exist prior to, and are not specified in, the contract. The cohesive force implicit in a system of contractual relations derives, then, not from the mutual advantage of the parties to the transaction, but from the presence of an "organic solidarity" existing before the transaction is undertaken.[133]

To the extent that it contradicts these socially generated explanantes of the social, Blau's exchange theory fits no more easily into that category of explanations than does Homans' theory. Indeed, Blau implies the same premises of innate (therefore imposed) psychological qualities that Homans does: "The basic social processes that govern associations among men have their roots in primitive psychological processes . . . ."[134]

Nevertheless, despite its excursions into imposed explanations, Blau's theory seems more rightfully to fall in the category of socially generated explanations of social phenomena, because one can set aside his discussion of "starting mechanisms" of complex social life as a preliminary to his principal theory. His avowed concern is not with what Homans has called the "elementary" forms of social life as such, but "with utilizing the analysis of simpler processes for clarifying complex structures."[135] Therefore, Blau's theory seeks to derive simple types of associations between persons from different types of exchange of different types of rewards, and from these associations to derive social integration, differentiation, opposition, and legitimation as dimensions of complex social structures. In the latter derivations socially generated values and norms play a central part: "Value consensus is of crucial significance for social processes that pervade complex social structures, because standards commonly agreed upon serve as mediating links for social transactions between individuals and groups without any direct

132. Blau, *Exchange and Power*, p. 92.
133. Lewis A. Coser, *The Functions of Social Conflict* (Glencoe, Ill.: Free Press, 1956), p. 123. See also Parsons, *The Structure of Social Action*, pp. 333–334.

134. Blau, *Exchange and Power*, p. 19 [p. 190, this volume].
135. *Ibid.*, p. 13.

contact. Sharing basic values . . . serves as functional equivalent for the feelings of personal attraction that unite pairs of associates and small groups."[136]

Thibaut and Kelley's exchange theory seems to be a more explicitly and exclusively social-generation-of-social-phenomena theory than Blau's: "The approach to be proposed takes as its independent variables the possibilities for reciprocal control possessed by the members of a collectivity. . . . The dependent variables are the various aspects of a relationship that can be viewed as outgrowths of the particular pattern of interdependence present there. These include properties of the interaction process, norms, and roles."[137] And although the exchange of costs and rewards is as crucial to their theory as it is to Blau's, Thibaut and Kelley note that

no stand has been taken [in our theory] as to the range of events that may constitute rewards for the individual. This we believe to be a matter for empirical research. . . . At times we have been tempted to invoke certain special social motives (e.g., a need for power or status) to explain specific phenomena. . . . However, since the list of such motives is still an open-ended matter and an indefinite number of plausible ones may be added, the appeal to a motive to explain any given social phenomenon seems both too "easy" and too unparsimonious.[138]

Blau does not acknowledge in this way the present insolubility of questions relating to the original genesis of complex social structures. In order to address questions of "primitiveness," "starting mechanisms," "intrinsicness," and the like, he must (and does) offer genetic as well as maintenance explanations of complex social phenomena.

Conflict Structuralism

"Conflict theory" is here treated as related to "exchange theory" in at least two ways. First, conflict theory may logically be considered a variety of exchange theory insofar as it pays primary attention to the exchange of acts, albeit acts defined as injurious or punishing. In exchange theory generally, interest is (or should logically be) in the exchange of any and all acts, whether beneficial or injurious, rewarding or punishing. Second, as Simmel pointed out, those exchanges that involve compromise (and "all exchange of things is a compromise")[139] are ordinarily substitutes for "robbery [which], along with gift, is the most obvious form of change in ownership."[140] To put this somewhat differently, a situation in which one party bestows a benefit on the other in return for a benefit received is viewed by Simmel as an alternative to

---

136. *Ibid.*, p. 24. This use of the term "functional" in his book on exchange calls to mind the fact that Blau's theoretic orientation has shifted, in perceptible stages during his career so far, from functional structuralism to exchange structuralism. In his first book, *The Dynamics of Bureaucracy*, Blau said "conceptions of functional analysis are used to organize the data of this study, taking as a starting point the conceptual scheme developed by Robert K. Merton" (p. 6), and discussed this scheme in some detail (pp. 6–12). But in his second book, *Formal Organizations* (San Francisco: Chandler, 1961), written with W. Richard Scott, Blau does not discuss "functional analysis" at all. Instead, considerable attention is paid to "the structural approach." This latter is defined as being "concerned with the influence of the present social conditions on conduct" (p. 82). The "structuralist" asks "how observed patterns influence social structure and social processes . . ." (p. 85). Thus, the critical point seems to have come for Blau when he divided structural-functional

analysis into two components and chose "the *structural* approach" over "*functional* analysis." Apparently, Blau thereby extinguished in his work the functionalist's nearly exclusive emphasis on the consequences of acts and began to incorporate the exchange theorist's equally strong emphasis on causes as well as consequences of acts. His most recent book, *Exchange and Power in Social Life*, therefore discusses neither "the structural approach" nor "functional analysis," but devotes its full attention to exchange, in which "give" as well as "take," cause as well as consequence, are examined.

137. John W. Thibaut and Harold H. Kelley, *The Social Psychology of Groups* (New York: John Wiley, 1959), p. 4.

138. *Ibid.*, p. 5.

139. Georg Simmel, "Conflict," in *Conflict and the Web of Group Affiliations* (Glencoe, Ill.: Free Press, 1955), p. 116.

140. *Ibid.*, p. 115.

situations in which one party bestows a benefit on the other in return for an injury (i.e., robbery), or in return for nothing (i.e., gift). Exchange of benefits can thus substitute for conflict: "The fight can be avoided by offering the owner of the desired object another object from one's own possession."[141] But in order to accomplish this, Simmel argues, the social invention of "value"—an abstraction that enables relatively dispassionate comparisons and equations among dissimilar concrete things to which the passion of possessiveness often becomes uniquely attached—is necessary. Simmel says:

Every exchange presupposes that valuations and interests have taken on an objective character. The decisive element is no longer the mere subjective passion of desire, to which only fight is adequate, but the value of the object which is recognized by both sides and which, objectively unchanged, can be expressed by several other objects. Renunciation of the valued object, because one receives the value quantum contained in it in some other form, is the means, truly miraculous in its simplicity, of accommodating opposite interests without fight.... Compromise through representability, of which exchange is a special case, means the fundamental, even though only partly realized, possibility of avoiding conflict or of terminating it before the mere strength of the parties has sealed the decision.[142]

The exchange nature of conflict is also clearly revealed in Coser's statement that "conflict . . . is always a trans-action,"[143] and in Boulding's resumes and elaborations of Richardson processes and game theory.[144] In all these cases, it is clear that exchanges—of different kinds of acts, between various kinds of parties, and structured in various ways—are interpreted to

give rise to new social phenomena. Thus, in a statement stressing the characteristics of conflict as a mechanism for social change, Dahrendorf indicates that "three questions come especially to the forefront, which conflict theory must answer: 1. How do conflicting groups arise from the structure of society? 2. What forms can the struggles among such groups assume? 3. How does the conflict among such groups affect a change in the social structures?"[145]

Blau offers the view that conflict is a causal product of exchange, once removed: "Exchange processes . . . give rise to differentiation of power,"[146] and then:

differentiation of power in a collective situation evokes contrasting dynamic forces: legitimating processes that foster the organization of individuals and groups in common endeavors; and countervailing forces that deny legitimacy to existing powers and promote opposition and cleavage. Under the influence of these forces, the scope of legitimate organization expands to include ever larger collectivities, but opposition and conflict recurrently redivide these collectivities and stimulate reorganization along different lines.[147]

Blau therefore sees conflict as a major engine of social change:

Opposition is a regenerative force that introjects new vitality into a social structure and becomes the basis of social reorganization. It serves as a catalyst or starting mechanism of social change. . . . There are tendencies toward change in social structures that do not depend on opposition movements such as those generated by technological developments. But there are also structural rigidities due to vested interests and powers, organizational commitments, and traditional institutions. These defy modification and adjustment except through social conflict and opposition.[148]

141. Ibid., p. 115.
142. Ibid., p. 116.
143. Coser, op. cit., p. 37.
144. Kenneth E. Boulding, Conflict and Defense (New York: Harper Torchbooks, 1962). See also Jessie Bernard, "Some Current Conceptualizations in the Field of Conflict," American Journal of Sociology (January, 1965), 70:442–454.

145. Ralf Dahrendorf, "Toward a Theory of Social Conflict," Journal of Conflict Resolution (1958), 11:176 [p. 218, this volume].
146. Blau, Exchange and Power, p. 22 [p. 192, this volume].
147. Ibid., p. 24 [p. 193, this volume].
148. Ibid., p. 301.

To close this discussion of the three social structuralist viewpoints—functional structuralism, exchange structuralism, and conflict structuralism—consider Figure 3, wherein an attempt is made to summarize their relationships. Figure 3 can offer only crude generalizations because, among other things, it assumes that all definitions are mutual to the participants (i.e., it assumes that A and B agree on what constitutes "benefit," "nothing," and "injury") and obviously this is not necessarily true, and also because it ignores the nuances that gradually shade "benefit" into "nothing," and "nothing" into "injury." But in spite of these short-

Social Actorᵃ A Gives to B:

Social Actorᵃ B Returns to A:	Benefitᵇ	Nothing	Injuryᵇ	
Benefitᵇ	A and B "exchange"ᶜ	B "gifts" A	A "robs" B	B is "functional" for A
Nothing	A "gifts" B B is "ungrateful"	No Interaction	B "turns other cheek"	
Injuryᵇ	B "bites the hand that feeds him"	B "attacks" A	A and B "conflict"ᶜ	B is "dysfunctional" for A
	A is "functional" for B		A is "dysfunctional" for B	

Figure 3. *The Primary Explanantes of Functional, Exchange, and Conflict Structuralism Seen as Various Combinations of Given and Returned Acts.*

a. Any individual or collectivity of some relatively clear and established social status.

b. Note that "benefit" and "injury" are more general terms than "reward" and "punishment," since the latter terms necessarily imply reciprocation. That is, a reward is a benefit returned for an act already received and a punishment is an injury returned for an act already received. But as the diagram suggests, both benefits and injuries may be initiated as well as returned.

c. For simplicity, only the injury-for-injury type is called "conflict" here; actually, each cell in the third row and each in the third column represents a type of conflict. Similarly, although only the benefit-for-benefit type is called "exchange" here, all of the cells (except the "no interaction" cell, of course) represent types of exchange.

comings, Figure 3 may help to clarify two major conclusions. First, it represents each structuralist viewpoint as concentrating on different selections made among eight types of social interactions (plus non-interaction). Second, functional structuralism is again described as a one-way or "marginals" viewpoint, whereas exchange and conflict structuralism (in the conventionally restricted sense in which these terms are most often used) are shown as two-way viewpoints, since they explicate B's action on A as well as A's action on B. (Perhaps it is superfluous to note that a two-way perspective is not necessarily superior to a one-way perspective; everything depends, of course, on what one wishes to see.)

A Missing Viewpoint

There does not seem to be current in sociology a theoretic viewpoint whose explanandum consists chiefly of objective behavior relations and whose explanans is chiefly generated by the social and operates via "not-nervous system" characteristics of the participants themselves (see Figure 2). Of course, all the viewpoints discussed here imply such an explanans, insofar as they at least allow for the possibility that participants' physiological structure and functioning can affect and be affected by social phenomena. But no viewpoint seems to make this one of its central propositions. Although Figure 2 indicates that Parsonian social actionism refers to the "actor," this is the least well-developed concept in the social actionist repertoire.

Presumably, a viewpoint that filled this vacancy would stress the shaping of objective behavior relations by socially generated differences in participants'

height, weight, brain structure, musculature, or other physiological attributes. Occasionally, especially in efforts to explain the social behavior of the poor, references are made to socially generated physiological differences, but so far they have not received the emphasis that other explanantes have. In sharp contrast with this theoretic deëmphasis in the study of human social phenomena is the entomologist's heavy reliance in explaining insect social phenomena on socially generated (via differential nursing of young) physiological (caste) differences. But in the now-foreseeable future, when the physical and biological sciences and technologies will have achieved the ability to manipulate the genetic (and therefore physiological) constitution of each new human social participant, this theoretic viewpoint may become as essential to sociology as it now is to entomology.

Symbolic Interactionism

One writer has suggested a sociologically useful contrast between the strategy of a game and the script of a play, such that the player of a game is allowed a wider range of specific "tactical" choices than is the player in a play, who is bound to say only his written lines at times and places specified for him by the playwright. Farber says, "probably, social relations can be placed on a continuum with the dramatic or completely restricted kind of social relations at one extreme and strategic or infinite kinds of social relations at the other."[149] On such a continuum, the social structuralisms would tend toward the dramaturgical end and symbolic interactionism would tend toward the strategical end. But as a counter

149. Bernard Farber, "A Research Model: Family Crises and Games of Strategy," in Bernard Farber (Ed.), *Kinship and Family Organization* (New York: John Wiley, 1966), p. 432. It is perhaps an overstatement to use theatre as illustrative of "completely restricted" social relations; the play-actor always has some control at least over *how* he speaks his lines—i.e., over "interpretation". Nevertheless, although the metaphor may have its weaknesses, Farber's analytical point seems a strong one.

to its emphasis on the uncertainties of participants' environments, symbolic interaction stresses emergent certainties within the participants themselves—i.e., the development of "self" and "commitment".

Thus Mead says:

I want to call attention particularly to the fact that this response of the "I" is something that is more or less uncertain. The attitudes of others which one assumes as affecting his own conduct constitute the "me," and that is something that is there, but the response to it is as yet not given. When one sits down to think anything out, he has certain data that are there. . . . He says, in effect, "I have done certain things that seem to commit me to a certain course of conduct." . . . And when the response does take place, then it appears in the field of experience largely as a memory image.[150]

More recently, Blumer emphasizes that:

Human interaction is a positive shaping process in its own right. The participants in it have to build up their respective lines of conduct by constant interpretation of each other's ongoing lines of action. As participants take account of each other's ongoing acts, they have to arrest, reorganize or adjust their own intentions, wishes, feelings, and attitudes; similarly, they have to judge the fitness of norms, values, and group prescriptions for the situation being formed by the acts of others. . . . Because of [symbolic interaction] human group life takes on the character of an ongoing process—a

continuing matter of fitting developing lines of conduct to one another.[151]

The sense of emergence, of flexible strategy and tactic, and of cumulative memory and commitment, in Mead's and Blumer's statements (and in Garfinkel's discussion of ethnomethodology)[152] is clearly missing from Merton's more strictly dramaturgical statement that:

Among the several elements of social and cultural structures, two are of immediate importance. . . . The first consists of culturally defined goals, purposes and interests, held out as legitimate objectives for all or for diversely located members of the society. . . . A second element of the cultural structure defines, regulates and controls the acceptable modes of reaching out for these goals.[153]

But again, the difference is largely one of emphasis. On the one hand, Blumer notes that in the perspective of symbolic interactionism:

Each joint action must be seen as having a career or history . . . [which] is generally orderly, fixed and repetitious by virtue of a common identification or definition of the joint action that is made by its participants. . . . Such common identifications serve, above everything else to account for the regularity, stability, and repetitiveness of joint action in vast areas of group life.[154]

This emphasis on fixity, repetition, orderliness, and common definitions is rather

---

150. George Herbert Mead, in Anselm Strauss (Ed.), *The Social Psychology of George Herbert Mead* (Chicago: Phoenix Books, 1956), pp. 244–245.

151. Blumer, *op. cit.*, p. 538 [p. 237, this volume]. See also, by the same author, "Society as Symbolic Interaction," reprinted in Jerome G. Manis and Bernard N. Meltzer (Eds.), *Symbolic Interaction* (Boston: Allyn and Bacon, 1967), pp. 139–148.

152. Insofar as ethnomethodology embraces a theoretic (rather than methodologic) viewpoint, it is clearly symbolic interactionist. Although it is difficult to cite a short and self-contained quotation to this effect, the following statements from Garfinkel are pertinent: "I use the term 'ethnomethodology' to refer to the investigation of the rational properties of indexical expressions and other practical actions as contingent ongoing accomplishments of organized artful practises of everyday life" (p. 11). The crucial phrase here, of course, is "rational

properties of indexical expressions." By "indexical expressions" Garfinkel means expressions for making the "settings of everyday affairs" "account-able"— i.e., "observable-and-reportable, . . . available to members as situated practises of looking-and-telling" (p. 1). And the "rational properties" of such indexical expressions are said to "consist of what members do with, what they 'make of' the accounts in the socially organized actual occasions of their use. Members' accounts are reflexively and essentially tied for their rational features to the socially organized occasions of their use for they are *features* of the socially organized occasions of their use" (pp. 3–4). Harold Garfinkel, *Studies in Ethnomethodology* (Englewood Cliffs, N.J.: Prentice–Hall, 1967).

153. Merton, *Social Theory and Social Structure*, pp. 132–133 [p. 163, this volume].

154. Blumer, *op. cit.*, p. 541.

more like a social structuralist position. On the other hand, Merton argues that:

Sociologists often speak of these controls as being "in the mores" or as operating through social institutions. Such elliptical statements are true enough, but they obscure the fact that culturally standardized practises are not all of a piece. They are subject to a wide gamut of control. . . . In assessing the operation of social control, these variations—roughly indicated by the terms presciption, preference, permission, and proscription—must of course be taken into account.[155]

And this emphasis on standardization and control as capable of existing in low degree as well as high degree is rather more like a symbolic interactionist position. Finally, in this connection, note Blumer's moderated reference to both positions:

Usually most of the situations encountered by people in a given society are defined or "structured" by them in the same way. Through previous interaction they develop and acquire common understandings or definitions of how to act in this or that situation. These common definitions enable people to act alike. The common repetitive behavior of people in such situations should not mislead the student into believing that no process of interpretation is in play; or the contrary, even though fixed, the actions of the participating people are constructed by them through a process of interpretation. Since ready-made and commonly accepted definitions are at hand little strain is placed on people in guiding and organizing their acts. However, many other situations may not be defined in a single way by the participating people. In this event, their lines of action do not fit together readily and collective action is blocked. Interpretations have to be developed and effective accommodation of the participants to one another has to be worked out. In the case of such "undefined" situations, it is necessary to trace and study the emerging

process of definition which is brought into play.[156]

Social Actionism and Functional Imperativism

In discussing the final two viewpoints, attention will be paid almost exclusively to the work of Talcott Parsons and his collaborators, who, though not alone in adopting either viewpoint, present the best opportunity of examining certain relations between them. The discussion itself should be understood as an attempt to radically simplify and compress Parsonian theory, which is very far from simple or brief in its natural state. For this reason, much important but complicated detail is deliberately left out here (most notably, the specific definitions of the pattern-variables and of the functional imperatives), but the reader is encouraged to pursue the footnotes to satisfy his interest in these matters.

Parsons, in his early statement (1937) of the "theory of action," is both sweeping and absolute concerning its intended scope: "There are no group properties that are not reducible to properties of systems of action and there is no analytical theory of groups which is not translatable into terms of the theory of action."[157] I have already indicated the subjective behavior definition of the unit act that characterizes Parsons' social actionism, and it may be noted that Hinkle lists this emphasis on the subjective first among the "core of suppositions held in common by MacIver, Znaniecki, and Parsons."[158] To this general characterization, however, one should add that Parsons has not been equally interested in all possible kinds of subjective behavior relations. Rather, he and his collaborators have

155. Merton, *Social Theory and Social Structure*, p. 133 [p.163, this volume].
156. Herbert Blumer, "Society as Symbolic Interaction," in Arnold Rose (Ed.), *Human Behavior and Social Processes: An Interactionist Approach* (Boston: Houghton Mifflin, 1962), pp. 187–188.

157. Parsons, *The Structure of Social Action*, p. 747.
158. Roscoe C. Hinkle, "Antecedents of the Action Orientation in American Sociology Before 1935," *American Sociological Review* (October, 1963), 28:706.

focused on *the making of choices* among the possible means and ends of action[159]—under the assumption that human behavior, in contrast with the behavior of other organisms (whose ends and means seem more genetically determined), necessarily involves such volitional processes, no matter what social entity may be defined as "actor." For Parsons, then, a social phenomenon is constituted by at least two actors' subjective and mutually complementary choice-making; but since each actor must be subjectively oriented toward the other, the orientation of either is taken as the basic unit of social actionist analysis. Thus, "the unit act involves the relationship of *an* actor to a situation composed of objects, and it is conceived as a choice (imputed by the theorist to the actor) among alternative ways of defining the situation,"[160] and "the concept 'actor' is extended to define not only individual personalities in roles but other types of acting units—collectivities, behavioral organisms, and cultural systems."[161]

Parsons' social actionism may thus be understood as offering answers to the following questions: (1) How may the alternative means–ends relationships that social actors confront, and the criteria of choice among them that such actors employ, be most intelligibly defined? (2) What factors explain the stability of such criteria, hence the regularity with which given choices are made by given actors, and hence social life itself? In his first major exploration of these questions, Parsons argued against utilitarian and positivistic answers to them, and defended the proposition that:

In the choice of alternative means to the end, in so far as the situation allows alternatives, there is a "normative orientation" of action. Within the area of control of the actor, the means employed cannot, in general, be conceived either as chosen at random or as dependent exclusively on the conditions of action, but must in some sense be subject to the influence of an independent, determinate selective factor, a knowledge of which is necessary to the understanding of the concrete course of action.[162]

For present purposes, two terms in this statement are clearly pivotal: "norm" (or its apparent equivalent, "independent, determinate selective factor") and "situation." These terms seem to contain Parsons' primary explanation of human choice, and therefore of social action.

Regarding the first term, Parsons says: "A norm is a verbal description of the concrete course of action . . . regarded as desirable, combined with an injunction to make certain future actions conform to this course."[163] Although the origins of norms in general—and of the "independent, determinate selective factor"—are not made clear in this early statement,[164] Parsons does indicate that "economic rationality" (which may tentatively be taken to be a particular norm) and also "value integration" are "emergent properties of action which can be observed only when a plurality of unit acts is treated together as constituting an integrated system of action."[165] To this extent, then, even the early statement of the theory relied on socially generated (Parsons' term is "emergent") explanations of the social. But the emphasis on

159. See especially Parsons and Shils, *op. cit.*, pp. 63–64.

160. Parsons, "Pattern Variables Revisited," p. 467 [p. 270, this volume]. Emphasis changed.

161. *Ibid.*, p. 467 [p. 270, this volume].

162. Parsons, *The Structure of Social Action*, pp. 44–45.

163. *Ibid.*, p. 75.

164. John Finley Scott, in "The Changing Foundations of the Parsonian Action Scheme," argues that Parsons believed the origin to be in some non-natural realm of man's existence. In this

connection, note Parsons' more recent description of "the environment above action" as "the 'ultimate reality' with which we are ultimately concerned . . . —e.g., evil and suffering, the temporal limitations of human life, and the like. 'Ideas' in this area, as cultural objects, are in some sense symbolic 'representations' (e.g., conceptions of gods, totems, the supernatural) of the ultimate realities, but are not themselves such realities" (*Societies*, p. 8).

165. Parsons, *The Structure of Social Action*, pp. 739–740.

socially generated normative orientations is revealed more clearly in Parsons' and Shils' 1951 statement:

Systems of value standards (criteria of selection) and other patterns of culture, when institutionalized in social systems and internalized in personality systems, guide the actor with respect to both the orientation to ends and the normative regulation of means and of expressive activities, whenever the need dispositions of the actor allow choices in these matters.[166]

Here too, Parsons and Shils discuss the key theoretic inventions of Parsonian social actionism, namely, the "pattern variables":

An actor in a situation is confronted by a series of major dilemmas of orientation, a series of choices that the actor must make before the situation has a determinate meaning for him. The objects of the situation do not interact with the cognizing and cathecting organism in such a fashion as to determine automatically the meaning of the situation. . . . Specifically, we maintain, the actor must make five specific dichotomous choices before any situation will have a determinate meaning. The five dichotomies which formulate these choice alternatives are called the pattern variables.[167]

They go on to say:

In principle, therefore, *every* concrete need disposition of personality, or every role-expectation of social structure, involves a combination of values of the five pattern variables. The cross-classification of each of the five against each of the others, yielding a table of thirty-two cells, will, on the assumption that the list of pattern variables is exhaustive, produce a classification of the basic value patterns. Internalized in the personality system, these value patterns serve as a starting point for a classification of the possible types of need-dispositions; as institutionalized in the system of social action, they are a classification of components of role-expectation definitions.[168]

The pattern-variables thus offer direct answer to the first question cited above that social actionism poses, namely: How may we most intelligibly define the alternative means–ends relationships that social actors confront, and the criteria of choice among them that such actors employ? The other conceptual inventions that seem essential to Parsons' social actionism jointly answer the second question posed by that viewpoint, namely: What factors best explain the stability of choice criteria (etc.)? Parsons' reply is: (1) socialization (through which the criteria of choice—the "need-dispositions"—become "internalized in the personality system" of the actor), and (2) role differentiation and social control mechanisms (through which each actor's conformity to a particular set of internalized criteria is maintained, and deviations from that pattern are corrected (by external pressures from other actors).[169] In short, Parsons' social actionism claims that one or the other alternative in each pattern-variable pair is engendered and maintained within the incumbents of a given role by the incumbents of other roles, and that the five-fold system of criteria thus socially generated serves as the actor's most fundamental guide in making the action choices required by his day-to-day role performance. For example, the role of physician vis-à-vis patient[170] might be characterized by the pattern-variable combination of universalism, performance, specificity, neutrality, and collectivity orientation. The physician's socialized adherence to this set of orientations, the patient's socialized adherence to a different but complementary set, and the exercise by each (and by others as well) of social control over the other's conformity and deviance, explain social relations between physician and

---

166. Parsons and Shils, *op. cit.*, p. 56.
167. *Ibid.*, p. 76.
168. *Ibid.*, p. 93.
169. See Parsons, *The Social System*, Chaps. VI

and VII; and Talcott Parsons and Robert F. Bales, *Family, Socialization and Interaction Process* (Glencoe, Ill.: Free Press, 1955).
170. See Parsons, *The Social System*, Chapter X.

patient insofar as these propositions account for the way physician and patient regularly choose among all possible behaviors toward each other. Through such interrelations between two or more choice-making actors, social systems— the explicit concern of functional imperativism—emerge, and at this point the essentially micro explanandum of social actionism (i.e., the "unit act") is transformed into the more macro one of functional imperativism. (This point will be discussed further below.)

Note that although the emphasis in social actionism is explicitly on the *social generation and maintenance* of subjective dispositions in role incumbents, a major *imposed* limitation is clearly implied when social actionism holds that one or the other member of each pattern-variable pair must always be chosen for any given role, and that both members of a given pair must never be chosen for any given role. This is indicated when Parsons speaks of "pattern-variable dilemmas" and remarks that "the *imperatives* of specificity and diffuseness cannot be maximally satisfied at the same time."[171]

More generally, as Scott has suggested, "the decline of voluntarism" is visible in the historical development of Parsons' action theory.[172] In the terms of the present essay, this means that socially generated elements declined in explanatory weight, while imposed elements increased in weight, as Parsons and his collaborators developed social action theory itself and, of course, moved into functional imperativist theory. It also

means that whereas Parsonian social actionism concentrates on *choice-making*, Parsonian functional imperativism concentrates on *selection among alternatives*. I wish to imply here the difference between social actionism's requirement of a *human* actor, capable of volition, and functional imperativism's reduced anthropocentrism and greater generality in seeking reference to *any* entity capable of selecting in some regular fashion among alternatives, whether one would call such selection voluntary or not.

The development of Parsonian theory from social actionism to functional imperativism[173] will not be traced here in detail, nor will more illustrations of imperativism be given than have already appeared in this paper. However, certain foreshadowings of the imperativist position—other than those already indicated —should be pointed out in quotations that have been given above. Note that in the first quotation from *The Structure of Social Action* (n. 162, above) Parsons argues that "in the choice of alternative means to the end, *in so far as the situation allows alternatives*, there is a 'normative orientation' of action" [emphasis added]. And in the first quotation from *Toward a General Theory of Action* (n. 166, above), Parsons and Shils propose that systems of value standards guide the actor "*whenever the need dispositions of the actor allow choices* in these matters" [emphasis added]. In other words, attention, albeit secondary in both instances, is here being paid to two types of *imposed* conditions—one pertaining to the environments of participants (i.e., "situation"), and one

171. Parsons, "Pattern Variables Revisited," p. 471 [p. 275, this volume]. Emphasis added.
172. Scott, "The Changing Foundations of the Parsonian Action Scheme."
173. It may be noted that Parsons' and others' lists of functional imperatives are all *positive* imperatives, in the sense that they seek to specify things that *must* be done. They do not include what might be called *negative* imperatives, or "proscriptions," in the sense of things that must *not* be done. A typology of functional proscriptions would classify all possible social consequences that lead to the disintegration of

any conceivable social system. Presumably, the simple nonperformance of functional imperatives would be included here, but functional proscriptions certainly need not be limited to this condition. Within such a more complete perspective, a persistent social system could be considered to be the joint result of fulfilling imposed functional imperatives and avoiding imposed functional proscriptions. See Parsons' typology of deviance, in *The Social System*, p. 257, for a possible typology of functional proscriptions.

pertaining to the participants themselves (i.e., "need dispositions of the actor"). In functional imperativism, such imposed conditions are pressed forward into the role of prime explanations of the social.

The part played by imposed conditions in functional imperativism closely parallels that of the socially generated pattern-variables in social actionism: the imperatives are meant to define the types of problems that a social system must confront, as the pattern-variables are meant to define the types of choices that a social actor in such a system must make. Similarly, Parsons' use of the concepts "structural differentiation"[174] and normative "specification," coupled with "input-output exchanges"[175] between differentiated substructures, parallels his use of role differentiation and socialization, coupled with social control,[176] insofar as the former set of concepts is meant to explain the way social system problems are met, and the latter set is meant to explain the way a social actor's choices are made. Indeed, one gets the

impression that in Parsons' view, socialization is a kind of structural differentiation—beginning with the differentiation that occurs inside the infant's brain structure between self and other[177]—that role differentiation is a kind of normative specification, and that social control is a kind of substructural exchange wherein normatively defined reciprocity from outside the actor is conditionally granted or denied.[178]

Such correspondences between the two viewpoints' explanantes seem matched by correspondences between their respective explananda. Thus, as has already been pointed out in an earlier section of this essay and in Figure 2, the two viewpoints share a subjective behavior relations definition of the social. It should now be reiterated that when the most elemental explanandum of social actionism—the "unit act"— is aggregated, it becomes identical with the most elemental explanandum of functional imperativism—the "social system." Given this strong definitional relation

174. "The primary, over-all principle is that of differentiation in relation to functional exigency; this is the master concept for the analysis of social structure" (Parsons, "An Outline of the Social System," in Talcott Parsons, Edward Shils, Kaspar D. Naegele, and Jesse R. Pitts Ed., *Theories of Society* [New York: Free Press of Glencoe, 1961], I:44). Parsons adds, however, that this principle alone is insufficient; the principles of "segmentation" and "normative specification" are also needed (see pp. 44–47). Cf. Parsons, *Societies*, pp. 22–24, where differentiation is said to be accompanied by "adaptive upgrading," by "integration," and by both normative "specification" and normative "generalization."

175. By the process of normative specification each differentiated substructure develops norms that give detailed and differentiated expression to the general norms of the parent structure. For example, Parsons argues that the adaptive substructure of the American society gives business entrepreneurial expression to the general American norm of "freedom," while the goal attainment substructure gives political expression to the same general norm (see Parsons, "An Outline of the Social System," pp. 44–47, and *Societies*, pp. 22–24). In making input-output exchanges, each differentiated substructure produces goods and/or services that become resources of other substructures, and receives, in turn, the products of other substructures as its own resources. For example, Parsons and Smelser argue

that an exchange of labor services for consumer goods occurs between households in the pattern-maintenance-and-tension-management substructure and business firms in the adaptive substructure (see Talcott Parsons and Neil J. Smelser, *Economy and Society* [Glencoe, Ill.: Free Press, 1956], p. 71).

176. The same pair of ideas was used by Durkheim in his typology of explanantes of suicide rates: (1) the anomie-fatalism explanans refers to extremes in the degree to which individuals may be socialized to accept a particular normative system (anomie = extremely low; fatalism = extremely high), and thus also maximally or minimally differentiated internally from one another with respect to their subjective goals or criteria of action; (2) the egoism-altruism explanans refers to extremes in the degree to which individuals may be subjected to external social control (egoism = extremely low; altruism = extremely high), and thus also poorly or well integrated into a pattern of objective benefit and injury exchanges among individuals. (Cf. Barclay D. Johnson, "Durkheim's One Cause of Suicide," *American Sociological Review* [December, 1965], 30:875–886.) The egoism-altruism explanans is another view of the "moral density" explanans that Durkheim used to account for the difference between mechanical and organic solidarity. (See also the discussions in this essay of demographism and exchange structuralism.)

177. See Parsons and Bales, *op. cit.*

178. See Parsons, *The Social System*, Chapter VII.

between the two viewpoints, the explanatory relations described above seem to follow logically, and each theory's explanantes have their analogues in the other's, as do their explananda. These correspondences seem to be part of what Parsons means when he says that from the social actionist viewpoint, "the concept 'actor' referred to individual human beings as personalities in roles, and the analysis . . . 'looks' out to the social system from the vantage point of the actor."[179] This implies that when social actionism is employed to explain the macro social system, it treats the latter as an aggregation of micro unit acts and concludes that the unit act must therefore be its primary explanandum. By accounting for the unit act, then, social actionism claims to account for all social phenomena that may be synthesized from it. Such a claim follows the familiar analytic credo that in order to understand the whole, its most elemental parts must first be understood. But in contrast with this credo, of course, is the equally familiar synthetic or gestaltist view that in order to understand the parts of any whole, the whole itself must first be understood. Functional imperativism follows this latter tradition. Thus Parsons says: "the conceptual scheme of the four system-problems [imperatives] has added a set of rules and procedures whereby the analysis of components of action in terms of pattern-variables can be carried out by 'looking down' on them . . . from the perspective of the social system."[180] This implies that when functional imperativism is employed to

explain a micro unit act, it treats the latter as the consequence of structurally differentiated functioning of the macro social system as a whole, and concludes that the latter must therefore be its primary explanandum. The relations between social actionism and functional imperativism that have just been discussed are summarized in Figure 4.

Quite apart from its relation to social actionism, functional imperativism's own central propositions may be briefly noted. If any given social system is to persist, this theoretic viewpoint claims, the system must "solve" four "system-problems" that are imposed on it by the nature of the universe. And in order to solve these problems, every social system will develop, in varying degree, an internal structural differentiation that will be temporal (i.e., phases), or subsystemic (i.e., institutions), or both.[181] Moreover, insofar as each subsystem is itself confronted with the system-problems, it too will develop internal differentiation, and so on down to the unit act.[182] At every level, however, such differentiation is prevented from leading to the total independence of a social system's parts (thus bringing about the destruction of the system itself) by the interconnecting exchanges and normative specifications that arise between them.[183] This emphasis on established differentiation, specification, and exchange between subsystems as ways of continuously satisfying imposed requirements raises the question of which particular subsystem (or, more generally, which social phenomenon) satisfies a given imposed

179. Parsons, "Pattern Variables Revisited," p. 467 [p. 270, this volume].
180. *Ibid.*, p. 468 [p. 272, this volume].
181. See Talcott Parsons and Robert F. Bales, "The Dimensions of Action Space," in Talcott Parsons, Robert F. Bales, and Edward A. Shils, *Working Papers in the Theory of Action* (Glencoe, Ill.: Free Press, 1953), pp. 63–109.
182. See Parsons, "An Outline of the Social System," p. 44.
183. At this point, of course, functional impera-

tivism joins functional structuralism in viewing the persistence of the social as a "function" or consequence of established, structurally differentiated, and socially generated interaction. The distinction between the two viewpoints remains, of course, because whereas functional structuralism (and social actionism as well) does not emphasize the existence of systematic limitations on this interaction and on its structural differentiation, functional imperativism makes this emphasis its main task.

	Social Actionism	Functional Imperativism
Social Phenomenon to be Explained (*Explanandum*)	Unit Act	Social System
Alternatives/Problems (*Explanans*)	Pattern-Variables	Functional Imperatives
Internal Selector and Stabilizer of Choices/ Solutions (*Explanans*)	Socialization	Structural Differentiation
External Selector and Stabilizer of Choices/ Solutions (*Explanans*)	Role Differentiation and Social Control	Normative Specification and Input-Output Exchanges

Figure 4. *Some Relations between Social Actionism and Functional Imperativism.*

requirement. In reply to this question, Parsons argues that the pattern-main-tenance-and-tension-management imper-ative explains and is satisfied by social values and cultural subsystems; the integrative imperative explains and is satisfied by social norms and social subsystems; the goal-attainment impera-tive explains and is satisfied by social collectivities and political subsystems; and the adaptive imperative explains and is satisfied by social roles and economic subsystems.[184] (Incidentally, the func-tional imperatives therefore also contri-bute to the existence of, and are presum-ably satisfied by, sociology, political

184. See Talcott Parsons, "An Outline of the Social System," pp. 41–44, 47–60; and *Societies*, pp. 18–19, 24–25. It may be noted that the present analysis of Parsons' schemes regards them as theories, rather than as conceptual frameworks or typologies. Issue is therefore taken with Parsons' critics (e.g., Homans, "Bringing Men Back In," p. 812) as well

as Parsons himself ("The Point of View of the Author," in Max Black [Ed.], *The Social Theories of Talcott Parsons* [Englewood Cliffs: Prentice-Hall, 1961], p. 321). But note Parsons' more recent suggestion that his work "outline[s] a *theory* of action" (Talcott Parsons, "Pattern Variables Revisited," p. 468) [p. 271, this volume].

science, and economics as fields of study.)[185]

Now some final remarks regarding the placement in Figure 2 of key social actionist and functional imperativist concepts can further clarify relations between these viewpoints and between them and the other viewpoints discussed here. First, although the social actionist's attention is focused on the actor's orientation, the complete "frame of reference of the theory of action involves actors [and] a situation of action [as well as] the orientation of the actor to that situation,"[186] and the situation is further divisible "into a class of social objects (individuals and collectivities) and a class of nonsocial (physical and cultural) objects."[187] Social actionism may therefore be described as comprising four main concepts: actor, orientation, social objects, and nonsocial objects. A brief examination of how these are defined will explain their arrangement in Figure 2.

First, note that an "actor" is said to be "an empirical system of action," and that "the orientation of the actor . . . is the set of cognitions, cathexes, plans, and relevant standards which relates the actor to the situation."[188] The important thing is that these latter "nervous system" characteristics of the social participant, are conceptually distinguished from all other "not-nervous system" characteristics that participant might have—which, incidentally, make him capable of acting *on* anything outside himself. Second, the "situation" is defined as "part of the external world [of] the actor"[189]—i.e., it is a characteristic of his environment. "Social objects" in that situation "include actors as persons and collectivities"[190] —i.e., they are "people" environment characteristics—and "nonsocial objects are any objects which are not actors"[191]— i.e., they are "not-people" environment characteristics.

Regarding the placement of the functional imperatives in Figure 2, note Parsons' and Smelser's statement that "the first functional imperative . . . is 'pattern maintenance and tension management' relative to the stability of the institutionalized value system."[192] Because "values" are characteristics of social participants' nervous systems (i.e., they are subjective dispositions rather than objective behavior), the location of the pattern-maintenance imperative in Figure 2 seems reasonable.

In describing the goal attainment imperative, Parsons and Smelser say that "a goal state . . . is a relation between the system of reference [i.e., the actor] and one or more situational objects which (given the value system and its institutionalization) maximizes the stability of the system. . . . The system must 'seek' goal states by controlling elements of the situation."[193] Note that the criterion of goal attainment put forward here is *stability*—analogous to the *homeostasis* that is often treated as essential to living organisms—and in which the controlling nervous system conditions (i.e., values) are taken as given.

The "adaptive" imperative is said to "deal with the problem of controlling the environment for purposes of attaining goal states."[194] Note that although the environments of individuals and collectivities *may* include other individuals or collectivities, such environments *must* include nonhuman features, and must include *only* the latter whenever a given social system is isolated from others or

185. See Parsons, "An Outline of the Social System," p. 34.
186. Parsons, *et al.*, *Toward a General Theory of Action*, p. 56.
187. *Ibid.*, p. 57.
188. *Ibid.*, p. 56.
189. *Ibid.*, p. 56.

190. *Ibid.*, p. 57.
191. *Ibid.*, p. 58.
192. Parsons and Smelser, *Economy and Society*, p. 17.
193. *Ibid.*, p. 17.
194. *Ibid.*, pp. 17–18.

when the entire world is taken as a single social system. Therefore, it would seem that the environment to which the adaptive imperative is *necessarily* addressed is the "not-people" one, and it may or may not be addressed to a "people" one also.

Finally, Parsons and Smelser argue that "the fourth functional imperative for a social system is to maintain solidarity 'in the relations between the units in the interest of effective functioning,' this is the imperative of system integration."[195] Note that the "units" referred to here are individuals and collectivities—i.e., "people."

In the light of this exposition of the underlying phenomenal referents in the social actionist and functional imperativist viewpoints,[196] let me call attention, briefly, to their relationships to each other and to viewpoints in the "objective" column of Figure 2. First, note that the discussion above of Figure 2 supplements Figure 4 by suggesting further correspondences between social actionism and functional imperativism: for example, there appears to be a correspondence between "nonsocial objects" and the "adaptive" imperative, between "actor" and the "goal attainment" imperative, and so on. Second, Figure 2 suggests that the Parsonian viewpoints attempt to synthesize the "objective" viewpoints by abstracting and integrating characteristics of the latter's chief explananates (though always, of course, under a "subjective" definition of the explanandum). For example, the "adaptive" imperative may be said to be a

capsule representation of the ecologistic viewpoint, and so on. Perhaps it is for this reason that the Parsonian theoretic viewpoints are so often referred to as archetypes of "grand" theory.

FOUR ADDITIONAL COMPLICATIONS OF THE BASIC TAXONOMY

In the preceding discussion I have tried to demonstrate some complementarities of content among eleven (plus one) leading theoretic viewpoints in the study of human social phenomena. To enable this demonstration, a basic taxonomic scheme —founded on the idea that the viewpoints in question may vary in their explananda and also in their explanantes —has been presented. In other words, this scheme classifies the theoretic viewpoints' specifications regarding "what" is to be observed and generalized about, and regarding the logical status (i.e., explanandum or explanans) that is to be assigned to the generalizations.

Four complications will now be added. In the first, provision will be made for *mixed as well as unmixed types of explananda and explanantes*. This first complication may be regarded as a further specification of "what" is to be observed. In the second complication, attention will be paid to the distinction between the *micro and macro* "*levels*" of the specified observations— i.e., to "where" the relevant observations are to be made, so to speak. The third and fourth complications rest on the fact that time must be of central concern when one analyzes the apparently irreversible processes that involve living

195. *Ibid.*, p. 18.

196. It must be emphasized that different definitions of social actionism's and functional imperativism's central concepts have been given by Parsons in different works. Therefore the definitions used here to locate these concepts in Figure 2 are selections from the several available definitions. For example, in *The Structure of Social Action*, "situation" is divided differently from the way used in Figure 2—i.e., into elements "over which the actor has no

control . . . and those over which he has such control. The former may be called the 'conditions' of action, the latter the 'means'." (Parsons, *The Structure of Social Action*, p. 44.) Similarly, other definitions of the functional imperatives may be found in Parsons, Bales, and Shils, *Working Papers in the Theory of Action*, Parsons, "An Outline of the Social System"; and Parsons, "Pattern Variables Revisited."

things, in contrast with certain more readily reversible chemical and physical processes. Attention must therefore be paid to the reflection of this fact in theoretic questions regarding the *genesis and maintenance* of social phenomena, and regarding the *stability and change* of social phenomena. Inasmuch as time is the new element being added here to the classificatory scheme, this part of the discussion may be said to concentrate on theoretic specifications of "when" the relevant observations are to be made (e.g., at what stage in the development of the social, how far apart in time, etc.).

In sum, therefore, the following remarks will deal with a further theoretic specification of *what* is to be observed, then with two specifications of *where*, and finally with a specification regarding *when* it is to be observed. The question of *how* observations are to be made is methodological, and the question of *why* they are to be made is ultimately ethical; neither question will be discussed here.

ate mixed types of explananda and explanantes.

Parsons and Shils,[197] and Merton,[198] provide partly conflicting names for the types yielded by cross-classifying objective and subjective behavior relations definitions of the social (Figure 5). Blau's stress on "emergent" qualities, as distinct from what might be called "elemental" qualities,[199] leads to naming the cross-classifications of explanations as shown in Figure 6. The resultant expanded version of Figure 2 is Figure 7, except that for simplicity's sake the "medium" dimensions (which would be applicable to each type of explaining phenomena separately) have been omitted. It should be emphasized that what is important here is the conceptual *content* of the types of explanandum and explanans, not how (or whether) these types are *named*. Therefore it is not the terms entered in the cells of Figures 5 and 6, (and their ambiguities) that should be taken as definitive, but rather the dimensions of these figures, no matter how their coincidences are named.

Unmixed and Mixed Types of Explanandum and Explanans

Until now, the discussion has assumed that every theoretic viewpoint can be classified with respect to a *single* principal explanandum and a *single* principal explanans. The focus, therefore, has been on unmixed types of explananda and explanantes. But of course, no such "purity" is logically required of sociological studies, and precisely equal stress on both types of definitions and on both types of explanations of the social is entirely possible, although not usual. It is therefore desirable to lift the prime-emphasis requirement in order to give the scheme an opportunity to incorpor-

Micro and Macro "Levels" of Explanandum and Explanans

The above mention of variation in the elemental or emergent character of the phenomena to be observed leads directly to the parallel question of variation in the "level" of such phenomena. (It should be emphasized at the beginning that although I shall speak of only two such levels— "micro" and "macro"—this is merely for analytical convenience, since variation in level is to be thought of as continuous and therefore many-levelled.) In order to make the argument as clear as possible, let me begin by explicating the definition of "emergent" that is quoted in Figure 6, in a way that the author of that quotation

197. Parsons and Shils, *op. cit.*, pp. 192–193.
198. Merton, *Social Theory and Social Structure*,

pp. 285–287, 299.
199. Blau, *Exchange and Power*, p. 3.

Objective Behavior Relations Definition

	yes	no
yes	"Group" (Merton)[a] "Collectivity" *(Parsons and Shils)*[b]	"Collectivity" *(Merton)*[c]
no	"Group" *(Merton)*[a] "Ecologically inter- dependent aggregate" *(Parsons and Shils)*[d]	"Category" *(Merton)*[e] "Category" *(Parsons and Shils)*[f]

*(Left vertical axis label: **Subjective Behavior Relations Definition**)*

Figure 5. *Variations in the Sociological Explanandum.*

This typology is suggested (but not unambiguously indicated) by the following remarks:

a. "The sociological concept of a group refers to a number of people who interact with one another in accord with established patterns. . . . A second criterion of a group . . . is that the interacting persons define themselves as 'members,' i.e., that they have patterned expectations of forms of interaction. . ." (Robert K. Merton, *Social Theory and Social Structure*, revised and enlarged [Glencoe, Ill.: Free Press, 1957], pp. 185–186).

b. "A social system having the three properties of collective goals, shared goals, and of being a single system of 'interaction' with boundaries defined by incumbency in the roles constituting the system, will be called a collectivity" (Talcott Parsons and Edward Shils, *Toward a General Theory of Action* [Glencoe, Ill.: Free Press, 1951], p. 192).

c. "Collectivities [are] people who have a sense of solidarity by virtue of sharing common values and who have acquired an attendant sense of moral obligation to fulfill role-expectations. All groups are, of course, collectivities, but those collectivities which lack the criterion of interaction among members are not groups" (Merton, *op. cit.*, p. 299).

d. "A plurality of persons who are merely interdependent with one another ecologically [will be called] an ecologically interdependent aggregate" (Parsons and Shils, *op. cit.*, p. 193).

e. "Social categories are aggregates of social statuses, the occupants of which are not in social interaction. These have *like* social characteristics—of sex, age, marital condition, income, and so on—but are not necessarily oriented toward a distinctive and common body of norms" (Merton, *op. cit.*, p. 299). For present purposes, this is an empty cell.

f. "A category [consists] of persons who have some attribute or complex of attributes in common, such as age, sex, education, which does not involve 'action in concert'" (Parsons and Shils, *op. cit.*, p. 193).

Explanatory Conditions
Imposed on **the Social**

	yes	no
yes	"Elemental-Emergent"	"Emergent"[a]
no	"Elemental"	[b]

Explanatory Conditions Generated by the Social (left vertical axis)

Figure 6. *Variations in the Sociological Explanans.*

a. Blau says "Emergent properties are essentially relationships between elements in a structure. The relationships are not contained in the elements . . ." (*Exchange and Power in Social Life* [New York: John Wiley, 1964], p. 3).

b. Empty cell.

does not.[200] Suppose I define as "elemental" any theoretic variable indicating an observation of some phenomenon that is treated as though it were internally homogeneous—that is, as though it were "unitary," "part-less," literally "atomic," without any internal components or relations. I may then more precisely

200. Blau also implies a second and entirely different definition of "emergent" when he contrasts two sorts of interaction: one which is "the emergent aggregate result of the diverse endeavors of the members of the collectivity," and another which is "organized and explicitly focused on some common, immediate or ultimate, objectives" (*Ibid.*, p. 313).

The definition of "emergent" that is implied here seems in the same category as "informal organization" (versus "formal organization"), "internal system" (versus "external system"), and "latent" (versus "manifest"), insofar as the social participants' conscious *intention* is the crux of distinction.

The Principal Phenomena that *Explain* the Social are:		The Principal Behavioral Relations that *Define* the Social are:			
		Objective *(Interaction)*			
Imposed on the Social	Generated by the Social	yes		no	
		Subjective *(Values)*			
		yes ("group")	no ("aggregate")	yes ("collectivity")	no
yes	yes ("Elemental-Emergent")				a
	no ("Elemental")				a
no	yes ("Emergent")				a
	no	a	a	a	a

Figure 7. *Variations in the Sociological Explanandum and Explanans.*

a. Empty cell.

define as "emergent" any theoretic variable indicating an observation of some phenomenon that is treated as though it were internally heterogeneous —that is, consisting of or resulting from internal components and relations. For

convenience, then, one may speak of "elements" and "systems" as two contrasting forms that variables can take in theories.[201] By way of illustration, it may be noted that ecologism treats the individual person merely as a component

201. Stinchcombe makes a parallel distinction between "variables" and "types": "The simplification of scientific theory by typologies is due to the fact that many times the operative variable, either as cause or effect, is the type rather than the variables which make up the type" (*op. cit.*, p. 44). Of course it is probably more useful to allow "type" to denote *any* discontinuity, whether it resides in what may be currently treated as values of a single variable (e.g., electron energy levels) or as values of a combination of several variables (e.g., the chemical elements).

element in a larger system of explanatory interest ("the subject of ecological inquiry then is the community. . ." and "life viewed ecologically is an aggregate rather than an individual phenomenon. The individual enters into ecological theory as a postulate and into ecological investigation as a unit of measurement; but as an object of special study he belongs to other disciplines."),[202] while social actionism treats the individual person as a system that is itself composed of more unitary elements ("actors are conceived as systems; they are never oriented to their situations simply 'as a whole,' but always through specific modes of organization of independent components").[203]

It is highly important to note that nothing is phenomenally *given* as either elemental or emergent, and that this question depends entirely on how a given observation is *treated* by a science as a whole and by an individual analyst in particular. Physics, for example, has passed through several stages that may be roughly described as follows: in an early stage, phenomena like earth, air, water, and fire were thought to be elemental; this notion was eventually rejected when earth, air, water, and fire were conceived as emergent systems and the molecular phenomena that are still called chemical "elements" came to be accepted as their constituents. Of course, in increasingly rapid succession thereafter, atoms, and then atomic and nuclear particles have appeared to be most elemental. Thus, whatever the preceding eras thought were elemental variables, succeeding eras have shown can be treated as systemic ones. This progression (which is in large measure general in the sciences) has presented the individual analyst with more and more options: he can now reasonably decide to treat almost any

phenomenon either as element or as system. For example, in a geological theory one can deal with earth, air, water, and fire as elements without mentioning the electrons, protons, mesons, neutrinos, positrons, etc. of which physics now says they are composed. Or to put the same idea more generally and in different but equivalent terms, if one is interested in a theory of emergent, or "macro-level," phenomena, one can, but need not, make explicit reference to the elemental, or "micro-level," phenomena of which they may be composed, and vice-versa. On the one hand, therefore, an ecologistic theory may seek to explain the geographical location of cities without referring to (for example) interpersonal relations among the inhabitants, and a symbolic interactionist theory of decision-making need not make reference to (for example) the size of the city inhabited by the individual decision-makers. On the other hand, a theory may build up from extremely micro explanantes to increasingly macro explanantes, such that elements at any given lower level yield emergents which then are treated as elements at the next higher level, and so on.

This pyramiding of emergents into elements has already been pointed out in connection with Parsonian social actionism and functional imperativism. A similar pyramiding is evident in Blau's argument. Blau views "power" as a social creation that emerges from the coincidence of two elements: (a) participants being attracted to a social interaction by the anticipation of "extrinsic" benefits, and (b) participants engaging in "unilateral" (or "imbalanced") transactions. "Legitimation" is similarly an emergent, but from the coincidence of two other elements: (c) "universalistic" standards of preference, and (d)

202. Hawley, "Ecology and Human Ecology," p. 403.

203. Parsons, "Pattern Variables Revisited," p. 471 [p. 275, this volume].

"goal-focused" social interaction. The coincidence of these two emergents (power and legitimation), now treated as elements, creates "authority," which may therefore be regarded as a second-order emergent, and so on up to society, the nth-order emergent: "Legitimation . . . transforms power into authority and thereby into an important resource for the stable organization of collective endeavours."[204]

The analyst's freedom to choose whether his explanandum calls for a relatively elemental (micro-level) observation, or a relatively emergent (macro-level) observation should not be understood as a denial of the definition of the social that was proposed early in this Overview as being common to all sociological viewpoints and theories. That definition stressed what may be termed the fundamentally micro character of the explananda of all sociological theories, since reference was made there to inter-*organism*, rather than inter-*group*, behavior relations as the *sine qua non* of social phenomena. This means that even when a given theory (e.g., of intersexual, or intergenerational, or interracial, or inter-city, or international relations) seeks to explain intergroup relations alone, such relations have interindividual relations as their necessary, though sometimes implicit, presumption.[205] In other words, the macro idea of intergroup relations necessarily implies the micro idea that individuals in the same group have relations among themselves that in some way differ from those that individuals in different groups have. And since the converse—that interindividual relations necessarily imply intergroup relations—

obviously does not hold, the logical dependence is not mutual, and inter-individual relations are therefore the more basic of the two.

Again, no denial is being made of this argument as fundamentally defining the sociological explanandum. What is being suggested, however, is that this definition may or may not be made explicit in any given theory or theoretic viewpoint. A given theory may legitimately define its particular explanandum as consisting only in macro phenomena, or only micro phenomena, or any variety of phenomena between the two extremes. Similar considerations hold for theories' explanantes (see the preceding discussion of social actionism and functional imperativism). In other words, while the underlying, most fundamental, reference is always to the *individual* "participant" and his individual "environment," this reference is not a limitation; participants are often conceived to be groups of individuals, and therefore explanations may be conceived as being imposed on *groups* or generated by their interaction as well as imposed on *individuals* or generated by their interaction.

The four taxonomic possibilities of micro and macro explanandum and explanans are shown in Figure 8. Wagner has discussed theories that would fall in cells (c) and (b): the former cell seems indicated by his analysis that "structure functionalism . . . sees smaller units, down to the individual, as structural subparts whose functions are essentially defined and confined by the whole system."[206] The latter cell seems indicated by his judgment that "interpretative-interactional theories, by contrast . . .

204. Blau, *Exchange and Power*, p. 9.

205. Helmut R. Wagner, in "Displacement of Scope: A Problem of the Relationship between Small-Scale and Large-Scale Sociological Theories," *American Journal of Sociology* (May, 1964), 69:574, quotes Weber: "In sociology, concepts like 'state', 'cooperative', 'feudalism', and similar ones, in

general designate categories of specific kinds of human interaction; thus, it is its task to reduce them to 'understandable' action, and this means without exception: to the actions of specific individuals." Kunkel, *op. cit.*, makes the same point.

206. Wagner, "Displacement of Scope," p. 575, and also Kaplan, *op. cit.*, pp. 299–300.

**The Principal Behavior Relations
that *Define* the Social are:**

Micro   Macro

<table>
<tr><td rowspan="2" style="writing-mode:vertical-rl">The Principal Phenomena
that Explain the Social are:</td><td>Micro</td><td>a</td><td>b</td></tr>
<tr><td>Macro</td><td>c</td><td>d</td></tr>
</table>

Figure 8. *Variations in "Level" of Explanandum and Explanans.*

view larger wholes as results of the interlinkages and interrelations among a multiplicity of individual actors."[207] (It should be noted that the validity of these generalizations is not now at issue. Indeed, in light of the discussion earlier in this essay of functional structuralism and functional imperativism, it appears that Wagner's first generalization is true for functional imperativism but not necessarily true for functional structuralism, for which his second generalization

often holds.) Wagner does not discuss the remaining two possibilities shown in Figure 8, but in cell (a) one would be likely to find theories made up of propositions like "the more frequently persons interact with one another, the stronger their sentiments of friendship for one another are apt to be."[208] And in cell (d) one would find theories made up of propositions like "the mode of production in material life determines the general character of the social,

207. Wagner, *ibid.*, p. 575. Blumer, for example, defines the symbolic interactionist view of the social as follows: "Fundamentally, group action takes the form of a fitting together of individual lines of action ("Society as Symbolic Interaction," p. 184).

208. Homans, *The Human Group*, p. 133.

political, and spiritual processes of life."[209]

In a somewhat different analysis, Leo Schnore has discussed a taxonomy that closely approximates the one shown in Figure 8,[210] and would place the studies of individual psychology and of social psychology in cells (a) and (c), respectively. Cell (b) would contain what Schnore calls "psychological sociology" (which "subsumes all efforts to explain properties of populations by reference to the properties of the individuals who . . . may be said to compose these populations").[211] Cell (d) would contain, according to Schnore, "macro-sociology" and, especially, human ecology—"a type of 'macro-sociology' [whose] most distinctive feature can perhaps be seen in its adherence to a single level of analysis, in which properties of whole populations are at issue."[212] By the latter statement, Schnore means that in ecologism certain macro phenomena (e.g., population size, density) are taken as the explanantes for other macro phenomena (e.g., division of labor, stratification).

The independence of the micro-macro explanandum and explanans dimensions seems further illustrated by the fact that in their respective careers to date, Parsons and Homans have moved in opposite directions along both. That is, Parsons seems to have had an early interest in accounting for the micro "unit act" and then moved increasingly toward explaining macro "social systems," and "societies" in particular. Homans, by contrast, seems to have given early attention to explaining the relatively macro, emergent, human "group" and later developed an interest in the relatively micro and "elementary" exchanges that occur between "person" and "other."[213] More-

over, Parsons has shifted from social actionism's early attempt to explain the macro social by the micro social to the reverse of this in functional imperativism, while Homans seems to have made the opposite move. Thus Parsons now writes of "a hierarchical series of . . . agencies of control of the behavior of individuals or organisms" wherein "the personality system is . . . a system of control over the behavioral organism; the social system, over the personalities of its participating members; and the cultural system, a system of control relative to social systems."[214] Homans argues the reverse: that explanantes operate from the micro individual psyche "upward" to the macro human group. In Homans' words, "from the laws of individual behavior, follow the laws of social behavior when the complications of mutual reinforcement are taken into account."[215]

Blau's social exchange theory is an example (similar to Homans') in which the chief explanans shifts from imposed to socially generated as the explanandum changes from micro to macro. Thus, Blau shows (a) that micro social phenomena have micro imposed explanations (i.e., face-to-face social exchanges arise from "primitive" psychological processes lodged in each individual); but his primary interest is in the propositions (b) that different socially generated micro conditions (balanced exchanges versus imbalanced exchanges) explain the emergence of different macro phenomena (integrative values, power differentiation, and opposition and legitimation norms), and (c) that these macro phenomena, once they are socially generated, explain their own maintenance as well as that of certain micro phenomena.

209. Karl Marx, A Contribution to the Critique of Political Economy, quoted in Feuer, op. cit., p. 43.
210. Leo Schnore, "The Myth of Human Ecology," Sociological Inquiry (1961), 31(2):128–139.
211. Ibid., p. 134.
212. Ibid., p. 139.
213. James A. Davis (op. cit., p. 458) also has

pointed out that "Homans has . . . written his Structure of Social Action a decade after writing his Social System," but Davis had in mind a contrast between a conceptual framework and a theory.
214. Parsons, "An Outline of the Social System," p. 38.
215. Homans, Social Behavior, p. 30.

Genetic and Maintenance Explanations

The above observation suggests that a given theory may account for the genesis of the social differently from the way it accounts for the maintenance (or elaboration) of the social. That is to say, the things that *start* a ball rolling may not be the same things that *keep* it rolling. Of course, it is precisely this possibility that Newton recognized in distinguishing the concepts "force" and "inertia." In the same general way, the things that originate social phenomena need not be the same ones that maintain them, and it will therefore be useful to distinguish between the two sorts of explanation.

The first observation to make in this connection is that the class of viewpoints that explain the social through phenomena generated by the social itself (technologism, the social structuralisms, symbolic interactionism, and social actionism) must finally be maintenance (more precisely, *self*-maintenance) theories, rather than genetic theories. That is, such viewpoints cannot explain how the first social phenomenon came into existence. However, viewpoints that explain the social through imposed phenomena (ecologism, demographism, materialism, psychologism, and functional imperativism), by definition of "imposed," are logically able to explain the genesis of the social as well as its maintenance. That is,

such viewpoints propose certain non-social factors which, if they operated prior to the social, can account for the latter's coming into existence, and, if they continue to operate alongside the social, can account for its persistence.

In this light, one could read Figure 2 as follows: viewpoints that rely on imposed explananda are certainly genetic ones and may also be maintenance ones, but viewpoints that rely on socially generated explananda are exclusively maintenance viewpoints.[216] It should also be noted that both types of viewpoints (genetic-maintenance and exclusively maintenance) can, in principle, account for the elaboration or development of social phenomena, although they recommend the primacy of different sources (usually called system-exogenous and system-endogenous,[217] respectively) of such elaboration.

By way of illustration, consider the relationship between the viewpoints expressed by Homans in *The Human Group* and in *Social Behavior*: the former seems concerned primarily with how groups are maintained, while the latter seems concerned primarily with how groups are generated.[218] Perhaps this difference is part of what Homans means when he says that "*The Human Group* did not try to explain much of anything, while *Social Behavior* will at least try to explain."[219]

216. The difference between the two groups of viewpoints, both of which are maintenance theories, may be summed up by noting Stinchcombe's two possible explanations of "why this year is like last year. One is that this year's phenomena are produced by . . . the same causes that produced last year's phenomena. . . . The second . . . is that some social patterns cause their own reproduction" (*op. cit.*, p. 101). Stinchcombe terms the latter, social *self*-maintenance, explanation an "historicist" explanation (pp. 101–29).

217. See Pierre van den Berghe, "Dialectic and Functionalism," *American Sociological Review* (October, 1963), 28:695–705 [pp. 202–213, this volume].

218. There are four main concepts employed in *The Human Group*, out of which Homans constructs "external" and "internal" analytic systems whose interaction, he proposes, explains the persistence of

human groups over time. But of these four concepts, two can have only maintenance potential, and two can have genetic potential (and of course, insofar as they persist alongside the social, also maintenance potential). Thus, the concepts "interaction" and "norms"—because they have relational, interparticipant, referents—can only be maintenance explanantes. "Sentiments" and "activities," however, can be genetic as well as maintenance explanantes, since they pertain to individual organisms and can be prior to (as well as subsequent to, of course) relational variables. In *Social Behavior*, Homans chooses sentiments as the more central of the two possible genetic factors that are set forth in *The Human Group*, and thus moves his viewpoint toward the psychologistic.

219. Homans, *Social Behavior*, p. 8.

In a second illustration, Buckley's recent discussion of systems theory may be mentioned briefly, although, as Buckley warns the reader, one "will not find [in his book] a new sociological theory in the stricter sense of that term."[220] Buckley's principal argument seems to be two-fold. It is (1) that systems theory is a superior explanatory theory, not of the genesis, but of the maintenance and, especially, the elaboration ("morphogenesis") of "sociocultural" systems, and (2) that symbolic interactionism is the sociological viewpoint that has made the closest approach to systems theory in this regard. Thus, Buckley claims that the special promise of systems theory lies in its ability "to get at the full complexity of the interacting phenomena ... to see the total emergent processes as a function of possible positive and/or negative feedbacks mediated by the selective decisions, or 'choices,' of the individuals and groups directly or indirectly involved."[221] Thus also, Buckley applauds "the fully cybernetic nature of [Mead's] analysis of human action as a feedback communication and control system."[222]

Finally, it may be noted that the Marxian *genetic* explanation for social phenomena rests on the imposed physiological nature of man. This is the "materialism" in dialectical materialism. However, Marxism's *maintenance* explanations include with these the social generation of differences in participants' environments (i.e., ownership of the means of production, wage-labor, differential association between and within classes, etc.), and of differences within the social participants themselves (i.e., ideology, class consciousness, etc.). The result of these socially generated differences,

against a background of imposed and universal physiological goals, is social conflict. This is the "dialectic" in dialectical (historical) materialism. In Marx' and Engels' words:

The history of all hitherto existing society is the history of class struggles. Free man and slave, patrician and plebian, lord and serf, guild master and journeyman, in a word, oppressor and oppressed, stood in constant opposition to one another, carried on an uninterrupted, now hidden, now open fight, a fight that each time ended either in a revolutionary reconstitution of society at large or in the common ruin of the contending classes.[223]

Undoubtedly, one of Marxism's chief theoretic appeals is its explicitly dual reference to imposed and socially generated explanantes, to the common physiological goals of men and the different social means of men, which enables the theory to address the problems of social genesis and social maintenance with equal directness.

Change and Stability Explanations

Buckley explicitly rejects the assumption that sociocultural systems, once begun, are normally "homeostatic," self-maintaining, and stability-seeking, in favor of the idea that such systems are normally "morphogenic," self-elaborating, and change-seeking. This brings us to the final dimension of sociological viewpoints to be considered here.

In one sense, it is unnecessary to add a specific change-stability dimension to the taxonomic scheme. Every sociological theory necessarily implies a theory of social change and every one implies a theory of social stability.[224] Obviously, to propose the existence of an empirical

---

220. Walter Buckley, *Sociology and Modern Systems Theory* (Englewood Cliffs, N.J.: Prentice-Hall, 1967), p. viii.
221. *Ibid.*, p. 80.
222. *Ibid.*, p. 96.
223. Karl Marx and Friedrich Engels, from *The Communist Manifesto*, quoted in Feuer, *op. cit.*, p. 7.

224. As Homans says, "in studying social change, as in studying social control, we discovered nothing new in the relationships between the elements of behavior.... What we did was watch how a change in the value of one of the elements effected changes in the values of the others" (*The Human Group*, p. 450).

relationship between the social and some other class or subclass of phenomena is exactly equivalent to proposing that a change in the latter will accompany (i.e., precede, follow, or occur simultaneously with) a change in the former. Conversely, it is also implied that stability in the latter will accompany stability in the former.

But it is also clear that some sociological theories more explicitly take change in a social phenomenon (e.g., industrialization, urbanization, bureaucratization) as the explanandum; others take stability in—or a stable state of—a social phenomenon (e.g., industrialism, urbanism, bureaucracy) as the explanandum; still others are ambiguous in this regard. This observation stresses that although all theories necessarily imply change and stability, some are more explicit about it than others, and moreover, some identify a particular social change, or sequence of changes, or stability that is to be explained. Consequently, direct attention here to the change-stability dimension of theories seems to be in order.

Early in this essay, I remarked on some of the broadly philosophical connotations of sociological theorists' objective-vs.-subjective preferences in defining the social, and of their imposed-vs.-socially-generated preferences in explaining the social (see Figure 1). I also suggested that these world-view connotations may be partly responsible for the heat with which sociologists sometimes debate their respective views of social life. The same is true of another, equally incendiary and equally hoary, philosophical problem: the relation between stability and change, between Heraclitus and the river. In this regard, it seems that one of two possible premises underlies every sociological theory (indeed, perhaps any theory whatever). One of these asserts that stability is the fundamental and "normal" given in social phenomena.[225] That is, steadiness of state unless disturbed is assumed here rather than change of state unless constrained. Change, in the face of this normal tendency toward stability, is therefore treated as an aberration that is to be explained. As Dahrendorf (who rejects this assumption) puts it,

... many sociologists seem convinced that, in order to explain processes of change, they have to discover certain special circumstances which set these processes in motion, implying that, in society, change is an abnormal, or at least an unusual, state that has to be accounted for in terms of deviations from a "normal" equilibrated system.[226]

And as Parsons (who accepts this assumption) argues,

The definition of a system as boundary-maintaining is a way of saying that, relative to its environment . . . it maintains certain constancies of pattern, whether this constancy be static or moving. These elements of the constancy of pattern must constitute a fundamental point of reference for the analysis of process in the system.[227]

Under an assumption such as this, one

---

225. It should be emphasized, however, that the assumption of the "normality" of stability in social phenomena may rest on the still more basic assumption that certain non-social phenomena "normally" induce disorder in social phenomena. Under this assumption, the social can persist only on condition that it normally, routinely, meets this constant threat to its existence. Thus Parsons argues that there are "two classes of tendencies *not* to maintain this [social] interaction" (*The Social System*, p. 205). One is that social actors may not be born with the orientations that support given interactions and, without learning, they may act so as to break down the interactions. The second is that

social actors, having once learned the appropriate orientations, may deviate from them and, again, act so as to break down the interactions. Hence, in order to exist, a social system must, according to Parsons, embrace processes of socialization and processes of social control. Such processes are "not problematical" for Parsons (*ibid.*, p. 204): if a social system exists at all these processes *must* exist within it, because without them, the unstabilizing tendencies of the universe-at-large would destroy the social system.

226. Ralf Dahrendorf, "Out of Utopia," *American Journal of Sociology* (September, 1958), 64:126.

227. Parsons, *The Social System*, p. 482.

may investigate the nature of the stability or equilibrium itself and its explanations, and one may also investigate the nature of "abnormal" deviations from stability. For example, one may examine the problems of social "consensus" and "control," and also of social "dissensus" and "deviance."

An alternative to assuming that stability is normal is, of course, to assume—again essentially without further explanation—that change is normal. As Dahrendorf (who accepts this assumption) argues, "all units of social organization are continuously changing, unless some force intervenes to arrest this change. It is our task to identify the factors interfering with the normal process of change. . . ."[228] It should be noted that the results of "interference with the normal process of change" may take more than one form. One possible result is non-change or stability, and a second is some "abnormal" pattern of change. At this point, of course, one may note a certain equivalence between one theorist's "normal change" and another's "moving constancy", and between the first's "abnormal change" and the second's "system change". For example, the similarity between the just-quoted assertion by Dahrendorf and the following by Parsons is striking: "We are assuming that the continuance of a stabilized motivational process in a stabilized relationship to the relevant objects is to be treated as non-problematical. . . . the problems . . . concern not what makes bodies move, but what makes them change their motion."[229]

Thus, under each assumption (i.e., that stability in the social is normal, or that change in the social is normal) in the very long run, one arrives at studies and theories of the very same things: stability and various kinds of change. In the shorter run, however, each assumption points to distinctive theoretic emphases and therefore to distinctive investigative strategies. But as in the case of all the other emphases discussed here, these too may be mutually complementary rather than contradictory, insofar as neither stability nor change is phenomenally given or absolute in the social but both are relative and dependent on analytical treatment. It therefore seems advisable to encourage work under whatever change-stability assumption the analyst finds most suitable, but to systematize each theory's implications in this regard for easy reference and comparison. Accordingly, the discussion so far suggests several questions regarding the social change implications of a given theory, and several corresponding questions regarding its social stability implications: (a) What type of phenomenon is defined as the change (or stability) to be explained by the theory? To what extent is the change (or stability) defined in terms of objective behavior relations or in terms of subjective behavior relations? A further, subsidiary question here is: What course of change (or stability) is to be explained—evolutionary, revolutionary, permanent, temporary, radical, sudden, violent, intense, non-violent etc.?[230] (b) What is the proposed explanation of change (stability)? To what extent is the explanation looked upon as imposed upon ("system-exogenous" source), or generated by ("system-endogenous" source), the social?[231] (c) What is the medium through which the change (stability) is induced? Is the medium chiefly the participants' external environments ("stimulus," "situation"), or chiefly the participants themselves ("disposition," "perception," "definition")?

228. Dahrendorf, "Out of Utopia," p. 126.
229. Parsons, The Social System, p. 204.
230. See Wilbert E. Moore, Social Change (Englewood Cliffs, N.J.: Prentice-Hall, 1963), and

Ralf Dahrendorf, Class and Class Conflict in Industrial Society (Stanford, Calif.: Stanford University Press, 1959).
231. See van den Berghe, op. cit.

It should be emphasized that the above three types of questions must be asked regarding change and stability *separately*, since it does not follow that the simple and unelaborated absence of the principal change-inducing factor must be the principal change-inhibiting factor, or vice-versa. More specifically, although a theorist must not employ exactly the same class of phenomena to explain change as he does to explain stability, once he has chosen the class that explains the one, he still has an extremely wide range from which to choose his principal explanation of the other. For example, a theorist can claim that certain socially generated value orientations are the principal factors in stabilizing a given social phenomenon, and still be free to claim that other socially generated participant characteristics, and/or certain socially generated environmental situations, and/or certain imposed characteristics of environmental conditions, and/or certain imposed characteristics of participants themselves, are the principal factors in changing the same social phenomenon.

Given this degree of independence between the theoretic explanation of change in the social and the explanation of stability in the social, it follows that the property-spaces used here for analyzing theoretic viewpoints should be duplicated, so that one complete set will be labeled "change" and the other will be labeled "stability." Each theory may then be analyzed with regard to its change propositions and also its stability propositions.

One further consideration regarding change and stability is highlighted by Buckley's discussion of general systems theory and sociology. In conceptualizing "system," Buckley puts forward two quite different alternatives (he does not discuss the difference) and thereby affords an illustration of a dimension of vari-

ability in the explananda and explanantes of sociological theories that is not otherwise treated here. To fix this dimension in mind, consider first Kaplan's distinction between "field theories" and "monadic theories" (or perhaps more properly and generally, field and monadic definitions of explanandum and/or explanans):

A theory may take as fundamental a system of relations among certain elements, explaining the elements by reference to these relations [a field theory], or it may give primacy to the relata, explaining the relations by reference to the attributes of what they relate [a monadic theory]. . . . Thus a theory of personality in terms of roles might be contrasted with a theory in which roles are explained by reference to sets of needs of the individual personalities participating in the system.[232]

Now consider one of Buckley's two definitions of "system":

The kind of system we are interested in may be described generally as a complex of elements or components directly or indirectly related in a causal network, such that each component is related to at least some others in a more or less stable way within any particular period of time.[233]

Note that the method of identifying a system suggested by this definition rests on finding a characteristic and stable set of *relations*. This is obviously a field definition of system. In an earlier definition (the first in the book), however, Buckley takes a different tack: "A system, as a continuous, boundary-maintaining, variously related assembly of parts, is not to be confused with the structure or organization its components may take on at any particular time."[234] Here the emphasis is clearly on system identification via the continuity of *components*, and the definition is clearly monadic.

The contrast forces us to note that when two analysts point to the "same" systemic or emergent phenomenon (or

232. Kaplan, *op. cit.*, p. 301.
233. Buckley, *Sociology and Modern Systems*

Theory, p. 41.
234. *Ibid.*, p. 5.

even when the same analyst regards it at different times), and when they disagree about whether it is changing or stable, one of them may be pointing to relational change (or stability) in the phenomenon, while the other points to componential change (or stability) in it.[235] For this additional reason, then, one analyst's "change" may be another's "stability" and careful analysis is sometimes required to discover whether they mean the same thing by the same term.

CONCLUSIONS

The above examination of theoretic viewpoints in sociology suggests three broad conclusions. First, a set of questions may be stated that every sociological investigator should address twice—once early in his study to guide its basic design (i.e., to guide the selection of a theoretic viewpoint from which to derive hypotheses), and again late in the study to guide the interpretation of its results (i.e., to guide the induction of theoretic conclusions from its empirical generalizations). In simplified form, these questions are as follows:

With respect to each social phenomenon that is to be explained:

1. To what extent does it consist in objective or in subjective behavior relations?
2. To what extent is it micro or macro?
3. To what extent is its genesis or its maintenance to be explained?
4. To what extent is its change or its stability to be explained?

With respect to each phenomenon that is proposed as an explanation:

5. To what extent is it imposed on the social phenomenon that is to be explained or generated by it?
6. To what extent does it operate through the medium of the environments of social participants or through the participants themselves? If through environments, is it the people there, or other, nonhuman, objects there, that are primarily involved? If through the participants themselves, is it the nervous system there, or other systems there, that are primarily involved?
7. To what extent is it micro or macro?

The answers to these questions should orient a given research toward current theories and their literatures when hypotheses are being formulated, and toward appropriate methods and techniques (e.g., panel techniques are appropriate for change studies; attitude questionnaires are appropriate for studies of subjective behavior relations, etc.) when observational work is being planned. Further, they should help systematize the comparison and accumulation of research results and thereby help facilitate the consolidation of sociological conclusions within a single frame of reference.

Second, if each of the seven questions listed above is viewed as dichotomizing an independent dimension of variability in sociological theories (and if the subquestions of question 6 are ignored), then the property-space thus described has $2^7 = 128$ cells, and each cell indicates a possible type of sociological theory. In this light, the eleven theoretic viewpoints discussed in this book may be thought of as real instances that have so far emerged at particular locations in this property-space. Needless to say, the few real instances should not be taken to exhaust all future possibilities; other varieties of sociological theory are undoubtedly forthcoming. Perhaps the analytical scheme discussed in this essay and grossly summarized by the above seven questions can stimulate the realization of such

235. See Caplow, *op. cit.*, p. 15.

future possibilities, and can connect, distinguish, and catalogue them once they have been realized.

Third, a somewhat more precise meaning than previously can now be assigned to the term "generality" when it is applied to sociological theory: to the extent that such a theory purports to explain objective behavior relations as well as subjective behavior relations (and different kinds of each), micro as well as macro social phenomena, social genesis as well as social maintenance, and social change as well as social stability—to that extent, the theory is a general one (or, more precisely, to that extent the theory's explanandum is a general one). Special, or "middle-range," theories may be said to relate to general ones (and to the theoretic viewpoints discussed here) chiefly as particular combinations of features that are contributed to, or borrowed from, the latter. By this I mean that theories of reference groups and role-sets, of the spirit of capitalism, of suicide, bureaucracy, oligarchy, collective behavior, the family, crime, revolution, wars, socialization, voting, etc., may be thought of as combinations of features that are peculiar to various of the theoretic viewpoints discussed here, or at least peculiar to the property-space that has systematized that discussion. Of course, the flow of information between general and special theories is (or should be) two-way: the special theories are (or can be) the chief intermediaries between empirical generalizations and general theories, and between general theories and hypotheses.[236] Special or middle-range theories can thus perform the vital scientific functions of informing general theory with the findings of empirical research and also informing specific hypotheses with the speculations and conclusions of general theory.

Sociology as a whole—including all the components and relationships set forth in the Preface to this book—may be described as an ultimately vain but irresistible search for a single general theory incorporating at least the dimensions discussed in this essay, and to which all special theories, all empirical generalizations, all hypotheses, and all observations regarding social phenomena can be accurately related and thereby made intelligible.

---

236. See the Preface to this book. In a recently published essay, "On Sociological Theories of the Middle Range," in Robert K. Merton, *On Theoretical Sociology* (New York: Free Press of Glencoe, 1967), pp. 39–72, Merton identifies as one distinguishing characteristic of "theories of the middle range" the fact that they "have not been logically *derived* from a single, all-embracing theory of social systems, though once developed they may be consistent with one" (p. 41, emphasis in original; see also p. 64). Clearly, the emphasis here is on ruling out one possible functional mediation that theories of the middle-range might logically perform—namely, assisting in the derivation of specific hypotheses from general theory. (This would seem to leave one other possible functional mediation by middle-range theories—namely, that from empirical generalizations to general theory—and indeed Merton stresses this: "We sociologists can look . . . toward progressively comprehensive sociological theory which . . . gradually consolidates theories of the middle range, so that these become special cases of more general formulations"—p. 51). In this and other ways, one gets the impression that when a *satisfactory* (i.e., "comprehensive") general theory will have been produced (presumably through the abovementioned gradual consolidation of theories of the middle-range), then Merton will favor the logical derivation of *other* middle-range theories from it and of other specific hypotheses from them. Then, presumably, the fact that they "have not been derived from a single, all-embracing theory of social systems" will no longer be true of middle-range theories, and they will be able to perform both mediations—i.e., between empirical generalizations and general theory, and between general theory and hypotheses—equally well.

PART II

READINGS IN
CONTEMPORARY
SOCIOLOGICAL THEORY

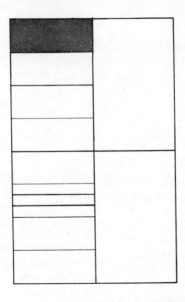

1. ECOLOGISM

The ecologistic viewpoint typically defines the social in terms of objective behavior relations, and seeks to explain it by referring to phenomena imposed on the social through characteristics of the participants' non-human environments. The following chapter by Hawley and article by Duncan and Schnore complement each other in describing this view-point: Hawley points out differences between human ecology and other general scientific disciplines, while Duncan and Schnore carry this effort further by distinguishing the ecological perspective from others that are relevant specifically to the study of social phenomena.

HUMAN ECOLOGY

AMOS H. HAWLEY

RELATION TO GENERAL ECOLOGY

We have attempted in the preceding chapters to show how the ecologist conceives the world of life as a subject for investigation. Our aim has been to outline the theoretical framework not of any special subdivision of the field but of ecology in general. We have sought to emphasize that ecology is a point of view which embraces life as a whole as well as particular populations of living things. All this, of course, has been preliminary to a statement of the nature of human ecology. Human ecology represents a specialization within the broader field of ecology and can be comprehended only when viewed against the background of the parent discipline. Before proceeding with our discussion let us summarize briefly what has been said by way of defining ecology as a general point of view.[1]

Implicit in the foregoing discussion has been the conception of ecology as the study of both the form and the development of organization in populations of living things. Ecology begins, as we have seen, with the problem of how growing, multiplying beings maintain themselves in a constantly changing but ever restricted environment. It proceeds, in other words, with the conception of life as a continuous struggle for adjustment of organisms to environment, a struggle initiated and continued essentially by the differential modes of change of these two components of the life process. In the ecological view, however, life is not an

individual but an aggregate phenomenon. Hence the underlying assumption of ecology is that adjustment to environment is a mutual, in fact a communal, function. The adjustment of a population to its physical world occurs not through the independent actions of many individuals but through the coordination and organization of individual actions to form a single functional unit.

The inevitable crowding of organisms upon limited resources produces a complex interaction of organism with organism and of organism with environment in the course of which individuals adjust to one another in ways conducive to a more effective utilization of the habitat. In consequence there arises among the organisms occupying a given habitat an equilibrium of relationships which approximates a closed system; that is, the aggregate assumes the characteristics of an organic unit as each type of life accommodates its behavior to that of every other. The community, as the ecologist is wont to call the pattern of symbiotic and commensalistic relations that develops in a population, is in the nature of a collective response to the habitat; it constitutes the adjustment of organism to environment.

The subject of ecological enquiry is therefore the community, the form and development of which are studied with particular reference to the limiting and supporting factors of the environment.[2] Ecology, in other words, is a study of the morphology of collective life in both its static and its dynamic aspects. It attempts to determine the nature of community structure in general, the types of communities that appear in different habitats, and the specific sequence of change in community development.

The unit of observation, it should be emphasized, is not the individual but the aggregate which is either organized or in process of becoming organized. The individual enters into ecological studies, on the theoretical side, as a postulate, and, on the practical side, as a unit of measurement. As something to be investigated in and of itself, however, the individual is subject matter for other disciplines. Ecology, as we have described it, then, is virtually synonymous with what plant ecologists call "synecology"—the study of the interrelations among organisms.[3] However, what plant ecologists term "autecology"—the study of the adaptations made by the individual organism throughout its life history[4]—is excluded from the conception as set forth in these pages. To include this latter phase would appear to be an unwarranted invasion of the fields of physiology and psychology, disciplines which are much better equipped to deal with problems concerning the individual.

It is to be emphasized that ecology in all its applications necessarily involves a sociological, not a biological, enquiry. The identification of plant and animal ecology with botany and zoology in no way alters this fact. If the study of behavior and particularly collective behavior is biology, then it follows that all social science is biology laboring under an assumed name. But it is not our desire to higgle over terms; we wish merely to underscore the essentially sociological background of human ecology.

AS A SPECIAL FIELD OF STUDY

Human ecology, like plant and animal ecology, represents a special application of the general viewpoint to a particular class of living things. It involves both a recognition of the fundamental unity of animate nature and an awareness that there is differentiation within that unity. Man, as we have seen, not only occupies a niche in nature's web of life, he also develops among his fellows an elaborate community of relations comparable in many important respects to the more inclusive biotic community. In at least one of its aspects the human community is an organization of organisms adjusted or in process of adjustment to a given unit of territory. Hence the rise of human ecology has meant a logical extension of the system of thought and the techniques of investigation developed in the study of the collective life of lower organisms to the study of man. Human ecology may be defined, therefore, in terms that have already been used, as the study of the form and the development of the community in human population.

Ecology as applied to man differs in important respects from its application to other forms of life or even to life as a whole. To reason from "pismires to parliaments or from mice to men" would be to commit a gross oversimplification. Man is an organism, to be sure, and as such he has much in common with other forms of organic life.

But at the same time he is capable of an extraordinary degree of flexibility and refinement in behavior. This is to be observed in man's extensive control over his surroundings, as manifested in the degree to which he modifies and reconstructs his environment through invention and the use of tools, and again in the complex cooperative arrangements entered into with his fellowmen. Furthermore, man's great facility for devising and accumulating methods of coping with life situations is evidence of a dynamics in human behavior that is without counterpart elsewhere in the animate world. It is this that constitutes man an object of special inquiry and makes possible a human as distinct from a general ecology.

Yet it is necessary to keep the phenomenon of human culture in proper perspective. When man by nature of his culture-producing capacity is regarded as an entirely unique type of organism the distinction has reached a point of overemphasis. Human behavior, in all its complexity, is but a further manifestation of the tremendous potential for adjustment inherent in organic life. Thus if we look upon culture as the totality of the habitual ways of acting that are general in a population and are transmitted from one generation to the next, there exist for human ecology no peculiar problems other than those involved in the fact of its complexity. The term simply denotes the prevailing techniques of adjustment by which a population maintains itself in its habitat. The elements of human culture are therefore identical in principle with the appetency of the bee for honey, the nest-building activities of birds, and the hunting habits of carnivora. To say that the latter are instinctive while the former are not is to beg the question. Ecology is not concerned with how habits are acquired—that is a psychological problem; it is interested rather in the functions they serve and the relationships they involve.

The definition of human ecology given here differs noticeably from earlier statements which seem to indicate a subordination of interest in functional relations to a concern with the spatial patterns in which such relations are expressed. For example, "Human ecology deals with the spatial aspects of the symbiotic relations of human beings and human institutions."[5] While such a statement possesses the merit of concreteness, it has had the unfortunate effect of permitting human ecology to be construed as the study of the distributive aspects of village and urban agglomerations. Much of the research carried on under the name "ecology" has consisted of compiling inventories of the observable characteristics of human settlement and of plotting the distributions of such findings on maps. Such a narrow interpretation of human ecology is incompatible with the fundamental logic of ecological theory and is not in accord with the subject as it is being developed in its other applications.

ITS PLACE IN SOCIAL SCIENCE

The collective life of human beings, especially as it bears upon the habitat, is also the focus of interest of a number of other branches of social science, such as demography, human geography, economics, and sociology. It is because of the close convergence of interest of these several disciplines and the consequent danger of confusion as to the nature of their respective fields that we need to consider the place of human ecology among the social sciences.[6]

The simplest way of viewing the human community is as a statistical aggregate. A population may be regarded as a collection of discrete and definite units which as a whole possesses certain interrelated tendencies to change that lend themselves to mathematical analysis. This type of approach to the study of population has become known as demography.[7] In the words of Wolfe, demography is the "numerical analysis of the state and movement of human population inclusive of census enumeration and registration of vital processes . . ."[8] However, while the demographer takes an abstract view of population, it does not follow that he deals with population in general. Demographic analysis is usually limited to the study of the conditions of community life as revealed in birth, death, and migration statistics.[9]

The distinction between demography and human ecology is more or less apparent. Although both study the community, the one is concerned with vital processes in the communal population while the other is interested in the organization of the population constituting the community. Demography may be considered as a service discipline to the other branches of social science. Its data and findings are basic to every other social science because of their immediate descriptive value and, what is even more important, because of their use in suggesting problems for research in other disciplines.

The relation of man and his activities to the physical condition of the earth has long been a concern of geography. Human geography, however, which explicitly emphasizes the influence of the geographic environment on man, had its inception in systematic form in the latter part of the nineteenth century, with the publication of Friedrich Ratzel's *Anthropogeographie*.[10] This new emphasis was at first greatly exaggerated, as the result of Ellen Churchill Semple's English interpretation of Ratzel,[11] to mean a thoroughgoing environmental determinism. But for the most part human geographers have adopted the more modest conception of their task as outlined by Paul Vidal de la Blache,[12] Jean Brunhes,[13] and others, namely, that of discovering in detail the manner and extent in which geographic factors influence human behavior. Confronted, however, with the indubitable fact that man characteristically responds to his physical environment in ways that are customary rather than mechanical, geographers have tended to invert the original form of the problem, thus making human geography the study of man's adaptations to his geographic environment. Barrows asserts that "geography is the science of human ecology."[14] Elaborating further, this author states: "Geographers will, I think, be wise to view this problem in general from the standpoint of man's adjustment to environment, rather than from that of environmental influence."[15] Not all human geographers[16] concur with Barrows although his viewpoint has found support among ecologists as well as geographers.[17]

The geographer, in point of fact, despite his increasing interest in human phenomena, has not been distracted from his initial preoccupation with the physical environment. Human geography simply involves carrying the analysis through to man.[18] Man, in a sense, is read into the field of study; since he occupies the earth's surface, he is a part of the natural landscape.[19] Accordingly, the geographer may concern himself with population, in which case he seeks correlations between population and other elements of the natural landscape. He describes the changing pattern of population distribution and explains it in terms of geographic factors. But man not only occupies the earth, he alters its form through his removal of forests, cultivation of fields, construction of buildings, roads, dams, and the like. Modifications of the physical landscape of this character form, in the German phrase, "cultural landscape."[20] This latter may itself, apart from population, be treated as an object of study by the cultural geographer who is interested in finding correlations between the cultural and the natural landscapes. The influence of geographic factors on man or man's adaptation to the geographic environment, as the case may be, is reflected in part in his distribution and in part in the changes he effects in the natural landscape.

Human ecology is therefore something different from human geography. Geography treats men and their activities in their visible aspects and so far as they may be regarded as distributed phenomena. It does not concern, except incidentally, the interrelations among men. Human ecology, which is also interested in the relations of man to his geographic environment, fastens its attention upon the human interdependences that develop in the action and reaction of a population to its habitat. In other words, while geography views the adjustment of man from the standpoint of modifications of the earth's surface, human ecology makes a detailed analysis of the process and organization of relations involved in adjustment to environment. This brings us to a second point of distinction between the two disciplines. Geography involves a description of things as they are at a point in time; its interest is in distribution rather than development. Ecology, on the other hand, is evolutionary.[21] It undertakes to describe the developmental process as well as the form of man's adjustment to his habitat. Human geography and human ecology thus constitute diverse approaches to the question of man's relation to environment; the one proceeds by way of environment, the other by way of organism.

The line of demarcation between economics and human ecology is somewhat less clear. Indeed, ecology has been described as but an extension of economics—if this term may be considered in a broader sense than implying a conscious economy—to the whole realm of life.[22] Such a statement is equally appropriate, though in a more limited sphere, of human ecology. Economics, which deals with those human interrelations that are mediated through a set of exchange values, does not include within its purview the whole of collective life. It does not, for instance, investigate the nonpecuniary aspects of economic relationships. Nor does it treat those subsidiary but contingent relationships which do not find expression in a pricing system, such as occur in the family and between nonprofit institutions.[23] Yet the community is fundamentally an economy and one which involves a far more intricate division of labor than that with which the economist ordinarily deals. It is in this conception of the community that human ecology represents an extension of economics beyond its nominal scope.

But it should not be supposed that human ecology is simply economics on a grand scale. Although the terms derive from a common origin, the disciplines differ both in problem and approach. Economics is concerned with the efficiency, as measured in units of cost, of the interrelations required in a given task of production, and with the changes in those producing relationships resulting from changes in costs. The point of view may be characterized as that of an entrepreneur planning and managing the production and sale of goods or services. This is in contrast to ecology in which attention is directed more to the form or pattern of human sustenance relations, the process of development of such patterns, and the factors that affect their development. The ecological viewpoint is that of individuals and groups seeking position in a developing system of relationships.

Human ecology emerged as and remains primarily a sociological concern. It deals with the central problem of sociology, that is, the development and organization of the community. Human ecology, however, does not pretend to exhaust that problem. The human community is more than just an organization of functional relationships and to that extent there are limitations to the scope of human ecology. Man's collective life involves, in greater or less degree, a psychological and a moral as well as a functional integration. But these, so far as they are distinguishable, should be regarded as complementing aspects of the same thing rather than as separate phases or segments of the community. Sustenance activities and relationships are inextricably interwoven with sentiments, value systems, and other ideational constructs. Human ecology is restricted in scope, then, not by any real or assumed qualitative differences in behavior but simply by the manner in which its problem is stated. The question of how men relate themselves to one another in order to live in their habitats yields a description of community structure in terms of its overt and measurable features. It does not provide explanations of all the many ramifications of human interrelationships, though it may serve as a fruitful source of hypotheses concerning those aspects of the community.

The definition of human ecology presented in this volume is not the only conception that is recognized.[24] It is one, however, which builds upon the contributions of plant and animal ecologists

and seeks to follow the logical implications of general ecological theory. As such it leads to the investigation of a fundamental and otherwise neglected sociological problem. The remaining chapters outline that problem and review the existing knowledge relevant to it. That there are many gaps in that knowledge is a commentary on the youth of human ecology.

NOTES

1. The content of this chapter is reproduced, with modifications, from Amos H. Hawley, "Ecology and Human Ecology," *Social Forces*, XXIII (May, 1944), 398–405.

2. This definition differs but slightly from others. For example: (1) Ecology is the science of "the correlations between all organisms living together in one and the same locality and their adaptations to their surroundings." Ernest Haeckel, *History of Creation*, Vol. II, 354; (2) "Ecology is the science of the relation of organisms to their surroundings, living as well as nonliving; it is the science of the 'domestic economy' of plants and animals." R. Hesse, W. C. Allee, and K. P. Schmidt, *Ecological Animal Geography*, 6; (3) ". . . the essence of ecology lies in its giving the fullest possible value to the habitat as cause and the community as effect, the two constituting the basic phases of a unit process." F. E. Clements and V. E. Shelford, *Bio-Ecology*, 30; and (4) "The descriptive study of the interrelations between coexisting species, and, more generally, their environment, is the province of ecology." (A. J. Lotka, "Contact Points of Population Study with Related Branches of Science," *Proceedings of the American Philosophical Society*, LXXX (February, 1939), 611.)

It is of interest in this connection to note that Charles Elton, the eminent British ecologist, eschews formal definition of the subject, preferring to describe what the ecologist does and allowing the reader to formulate his own definition. "Ecology, Animal," *Encyclopaedia Britannica* (14th ed.), VII, 915–916.

3. See Braun-Blanquet, *Plant Sociology*, 81.

4. *Ibid.*

5. R. D. McKenzie, "Human Ecology," *Encyclopedia of the Social Sciences*, V, 314.

6. See McKenzie, "The Field and Problems of Demography, Human Geography and Human Ecology," chap. iv, in *The Fields and Methods of Sociology*, ed. L. L. Bernard (New York, 1934).

7. Term first used by Achille Guillard, *Elements de statistique humaine ou demographic comparie* (Paris, 1855), XXVI.

8. "Demography," *Encyclopedia of the Social Sciences*, V, 85–86.

9. *New English Dictionary on Historical Principles*, Vol. III, 184.

10. Two vols. (Stuttgart, 1882–1891).

11. *Influences of the Geographic Environment* (New York, 1911).

12. *Principles of Human Geography*, trans. C. F. Brigham (New York, 1926).

13. *La geographie humaine* (3rd ed.), 3 vols. (Paris, 1925).

14. "Geography as Human Ecology," *Annals of the Association of American Geographers*, XIII (1922), 3.

15. *Ibid.*

16. "Geography as the study of responses or adjustments is in the stage of medieval alchemy, geography as the study of the mutual space relationships of phenomena on the face of the earth is a science." Preston E. James, *An Outline of Geography* (New York, 1935), ix.

17. See C. Langdon White and George T. Renner, *Geography: An Introduction to Human Ecology* (New York, 1936); and Barrington Moore, "The Scope of Ecology," *Ecology*, I (January, 1920), 4.

18. See Charles C. Colby, "The California Raisin Industry: A Study in Geographic Interpretation," *Annals of the Association of American Geographers*, XIV (1924), 49–108; and Robert B. Hall, "The Cities of Japan: Notes on Distribution and Inherited Forms," *ibid.*, XXIV (1934), 175–199.

19. "The people on the land are in the geographer's province because they are on and of the land and the relative density of population is a matter of geographical concern." Stanley Dodge, "World Distribution of Population: Preliminary Survey and Tentative Conclusions," *Papers of the Michigan Academy of Sciences, Arts and Letters*, XVIII (1932), 138.

20. Carl Sauer indicates a distinction between human and cultural geographers. "The one group asserts directly its major interests in man; that is, in the relationship of man to his environment, usually in the sense of adaptation of man to physical environment. The other group . . . directs its attention to those elements of material culture that give character to area." "Geography, Cultural," *Encyclopedia of the Social Sciences*, VI, 621.

21. Cf. Patrick W. Bryan, *Man's Adaptation of Nature* (New York, 1933), 8–10.

22. Wells, Huxley, and Wells, *The Science of Life*, 961–962.

23. Cf. Allyn Young's definition of economics in *Encyclopaedia Britannica* (14th ed.), VII, 925.

O. A. Taylor declares: "The three non-economic elements to be considered are (1) technology; (2) the power element, i.e., the pursuit and use by members of society of coercive power to control the actions of other members and (as one use of power) exploit others for their own gain; and (3) the element of prevailing ethical attitudes." "Economic Theory and Certain Non-Economic Elements in Social Life," *Explorations in Economics,* Essays in Honor of F. W. Taussig (New York, 1936), 381.

24. See J. A. Quinn, "Topical Summary of Current Literature in Human Ecology," *American Journal of Sociology,* XLVI (September, 1940), 191–226.

CULTURAL, BEHAVIORAL, AND ECOLOGICAL PERSPECTIVES IN THE STUDY OF SOCIAL ORGANIZATION

OTIS DUDLEY DUNCAN *and* LEO F. SCHNORE

Although there are various understandings as to the scope and problems of sociology, many would grant that the study of society as a system or pattern of organization constitutes the core problem, whatever other preoccupations it may have. As a result, a rather amorphous area, usually called "social organization," seems to provide sociology's central concern. Admittedly, the boundaries of the area are indistinct, and its conceptual apparatus is notably eclectic.

Tangential to this central area, three distinctive approaches to the study of society have developed within American sociology within the last few decades— the *cultural, behavioral,* and *ecological.* The terms may recall the tripartite scheme of Sorokin and Parsons: society, culture, and personality.[1] The purposes of these authors differ from ours. Focusing on the nature of society as the *explanandum* of sociological theory, we attempt to make clear that the concepts and assumptions

Reprinted from *American Journal of Sociology* (September, 1959), pp. 132–146, by permission of the authors and the University of Chicago Press. © 1959 by the University of Chicago Press.

in use in sociology today were fashioned largely from these three different ways of regarding society. However, no prospect of integrating them into a "socio-cultural" theory or a "general theory of action" is here entertained; the relationships among the three are not taken as evidence that they are special cases of some master scheme.

"Cultural sociology," whose "father" might be identified as Sumner, was picked up as a label in the 1920's following the popularization of concepts of culture by Ogburn, Chapin, and others who leaned heavily on such authorities in anthropology as Kroeber, Lowie, and Wissler. The pervasive impact of cultural sociology as a school of thought has waned, but virtually all general texts on sociology continue to give considerable play to concepts derived from culture theory. Znaniecki's recent magnum opus, *Cultural Sciences,* persuasively restates his position that social systems are a subclass of cultural systems and that the methods of studying social and cultural systems are generically the same. However, Znaniecki's work draws heavily on European sources of culture concepts and stands somewhat outside the main stream of cultural sociology in this country.[2] A splendid statement that is of greater relevance to developments within American sociology is given in the collection of Kroeber's papers, *The Nature of Culture*.[3]

"Behavioral science," of course, is little more than a new label for what has long gone under the name of "social psychology." The current popularity and even dominance of "behavioral" studies in sociology reflect, in part, the vigor of recently developed sociometric and small-group interests, the convergence of certain social-psychological concepts, stemming, respectively, from sociological and psychological traditions, and the current preoccupation of sociologists with such problems of method as scaling, experimental design, and analysis of opinion-survey data. The contemporary version of behavioral science seems to find little place for the older tradition of "collective behavior." This is unfortunate, inasmuch as the latter was explicitly an approach to the study of society, as distinguished from the study of attitudes, personality, socialization, and the processes of interaction emphasized in recent social psychology. It is in the relatively unstructured collective behavior of aggregates that we are sometimes able to observe organization in an incipient form. Thus the study of social movements may give clues to the emergence of organizational forms prior to their becoming viable, that is, before they possess unit character. This possibility assumes some practical importance when it is recognized that most societal origins are lost in the past. The recent appearance of a comprehensive treatise on collective behavior and the apparent renewal of interest in the study of social movements may indicate that this tradition has more vitality than seemed apparent for some time.[4] Should this prove to be the case, perhaps it would be well to regard collective

behavior as a fourth major perspective.

"Human ecology" has had a curious history, arising as it did in the context of a series of specialized empirical studies of contemporary urban life. Its early exponents can hardly be said to have grasped its possibilities and implications. In fact, the leading spokesman of the first sociological version of ecology denied that he and the other early writers were attempting to construct a theory.[5] Consequently, when the urban studies lost their novelty, ecology was relegated to a minor theoretical role at best and virtually became identified with a rather narrow preoccupation with urban areal distributions and the elementary techniques applied to their analysis. The belated summary of this "classical" point of view appeared in 1950 in Quinn's *Human Ecology*.[6] By coincidence, the same year witnessed the appearance of Hawley's *Human Ecology*, which developed human ecology as "a theory of community structure."[7] This treatise presented not only a systematic account of human ecology as the study of social organization but also a statement of its basic assumptions, elaborated in a number of important conceptual contributions and a host of researchable hypotheses. In the light of subsequent thinking the fact that Hawley's volume tended to stop short at the community level of organization must be viewed as a temporary expedient, for there is nothing in the basic framework of ecology that precludes its attention to more-inclusive forms of organization. A flurry of interest in the ecological viewpoint on the part of disciplines other than sociology seems certain to force human ecologists working in the sociological tradition into more ambitious conceptions of their task.

None of the three perspectives can be regarded as an exclusively sociological specialism. Certainly, each has ramifications carrying it into a whole range of problems lying well beyond the study of society, which is the focus of interest here. Unless sociology is willing to revert to a Comtean encyclopedism, it will hardly wish to claim the entirety of behavioral science, culture theory, and human ecology. In discussing their contributions to the study of society, therefore, one must avoid the appearance of evaluating them as fields or disciplines in their own right—on their "home territory," so to speak. At the same time the character of their extra-sociological preoccupations manifestly directs and limits their mode of attack on the core problems of sociology. This is seen readily in their key problems.

The cultural approach is derived from classical anthropological theory, which conceives of culture as a more or less integrated totality, comprising cultural patterns or sub-systems of which society is one, along with art, religion, language, technology, and others. A volume such as Kroeber's *Configurations of Culture Growth*, for example, scarcely makes reference to social structure and can hardly be called a contribution to knowledge of *social* change, except indirectly.[8] The original intention of the cultural sociologists was to bring over from culture theory its general concepts and major hypotheses, demonstrating their applicability and fruitfulness in the study of society and of social change in particular. Thus society, like other parts of culture, was described in terms of cultural continuity ("social heritage"), invention, cultural diffusion, and the like.

The enduring contribution of this school, as it turned out, was not the strangely static "cultural determinism" of certain of its epigoni, or the theory which explains social systems in terms of "institutions" derived from "cultural value patterns," or yet the abortive effort to construct a global "sociocultural" theory. It was rather the interpretation of social change as an adjustment to cultural, and particularly technological, accumula-

tion. (As is suggested below, the ecological perspective is perhaps a more congenial milieu for this type of interpretation than culture theory per se.) Hence the theoretical weakness of behavioralism in regard to change is not characteristic of the best cultural sociology. The latter has a well-developed interest—at least on the conceptual level—in innovation and invention and in diffusion and borrowing, all conceived as processes. In practice, except for the global theorists, cultural sociologists seldom concerned themselves with such problems of culture theory as the structure and evolution of linguistic systems, movements in styles of art and philosophy, or diffusion of items of ceremonial culture. But culture theory, insofar as it suggests an effort to treat these matters as aspects of an integrated whole, may distract the student whose business is to deal with social organization.

The *behavioral* approach (we shall refer primarily to the social-psychological version rather than that of "collective behavior") is centrally concerned with how the individual participates in social life: how the person reconciles himself to the necessity of living with others, how he relates to other persons, how he is socialized, how his behavior is controlled or influenced by that of others, and how all these problems are related to the structure of his personality and the content of his attitudes, commitments, orientations, and personal adjustment. The sociological viewpoint appropriate for this range of problems regards society as a pattern of interpersonal relationships or as an arena of social interaction. Here, however, the relevant "structure" is that which is perceived by the individual, just as the relevant "environment" is the social environment, which is again conceived in terms of individual perceptions. One searches this literature in vain for more than superficial reference to the brute facts that men live in a physical environment and that they employ material technology in adapting to it. More important, adaptation itself is conceived in individualistic terms rather than as a collective process.[9]

As a consequence of the behavioralists' focus on the individual, his motivation, and his "tensions . . . as he fits himself into the social system,"[10] they find little need for structural or organizational concepts, nor do they like to entertain hypotheses calling for an explanation of social change other than through such intervening variables as dispositional changes or modifications of character structure. Many behavioralists have a thoroughly nominalistic view of societies and groups; as a result, they are methodological reductionists and have a trained incapacity to view social organization as a reality *sui generis* in functional and evolutionary terms. (These remarks do not apply so forcefully to the student of collective behavior, who examines social organization in the process of its emergence from relatively unstructured interaction. But this view, of course, has a built-in bias that precludes its yielding an adequate account of society as a going concern or the underlying factors of social change.)

In fact, the most glaring weakness of the behavioral approach to problems of organization can be seen in the treatment accorded change. One is hard put to find the source of societal dynamics—the causes of the changing objective circumstances perceived by the individual, to which he attends. Thus the overwhelming stress upon the individual's "adjustment" to altered external circumstances and the almost total lack of attention to the mainsprings of change, wherever they may reside. Actually, by adopting a patently static conception of culture as "that which is socially transmitted between generations," the behavioral approach is forced to an impasse: it can "explain" stability over time, but it is unable to cope with change within its

own frame of reference without invoking "deviation" from norms. A circular argument often results, for social change is defined as a new pattern of individual behavior, which is brought about by "deviation"—a new pattern of behavior.

The *ecological* viewpoint likewise is easily deflected, in its turn, into studies of the environment in strictly geographic terms or into exercises in formal demography. However, its view of social organization as the collective adaptation of a population to its environment avoids the reductionism of behavioral concepts and the etherealism of the "value-pattern" concepts of some culture theorists. In this sense ecology deals with society in somewhat more concrete terms than either of the other approaches. The concept of a "population" as a system with emergent properties is not found in the behavioral or cultural perspectives, nor is the version of the functions of social organization to which this concept leads.

Judged by their research interests and theoretical concerns, as mirrored in current publications, most sociologists today are inclined to be behavioralists. Some have a familiarity with culture theory, and they eclectically accept elements of the cultural approach; few have an acquaintance with human ecology that goes beyond the chapters on urban ecology in their undergraduate textbooks. A brief exposition of this perspective may be appropriate at this point.

In the most general terms the framework of human ecology embraces four main referential concepts: population, environment, technology, and organization, which define what may be called the "ecological complex."[11] Organization is assumed to be a property of the population that has evolved and is sustained in the process of adaptation of the population to its environment, which may include other populations. Insofar as it is amenable to ecological study, organization tends to be investigated as a ramification of sustenance activities, broadly conceived, which utilize whatever technological apparatus is at the population's disposal or is developed by it.

While in its crudest version this framework suggests that organization is to be viewed as the "dependent variable," influenced by the other three "independent variables," upon a more sophisticated view, organization is seen as reciprocally related to each of the other elements of the ecological complex. In fact, to define any of the elements of this complex adequately, one has to take account of their relationship with organization. The notion of an "ecosystem" may be used as a heuristic designation for the ecological complex in order to bring out this aspect of interrelatedness which some writers have identified as the most fundamental premise in ecological thinking. That to others this notion is one of the central postulates of sociology itself only serves to underscore the sociological character of ecology—whether in its plant, animal, or human version. Darwin's conception of the "web of life" refers to a system of organization first and foremost.

Although ecology is not to be identified with the study of areal distributions, and its subject matter is by no means limited to the "territorial arrangements that social activities assume,"[12] the study of spatial relationships continues to play a key role in ecology for several reasons. First, territoriality is a major factor giving unit character to populations. Second, space is simultaneously a requisite for the activities of any organizational unit and an obstacle which must be overcome in establishing interunit relationships. Finally, space—like time—furnishes a convenient and invariant set of reference points for observation, and observed spatiotemporal regularities and rhythms furnish convenient indicators of structural relationships.[13]

In comparing the three alternative approaches, it is instructive to raise two closely related questions: What are the unit parts that are analytically manipulated? What emerges as a "system" when these unit parts are ordered?

In the case of the cultural approach, the units turn out to be "culture traits," such as the elements of language, aesthetic values, or material artifacts, and they are organized into "trait complexes" and, less frequently, cultural and subcultural systems. With respect to the behavioral perspective, the ultimate focus is upon one or another variety of mental behavior (e.g., attitudes, aspirations, and expectations), and these elements are organized most often into "personality systems" or "character types." From the ecological standpoint, however, the elementary unit of analysis—the "atom," so to speak—is the "pattern of activity," or simply "activity." The system envisioned is an organization of activities, arranged in overlapping and interpenetrating series of activity constellations, or groups.

From the standpoint of the individual engaged in it, the activity or the individual's share in the activity is commonly designated as his "role." This term would be quite serviceable for ecological analysis[14] were it not for the psychological connotations that have become attached thereto in the work of writers like Linton, Parsons, and Stouffer. The ecologist is interested in the pattern of observable physical activity itself rather than the subjective expectations that individuals may entertain of their roles. Ecological analysis does not attempt to explain the individual's feelings of obligation, the stresses he suffers as a consequence of performing several roles simultaneously or sequentially, or his motivational syndromes when he is engaged in different sorts of activities. At the common-sense level the closest approximation to the ecological conception of "activity" is the notion implied by the term "occupation," although our interest includes activities that do not ordinarily receive monetary compensation (e.g., those found within the household complex). "Functionary" is a less frequently used term that carries a similar connotation, and—within general ecology—the concept of "niche" designates practically the same.[15]

Although the notion of subjective obligation emphasized in role theory is irrelevant for our purposes, there is a strong emphasis upon reciprocity in the ecological conception of activity, for the activity is not conceived individualistically or *in vacuo*. It cannot be conceived of apart from other activities. The logic of ecological theory compels the analyst to view distinctive activities—their numbers and kinds—as *properties of aggregates or populations*. Thus an aggregate may be labeled as relatively "undifferentiated" if it is found to engage in few distinctive activities. Actually, however, that portion of the ecological notion of activities that points to their *interdependence* is perhaps the crucial element of the concept. This stress, it might be added, indicates the intrinsically sociological character of ecological thought, for, if sociology can be credited with any one major insight, it is its recognition of the inescapable interdependence of human activities.

Such a conception gives immediate rise to a range of essentially *taxonomic* problems. Most abstractly, what are the generic forms of activity constellations or groups? Unfortunately, this basic taxonomic work has been studiously avoided by sociologists in general and by ecologists in particular. Ecologists themselves are currently obliged, for example, to work with crude polar types of communities and societies. In many respects a perusal of the recent literature suggests that taxonomic work is being carried forward largely by anthropologists, economists, geographers, and political scientists rather than sociologists.[16]

Another line of inquiry is to ask to what extent the alternative approaches might serve to inform major areas of current interest for students of social organization. For illustrative purposes we may raise this question with respect to three topics of much current theoretical and empirical interest: bureaucracy, stratification, and urbanization. We shall then allude to the issue of functional analysis.

In the case of the cultural approach to these three topics there seem to be almost no immediate contributions in view, beyond certain broad generalities regarding the indigenous appearance of such "trait complexes" as written language, monetary systems, and rational techniques and devices for the measurement of time, space, and weight with the emergence of urban forms of organization. If it offers any special contribution to an understanding of bureaucracy, it escapes most writers on the subject. With respect to stratification, the only relevant contribution is the notion of distinctive "subcultures" in various strata; this term, however, merely provides another label for the phenomena under investigation.

As to the behavioral approach, to the extent that it is employed in these areas of investigation, the main focus is upon the effects upon the individual of a position in a bureaucratic setting, of a particular locus in the stratification system, or of living in an urban area. When behavioralists study bureaucracy, they study the stresses on the individual in a bureaucratic context and his accommodations thereto rather than the functions of bureaucratic systems as such or the societal and technological matrix within which bureaucracy evolves. In the analysis of stratification, behavioralists avoid the problem of the determinants of systems of rank. Rather their overwhelming concern is with such matters as the criteria employed by individuals in their evaluations of others, the processes of socialization in the various strata, or the development of stratum-specific clusters of attitudes, values, and modes of thought. Regarding urbanization, behavioralists have not proceeded very far beyond the hypotheses sketched by Wirth in his essay, "Urbanism as a Way of Life," in which he suggested certain consequences for the individual living in a community of great size, density, and heterogeneity.[17] As yet, no one has seriously put forward a causal account of the rise of cities in which social-psychological factors take precedence, although there has been some recent effort to deal thus with "suburbanization."[18] In each of these problems, then, the focus is almost inevitably upon the *consequences* for the individual of the very forms that the student would like to explain.

In contrast, the *ecological* perspective apparently holds great promise for the student of organization, although, frankly, it is at present largely a matter of potential rather than of solid performance in the areas of stratification and bureaucracy. But in the study of urbanization, of course, a well-documented case can be argued that ecology provides an appropriate mode of causal analysis; for this reason, we shall not elaborate the point. However, ecologists themselves are not entirely satisfied with the present state of their own research on urbanization. Much more work is required, detailing the precise technological, demographic, and environmental conditions under which various urban forms of organization may be expected to appear and—once established—to develop at given rates.[19] But the absence of comparative data of historical depth and on a world-wide scale poses a major problem.

In the two remaining areas—bureaucracy and stratification—the ecological conception of "activity constellations" could be fruitfully extended, to the benefit of the analysis of social organization and to ecology itself. If one does not become deflected by an interest in certain institutional mechanisms, such as provisions for promotion and job security, the salient features of a bureaucracy are its great size, its high degree of differentiation, and its internal stratification—properties of the aggregate itself which suggest that the bureaucracy, as a mode of organization, shares certain key features with the urban community and the urban society in which it typically appears. Further, these common formal characteristics suggest that the causation may be similar and that the study of a bureaucracy in terms of the ecological complex may be more than an idle exercise. On the face of it, the impact of technological developments would appear to warrant further study. It is a commonplace to speak of the historical emergence of the factory, a large, differentiated, hierarchically organized system, as an organizational response to the development of steam power and other technological innovations. Longitudinal study of growing business enterprises or governmental bureaus might also establish whether or not mounting numbers and spatial expansion of functions tend to exert a pressure in the direction of increasing "bureaucratization."[20] Boulding's recent attempt to account for the rise of the type of large-scale social unit that lends itself to bureaucratic organization makes explicit reference to what the author regards as an "ecological" framework.[21] Had his argument availed itself more explicitly of the ecological conceptions of sociologists, it might have provided even more convincing evidence of their relevance. Reference may also be made to a study which demonstrates the mutual relevance of studies in bureaucratic organization and in metropolitan dominance.[22]

In the area of stratification, of course, the "prestige dimension" in the subjective sense in which it is generally understood is beyond ecology's immediate purview. The primary contribution would consist of aiding the student of organization in attacking the problem of power. However, precisely this aspect of stratification is widely regarded as the most neglected in American sociological thought.[23] For the moment, the ecologist's contribution to the analysis of power may be confined to the context of the local community. Hawley has suggested that "dominance" in the local community attaches to those functional units that control the flow of sustenance into it.[24] Comparative analysis would be required to test this hypothesis adequately; however, informal observation leads one to conclude that cities of different size and functional type do comprise significantly different arenas for the struggle between contending power groups. The "town-and-gown" splits in small university towns present somewhat different situations from those in the traditional "company town," and both differ significantly from the complexities of the metropolis, where dominance is diffused.

Indeed, there are striking formal similarities between the very concept of "power" and that of "dominance" which, in general ecology, is treated as a subcategory of symbiotic relation between dissimilar functions and is ordinarily given a species referent. Both concepts point to the ability of one cluster of activities or niches to set the conditions under which others must function. One promising line of inquiry is the elaboration of the related ecological concepts of "subdominant" and "influent." These are also positional concepts that refer to a system of interdependent relationships between activities. Consideration of their formal analogues in the study of stratification in the human community might eliminate the too-frequent conceptualization of power as a "one-way street." In this connection a problem that has

yet to be adequately explored is the relationship between occupational differentiation and stratification: occupations hold central positions in theories of stratification that are otherwise strikingly dissimilar.

Coming at the problem in another way, strata may be viewed as assemblages of household units, although the precise conditions under which they are likely to act in concert have yet to be specified. In another guise this is the question of whether strata are "really" groups or merely statistical categories.[25] An unequivocal answer is, of course, impossible; rather it seems that under certain circumstances households do act together to such an extent that they can be literally regarded as groups. "Castes" are cases in point, although probably too much attention has been given such institutional mechanisms as caste endogamy and occupational inheritance. A somewhat related problem—although it requires analysis outside the confines of the local community—is that of the circumstances under which occupational coalitions appear. The standard answer is that they emerge in response to some external threat. Systematically overlooked, however, is the simple matter of spatiotemporal accessibility. The difficulty of unionizing workers in industries widely scattered or subject to seasonality is instructive.

One recent approach to stratification that has come into some prominence is by way of the concept of "class crystallization."[26] Although the form of the data with which most investigators of this phenomenon have worked (the products of sample surveys) has tended to turn them in the direction of analyzing the extent to which the individual's ranked roles may be in alignment, the writers seem to appreciate fully the possibility of characterizing whole aggregates—communities and even societies—as more or less crystallized. Just as an aggregate may be more or less differentiated by the number of its distinctive activities, it seems possible that degrees of stratification may be shown by the extent of its crystallization. The usual approach, of course, is to conceive societies as possessing varying degrees of permeability between strata, with "open" and "closed" societies as polar types; individual mobility is used as an index. However, this method requires "dynamic" data, for example, career mobility or father's occupation—measures that inevitably involve thorny methodological problems, including controls for age and estimates of structurally induced mobility. In contrast, crystallization can be used with data referring to only one point in time; however, this does not prevent its use in longitudinal analysis. Given comparable data of appropriate form, a series of "snapshot" observations would provide a "moving picture" and might incidentally settle the current controversy over whether the United States is tending toward a "closed" society.

But the point is that the concept of crystallization permits one to define stratification operationally as a variable property of the aggregate, without further reference to the individual. For ecological analysis this may then be related to other attributes of the aggregate—for example, its size, rate of growth, degree of urbanization, and technological equipment.[27] However, it soon becomes evident that there will be inevitable difficulties in the analysis of stratification in the absence of a well-defined taxonomy of societies.[28] Moreover, a coherent typology of communities would also be of enormous value, especially in view of the usual research strategy of making case studies of single communities. Again, the single-industry town presumably reveals a different degree of class crystallization from that of the metropolis.[29] At this point the ecologists can be of some assistance, for at least they have done some exploratory typing of communities according to major functions.

The human ecologist is, of course, in a unique position by virtue of his skills and preoccupations to contribute to knowledge of the sheerly demographic and territorial aspects of stratification.[30] But the test of ecological theory is its ability to clarify issues and suggest hypotheses. One issue which has been much discussed in the last decade is that of the relation between patterns of stratification in the local community and those of the mass society[31] or of the reasons for variation in stratification patterns.[32] It is difficult to see how a behavioral approach can explain such variation, while the cultural viewpoint has contributed little more than the virtually tautological suggestion that differences among communities or their deviations from a national pattern may be regarded as "substitute profiles of cultural orientation."[33] But, if social stratification is conceived to be related to other aspects of organization, the ecologist is in a position to indicate reasons for both similarities and differences in a community's patterns of stratification. On the one hand, modern communities are highly interrelated by function, as is shown by the volume of intercommunity economic and migratory flows; they share a common technology for the most part; and communities of comparable size have fairly similar local service structures and perform fairly similar repertories of services for outlying areas. On the other hand, each community holds a more or less specialized position in the complex of intercommunity relationships, reflected in variations in occupational structure and levels of living. Moreover, given unequal rates of change in the several sectors of the economy, communities with differing economic bases are expected to evidence differing rates of growth and hence differential opportunities for social mobility. Finally, ecologists have amassed a considerable amount of information on variation in social structure according to community size, which is highly relevant to the differences in stratification pattern. In short, it seems good scientific strategy to couch analysis of structural variation in structural terms, at any rate until such time as it is shown that the only recourse is to another level or type of abstraction.[34]

We believe that the acceptance of an ecological approach would go far toward clarifying contemporary issues in organizational theory concerning "functionalism." Although "functional analysis" arose in the cultural approach to society, it has been taken over by the behavioralists. Consequently, recent statements of the "functional requisites of society" have been confounded by the attempt of their authors to proceed simultaneously from both an individual and a social perspective. What are called "functions" are, as often as not, aspects of individual motivation, and the necessity for a clear distinction between motivation and function has yet to be clearly recognized.[35] A coherent statement of functionalist principles as applied to the study of society will follow from the recognition that functions should be attributed to units of social organization—activity constellations—and not to individuals as persons or to symbols, values, or other cultural items.

Ecological structure is conceived as an organization of functions—activities that are dependent upon other activities. Ecologists have usually bypassed the question of "contributions to the maintenance of the system," although this problem logically does not lie beyond their purview. However, they have deliberately avoided the blind alley of exploring "functions versus dysfunctions," recognizing that what is functional for one part of the total system is often dysfunctional for another. (This fact, incidentally, appears to be the source of many conflicts of power.) Moreover, the ecologist makes no use of the distinction between latent and patent functions, since this rests with the individual's knowledge and judgment, and the individual's personal view of things is, as such, of no ecological interest. Parenthetically, it might be remarked that the ecologist—for all his lack of skill in social-psychological matters—has come to recognize that what is obvious, intended, and anticipated by one person may be unknown, unanticipated, and unintended by another. Perhaps his acumen has been fortified by wrestling with what now appears to be an irrelevant distinction between "natural" and "planned" processes. At any rate, it is clear to the contemporary ecologist, though it was not to the classical, that the subject matter of human ecology cannot be defined residually in terms of an unmanageable psychological distinction.

It is significant that, while theorists of culture and behavioralists have been propounding confused hypothetical versions of functionalism, ecologists have been busy making inductive studies of the functions of communities and correlating functions with aspects of organization, location, and demographic structure. This suggests that the ability to manipulate ideas about function effectively in research develops rather easily after an ecological perspective is adopted.

The ecological approach, in comparison with the two alternatives, holds out special promise of enriching the fund of systematic knowledge on social change—here conceived as the transformations of patterns of social organization occurring over time rather than as, say, shifts in value systems or modal character structure. Recent contributions exhibit a wide range of ecological hypotheses which illuminate broad patterns of social evolution, help to explain contemporary social trends, and provide a sociological matrix for studies of "economic development."

In contrast, the efforts of present-day behavioralists contribute little to our understanding of where modern society came from or where it is going, and the limited potentialities for providing a comprehensive account of social change within the framework of "collective behavior" remain largely latent, as a recent statement admits.[36] Culture theory, too, except as it implicitly or explicitly incorporates an ecological viewpoint, fails to come to grips with many salient aspects of social change, particularly insofar as it remains preoccupied with global theories of cultural evolution or sociocultural dynamics.[37]

Ogburn's theory of social change continues to be the most influential one in American sociology.[38] Although it developed in the tradition of cultural sociology, actually it has assumed a quite different emphasis. Ogburn's theory falls into two main parts: the theory of cultural accumulation, expounded with primary reference to technology, and the hypothesis that a large part of social change amounts to an adjustment to technological change. In the first part, the theory depends upon such concepts as invention, culture base, cultural accumulation, and, quite incidentally, cultural diffusion. Invention is regarded as fundamental and is viewed, in turn, as a function of "demand," the culture base, and mental ability. The last-named is regarded as essentially a constant, while the inability of demand to stimulate invention in the absence of an adequate culture base is emphasized.

Ogburn's theory of invention could doubtless be improved by casting it in ecological terms, that is, by examining technological innovation as a response to demographic, environmental, and organizational variations over space and time. "Demand," for example, may be viewed as rather sensitive to population change. Moreover, while the relative distribution of mental ability may be viewed as a constant, the absolute number of persons of superior ability is, of course, directly related to size of population. Moreover, ability as such makes no inventions, but organized ability does, for the more and more elaborate organization of inventive effort is a trend nearly equal in importance to technological accumulation itself. Studies of such organization would reveal the role of mobilized resources in making inventions possible; no amount of progress in pure science accomplished through the exercise of "mental ability" would have produced the atom bomb without a tremendous mobilization of resources and personnel. Finally, the character of the problem of collective adjustment facing a population rather than "demand"—in the somewhat anemic sense of the economist—may be what gives direction to invention. Thus the environment itself must be taken into account from the standpoint of the limitations and the possibilities that it presents: the arts of navigation are not perfected by landlocked peoples; and the irrigation systems developed where there are monsoons differ from those devised in arid regions.

The second part of Ogburn's theory—social adjustment to technological change—requires little restatement to bring it well within the compass of an ecological framework. In fact, the voluminous evidence that he has amassed on behalf of this general hypothesis is one of the major claims of technology to its status as a prime element in the ecological complex, along with population, environment, and organization. Here again, however, Ogburn's analysis of the implications of technology for organization seems to require supplementary exploration of the demographic situations and environmental contexts in which technology modifies organization.[39]

The most recent theory of cultural change to attract widespread attention is one that espouses a frankly ecological view: Steward's "cultural ecology" and his theory of "multilinear evolution."[40] Steward's position differs in a number of details from the ecological perspective as it has developed within sociology. The key difference, however, can be seen in his choice of "culture," in the usual broad sense, as his dependent variable. This is not to say, however, that he fails to offer a great deal to the student of social organization, for organizational arrangements comprise part of the totality of culture that he sets out to explain. Thus, in the course of his analysis of the culture of the Great Basin Shoshone, Steward includes an admirably lucid account of the forms of community and family organization and how they evolved in response to technological, demographic, and environmental forces. In short, a great deal of his empirical work makes use of the "ecological complex" described above. Moreover, he does not feel compelled to invoke subjective "values" or any other attributes of individuals in detailing his causal explanation.

Steward apparently does consider his version of ecology as significantly different from the sociological variety, as shown by his choice of the "cultural ecology" rubric. From his brief remarks on the difference between his viewpoint and that of the human ecologist, one gathers that he is especially critical of human ecologists like Hawley for giving too little recognition to the physical environment as a causal factor. His different emphasis is very probably the result of his greater interest, as an anthropologist, in smaller and technologically less advanced societies, where adaptations to the environment are more direct and immediately evident. In his discussion of other larger and more complex societies (e.g., Puerto Rico) the environment receives notably less weight. And, further, Steward accuses the human ecologists of seeking "universal" relationships and thus tending to develop hypotheses that resemble those of the unilinear evolutionists of the late nineteenth century.[41]

It must be abundantly clear by now that the ecological view—alone among these three perspectives—focuses upon organization as a property of an aggregate or population. Eschewing a formulation of his problem in terms of the individual or the culture trait, the ecologist takes the aggregate as his frame of reference and deliberately sets out to account for the forms that social organization assumes in response to varying demographic, technological, and environmental pressures. In this way, the ecologist seems to be contributing to the maintenance of a traditional sociological interest in explaining forms of organization and changes therein. Were it not for the recent ascendancy of the behavioral approach, one would be tempted to say that these two problems—structure and change—pose the key questions for sociology. However, the behavioral approach has shifted the focus of sociological attention to an individualistic frame of reference.

Our intention here is not to engage in bootless argument regarding the "ultimate reality" of either the individual or the aggregate. Suffice it to say that both are abstractions and thus unreal in equal degree. As Cooley noted, and as many of his alleged followers choose to forget, the individual and the group are but aspects of the same reality.[42] Nor is it our intention to establish false divisions where none exist. None of these perspectives is independent of the others. Empirically, they all examine the same thing—society —albeit different aspects of that "thing." As frames of reference each must borrow certain assumptions from the empirical generalizations of the others or else substitute "homemade" versions. Underlying any elaboration of ecological theory, for example, are certain minimal assumptions about the plasticity of the individual's behavior, permitting him to engage in numerous activities. From the cultural approach, ecology borrows presuppositions about cultural continuity and the diffusibility of culture patterns, as well as assumptions regarding the cumulative character of technological change. The uses made of such premises, however, are unlikely to be the same by the borrower as by the lender, inasmuch as they are combined with other assumptions and empirical generalizations to yield distinctive hypotheses.

Consequently, emphasis on the indebtedness of each perspective to the others must not obscure the genuine distinctiveness of their concepts and assumptions: the behavioral scientist studies society as a system of social interaction and interpersonal relations, the culture theorist approaches it as a culture pattern or value system, and the human ecologist examines society as the functional organization of a population in process of achieving and maintaining an adaptation to its environment. If our experience is typical, these perspectives are not only different; they are so different that it is difficult to explain and justify one of them to a sociologist committed to another. The usual reaction is that the other two perspectives are wrong, or at least incomplete, whereas the favored one is sufficient for virtually all purposes of sociological research. Let it be very clear that our intention is not to assert the superiority of the ecological approach per se, for all sociological uses, except perhaps for the particular range of organizational problems emphasized here.

Our intention, rather, is to argue—with as much force as may be at our disposal—that a point of view that transcends the view of the individual as the ultimate significant unit, and that confines attention to a limited aspect of the totality of culture, is not somehow doomed from the outset, nor is it to be dismissed out of hand as intrinsically incapable of a very high degree of pre-

dictive power. On the contrary, the partial results available at this point lead us to the conclusion that an aggregate approach—not framed in terms of the individual or value systems—holds more promise for exploring problems of organization than any alternative yet put forward.

It is true that the behavioral approach, in particular, will probably continue to illuminate the human situation, offering insight into the nature of life in society, but it does not promise to yield much in the way of explanation of social organization per se. These two approaches may be expected to make further contributions, respectively, to theories of personality and of culture, but their current preoccupations are such that they offer relatively little promise of advancing the study of society itself. Needless to say, this point of view is subject to empirical test. We are unable to wait for a happy millennium, when "all the evidence is in." The internal dynamics of the cultural system called "social science" seem to demand that theory and research press forward even in the absence of complete logical closure.

One further observation may be pertinent to our argument for the fruitfulness of an ecological approach. While behavioralists have recently emphasized the advantages of interdisciplinary co-operation, ecologists for a long time have been engaged in cross-disciplinary activity. A comprehensive bibliography of work embodying the ecological approach would show titles from economics, demography, geography, and biology, along with contributions of sociologists (the latter representing a minority). Not only do the several disciplines add to the general stock of ecological research but, in regard to many specific problems, the contributions of each discipline are hard to isolate.[43] That an ecological outlook lends itself so well to fruitful exchanges among disciplines is due to its strong empirical base and its relatively concrete view of society, which brings sociological investigation down from the spaceless, timeless abstractions of culture theory but preserves it from the aimless empiricism of detailing the manifold behavioral nuances of interpersonal relations. The cross-disciplinary tendency of human ecology also accounts for the fact that one need not call himself an ecologist to do ecological research or to employ essentially ecological concepts. Thus geographers balked when urged to regard geography as human ecology, but, first and last, they have not been able to pursue geographic research without making notable contributions to ecological knowledge.[44] The same can be said, of course, about those sociologists who (as implied in respect to Ogburn) are at least half-ecologist, in spite of their labels.

At any rate, this paper is no mere prolegomenon to ecology or a statement of a suspicion that an ecological perspective might be a valuable way to look at society. Contributions of the highest importance to an understanding of the nature of social organization and social change are being made by investigators more or less explicitly adopting an ecological outlook.[45] The performance and promise of human ecology should be judged in terms of the caliber of such contributions, and judgments should be based on an analysis of patterns of inquiry, not on slogans. It matters little if an investigator, breaking somewhat with anthropological tradition but wishing to maintain his affiliation with it, attaches importance to the rubric "cultural ecology" as distinct from "human ecology." What does matter is whether an important insight has been gained by taking an ecological perspective.

NOTES

1. Pitirim Sorokin, *Society, Culture, and Personality* (New York: Harper & Bros., 1947); Talcott Parsons, *The Social System* (Glencoe, Ill.: Free Press, 1951); Talcott Parsons and Edward A. Shils (Eds.), *Toward a General Theory of Action* (Cambridge, Mass.: Harvard University Press, 1951). In some respects the perspectives identified here correspond more closely to those sketched by Harold W. Pfautz in his "Social Stratification and Sociology," *Transactions of the Second World Congress of Sociology* (London: International Sociological Association, 1954), II, 311–320.

2. Florian Znaniecki, *Cultural Sciences* (Urbana: University of Illinois Press, 1952).

3. A. L. Kroeber, *The Nature of Culture* (Chicago: University of Chicago Press, 1952).

4. Ralph H. Turner and Lewis M. Killian, *Collective Behavior* (Englewood Cliffs, N.J.: Prentice-Hall, Inc., 1957); Rudolf Heberle, *Social Movements* (New York: Appleton–Century–Crofts, 1951); Herbert Blumer, "Collective Behavior," in J. B. Gittler (Ed.), *Review of Sociology: Analysis of a Decade* (New York: John Wiley & Sons, 1957).

5. Robert E. Park's review of Milla A. Alihan's *Social Ecology* in the *Annals*, CCII (March, 1939), 264–265.

6. James A. Quinn, *Human Ecology* (New York: Prentice-Hall, Inc., 1950).

7. Amos H. Hawley, *Human Ecology* (New York: Ronald Press Co., 1950).

8. A. L. Kroeber, *Configurations of Culture Growth* (Berkeley: University of California Press, 1944).

9. The *Handbook of Social Psychology*, ed. Carl Murchison (Worcester, Mass.: Clark University Press, 1935), contained a long chapter on "The Physical Environment" by the ecologist V. E. Shelford. But in the two-volume *Handbook of Social Psychology*, ed. Gardner Lindzey (Cambridge, Mass.: Addison–Wesley Publishing Co., 1954) only 2 out of 1,175 pages are explicitly devoted to physical-environmental features (see Henry W. Riecken and George C. Homans, "Psychological Aspects of Social Structure," section on "Social Structure and the Environment," *ibid.*, pp. 801–802). Clyde Kluckhohn dismisses the relevance of the physical environment for human activities by quoting Margaret T. Hodgen, that "the historically important thing in regard to natural resources is man's attitude toward them" ("Culture and Behavior," *ibid.*, p. 922).

10. Phraseology attributed to Wilbert E. Moore by Clyde V. Kiser in a summary of a round table on "Exploration of Possibilities for New Studies of Factors Affecting Size of Family," *Milbank Memorial Fund Quarterly*, XXXI (October, 1953), 477. (Moore is singled out for the aptness of his language, not necessarily because of his theoretical position.)

11. If one needs a mnemonic device, the initial letters of these terms spell P-O-E-T (see Otis Dudley Duncan, "Human Ecology and Population Studies," in Philip M. Hauser and Otis Dudley Duncan [Eds.], *The Study of Population* [Chicago: University of Chicago Press, 1959], pp. 678–716, and Leo F. Schnore, "Social Morphology and Human Ecology," *American Journal of Sociology*, LXIII [May, 1958], 620–634).

12. Walter Firey, *Land Use in Central Boston* (Cambridge, Mass.: Harvard Universitv Press, 1947), p. 3.

13. Hawley, *op. cit.*, and his succinct account of "The Approach of Human Ecology to Urban Areal Research," *Scientific Monthly*, LXXIII (July, 1951), 48–49.

14. Amos H. Hawley, in "Some Remarks on the Relation of Social Psychology and Human Ecology," a paper read at the 1950 meetings of the American Sociological Society, defines "role" as "a routinely performed activity which depends for its continuity on the routine performance of other activities." We are greatly indebted to this paper and to his other published and unpublished work.

15. Odum writes that "the habitat is the organism's 'address,' and the niche is its 'profession,' biologically speaking" (Eugene P. Odum, *Fundamentals of Ecology* [Philadelphia: W. B. Saunders Co., 1953], p. 15).

16. See Hawley, *Human Ecology*, chap. xii: "Community Structure," for a discussion of types of activity constellation; the household, the production unit, and the community itself are treated in some detail. One misses, however, a formal treatment of systems of local communities, regions, and societies, for which see Rutledge Vining, "A, Description of Certain Spatial Aspects of an Economic System," *Economic Development and Cultural Change*, III (January, 1955), 147–195, and the comment by Edgar M. Hoover, "The Concept of a System of Cities," Economic Development and Cultural Change, III (January, 1955), 196–198.

17. Louis Wirth, "Urbanism as a Way of Life," *American Journal of Sociology*, XLIV (July, 1938), 1–24.

18. Fava and Bell, respectively, stress a propensity for "neighboring" and "familistic values" in their discussions of the development of suburbs; both, however, eventually admit that they are attempting to account for the selectivity of migration to suburbs (even in the absence of controls) and that they are not presuming to explain the rise of suburbs themselves (see Sylvia Fleis Fava, "Suburbanism as a Way of Life," *American Sociological Review*, XXI [February, 1956], 34–37, and Wendell Bell, "Familism and Suburbanization: One Test of the Social Choice Hypothesis," *Rural Sociology*, XXI [September–December, 1956], 276–283).

19. Duncan, *op. cit.*

20. Frederic W. Terrien and Donald L. Mills, "The Effect of Changing Size upon the Internal Structure of Organizations," *American Sociological Review*, XX (February, 1955), 11–13.

21. Kenneth E. Boulding, *The Organizational Revolution* (New York: Harper & Bros., 1953).

22. Donnell M. Pappenfort, "The Ecological Field and the Metropolitan Community: Manufacturing and Management," *American Journal of Sociology*, LXIV (January, 1959), 380–385.

23. Seymour M. Lipset and Reinhard Bendix, "Social Status and Social Structure: A Re-examination of Data and Interpretations, I and II," *British Journal of Sociology*, II (June and September, 1951), 150–168 and 230–254.

24. Hawley, *Human Ecology*, pp. 229–230.

25. Gerhard Lenski, "American Social Classes: Statistical Strata or Social Groups?" *American Journal of Sociology*, LVIII (September, 1952), 139–144.

26. Hawley, *Human Ecology*, p. 231; Ronald Freedman, Amos H. Hawley, Werner S. Landecker, Gerhard E. Lenski, and Horace M. Miner, *Principles of Sociology* (rev. ed.; New York: Henry Holt & Co., 1956), chaps. vii and xiii; Gerhard Lenski, "Status Crystallization: A Non-vertical Dimension of Social Status," *American Sociological Review*, XIX (August, 1954), 405–413, and his "Social Participation and Status Crystallization," *American Sociological Review*, XXI (August, 1956), 458–464; Ralph Spielman, "A Study of Stratification in the United States" (unpublished doctoral dissertation, University of Michigan, 1953).

27. For an interesting use of census and other mass data in a "crystallization" framework see Leonard Blumberg, "The Relationship among Rank Systems in American Society," in Freedman *et al.*, *op. cit.*, pp. 540–544. In both the mobility and the crystallization approaches, of course, the sheer number of strata recognized by the observer will affect his judgment of the degree of "openness" or "crystallization" that obtains.

28. Pfautz (*op. cit.*) makes a similar observation with respect to mobility. For a provocative discussion of stratification in the context of types of community and society see Gideon Sjoberg, "Folk and 'Feudal' Societies," *American Journal of Sociology*, LVIII (November, 1952), 231–239, and his related discussion of "The Preindustrial City," *American Journal of Sociology*, LX (March, 1955), 438–445.

29. Lipset and Bendix, *op. cit.*

30. Otis Dudley Duncan and Beverly Duncan, "Residential Distribution and Occupational Stratification," *American Journal of Sociology*, LX (March, 1955), 493–503.

31. Paul K. Hatt, "Stratification in the Mass Society," *American Sociological Review*, XV (April, 1950), 216–222.

32. Otis Dudley Duncan and Jay W. Artis, "Some Problems of Stratification Research," *Rural Sociology*, XVI (March, 1951), 17–29.

33. Florence Kluckhohn, "Dominant and Substitute Profiles of Cultural Orientations: Their Significance for the Analysis of Social Stratification," *Social Forces*, XXVIII (May, 1950), 376–393.

34. Duncan and Artis, *op. cit.*, pp. 28–29.

35. See David Aberle *et al.*, "The Functional Prerequisites of a Society," *Ethics*, LX (January, 1950), 100–111.

36. Turner and Killian, *op. cit.*, chap. xxii, pp. 515–529.

37. Sorokin, *op. cit.* A "culturological" view that has had less influence in sociology is that of Leslie A. White (see his *The Science of Culture* [New York: Farrar & Strauss, 1949]).

38. William F. Ogburn, *Social Change* (New York: B. W. Huebsch, 1922; rev. ed., New York: Viking Press, 1950).

39. At least three of Ogburn's essays deal explicitly with population as a variable, although in different ways. In his "Inventions, Population and History," in Percy Long (Ed.), *Studies in the History of Culture* (Menasha, Wis.: George Banta Publishing Co. [for the American Council of Learned Societes], 1942), pp. 232–245, population size is explicitly

treated as the dependent variable. A more general discussion is contained in his essay, "On the Social Aspects of Population Changes," *British Journal of Sociology*, IV (March, 1953), pp. 25–30. Finally, "Population, Private Ownership, Technology, and the Standard of living," *American Journal of Sociology*, LVI (January, 1951), 314–319, contains a formulation almost identical with the "ecological complex" discussed above.

40. Julian Steward, *Theory of Culture Change* (Urbana: University of Illinois Press, 1955).

41. *Ibid.*, p. 34.

42. See Charles Horton Cooley, *Human Nature and the Social Order* (New York: Charles Scribner's Sons, 1902; rev. ed., Glencoe, Ill.: Free Press, 1956), esp. chap. I, "Society and the Individual."

43. E.g., the recent work on the functions of communities has been carried forward by land economists, location economists, human and urban geographers, political scientists, and sociologists (see the references cited in Leo F. Schnore, "The Functions of Metropolitan Suburbs," *American Journal of Sociology*, LVII [March, 1956], 453–458). An earlier contribution was made by a sociologist who was a "territorial demographer" before he became a behavioralist interested in the looking-glass self (see Charles Horton Cooley, "The Theory of Transportation," *Publications of the American Economic Association*, Vol. IX [May, 1894]; reprinted in Robert Cooley Angell [Ed.], *Sociological Theory and Social Research* [New York: Henry Holt & Co., 1930], pp. 17–118).

44. See H. H. Barrows, "Geography as Human Ecology," *Annals of the Association of American Geographers*, XIII (March, 1923), 1–14. Barrows' view has not been widely accepted by geographers.

45. Among the more significant recent contributions are the following: Francis R. Allen *et al.*, *Technology and Social Change* (New York: Appleton-Century-Crofts, 1957); Donald J. Bogue, *The Structure of the Metropolitan Community* (Ann Arbor: University of Michigan Press, 1949); Boulding, *op. cit.*; Fred Cottrell, *Energy and Society: The Relation between Energy, Social Change and Economic Development* (New York: McGraw-Hill Book Co., 1955); William F. Ogburn and Meyer Nimkoff, *Technology and the Changing Family* (Boston: Houghton Mifflin Co., 1955); Julian Steward *et al.*, *Irrigation Civilizations: A Comparative Study* (Washington, D.C.: Pan-American Union, 1955); William L. Thomas, Jr. (Ed.), *Man's Role in Changing the Face of the Earth* (Chicago: University of Chicago Press, 1956); and Erich W. Zimmerman, *World Resources and Industries* (rev. ed.; New York: Harper & Bros., 1951). Only Bogue (a demographer), Boulding (an economist), Steward (an anthropologist) and a few of the contributors to the Thomas volume employ explicitly ecological approaches, and these differ.

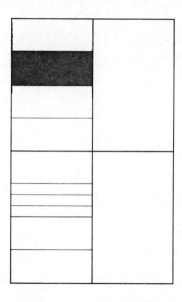

2. DEMOGRAPHISM

Demographism in sociology typically defines the social in terms of objective behavior relations, and seeks to explain it by referring to phenomena imposed on the social through characteristics of the participants' human environments. N. B. Ryder's is a relatively recent article examining the distinctive role of demographic concepts in sociological theory and research.

NOTES ON THE CONCEPT OF
A POPULATION[1]

N. B. RYDER

There are many peculiar aspects to demography as an academic calling. In some senses it is a field of sociology; in other senses it is neither a field nor even sociology at all. On the basis of its elegant models and quantitative rigor it has a claim to be considered the most advanced area in social science, and yet it might be rejected from that realm altogether as consisting essentially of a form of macrobiometry. It has endured for three centuries as "Political Arithmetic." As sometimes described, its scope seems to encompass the whole world of social statistics, but many social statisticians have neither training nor interest in demography. In the United States, where it has had its most extensive development, it has status nowhere as an independent academic discipline. Most often the demographer is found inside the Department of Sociology, but it is not always clear that he is either a welcome or a comfortable guest. When demographers gather, they manifest a host of varied and sometimes conflicting interests: natural and social, pure and applied, scientific and propagandistic.

This essay is an attempt to identify some distinctive characteristics of the demographic approach to social analysis, with emphasis on the contributions that can be made by the concept of a population. The effort has been prompted by several recent publications with similar intent but somewhat different conclu-

Reprinted from *American Journal of Sociology* (March, 1964), pp. 447–463, by permission of the author and the University of Chicago Press. © 1964 by the University of Chicago Press.

sions.[2] In the first section of this essay the basic population model is introduced and described. This model is then used to provide a basis for distinguishing the demographer's special contribution to the study of population composition and population processes. The penultimate section introduces the concept of a population into the controversy concerning the interrelationships of microanalysis and macroanalysis. Finally, some suggestions are made concerning the contributions a demographic approach can make to the study of social change. The pervasive theme of the article is the way in which the concept of a population forces the sociologist to give time a central place in his theory and research.

I. THE BASIC POPULATION MODEL

The backbone of population study is formal demography. The demographer is equipped with a special type of mathematical model which is adaptable to a wide range of problems and which yields proposals that particular kinds of data be studied with particular techniques of description and measurement. Formal demography is the deductive study of the necessary relationships between the quantities serving to describe the state of a population and those serving to describe changes in that state, in abstraction from their association with other phenomena.[3] The central features of demography as a body of knowledge and methods may be approached by considering the population as a model. The generic concept of a population is an abstract view of a universe of phenomena comprising recognizable individual elements. Although demography is concerned substantively with humans, it has formal affinity with the analysis of all such collectivities. The first contribution by Alfred J. Lotka, the man most responsible for modern demography, was a study of "the mode of growth of material aggregates."[4] In that paper, he presented the essence of demography in his opening observation that, in a material system, certain individual constituent elements may each have a limited life-period, but the aggregate of a number of such individuals may nevertheless have a prolonged existence, provided there is some process for the formation of new individuals as the old ones are eliminated.

The elements of the basic population model may be specified as follows:

1. The population is characterized as an aggregate of individuals which conform to a given definition. This definition is ordinarily at least spatial and temporal in specificity.

2. The central question concerns the change of the aggregate number of constituent elements through time. Population research is dynamic in this elementary sense.

3. The change through time in the aggregate number is conceptualized as the difference between the number of additions to, and number of subtractions from, that total during the time interval of observation.[5] Decomposition in this way is so characteristic of the demographer's behavior that it is often specified in a definition of the field.[6] If additions and subtractions are further distinguished as births and immigrations on the one hand, and deaths and emigrations on the other, the proposition becomes the so-called demographic equation.[7] In this section of the paper, the population is assumed to be closed to migration; in a subsequent section migration is given special attention.

4. The model is microdynamic as well

as macrodynamic. That is to say, the passage of time is identified for the individual constituent elements as well as for the population as a whole. This emphasizes, in Lotka's terms, the distinction between persistence of the individual and persistence of the aggregate. Individual entries and exits are dated, and the difference between date of entry and date of observation, for the individual, is his age at that time. Age is the central variable in the demographic model. It identifies birth cohort membership (as discussed below). It is a measure of the interval of time spent within the population, and thus of exposure to the risk of occurrence of the event of leaving the population, and more generally is a surrogate for the experience which causes changing probabilities of behavior of various kinds. Age as the passage of personal time is, in short, the link between the history of the individual and the history of the population.[8]

5. Once increases and decreases are identified in terms of both personal and population time, attention is focused on properties of the system that determine the limitation of the life-period of the constituents and the formation of new constituents. The emphasis passes from the deaths and births that occur to the individuals, to mortality and fertility, which are cohort processes.[9]

6. The population model is completed by linking together three kinds of functions. The first of these is the number of person-years of exposure of the population within each age interval and time interval; the second is the number of births occurring within each age interval and time interval per person-year of exposure; the third is the number of deaths occurring within each age interval and time interval per person-year of exposure. In brief, they are the age-time structure of the population, and the age-time processes of fertility and mortality. These three functions represent a network of identities within a complete deterministic

model. The formal theory of demography is concerned with working out the logico-mathematical relationships among these components and elaborating schemes for their analysis in terms suggested by the structure of the model.

At several points above, reference has been made to the distinction between individual occurrences and cohort processes. The significance of this may be exemplified by reference to mortality. An individual has a lifetime of, say, x years, which is begun at birth and terminated by death. In the population accounts this is recorded as an addition to, and then, x years later, as a subtraction from, the aggregate of one unit. From the standpoint of population size as a function of time, the age of the individual at death is irrelevant. Only the fact and time of death enter the accounting procedure, since the question of which individual dies does not affect the size of the population. The individual is assigned to a temporal aggregate on the basis of his time of birth, because this offers some obvious arithmetical conveniences. Such an aggregate is termed a (birth) cohort.[10] The mortality process for the cohort is the distribution of its membership by age at death (and, since time of birth is identical among the members, by the time of death as well). This distribution is a characteristic of the cohort as an aggregate, but the argument of the function representing it is individual time. Thus the events of subtraction of individuals from the aggregate are transformed into rates for each age-time interval, the numerator of the rate being the number of occurrences of the event of death, and the denominator the area of person-years of exposure of the aggregate to the risk of occurrence of that event during the particular time interval. By this form of calculation the event which characterizes the individual is transformed into the process which characterizes the cohort.

In considering the demographic history of a cohort, there is an obvious cause-and-effect relationship between its mortality process and its age-time structure, that is, the distribution through time of the person-years of exposure. Considered as an age structure, the population at any moment of time is a cross-section of cohorts as age structures, when the cohorts are viewed diagrammatically as if they were stacked in uniformly staggered fashion, each atop its predecessor in time. The procedure for relating the parameters of these two kinds of age structures has been developed by the writer and named the process of "demographic translation."[11]

To complete the basic population model as a web of structures and processes, some fertility mechanism is required. The size of any cohort at birth is provided by the number of births in the period that dates the cohort. Those births that occur in any period may be viewed as a product sum of the age structure of the population in the period and the fertility rates of the cohorts that occupy the various ages of parenthood at that time. These rates are of the occurrence-exposure type elaborated for mortality.[12] Now the period age structure is a cross-sectional translation of the age structures of the successive participant cohorts, and the fertility rates are a cross-sectional translation of the fertility rates of the same cohorts. Thus the process of demographic translation between period and cohort functions is intrinsic to the establishment of interdependencies among all three functions of the basic population model.

To summarize, the system provides a way of generating changes in population size through time, because of the continual destruction and creation of members, as a joint product of population structures and cohort processes. As noted, the population structure in any period is a translation of cohort age structures, and these are in turn the outcome of cohort mortality processes. The circle of formal analysis moves from (1) individual acts of procreation and death to (2) cohort processes of fertility and mortality, and thence to (3) cohort age structures. These are translated into (4) period age structures which combine with period translations of the cohort vital processes to yield (5) the births and deaths which change the size of the population. This mode of analysis presents the problem of structural transformation in terms of the processes that shape and reshape the structure. Thus it is attuned to the tendency of present-day science to regard events rather than things, processes rather than states, as the ultimate components of the world of reality.[13] The contributions of Lotka[14] have established the determinacy of the population structure implicit in fixed processes of cohort fertility and mortality and have provided, at this level, a comprehensive representation of the stable equilibrium model. Work is now proceeding on the establishment of the structural consequences of systematic change in the cohort processes, in order to develop models which are dynamic in the customary sense of the term.[15]

II POPULATION COMPOSITION

The basic population model presented above can be used in consideration of social composition and social mobility as topics for demographic inquiry.[16] Population composition has been defined as the relative frequency of any enumerable or measurable characteristic, quality, trait, attribute, or variable observed for individuals in a population, that is, as any view of an aggregate that recognizes any differences among its individual components. A list of such items would include residential location; ethnic group membership; religion; education; employment; occupation; industry; social roles and memberships; anthropometric, biometric, and psychometric traits; genetic constitution; health status; and attained skills.[17] From this vantage point the demographer's ken seems boundless. Perhaps it is impossible to draw a boundary line around demography and confine its scope to such-and-such phenomena and no others.[18] Perhaps the range of possibilities is limited only by convention, so that the choice of subjects for demographic purview is largely fortuitous.[19] And perhaps the criterion for labeling something as demographic is essentially the same as the criterion for its inclusion in the census, that is, any characteristic of an indivual that is useful in administration and policy determination and that can be collected by nonprofessionals.[20] While such specifications may indeed be apt characterizations of what demographers do, they are less than satisfying as guidelines for the future development of the field. The concern in this section is to attempt to identify some criteria for drawing a line between demographic and non-demographic variables, in order to arrive at an understanding of what it is about demographic analysis that could distinguish it from any other kind of statistical social analysis.[21] The position to be advanced is that limits can be established for the sphere of demographic competence by considering not so much the substance of any characteristic as its adaptability to formulation in the terms of the basic population model.[22]

The argument begins with consideration of a distinction that has been proposed between characteristics that are fixed and characteristics that are changeable.[23] Some characteristics are determinable at birth and fixed for life. These may be distinguished for convenience as the genetic inheritance and the cultural inheritance, in both cases derivative from the parents. The most prominent representatives of the former are sex and color. Under the latter heading come such non-biological characteristics of parents as ethnic origin, mother tongue, and place and date of birth. The last of these, which identifies cohort membership, is usually represented by age, which is, of course, an invariant function of time and in this sense a fixed variable. Other characteristics are subject to change throughout the course of an individual's life, such as educational attainment, marital status, and the various attributes associated with economic activities.

Now this distinction between changeable and unchangeable characteristics is an important convenience at an operational level, but it is scarcely defensible from the standpoint of the significance of such identifications for behavior, and it conceals a facet of almost all census questions which can be exploited by the demographer. Thus there is merely a distinction of degree rather than kind between inherited and acquired characteristics, since virtually all phenotypic characters manifest the interaction of genetic and environmental factors. From a sociological standpoint sex, race, age, and other "biological" characteristics are learned roles. Although the various types of non-biological identification that can be used to label a person at birth may be regarded as having a persistent influence on his lifetime behavior, their fixity is only a convenient approximation to a much more complex and dynamic reality.

There are several senses in which the changeable characteristics are fixed. Many of them endure for extended periods of time, and are frequently permanent within or beyond particular age limits. Thus educational attainment is by and large established during prematurity; marital status tends to be fixed for lengthy periods within each stage of the sequence of single, married, and widowed; labor-force participation for many involves a single entry early in life and a single departure late in life; religion and citizenship are fixed for life for the majority. Now it is not disputed that changes can and do occur in these variables. But the significant point for the student of the population as an aggregate is that these changes tend to occur within a narrow age range for most of the population.

This aspect of temporal persistence in most census characteristics is manifest in and enhanced by census practice. Thus it is accepted procedure to attempt to record those who habitually live in an area (including absentees and excluding transients) in order to get at "usual residence" —the place where a person "lives." A population is considered as consisting of inhabitants, a term that implies both spatial fixity and temporal endurance. Occupation and place of residence are among the characteristics that a person changes most frequently. But census procedures ordinarily involve the attempt to establish what these are usually rather than momentarily. This is a partial explanation for the fact that the census is primarily a classificatory rather than a measuring instrument. In the same way, migration is identified as only those changes of residence that carry some implication of permanency. In summary, population characteristics are for the most part the results of attempts to achieve relatively enduring labels by definitional devices, and changeable characteristics may be distinguished by the extent to which they manifest temporal persistence.

A further type of fixity in the realm of changeable characteristics concerns fixity of sequence. Several important population characteristics have high probabilities of change, but in relatively restricted ways. The classic case is age (which departs from its fixed sequence only through age misstatement, a form of intercohort migration). Reproductive parity and educational attainment in terms of years of schooling fall under the same heading. Likewise, specific marital statuses can only be changed, by law, into a limited number of particular other marital statuses. Some occupations can be arranged in career sequence, particularly if the earlier occupation is in some sense apprenticeship for the later. Sometimes one variable is characteristically sequential with another, for example, the close relationship between certain levels of education and certain categories of occupation, which in turn are closely related to income levels.

The aspect of fixity of characteristics and sequences has been stressed here because it makes possible the application in analysis of the array of demographic techniques based on the concept of a population. The argument is, in a sense, a generalization of the implications of Grauman's observation that the principal relevance of the distinction between fixed and changeable characteristics is that population segments which have the same fixed characteristics can be treated by estimating methods analogous to those which are employed in estimating population totals.[24] It is the writer's view that the special contribution of the demographer to social analysis is focused on those items of individual information which can be thought of as defining quasi-populations, because they endure. Thus a characteristic may be viewed as an individual's residence over a period of time. The time interval has a beginning and an end for the individual—an entry into and an exit from that particular quasi-population—and within the interval the individual is exposed to the risk of occurrence of various events, in particular, that of departure from that quasi-population. It is at least operationally conceivable that not only an enumeration of the individuals within these quasi-populations at successive times can be obtained, but also a registration of entries and exits. Full utilization of the power of the population model would also require determination of the length of time each individual has spent within the quasi-population. The most commonly used interval is age, and it ordinarily serves as a surrogate for more precise interval determination. Age is the outstanding

representative of a large class of measurements of the length of time elapsing since the occurrence of a cohort-defining event, but is a satisfactory substitute for the particular duration only to the extent that there is small variance in age at entry into the quasi-population in question.

To summarize this section, the cutting edge of methodology has been used to guard against the presumptuous position that the demographer is sole custodian of census materials. In the writer's view, the talents of the demographer are most usefully employed in considering such items of information about individuals as can be conceptualized as quasi-populations by virtue of their property of persistence through time. This perspective is designed not so much to inhibit the expansiveness of the demographer's statistical work as to suggest a program for extending his activities into areas in which his contribution is unique.

III. POPULATION PROCESSES

The position has been advanced that the criterion which identifies those situations in which the demographer has something special to offer is methodological rather than substantive. To exemplify further this viewpoint, the present section examines the applicability of the population concept in the study of the three processes that are clearly integral to the field of demography considered substantively—fertility, mortality, and migration—and to the closely associated process of nuptiality. The outcome of the presentation is that the basic population model is tailor-made for mortality analysis, plays an important but incomplete role in the measurement of nuptiality, has proliferated in several analytically advantageous ways in fertility research, and finally is appropriate for answering questions about one kind of migration but not about another.

The prototype of statistical analysis in

demography is the life-table. A cohort is taken from birth throughout the lifespan, with its numbers reduced age by age on the basis of the mortality rates, the ratios of occurrences of death to person-years of exposure to the risk of death. The area of exposure in each age and time interval is reduced successively by occurrences which depend in turn on previous areas of exposure and their mortality rates. Whatever other subpopulation or quasi-population may be studied, the events that reduce membership must include mortality as well as the departures that are specific to the particular definition of membership. The elegance of the system of life-table functions has inspired the whole array of attempts to convert other processes, often substantively quite dissimilar, into analogues of mortality.

In the sphere of nuptiality analysis, the parallel with mortality is readily drawn and the basic population model successfully applied. Every person begins life single and most persons suffer "death" as a single person by experiencing the event of first marriage, an event that is irreversible provided a strict definition of the single state is maintained. Similarly the successive stages of married life may be studied as attrition processes, for example, the dissolution of marriage by divorce or widowhood. But the population model is restricted in its usefulness to the situation in which the event may reasonably be considered as occurring to an individual. Now marriage is in fact an event that occurs to two persons simultaneously, and the exposure to the risk of occurrence of marriage is a function not only of the personal characteristics of the man and woman involved, but also of the general state of the marriage market—the relative availability of spouses of either sex. This problem has proven completely intractable to conventional modes of demographic analysis.[25] This is the reason for specifying above that the basic population model is non-sexual or monosexual. The

relationships between probabilities of marriage and the sex-age composition of the unmarried population are not expressible in terms of formal interconnections between occurrences and exposures. This is a clear-cut case of the need for measurements of properties of the aggregate in determination of probabilities of individual behavior, as discussed in more detail in Section IV.

In fertility research, one important improvement in methodology has been the extention and generalization of the basic notion of a cohort from its original signification of birth cohort to cohorts identified by common date of occurrence of other significant events. The variables that have been exploited in modern fertility measurement are number, age, marital status, marital duration, parity, and birth interval. These six variables may be grouped in three pairs, in order, each pair consisting of a status—which identifies quasi-population membership —and a time interval since acquiring that status—"age" within the quasi-population. The demographic characteristics pertinent to the act of parenthood are most succinctly identified as a series of time points: date of birth of the prospective mother; date of her marriage; date of birth of each preceding child; and date of current birth. The intervals, then, are the differences between pairs of successive time points. The statuses imply membership in various types of cohort: the birth cohort, the marriage cohort, the first parity cohort, and so forth. Temporal aggregation afresh on the basis of the most recent event in the reproductive history provides a mode of efficient analysis of the frequency and the time distribution of the next succeeding event.[26] The only formal problem in this sequence is the formation of marriage cohorts out of birth cohorts, as discussed in the preceding paragraph.

Migration is clearly the most complex demographic process to discuss from the standpoint of the basic population model. The problems that arise are discussed here first for external migration and then for internal migration. Immigration and emigration, the terms generally used in distinguishing the two directions of external migration, are on an equal footing with fertility and mortality as modes of entry and exit from the total population. This circumstance follows from the fact that the population is customarily defined in spatiotemporal terms: immigration and emigration represent the crossing of spatial boundaries just as fertility and mortality represent the crossing of temporal boundaries. The parallel may be extended to the conceptualization of emigration as a type of mortality. There are no unique difficulties of a formal kind in considering exposure to the risk of occurrence of emigration from the population, with a determination of the probabilities of emigration in each time interval, for members of successive birth cohorts, following the life-table format. Furthermore emigration, like mortality, is a process of exit from the total population, and therefore from every constituent subpopulation of quasi-population.

When attention is turned to immigration, the analogy immediately dissolves. This may indeed be an important mode of addition of new members to the receiving population, but the events that constitute it do not occur to members of the receiving population. In contradistinction to fertility, the initiation of immigration is exogenous to the population being studied and can be built into the model only on an *ad hoc* basis because the exposure to the risk of immigration lies outside the defined population. For this reason, immigration research has not been able to exploit the measurement techniques that emanate from the basic population model. The characteristics of the population which yield various patterns of immigration are characteristics of the aggregate rather than of individuals within the aggregate. In this sense, immigration is a subdivision of the general study of ecosystem inter-change, a branch of population theory which is much more developed for non-human than for human populations.[27]

The process of internal migration may be regarded on the one hand as a special application of the quasi-population concept, or on the other hand as the prototype of a different but related kind of population model. If the territory that defines a population is divided into subterritories, each with its own subpopulation, then the movement of an individual from one subterritory to another is formally analogous to passage from any one status to another. If the focus of interest is the subpopulation itself, then in-migration and out-migration are at that level analogous to the processes of immigration and emigration as discussed above for the total population. But if the total population within which the movements are occurring is the focus of attention, then it is more natural to speak of the movements not so much in terms of entry into and exit from particular subpopulations, as in terms of interstitial movement between subpopulations.[28] This way of describing the process places the subject within the reach of the theory of Markov chains, a type of mathematics that possesses great potentialities in demographic research. An initial distribution and a terminal distribution, termed column vectors, are related to one another by a square matrix of transition probabilities. These are the conditional probabilities of moving to a particular terminal location, given a particular initial location.[29]

The basic population model and the transition matrix are variants of a single formal system, which have their own special advantages for two different categories of problems. The basic concept of a population has been characterized as spatiotemporal. Accordingly, two types of changes may be distinguished: metabolism, or replacement in time, characterized by the processes of fertility and mortality; and migration, or replacement in space. An emphasis on metabolic transformation leads to a preference for the model of entry, exposure, and exit, as discussed above. An emphasis on migratory transformation leads to a preference for the transition-matrix model. The two types of models share one important feature. If the matrix of transition probabilities is held fixed, it may be shown that the column vectors move toward an equilibrium state which represents the latent structural propensities of the processes characterized by the matrix. This is, of course, a precise analogy to stable population theory. Both mathematical models direct analytic attention away from the consequent structures and toward the determinant processes. But a distinction of degree or emphasis remains. In considering the various census characteristics in the preceding section, it became clear that some of them were more adaptable to the quasi-population concept than others, and that the degree of adaptability hinged on the frequency of entry and exit, or, said otherwise, on the degree of temporal persistence. It seems resonable to propose that those characteristics that are too variable from time to time to be usefully conceptualized in quasi-population terms can be accommodated methodologically within the transition matrix approach. As an alternative mode of division of labor between the two models, it may be suggested that the transition-matrix approach is more suitable for comparative cross-sectional analysis, which focuses on short-run period-by-period changes in the population structure, while the population approach is more suitable for the study of behavior associated with the life-cycle, which focuses on long-run cohort-by-cohort transformation. But these should be considered as tentative and probably premature forays beyond a fecund methodological frontier.

IV. MACROANALYSIS AND MICROANALYSIS

The study of population comprises not only a system of formal relations but also various systems of substantive relations between parameters of the population model and other variables.[30] Now the parameters of the population model are expressed as concrete phenomena rather than as analytic abstractions. In its substantive component, demography is an observational proto-science, and the concrete objects of observation may be examined through various frames of reference and from various analytic perspectives. The study of systems of analytic relations between population parameters and other variables lies within the purview of the various abstract sciences. The term "analytic relations" is used here to convey the sense of appraisal of probabilistic co-variation within a particular frame of reference rather than analysis in the literal sense of decomposition.

Various consequences follow from the circumstance that the parameters of the population model are defined concretely. (1) Population studies may be located within the realm of any of the abstract sciences. In particular, the subject straddles the biological and social sciences. The term "science" is used to mean an abstract area of empirical inquiry determined by a particular orientation and frame of reference, as distinct from proto-scientific approaches to concrete phenomena in all their aspects, like geography, ethnography, and, as generally defined, demography. (2) The professional demographer is almost always identifiable also as a substantive specialist with competence in a particular science. The circumstance that most American demographers are also sociologists is somewhat fortuitous, but does help to explain the tendency to define demography by contiguity as a field within sociology. That this is an incomplete view is indicated by the array of different kinds of scientists found in the International Union for the Scientific Study of Population, and even in the Population Association of America. (3) The diffuseness of substantive interest in questions defined by the population model and the narrow limits of the formal core of the discipline are sufficient to explain why it does not have the dignity of academic autonomy as a department of university instruction. For convenience, demography is housed within particular other departments, the choice being to some extent historical accident and varying considerably from country to country.[31] (4) The concreteness of content and the sophistication of the special methodology account for the continued tolerance of the demographer as a resident alien within different disciplines. The data with which the demographer works are grist for almost everybody's mill, and the models he employs are adaptable to a wide variety of situations, although the former type of usefulness to colleagues has been much more widely exploited than the latter. Indeed, the neglect of demographic concepts by non-demographers is one justification for the present piece. The demographer's work, in other words, yields problems for investigation by various scientific disciplines and provides an orientation for the solution of these and other isomorphic problems. (5) Under the circumstances, the demographer is likely to participate in interdisciplinary research—because the limits of his subject extend into the provinces of various disciplines—and he is useful as a channel of scientific communication between otherwise disparate orientations. (6) Finally, the concrete definition of the subject makes the demographer more immediately useful than the abstract specialist in the realm of policies directed toward practical, as distinct from intellectual, problems.

The writer has described elsewhere an example of the way in which a concrete object of the demographer's attention may have its various aspects allocated among different abstract disciplines.[32] Research on fertility can be divided into the contribution of substantive analysis in the biological realm—using data about fecundity and fertility regulation to explain observed fertility—and the contribution of substantive analysis in the realm of the social sciences—using data about individuals and groups to explain observed fertility regulation (and even to some extent fecundity). Within the latter realm it is useful to distinguish between psychosocial and sociocultural research, or—to identify more precisely the point to be discussed—between microanalytic and macroanalytic inquiries. The relationships between these two levels of inquiry deserve attention because they are of peculiar relevance to the demographer and because the concept of a population contributes to their clarification.

Much of the discussion of analytic strategies in fertility research has consisted of assertions of the relative importance of microanalytic and macroanalytic levels of inquiry for the explanation of fertility. Thus Vance has called macroanalytic explanations inadequate because they fail to specify the ways in which macro-variables are translated into individual motivations.[33] In their commentary on this assertion, Hauser and Duncan have labeled the psychosocial variables as superficial, and proposed that the deep-seated macroanalytic causes underlie them.[34] The difficulty of adjudicating competing claims like these is that the criteria of relative success differ. If the individual is the unit of analysis, then success is measured by explanations of variance among individuals; if the population is the unit of analysis, then success is measured by explanation of variance among populations. The issue has not been confined to the field of fertility. Several influential demographers have decried the circumstance that most migration analysis ignores the study of the motivations behind particular individual movements by its macroanalytic focus on net migration.[35] Schnore has taken the opposite stand concerning sociological interest in mobility.[36] He has expressed concern that the majority interest in the correlates of individual behavior means short shrift for macroanalytic inquiries into interdependencies of population composition and social structure. In the field of mortality research, the microanalytic approach is winning by default, because almost no student of the subject seems interested in asking macroanalytic questions.

A final controversy deserves mention. The variables in individual correlation are descriptive properties of individuals; the variables in ecological correlation are descriptive properties of populations (although they are computed by deriving summary indexes of the properties of individual members of the respective populations). Robinson has asserted correctly that individual correlations cannot be inferred from ecological correlations, and has asserted incorrectly that the purpose of ecological correlations must be to discover something about the behavior of individuals.[37] This debate has special pertinence for the demographer because of one characteristic feature of the population concept. Given the definition of a population as an aggregate of members, it appears superficially that the characteristics of the population are merely derivative from the characteristics of individuals by summation. The situation is in fact much more complex than that. Just as the properties of individual members may be used in aggregate form as properties of the population, so the properties of a population may be used as properties of its individual members.[38]

The macroanalytic level of inquiry consists of propositions or statements of relationships among the properties of the population as the unit of reference. The microanalytic level of inquiry consists of propositions or statements of relationships among the properties of the individual as the unit of reference. In general it is invalid either to transform a proposition about populations into a proposition about individuals or to transform a proposition about individuals into a proposition about populations. The relationship among individual characteristics, expressed as a regression equation linking individual variables, will generally have different parameters from one population to another. Now most sociological theory is pitched at the microanalytic level and therefore requires a test based on observations of individuals. This does not imply that macroanalytic theory is a lesser breed of theorizing, nor that it is merely derivative and a temporary substitute employed for the sake of convenience.

The question of the relationships between macroanalysis and microanalysis is important in current economic thought. Most theories in economics (as in sociology) are microtheories, while most empirical descriptions contain measurements of macrovariables which are functions, such as averages, of microvariables. The parameters in the macroanalytic regression equations are weighted averages of the parameters in the microanalytic regression equations because the former system is dependent not only on the latter but also on the composition of the population.[39] One prominent direction of resolution of this and other problems which exploits the magnitude of the latest computers is the microanalysis of socioeconomic systems, an attempt to generate aggregate properties from properties of individuals.[40] As a general rule, the theoretical systems of the economists have not encompassed the problems of differences between systems *qua* systems through time or space.[41]

There is another respect in which the microanalytic and macroanalytic levels of inquiry differ in character, and it leads to an important example of the utility of the population concept. The properties of distributions of variables are specific to populations rather than to individuals. An important question about a population is how to explain the differential distributions of various populations in terms of some individual-specific characteristic. Now microanalytic relationships are of the form: If an individual has characteristic A, then he has a probability p of having another individual characteristic B. This may be used to predict the distribution of B, given the distribution of A, but it does not answer the question: What determines the distribution of A? The approach that uses the basic population model emphasizes the events of acquiring and losing some characteristic. From the standpoint of the individual, movement into and out of categorical locations is placed in the perspective of the life-cycle; from the standpoint of the population, the distribution by categories is viewed as a consequence of processual parameters of fertility and mortality, using these terms in the broad as well as the narrow sense. More specifically, attention is directed to the movement from one structure to another by means of two questions: "Given this kind of exposure, what is the probability of the occurrence of departure from exposure?" and "Given departure from exposure, what is the consequence for subsequent exposure?" Thus this approach places emphasis on changes through time. More precisely, the emphasis is on long-run time, or time as the biology of evolution considers it, as distinct from short-run time, or time as used in the equations of physics. The latter is the analogy for the study of covariation of individual and population characteristics; the former is the analogy for the study of population dynamics.

In the area of conjuncture between the macroanalytic and microanalytic approaches to the study of behavior, the cohort as a population element plays a crucial role. It is a device for providing a macroscopic link between movements of the population and movements of individuals. The conceptual gap between individual behavior and population behavior is provided with a convenient bridge, in the form of the cohort aggregate, within which individuals are located and out of which the population as a function of time is constructed from the sequence of cohort behavior patterns. Thus the cohort is a macroanalytic entity like the population, but it has the same temporal location and pattern of development as the individuals that constitute it. It seems to the writer that the analysis of cohort structures and processes is a valuable intermediary between the analysis of individual behavior and the analysis of population behavior, in attempting to increase the possibilities of cross-fertilization. The concept of a population, which is closely allied with the concept of a society, is brought closer to the concept of an individual, when the latter is viewed as a member of a cohort aggregate which is in turn a constituent of a population. Thus one avenue is provided in sociology for the perplexing questions of the relationships between the individual and the society.

To conclude this section, a note seems worthwhile concerning the partnership of demography and human ecology, a partnership manifest in the central position within each discipline of the concept of a population and in the frequency with which particular scientists have interests in both areas. Human ecology may be characterized as the study of social organization as a property of a population in interaction with its environment.[42] The characteristic method of this study is employment of the spatiotemporal orientation to provide dimensions for the observation and measurement of organization. The concrete definition of a population within both demography and human ecology implies that the two principal definitional axes of each are space and time, and that each discipline will have an expansive view across various spheres of learning. To some extent there has been a division of labor between the ecologic and the demographic orientations: the former has focused more on variations in space, and the latter more on variations in time. The central concept of the ecologist has been the community, defined minimally by spatial co-occupancy. To some extent it is possible to make the parallel assertion that the central concept of the demographer is the cohort, defined minimally by temporal co-occupancy.[43] The approaches converge in orientation and bring the demographer and the human ecologist together as the ecologist begins to ask dynamic questions and the demographer concerns himself with spatial distribution. The parallel between the cohort and the community is not to be pressed too far because the community is viewed by the ecologist as capable of being considered a self-sufficient societal organism, whereas the cohort is for the most part a statistical plural with common characteristics stemming from its definitional basis of temporal location but without the integration implicit in various community properties.

V. SOCIAL CHANGE FROM A DEMOGRAPHIC PERSPECTIVE

The purpose of this section is to present some ways in which the concept of a population may contribute to the analysis of social change. The first type of contribution is related to the definition of change. It is common in discussions of the topic to confine the term "social change" to transformation of the social structure, in contradistinction to the patterned sets of phases in the life-cycles of individuals and other relatively invariant systems of action and interaction.[44] Two contributions to this distinction may be drawn from stable population theory. In the first place, structural transformation is caused by a discrepancy at any point of time between the extant structure and the processes which are responsible for creating that structure. In the second place, life-cycle changes for individuals can be summarized by various indexes of cohort behavior as a function of age (or other appropriate interval). The definition of social change prompted by these considerations is the modification of processual parameters from cohort to cohort. Thus social change occurs to the extent that successive cohorts do something other than merely repeat the patterns of behavior of their predecessors. Given the far greater availability of structural than of processual data of all kinds, knowledge of the nuances of interdependency of period and cohort functions of fertility, mortality, and age distribution (or their analogous forms, if a quasi-population concept is employed) is likely to be essential in research on social change.

The proposed definition of social change is incomplete because it does not distinguish long-run from short-run change. Statistical contributions to the separate measurement of each for quantitative materials have been unimpressive because the distinction to be drawn does not actually hinge on the length of time elapsing but on the consideration that such changes have different determinants, and this can only be supplied by a person with knowledge of the content rather than the form of the data. Again the basic population model provides one direction of resolution of the difficulty. If functions of process are examined for a series of cohorts over their age spans, two distinct types of changes may be observed. One of these is the manifestation of a period-specific event or situation which "marks" the successive cohort functions at the same time, and thus at successive ages of the cohorts in question. Frequently such manifestations take the form of fluctuations, in the sense that a counteracting movement occurs subsequently which erases the impact of the situation in the eventual summary for the cohort. The other type of change is characterized by differences in functional form from cohort to cohort other than those betraying the characteristic age pattern of the period-specific event. With full recognition of the incompleteness of the view, it is suggested that among the various sense of "short run" and "long run," an important part of the distinction can be captured by statistical operations designed to segregate the period-specific and cohort-specific variations as functions of age and time. As a not entirely paren-thetical remark it may be suggested that one contrast between demography and other types of quantitative sociology has been the emphasis of the former on long-run change and of the latter on short-run or no change.[45]

Throughout this essay, attention has been focused almost exclusively if implicitly on the level of the total population and its less tangible partner, the society. But the concepts introduced are clearly applicable with little modification to the other levels of social organization. In particular the demographic approach provides some methodological resources for a dynamic approach to organizational structure. Any organization experiences social metabolism: since its individual components are exposed to "mortality," the survival of the organization requires a process of "fertility." The problem of replacement is posed not only for the total organization but also for every one of its differentiated components.[46] The

ineluctability of social metabolism is from one view a problem that any organization must solve in the interests of continuity and from another view a continual opportunity for adaptation and change.[47] Furthermore, a plausible case can be made that the processes of "fertility" and "mortality" provide revealing insights into the present character of an organization as well as predictions of its future shape. As a final note on the demography of organizations, it is evident that they themselves can be treated as individuals within a population of organizations of like type, to approach the changing structure of the larger society from another viewpoint.

It is probably true that many sociologists view population data with less than excitement because these seem to provide distributive descriptions of aggregates rather than structural information about groups. This perspective ignores the interdependency which must exist between the functioning of organizations and the demographic characteristics of the aggregates of members of these organizations. The institutional structure rests on a population base, in the sense that particular functions are dependent for their performance on the presence of particular categories of persons. The most elementary recognition of the point comes in the commonplace research practice of distinguishing three types of variables—dependent, independent, and control variables—with demographic data falling under the third heading. The implication is that the composition of the population plays a necessary role (almost tautologically so), but not a sufficient one, as a set of constraints on the degree and direction of change in the institutional structure.[48] Now abstracting from the population composition through the use of the control technique may be a useful practice in the static analysis of covariation, but these parameters become variables as time passes and the questions of social change arise. For analogous reasons, economic theory was able to progress without demographic variables only so long as economists failed to raise questions about economic development. Inquiry into the relationships between population composition and institutional structure promises large rewards for the person interested in developing a dynamic theory of society.

Finally the population model offers a strategy for helping to resolve one of the most frustrating methodological issues in the study of social change. Two modes of conceptualizing and describing change may be distinguished, termed loosely the qualitative and the quantitative. The former mode ordinarily appears as an approximately ordered sequence of discrete complexes which somehow replace or displace or merge with their temporal neighbors. Analysis relies on before-and-after comparisons or at the most on some variant of the idea of stages. With such conceptualizations it is most difficult to achieve operational precision, let alone statistical data. The latter mode of the study of change most commonly yields a precisely dated series of measurements of one or another particular element of a qualitatively homogeneous type. Precision of observation is achieved at the cost of qualitative richness. In some ways the demographic approach is a combination of these two procedures. The concept of a population suggests the examination of a succession of overlapping stages, based on elements of various qualitative (categorical) types, quantified in terms of the frequency of each and the temporal distribution of individuals within the type, and the progression of aggregate indexes for the total population. A satisfactory dynamic theory of society requires a frame of reference that can establish propositions relating quantitative changes in "inputs and outputs" to the organizational transformations that they manifest and induce.[49] One such frame of reference is the concept of a population.

The case for the demographic contribution to the study of social change can easily be overstated. Clearly there are alternative procedures of great promise which have no particular connection with the population model. For example, there are many aggregate data of major significance for structural transformations such as the content of material and normative technology, and there are compositional data based on units of observation such as roles or norms rather than individuals, which require different kinds of model. But at the very least, population change provides a reflection of social change, conceived in any way, a reflection that deserves a place in efficient research because its data are well defined and well measured and its methodology is sophisticated.

VI. CONCLUSIONS

In this essay the demographer has been characterized as an agent for a particular type of model, the use of which implies particular kinds of measurements and particular directions of substantive inquiry. The influence the population concept might have on the shape of social analysis is threefold. In the first place, the demographer's mode of conceptualization never strays far from the mathematical in substance if not in language. This emphasis implies not only quantification but also persistent attention to some of the necessary components of explanation of societal behavior. Second, the demographic approach is both aggregative and distributive. The basic model is macroanalytic in form, and inclines the student toward a view of social systems in their totality. Nevertheless the model is so designed that it offers a convenient confrontation with some central issues of theorizing at different levels of organized reality. In particular the cohort provides an aggregative format within which the phases and facets of the individual life-cycle are imbedded, and through which the events experienced by the individual may be translated into the population processes that shape population structures. Finally the questions that are of central interest to the demographer are by definition dynamic. He is forced by his methodology to ask not so much about the association of characteristics as about the correlates of changes in characteristics, or, in his terms, about the perpetual interplay between occurrence and ex-posure. The central place of time in the demographic schema is most evident in the conceptualization of structure as a consequence of evolving process. Now these emphases all require qualifications, and particularly warnings, about what they neglect, but the same is true of any model. In the long run the utility of any approach to research is determined by the test of survival as measured by the fruits of inquiry in its image. To this writer the concept of a population has a high probability of high fertility.

NOTES

1. Revised version of a paper entitled "The Demographer's Ken," which was delivered at the annual meetings of the Population Association of America, Madison, Wisconsin, May, 1962. The writer wishes to acknowledge the financial support of the Social Systems Research Institute, University of Wisconsin, and the intellectual support of O. Dudley Duncan and George J. Stolnitz in the preparation of this paper.

2. See the following papers in Philip M. Hauser and O. Dudley Duncan (Eds.), *The Study of Population* (Chicago: University of Chicago Press, 1959): Philip M. Hauser and O. Dudley Duncan, "Demography as a Science," Part I, pp. 29–120; John V. Grauman, "Population Estimates and Projections," pp. 544–575; and Amos H. Hawley, "Population Composition," pp. 361–382. See also Leo F. Schnore, "Social Mobility in Demographic Perspective," *American Sociological Review*, XXVI (June, 1961), 407–423.

3. Alfred J. Lotka, *Théorie analytique des associations biologiques*, Part 2: *Analyse démographique avec application particulière a l'espèce humaine* (Paris: Hermann & Cie, 1939).

4. "Studies on the Mode of Growth of Material Aggregates," *American Journal of Science*, XXIV (1907), 199–216. The author emphasized the generality he intended by using biological terms like "birth" and "death" only in quotation marks.

5. Boulding has called this proposition perhaps the most fundamental of all science (Kenneth E. Boulding, *A Reconstruction of Economics* [New York: John Wiley & Sons, 1950], p. 190).

6. See, e.g., Hauser and Duncan, "Demography as a Science," *op. cit.*

7. Kingsley Davis, "The Demographic Equation," in *Human Society* (New York: Macmillan Co., 1948), pp. 551–594.

8. Age is only the most useful case of the general category of intervals, measured from the time of entry into particular kinds of subpopulations or quasi-populations. These are discussed in Sec. II.

9. An important distinction can be made between biological populations, to which new members are added as a consequence of the event of parenthood occurring to existing members of the population, and other situations in which the population concept is applicable, but the additions are properties of the population as a whole and its total environment. Immigration is a case in point.

10. The cohort approach has analytical as well as arithmetical advantages. See my "Cohort Analysis," *International Encyclopaedia of the Social Sciences*, forthcoming.

11. See my "The Process of Demographic Translation" (paper presented at the 1963 annual meetings of the Population Association of America, Philadelphia), to be published in the *Demography Annual*.

12. The process is purposely described here as if parenthood were monosexual or non-sexual, for reasons to be amplified in Sec. III.

13. The philosophical term for this view is "actuality theory" (see "Actuality Theory" in *Encyclopaedia Britannica* (1957 printing), I, 138.

14. *Op. cit.*, 1939.

15. See my "The Translation Model of Demographic Change," in *Emerging Techniques in Population Research* (Milbank Memorial Fund, 1963), pp. 65–81.

16. See Schnore, *op. cit.*, for the ideas which prompted this section.

17. United Nations, Department of Economic and Social Affairs, *Multilingual Demographic Dictionary*, English Section ("Population Studies," No. 29 [New York, 1958]); Hauser and Duncan, "Demography as a Science," *op. cit.*

18. Hauser and Duncan, *op. cit.*

19. Schnore, *op. cit.*

20. Hawley, *op. cit.*

21. One of the beginnings of sociology as an academic discipline in the United States was the quantitative treatment of social problems. Some such departments were first called "Statistics" but later changed their name to "Sociology." "Population problems" gradually became identified as a major subdivision of these departments (F. Lorimer, "The Development of Demography," in Hauser and Duncan [Eds.], *op. cit.*, pp. 124–179).

22. An analogous approach has been adopted in the study of the economics of capital (see Boulding, *op. cit.*, p. 189).

23. Grauman, *op. cit.*; Schnore, *op. cit.* Status ascription is a process which ties some changeable characteristics to some fixed characteristics. Status achievement is a process which ties some changeable characteristics to other changeable characteristics.

24. Grauman, *op. cit.*

25. See my "Bisexual Marriage Rates" (paper read at the annual meetings of the Population Association of America, 1961).

26. See my "La mesure des variations de la fécondité au cours du temps," *Population*, XI (January–March, 1956), 29–46.

27. Boulding, *op. cit.*, chap. i.

28. Similarly immigration and emigration may be considered as species of internal migration from the standpoint of the population of the world. Indeed the world population as a model has considerable theoretical convenience because, thus far at least, there is only one mode of entry and one mode of exit.

29. The approach has been applied with success in solving some residual difficulties in stable population theory: see, e.g., D. G. Kendall, "Stochastic Processes and Population Growth," *Journal of the Royal Statistical Society*, XI (1949), 230–265; Alvaro Lopez, *Problems in Stable Population Theory* (Princeton, N.J.: Office of Population Research, 1961). Applications to the study of intergenerational occupational mobility have been less successful because the column vectors can be uniquely specified neither in temporal location nor in constituents. See, e.g., S. J. Prais, "The Formal Theory of Social Mobility," *Population Studies*, IX (July, 1955), 72–81, and his "Measuring Social Mobility," *Journal of the Royal Statistical Society*, Series A, CXVIII (1955), 56–66; Judah Matras, "Comparisons of Intergenerational Occupational Mobility Patterns: An Application of the Formal Theory of Social Mobility," *Population Studies*, XIV (November, 1960), 163–169, and his "Differential Fertility, Intergenerational Occupational Mobility, and Change in the Occupational Distribution: Some Elementary Interrelationships," *Population Studies*, XV (November, 1961), 187–197.

30. Lorimer (*op. cit.*, p. 165) has asserted that the concept of "pure demography" is an illusion except as the skeleton of a science.

31. David V. Glass (Ed.), *The University Teaching of Social Sciences: Demography* (Paris: UNESCO, 1957).

32. See my "Fertility," in Hauser and Duncan (Eds.), *op. cit.*, pp. 400–436.

33. Rupert B. Vance, "The Development and Status of American Demography," in Hauser and Duncan (Eds.), *op. cit.*, pp. 286–313.

34. *Op. cit.*

35. Donald J. Bogue, "The Quantitative Study of Social Dynamics and Social Change," *American Journal of Sociology*, LVII (May, 1952), 565–568; Vance, *op. cit.*; C. Horace Hamilton, "Some Problems of Method in Internal Migration Research,"

Population Index, XXVII (October, 1961), 297–307.

36. Schnore, *op. cit.*

37. W. S. Robinson, "Ecological Correlations and the Behavior of Individuals," *American Sociological Review*, XV (June, 1950), 351–357; H. Menzel, "Comment on Robinson's 'Ecological Correlations and the Behavior of Individuals,'" *American Sociological Review*, XV (October, 1950), 674. See also L. A. Goodman, "Ecological Regressions and Behavior of Individuals," *American Sociological Review*, XVIII (December, 1953), 663–664; O. Dudley Duncan, and B. Duncan, "An Alternative to Ecological Correlation," *American Sociological Review*, XVIII (December, 1953), 665–666.

38. J. A. Davis, J. L. Spaeth, and C. Huson, "A Technique for Analyzing the Effects of Group Composition," *American Sociological Review*, XXVI (April, 1961), 215–225.

39. H. Theil, *Linear Aggregation and Economic Relations* (Amsterdam: North-Holland Publishing Co., 1954).

40. Guy H. Orcutt, Martin Greenberger, John Korbel, and Alice M. Rivlin, *Microanalysis of Socioeconomic Systems* (New York: Harper & Bros., 1961).

41. The problems of distinction between analyses of individuals and of aggregates are not confined to the social sciences. For a brief view of the parallel dilemma in physics see William Feller, *An Introduction to Probability Theory and Its Applications* (2nd ed.; New York: John Wiley & Sons, 1957), I, 356.

42. Hawley, "Human Ecology," *International Encyclopaedia of the Social Sciences*, forthcoming.

43. It is interesting to observe that the word "cohort" originally had a spatial referent, because it identified a type of community. This etymological tie is manifested in its kinship with words like "garden"and "girdle."

44. T. Parsons, "Some Considerations on the Theory of Social Change" (1960). (Mimeographed); Hawley, "Change and Development," in *Human Ecology* (New York: Ronald Press Co., 1950), p. 319.

45. Cf. Boulding, *op. cit.*, p. 26; Lorimer, *op. cit.*, *passim*.

46. A penetrating early contribution to this discussion, which seems to have been ignored, is P. A. Sorokin, and C. Arnold Anderson, "Metabolism of Different Strata of Social Institutions and Institutional Continuity" (Comitato Italiano per lo studio dei problemi della popolazione [Rome: Istituto Poligrafico dello Stato, 1931]). Cf. Georg Simmel, "The Persistence of Social Groups," *American Journal of Sociology* (1897–1898), trans. Albion W. Small; abridged in Edgar F. Borgatta and Henry J. Meyer (Eds.), *Sociological Theory: Present-Day Sociology from the Past* (New York: Alfred A. Knopf, Inc., 1956), pp. 364–398.

47. Ryder, "Cohort Analysis," *op. cit.*

48. Cf. Hawley, *op. cit.*

49. T. Parsons, and Neil J. Smelser, "The Problems of Growth and Institutional Change in the Economy," in *Economy and Society* (Glencoe, Ill.: Free Press, 1956), pp. 246–294.

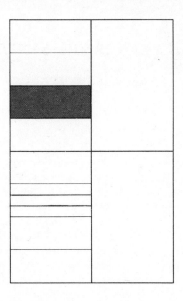

3. MATERIALISM

The materialist viewpoint typically defines the social in terms of objective behavior relations and seeks to explain it by referring to phenomena imposed on the social through the physiological characteristics of the participants themselves. In the following selection from The Human Group, *George Homans focuses on the "external system" as the group's means of surviving in its environment. Here the emphasis is on conditions determined largely by the physiological needs of the group's members for food, clothing, shelter, and so on. In a later chapter (not reprinted here) on the "internal system", Homans emphasizes largely psychological conditions that are socially generated within the group—sentiments such as friendship, loyalty, and the like. It is the causal primacy of the external system that most clearly identifies Homans' theory as materialistic.*

THE EXTERNAL SYSTEM

GEORGE C. HOMANS

In the next three chapters we shall make an analysis of the Bank Wiring group, using the concepts defined in Chapter 2, and at least one new concept which we shall introduce when necessary. In the first two of these chapters, we shall try to establish only a few general ideas, taking the Bank Wiring group as little more than a point of departure, but in the third chapter the analysis will get very detailed indeed.

There would be no reason for doing this work, which takes us, in analysis, over ground we have already covered in common-sense description, if it did not help us accomplish our main purpose. Human groups differ greatly in externals: one group is connecting wires to banks of terminals, while another is hanging out on a street corner, and a third is gathering coconuts on a South Sea island. Only if we apply the same scheme of analysis to all groups can we bring out the similarities in human relationships that underlie these differences in externals. Or perhaps, instead of speaking of similarities, we had better say that a general scheme of analysis helps us to see that the underlying human relationships differ from group to group in degree rather than in kind. The Bank Wiring Observation Room would be nothing to us if it did not let us show how such a scheme can be set up and used.

DEFINITION OF THE GROUP

The subject of this book is the human group. We all think we know what we

mean by this word, but if one of our purposes is to make explicit what we already understand intuitively, perhaps we should be more rigorous in defining it than we have been so far. Here, if anywhere, is the place for clarity. How do we determine that a certain number of persons form a group? Let us study one method of determination that is not far different from our intuitive attack on the problem. Suppose we are in a position to observe, or get records of, the social participation, within a given community, of a certain number of persons, let us say eighteen women.[1] We follow their participation over a period of time, and we notice that each woman is present on occasions or at events when some others of the eighteen are also present. The events are various: a day's work behind the counter of a store, a meeting of a women's club, a church supper, a card party, a supper party, a meeting of the Parent-Teacher Association, etc., but we make a note of the women present at each one. Then, since we are methodical social scientists, we begin to make a chart, divided into squares by lines and columns. Each column stands for a single social occasion or event, identified by date; each line, for a single woman. (See Fig. 1; but this is the chart in its final, not its original form.) Then we begin to fill in the squares. If Evelyn, Theresa, Brenda, and Charlotte were present at a bridge party at Brenda's house on September 26, we put a cross opposite each of their names in the column that stands for this social event, and so on for the other events, until we end with a chart showing for a period of

NAMES OF PARTICIPANTS	DATES OF EVENTS (MONTH AND DAY)													
	6/27	3/2	4/12	9/26	2/25	5/19	3/15	9/16	4/8	6/10	2/23	4/7	11/21	8/3
1. Evelyn	×	×	×	×	×	×		×	×					
2. Laura	×	×	×		×	×	×	×						
3. Theresa		×	×	×	×	×	×	×	×					
4. Brenda	×		×	×	×	×	×	×						
5. Charlotte			×	×	×		×							
6. Frances			×		×	×		×						
7. Eleanor				×	×	×		×						
8. Pearl						×		×	×					
9. Ruth					×		×	×	×					
10. Verne						×	×	×				×		
11. Myra								×	×	×		×		
12. Katherine								×	×	×		×	×	×
13. Sylvia						×		×	×	×		×	×	×
14. Nora						×	×		×	×	×	×	×	×
15. Helen						×	×			×	×	×		
16. Dorothy							×	×						
17. Olivia									×		×			
18. Flora									×		×			

Figure 1. *Social participation plotted so as to reveal group membership.*

time which women were present at social events at which at least one of the others was also present.

The chart in its rough form will not reveal very much. (If you do not believe this, try making such a chart for yourself.) For one thing, the columns are probably arranged in the chronological order of events, and the women are probably in no particular order at all. But then we begin to reshuffle lines and columns. As far as columns are concerned, we put in the center the columns representing events, such as a meeting of the Parent-Teacher Association, at which a large number of the women were present, and we put toward the edges the columns representing the events, such as supper parties, at which only a few of the women were present. As far as lines are concerned, we put together toward the top or bottom the lines representing those women that participated most often

together in social events. A great deal of reshuffling may have to be done before any pattern appears.[2]

The final form of the chart is shown in Fig. 1. It reveals that there were some events, such as those of March 15, April 8, and September 16, at which most of the women were present. It also reveals that Laura, to take one example, participated more often in events at which Evelyn, Theresa, Brenda, Charlotte, and Frances were present than in events at which Nora was present, and that Nora participated more with Myra, Katherine, Sylvia, and Helen than with Laura. Count the participations and see. We can make the same kind of analysis for the other women, and we generalize these observations by saying that the eighteen women were divided into two groups. The pattern is frayed at the edges, but there is a pattern. The first seven women, Evelyn through Eleanor, were clearly members of one group; numbers 11 through 15, Myra through Helen, were just as clearly members of another. Some women participated about equally with both groups but not very much with either; Pearl is an example. And some participated, though not very often, only with the second group. Pearl, Olivia, Flora, and their like are marginal group members. There may be a sense in which all eighteen women formed a group, distinct from the other groups in the community, but that would take further research to find out.

It should be clear that a modification of this method could have been used—in fact, was used—to map out the two cliques in the Bank Wiring Observation Room and to divide the Bank Wiring group as a whole from the other groups in the department. It could probably be applied to any group whatever. So let us generalize the method to give us a definition of the word *group*. We have been looking at the persons that participated together in social events. Our word for "participating together" is *interaction*: a group is defined by the interactions of its members. If we say that individuals A, B, C, D, E . . . form a group, this will mean that at least the following circumstances hold. Within a given period of time, A interacts more often with B, C, D, E, . . . than he does with M, N, L, O, P, . . . whom we choose to consider outsiders or members of other groups. B also interacts more often with A, C, D, E, . . . than he does with outsiders, and so on for the other members of the group.[3] It is possible just by counting interactions to map out a group quantitatively distinct from others. This is what we do crudely in everyday life when we say that certain persons "see a lot of one another," "go around together," "work together," or "associate with one another," and that they make up a clique, a gang, a crowd, a group. We are saying that they interact frequently

with one another, irrespective of the particular activities in which they interact.

A couple of further points about this definition need to be brought out. The definition certainly does not imply that a person belongs to only one group. That would run counter to common sense, and we are here to sharpen common sense, not to outrage it. In our stalking horse, the Hawthorne Plant, a wireman like Taylor (W3) was, in his working hours, a member of the Bank Wiring Observation Room and of clique A within it, but after working hours he was a member of other groups: his family, his church, his lodge, interacting in each of these groups only within limited spans of time.

Note also that our definition of the word *group* is relative: the meaning depends on what persons and groups one chooses to consider outsiders to the group in question. For some purposes we choose to consider cliques A and B in the Bank Wiring Room as groups in their own right, but they were at the same time sub-groups of the Bank Wiring Room, which was itself a group. In like manner, the room itself was a subgroup of the department, and the department a subgroup of the Hawthorne Plant. But we have now pushed our definition too far. We are especially concerned with those groups—an older generation of sociologists called them primary groups—each member of which is able to interact with every other member.

The decision, then, as to what will be called a group and what a subgroup depends on the level at which we wish to make the analysis. This does not mean that the division between groups is merely conventional, that we can draw the line where we please. Given the reported facts, a sociologist could hardly cut the Bank Wiring Observation Room into cliques in any other way than Roethlisberger and Dickson did. The cliques were matters of observation, not convention. At whatever level we look at the web of interaction, it always shows certain thin places, and the lines between groups fall there. Any group with a population larger than two can be divided into subgroups, but even in a group of three persons, the question as to which pair makes the "company" and which individual the "crowd" cannot be settled by a flip of a coin.

Perhaps we have gone far enough in spelling out our definition of the word *group*. How much of any theory needs to be set down for the record beyond the possibility of misunderstanding—though anyone can misunderstand if he is bound he is going to—and how much left to the intelligence of the reader is always a hard question, but certainly the reader will be insulted if he is not allowed to do any independent thinking of his own. One point does need to be made clear. Saying that a group is defined by interaction is not the same thing as saying that interaction is the whole of group life. Every page of this book will tell about other elements that need to be taken into account. Unfortunately one has to begin, and begin somewhere. The charm of interaction for some sociologists is that it can be observed rather unambiguously, that it can in fact be counted. It may be a good place to start.

SYSTEM AND ENVIRONMENT

This definition of the group implies, and is meant to imply, that the group has a boundary and that outside the boundary lies the group's environment. A scheme of analysis that breaks down the phenomena being studied into organized wholes, or systems, and environments in which the systems exist has turned up again and again, and has again and again been found useful, in sciences as far apart as physics and biology. Sometimes the organized wholes can be easily identified;

their boundaries are clear; they have skins. But even when the wholes are not so definitely marked off from the environment, much intellectual illumination is gained by stating what shall be taken as the boundary of the system— by drawing an imaginary line around it— and then studying the mutual relations between the system and its milieu. In thermodynamics—the study of phenomena such as hot, compressed gas in a cylinder—you may be able to say something about the energy generated by the system or the work done on the environment: energy and work are functions of the system as a whole. In biology and physiology —the study of animal bodies —you may be able to show how the system, this time the living organism, reacts as a unit to changes in the environment. Whitehead says that the idea of an organized whole, or system, existing in an environment is "a fundamental concept which is essential to scientific theory."[4]

Our definition of the group draws a line between the systems we shall study and their different environments. The activities, interactions, and sentiments of the group members, together with the mutual relations of these elements with one another during the time the group is active, constitute what we shall call the *social system*. The rest of the book will be made up of detailed analyses of social systems. Everything that is not part of the social system is part of the environment in which the system exists. Note that, as the definition of the group is relative, so must be that of the group's environment. If the group we are interested in is the Bank Wiring Observation Room, then the rest of the Hawthorne Plant is part of its environment, but if the Hawthorne Plant itself should be the group in question, then the environment would become everything outside this new system.

Whenever we use the words *organized*

whole or, still worse, *organism* in connection with groups and societies, we are laying ourselves open to misinterpretation. People will at once think we mean that a group is an organism like that most familiar one, the living body, and of course it is not. Organized wholes have some things in common with one another but also differ greatly among themselves, especially in the capacity to maintain a steady state in the face of changes in the environment. A thermodynamic system like hot coffee, cream, and sugar in a thermos bottle does pretty well in solving this problem, but only for a short time and for small changes in outside temperature. The healthy human body does very much better. Indeed the steady state kept by its internal organs sets it free to take agressive action on the environment. Somewhere in between, if we were arranging systems in the scale of their *organicity*, would come social systems. The group is never quite passive. The various attempts to show that it is the mere creature of its surroundings have never been clinching, though they have helped social scientists to be tough-minded. The demands of the environment cannot be disregarded, but they by no means wholly determine the constitution of the group. In fact, in the favorable instance, the group spontaneously evolves the behavior necessary to improve its standard of living in the environment. In the curious coincidence between the needs for survival and the organism's capacity to meet those needs, the group and the animal body are the same in kind if not in degree. The ability of the group to survive gross changes in its milieu seems less than that of the animal body, but both are struggling toward the free life.

THE NATURE OF THE ENVIRONMENT

We are getting too philosophical, though it is a man's philosophy that makes what he sees. In our standard procedure for analyzing social behavior, we ask first: What is the nature of the group's environment? and next: Given that the group is surviving in the environment, what are the limits that this condition places on the interactions, sentiments, and activities of the group? If you prefer the latter question in the form: What is the response of the group to the demands of the environment? you are welcome to it, but it is probably less rigorous. Answering these questions, in whatever form they are put, is the first step in the study of a social system.

The environment may be broken down into three main aspects: physical, technical, and social, all of which are interrelated, and any one of which may be more important than the others for any particular group. But let us get back to the Bank Wiring Observation Room, and first take the physical and technical aspects together. The men were working in a room of a certain shape, with fixtures such as benches, oriented in a certain way. They were working on certain materials with certain tools. These things formed the physical and technical environment in which the human relationships within the room developed, and they made these relationships more likely to develop in some ways than in others. For instance, the sheer geographical position of the men within the room had something to do with the organization of work and even with the appearance of cliques. In just the same way, we should begin with the physical and technical environment if we were studying some other kind of group, say a primitive tribe or a medieval village. Thus we might observe that the villagers worked in a cool, wet climate, on clay soils, using a wooden plow drawn by eight oxen to till the land for planting winter wheat. Then we should ask ourselves how these physical and technical factors helped determine the relationships between villagers. Note that we say "helped determine." Seldom does the environment wholly determine social relationships in the sense that, if the group is to survive, only *one* scheme of organization is possible.

As for the social environment, the Hawthorne Plant and the Western Electric Company in general was, through its supervisory force, an important influence on the wiremen. The management had chosen the men; it wanted them to accomplish results of a certain kind; it had an organization plan for reaching these results; it had a method of wage payment by group piecework, and so on. We do not need to repeat what we have said already. The management tried to put these plans into effect, and in a large measure succeeded, though not altogether. In output, in helping, in exchanging jobs much was going on in the room of which the higher-ups in the company would not have approved. In this respect, again, the environment set limits on the behavior of the group, which would certainly have been broken up if it had not conformed to the company's plans to some degree.

Another important influence—we cannot say which is the most important—came from the other workers that the wiremen met in the plant and department. Many of the ideas about the restriction of output must have been picked up from them. Important also was the Chicago of the early years of the depression, and so were the groups in which the men participated outside of their work. Their membership in families certainly had a direct effect on their behavior, particularly on their motives for work, and so did their looser membership in neighborhoods, social classes, and churches. We mention these aspects of the environment, not because we know enough about their effect on the wiremen, but because they ought to be looked at in the study of a group. We are not just analyzing the environment of the Bank Wiring Observation Room but setting up a check list for future use.

Another and pervasive environmental influence on the Bank Wiremen was *culture*, to use a word some anthropologists have taken as their central concept. The wiremen were Americans, and they were soaked in American culture: the values and norms of American society. We shall have something to say about culture later; it can be taken up most conveniently at another point in the study of the social system, so let us say no more about it now, except to underline its importance.

THE EXTERNAL SYSTEM

We have studied the nature of the environment and the kinds of influence the environment may exert on the behavior of a group. The environment and its influences will be different for each group considered, but we are now focusing on the Bank Wiring Observation Room. We turn next from the environment to the behavior of the group itself; we note that the group is, at the moment we study it, persisting or surviving in its environment; and we infer, not unnaturally, that the behavior of the group must be such as to allow it to survive in the environment. Then we turn to the elements of group behavior: sentiment, activity, and interaction, and we say that the *external system* is the state of these elements and of their interrelations, so far as it constitutes a solution—not necessarily the only possible solution—of the problem: How shall the group survive in its environment? We call it external because it is conditioned by the environment; we call it a system because in it the elements of behavior are mutually dependent. The external system, plus another set of relations which we call the *internal system*, make up the total social system.

At the risk of anticipating some later steps in our argument, let us take everyone into our confidence on what we are trying to do. When we study a group, one of the first observations we can make is that the group is surviving in an environment, and therefore we say of the group, as of other organisms, that it is, for the moment at least, adapted to its environment. But this word *adaptation* is ambiguous. Does it mean that the characteristics of the group are determined by the environment? No, it does not, for the second observation we can make is that the characteristics of the group are determined by two classes of factors and not one only. These characteristics are determined by the environment, in greater or lesser degree according to the nature of the environment and of the group in question, and also by what we shall call for the time being the internal development of the group. But we are not yet at the end of our difficulties, for the third observation we can make is that the two classes of factors are not independent of one another. Full explanation of our meaning will take the rest of this book, but we can outline our argument now. Assuming that there is established between the members of a group any set of relations satisfying the condition that the group survives for a time in its particular environment, physical and social, we can show that on the foundation of these relations the group will develop new ones, that the latter will modify or even create the relations we assumed at the beginning, and that, finally, the behavior of the group, besides being determined by the environment, will itself change the environment.

In short, the relationship between group and environment is essentially a relationship of action and reaction; it is circular. But perhaps it is safer to say that it sounds circular when described in words and sentences. When we describe a phenomenon in ordinary language, we are bound to start with a particular statement, going on from there to a sequence of further statements, and if the phenomenon is complex and organic, the sequence has a way of coming back sooner or later to the statement with which we started. No doubt a series of simultaneous equations could describe the characteristics of the group more elegantly than words and sentences can, but we do not yet have the equations, and it may be that the equations cannot be set up before the verbal description has been made. If, then, we are limited to ordinary language, and if the tendency of ordinary language is to make the analysis of complex organic wholes sound circular, we propose in this book to relax, to fall in with this tendency of language rather than fight against it, and to analyze the relationship between group and environment as if it were a process having a beginning and an end, even though the point at which the process ends may be the point from which it started. Let us be candid and admit the method is clumsy, though it may be the best we have.

Our method has many analogies in the verbal description of physical processes. In describing a group, our problem is, for instance, a little like the problem of analyzing without the help of mathematics what happens to a set of interlinked springs when one of them is compressed. How shall a man describe in words what happens to a set of springs in a cushion or mattress when he sits on them? If he begins by sitting on any one spring and tries to trace from there the changes that take place in the rest of the springs, he will always find that the last spring in the series is linked back to the first and prevents the first from giving way under his weight as much as he thought it would. This, in fact, is the virtue of the set of springs.

Now let us use a more complicated analogy. We are all more or less familiar with the operation of the gasoline, or internal-combustion, engine. Let us ask ourselves how the operation of this engine was originally explained to us, or, better, how we should go about explaining it to someone else. We should, perhaps, begin by considering only one cylinder, instead of all the cylinders a real engine would have, and we should, just to get our exposition going, assume the cylinder and its contents to be in a certain state. We might, for instance, assume that the piston has reached the top of its stroke, and that the mixture of air and gasoline above the piston is hot and compressed. From then on, we should describe the operations of the engine as proceeding in sequence. A spark explodes the hot mixture; the explosion drives the piston downwards, and the moving piston transmits turning energy to the shaft. As the shaft turns, a system of cams opens valves in the cylinder head that admit a fresh mixture and allow the burnt gas to escape. The turning shaft also causes the piston to rise once more in the cylinder, compressing and heating the fresh mixture; and we are back where we started from, except that we have yet to account for the spark that set the whole process going. A generator is turned by the shaft, and this generator produces the electric current that explodes the mixture in the cylinder. And so the process goes on as long as the gasoline holds out.

The point we want to make is that although these operations in fact take place in a continuing cycle, we must nevertheless, language being what it is, describe them as if they took place in a sequence having a beginning and an end. Therefore we must assume a certain state of affairs at the beginning of our exposition, the existence of which we can account for only at the end. Thus we assume at the beginning the hot, com-

pressed gas and the spark that ignites it, but we cannot account for the gas being in the cylinder, and being heated, compressed, and ignited, until we have reached the end of our explanation. At our convenience, we can choose any point in the cycle as the point from which our exposition starts, but, whatever point we choose, the problem of describing a cycle as a sequence of events still remains.

Now a group is obviously not an internal-combustion engine—our analogy is *only* an analogy—but we shall analyze the characteristics of the group as if we were dealing with some kind of ongoing circular process. No doubt this is not the only way in which the group could be analyzed, and no doubt, once we have finished making our analysis in this way, we shall be able to adopt a better way and throw away the old, just as one discards the scaffolding that has surrounded a house during construction. But having adopted this method of exposition, we encounter the same kind of difficulty we encountered with the gasoline engine. In describing the circular process in ordinary language, we are at liberty to begin at whatever point in the process we choose, but no matter what point that is, we must still assume at the beginning of our description the existence of certain conditions that we can account for only at the end. We choose to begin the analysis of the group with the external system, which we have defined as a set of relations among the members of the group that solves the problem: How shall the group survive in its environment? We do not say that the external system is the only possible solution to the problem. We do not say either that the group could do no worse or that it could do no better and still survive. We merely say that the external system is *one* solution of the survival problem. For us it is the equivalent of the assumption we made in describing the gasoline engine that the mixture was originally hot and compressed and that a spark was ready to explode it. Then, having assumed that some set of relations such as the external system must exist, we shall go on, as we did with the gasoline engine, and try to show why they do in fact exist or why the assumed relations are modified. The emphasis had better be on modification, for there is one great difference between describing the gasoline engine and describing the group. With the gasoline engine we show how the later events in the cycle create the very conditions we assumed in the beginning, whereas with the group we shall show that the later events in the cycle may modify the conditions we assumed in the beginning. We shall have to allow scope for emergent evolution.

Thus the external system first gives us a set of initial conditions from which our exposition can take its departure and then takes account of the fact that the adaptation of the group to its environment is partly determined by the nature of the environment, while leaving us free later to show how this adaptation is also in part determined by the internal development of the group.

To return from the general problem to the particular group we are studying at the moment, the first question we ask of the Bank Wiring group is this: What does this group need to have in order to keep going in its particular environment? It needs motives (sentiments) on the part of its members, jobs (activities) for them to do, and some communication (interaction) between them. In other words, the members of the group must meet in some degree the plans of the Western Electric Company, and they must be adequately motivated to do so. We shall first take up each element of the external system separately and then in its mutual relations with the others. Until we have done this job we had better not try to define the external system any more rigorously. We must show, and not just say, what we mean.

SENTIMENT

The Bank Wiremen came to the Hawthorne Plant in the first instance with certain motives. The motives were generated by the circumstances of their lives outside the plant, but they were also part of their behavior within it. Some of the motives the men would have recognized: they were working for money, money to get food, to support a family, to buy and keep a car, to take a girl to the movies. These motives were the only ones the planners in the company took into account in devising the wage incentive scheme. Perhaps these were the only motives they thought they could successfully appeal to. At any rate, the men must have had many other reasons for working at Hawthorne that they might not have admitted so easily: a feeling that a man was not a fully self-respecting citizen unless he had a job, a desire for the prestige outside the factory that comes from working up to a good job within it, the wish to belong to a company that was said to be a good place to work, and so on. These are all, by our definition, sentiments, and these were the motives for work that the men brought to the Bank Wiring Observation Room. Whatever other sentiments their association with their fellow workers might release in the men, these would still have had to be satisfied in some degree. Man does not live by bread alone, but he lives by bread at least. These sentiments were assets to the company in that they led to hard work; they were liabilities in that the company had to satisfy them. Sentiment as an element of co-operation always has this double aspect.

The sentiments we have been talking about are part of what is often called individual self-interest. Let us be clear as to what we mean by this famous phrase. In the first place, it may be that all motives are motives of self-interest in the sense that, given the situation in which he is placed, a man always tries to do as well as he can for himself. What he does may look to outsiders as if it were hurting rather than helping him; it may look impossibly altruistic rather than selfish, and yet modern psychology teaches us that, if we knew the full situation, both the social relationships and the psychological dynamics of the person concerned, we should find all his actions to be self-enhancing. But this is an aside; let us take up the question from another point of view. If we examine the motives we usually call individual self-interest, we shall find that they are, for the most part, neither individual nor selfish but that they are the product of group life and serve the ends of a whole group not just an individual. What we really mean by the celebrated phrase is that these motives are generated in a different group from the one we are concerned with at the moment. Thus from the point of view of the Bank Wiring Observation Room, the desire of a man to earn wages was individual self-interest, but from the point of view of his family it was altruism. Motives of self-interest in this sense are the ones that come into the external system. Sentiments, on the other hand, that are generated within the group we are concerned with at the moment include some of the ones we call disinterested. Friendship between wiremen is an example. While sentiments of self-interest affected or influenced the behavior of the men in the room, they did not solely determine that behavior. If these sentiments had been alone decisive, output would perhaps have been higher. That both self-interest *and* something else are satisfied by group life is the truth that is hardest for the hard-boiled—and half-baked—person to see. As Mayo says, "If a number of individuals work together to achieve a common purpose, a harmony of interests will develop among them to which individual self-interest will be subordinated. This is a very different doctrine from the claim that individual self-interest is the solitary human motive."[5]

ACTIVITY

The activities of the group were in the first instance planned by the Western Electric Company engineers. Some of the men, with tools and fixtures, wired one kind of equipment; some of the men wired another. Some of the men soldered the connected wires into place on the terminals. Two men inspected the completed switches, both visually and with testing sets. A group chief supervised the whole. A trucker brought supplies into the room and took completed equipments out. Here were a number of different kinds of activity, ranging from manual work with tools through visual observation to activity that was largely verbal: supervision and direction. The activities were in theory different for different persons, and they were organized: each had a part in the production of a completed whole. Furthermore, the men were paid for their work in different amounts, according to a complicated system of group piecework. Note that the Western Electric organization tried to control more of the activities of the group than it was actually able to control. Nevertheless, it did to a very large extent settle what the men should do.

INTERACTION

In the same way, observing the behavior of the men, one could have mapped out a scheme of interaction among them, in abstraction from their sentiments and their activities, and one could have recognized that a part of the scheme was set by the company. There were the necessary interactions between a solderman and the three wiremen he worked for, between an inspector and the wiremen and soldermen whose work he passed judgment on, between the group chief and all the men in the room. Then there were the almost inevitable interactions between the men who were thrown together by the physical geography of the room, especially between the wiremen and soldermen who worked together, some at the front, some in the middle, and some at the back of the room. Finally, the mere fact that all the men were together in a single room tended to increase interaction between each member of the group and every other.

PAIR RELATIONSHIPS

So far we have been doing with the description of the Bank Wiring Observation Room no more than we did, two chapters back, with the description of the Irish countryman's family. We have, to be sure, limited ourselves to that part of group behavior that is under the direct influence of the environment, but within this field what we have been doing is the same. We have been making a crude analysis, breaking the behavior of the men down into its elements of sentiment, activity, and interaction. We shall now take a new step in the application of our method, the first step in synthesis. What has been separated must be put together again. We shall study the relationships of mutual dependence among sentiment, activity, and interaction in the external system. More particularly, we shall study the relationships between pairs of elements, of which there are, logically, three: sentiment-activity, activity-interaction, and interaction-sentiment.

There is nothing complicated about the idea of mutual dependence. Just the same, we had better say what we mean by it, as it will come into our thinking over

and over again. In physics, Boyle's law states that the volume of a gas in an enclosed space varies inversely with the pressure upon it. The greater the pressure, the smaller the volume of the gas. This statement, which is usually put in the form of an equation, expresses a relationship of mutual dependence, mutual because if either pressure or volume changes, the other variable will change too. If pressure is increased, volume will decrease. But if we choose to begin with volume instead of pressure, we say that if volume increases, pressure must decrease. This kind of relationship is most elegantly expressed in an equation, but in the field of sociology we should not pretend to use equations until we have data that are thoroughly quantitive. Instead we shall have to describe this kind of relationship in ordinary language, and here we are at once in trouble, because this is just the kind of relationship that ordinary language—at least any of the Western languages—is least well equipped to describe. Ordinary language, with its subjects and predicates, is geared to handling only one independent factor and one dependent factor at a time: someone is always doing something to somebody. Cause-and-effect thinking, rather than mutual-dependence thinking, is built into speech. Yet a situation that can accurately be described in cause-and-effect terms is just the kind that is encountered least often in sociology. Here the cause produces an effect, but the effect reacts upon the cause. In these circumstances, the very first effort to use ordinary language shows how crude a tool it is. Yet we shall do what we can with it, as we have nothing else. We may, for instance, say that an increase in the complexity of the scheme of activity in the external system will bring about an increase in the complexity of the scheme of interaction, but that the reverse is also true. The two are mutually dependent.

One other point should be made but not elaborated at this time. According to

Boyle's law, the volume of a gas in an enclosed space varies inversely as the pressure put upon it only if the temperature is held constant during the process. If the temperature does vary, the relationship between volume and pressure will not have the simple form stated by the law. When we study the mutual dependence of two variables, we must somehow take account of the effect on these two of the other variables that enter the system. In the same way, when we make a statement about the mutual dependence of, for instance, interaction and activity, we must never forget that sentiment also comes into the system and may effect the relationships described. It is never enough to say that the relationship holds good "other things being equal." We must try to say what these other things are, and where they are "equal." This raises immense problems, which we shall not try to cope with at this time, if indeed we can ever cope with them adequately in social science.

MUTUAL DEPENDENCE OF SENTIMENT AND ACTIVITY

When we are thinking of the relationship of mutual dependence between sentiment and activity, we speak of sentiments as motives or drives. In the simplest form of the relationship, a motive gives rise to activity, and once the activity is successfully completed, the motive disappears. A man feels hungry; he gets something to eat and his hunger disappears. If his activity does not result in his getting something to eat, new sentiments, which we call frustration, will be added to his original hunger, and we say that the activity was unrewarding or even positively punishing. He may then try a new one; if it ends in his getting something to eat, his hunger is allayed, and he will tend to repeat the activity the next time he feels hungry. We now say that the activity is rewarding, but do we mean

anything more by this word than that we saw the man eat the food and repeat the activity leading to it?

This is the relationship at its simplest. It is much more complicated when the motive is not something like hunger but something like a man's fear that he will be hungry in the future. Suppose that a man is afraid he will be hungry in the future if he does not now start plowing his field and doing other tasks in co-operation with other men that will lead in the end to loaves of bread on his table. The man's hunger is allayed when he gets food, but the fear does not necessarily disappear when the appropriate activities are carried out. Future hunger is still a threat. In these circumstances, *both motives and associated activities persist, both continuously recreated, but if either side of the relationship is changed, the other will be affected.* Returning to our example, we can say that, if for any reason the man is less afraid he will be hungry, he may not work so hard. And if, on the other hand, he finds some new set of activities that will yield more food than the old, he may become less fearful. The relationship between motive and activity is mutual.

This relationship seems to hold good whether the activity in question is obviously and directly useful or, like magic, takes the place of a useful activity that is unknown or impossible. In the absence of anything better to do, men must find even magic rewarding. The relationship also seems to hold good both for the sentiments we share with all men, such as fear, hunger, thirst, cold, and the like, and for the sentiments generated in a particular social situation, such as the need to be paid wages. Note how in the Bank Wiring Observation Room the company's wage incentive plan tried to establish a particularly close link between one sentiment (the desire for money) and one set of activities (production). That the plan did not altogether achieve its intended results does not mean that this link was unimportant. It means that other sentiments besides the need for money affected output. It is clear, for instance, that the sentiments of Green (W9)—"I'd like a job reading"—, sentiments that presumably were generated by his whole past history and experience in groups outside the plant, were among the forces making his output the lowest in the room. If the interviews with the workers had been reported more fully, we should know much more about the outide influences on the motives of the men.

We need not go further into the mutual dependence of sentiment and activity. After all, most of the science of psychology, and particularly that part called "learning theory," is devoted to studying it, and if we tried to compete with psychology our hopeless inadequacy in that field would be revealed even more clearly than it is already. All we can do is show how some of the problems studied by psychology fit into a general scheme for analyzing group behavior. Remember also that we are now considering only the sentiments that come into the external system. The sentiments of the internal system are rather different in kind, though their mutual dependence with activities is the same as that we have just described.

MUTUAL DEPENDENCE OF ACTIVITY AND INTERACTION

In the external system, the relationship of mutual dependence between activity and interaction links the division of labor with the scheme of communication in the group. In the Bank Wiring Observation Room, the total job of turning out completed equipments was divided into a series of separate activities: wiring, soldering, inspection, trucking, and, not least in importance, supervision. Each separate activity was assigned to a different individual or subgroup, and in many of the activities each unit of work—for instance, completing a single level of connections—took a certain length of time. But what has been broken up must be put together again. If finished equipments were to be turned out, interaction had to take place in a certain scheme between the men doing the different jobs.

Thus when a wireman had completed a level on one equipment he moved over to a second one, and that act was the signal for the solderman to begin soldering in place the connections of the first terminal. The wireman had interacted with the solderman: remember that by our definition interaction takes place when the action of one man sets off the action of another. And note that, in this instance, the wireman originated interaction with the solderman: he gave the signal to which the other responded. We can without danger call interaction communication provided we remember that communication is not necessarily verbal. There was no need for words to pass between wireman and solderman in order that communication between them should be effective. In the same way, the solderman's completion of his part of the task was the signal for the inspector to go to work, and if he discovered any defect, he would initiate interaction, almost necessarily verbal this time, with the workman responsible. Thus a continuous process of interaction brought together the separate activities that went into the completion of the product. Finally, if one of the company's regulations was too flagrantly violated, or the process of co-ordination failed at any point, the problem would come to the group chief's attention. Someone would bring the matter up to him, or he himself would initiate interaction to restore the established order.

Generalizing from the Bank Wiring Observation Room, we can say, then, that any division, among the members of a group, of the partial activities that go into the completion of some total activity implies a scheme of interaction among the persons concerned, and that *if the scheme of activities is changed, the scheme of inter-action will, in general, change also, and vice versa.* The two are mutually dependent. Sometimes, and this is perhaps the more common situation, a man who is organizing a piece of work begins by dividing it up into separate activities, and then makes the scheme of interaction conform to his division. That is, he treats the scheme of activity as the independent or governing factor. Thus the management of a plant may decide how an operation shall be divided among the workers and then devise an appropriate method of co-ordination. But this presupposes that an appropriate method of co-ordination can be put into effect, and the presupposition may be wrong. That is, the scheme of interaction may sometimes be the governing factor. Surely certain forms of the division of labor among the members of an industrial group were prohibitively expensive in the days before the conveyor belt was invented and made new schemes of interaction possible. In most circumstances, *both* factors are important.[6]

The division of labor makes the cost of work less in human effort or money. For this reason all societies have gone some distance in making their members specialists. From Adam Smith to Henry Taylor the uncriticized assumption was apt to be that the further the division was carried, the greater were the savings effected, that the further a job like shoe-making was broken down into its component specialties, and each assigned to a workman who did nothing else, the less would be the cost of making the shoe. Now we have begun to understand that the division of labor, like any other process, has its point of diminishing returns. Peter Drucker has shown how, in World War II and in some kinds of industrial work where conventional assembly lines could not be set up, the assigning of all the component specialties of any one job to one person or a group of persons, rather than to a number of separate

individuals, turned out to be a cheaper way of manufacturing than any other.[7] Why the division of labor may reach a point of diminishing returns should be clear from our analysis. The division of labor is not something in itself; it always implies a scheme of interaction by which the different divided activities are co-ordinated. The indirect costs of setting up this scheme, including the costs that arise if supervision is inadequate, may offset the direct savings from specialization.

THE PYRAMID OF INTERACTION

What we said two paragraphs ago we must now take back in part. It is not universally true that as the scheme of activity changes, the scheme of interaction will change too. It is not true when the activity in question is supervision or leadership: the process by which departures from a given plan of co-operation are avoided or new plans introduced. In groups that differ greatly in the activities they carry on, the schemes of interaction between leaders of different levels and their followers tend nevertheless to be strikingly similar. Let us see what this means by taking up the problem of the *span of control*, as organization experts call it: How many men can be supervised by a single leader? When the activities of a group are of such a kind that they can be co-ordinated largely through one-way interaction from the leader to the followers, then the leader can supervise a rather large number of persons. An example is the conductor of a symphony orchestra, who may direct as many as a hundred men. But in general the interaction must be two-way: the leader gives orders, information, and exhortation to his followers, but they must also supply him with information about themselves and the situation they face. In these circumstances the span of control becomes much smaller. It is significant how often a group of between eight and a dozen persons crops up under the supervision of a single leader in organizations of many different kinds. The old-fashioned squad in the army is an example. And since the same kind of considerations govern the relations between the leaders of the first level and their own leaders, and so on for higher and higher leaders in groups of larger and larger size, it is easy to see how the scheme of interaction, especially in big organizations, piles up into its characteristic pyramidical, or hierarchical, form. The leader-in-chief appears at the apex of the pyramid, working with a small group of lesser leaders; each lesser leader, level by level, works with his own small group of leaders of still lower rank, until finally at the broad base the rank and file are reached.

No matter what activities an organization carries on, this characteristic form of the interaction scheme tends to appear; it appears in the Catholic Church as surely as it does in an industrial firm or an army. Therefore we must modify our earlier rule and say that *whatever changes occur in the scheme of activities of a group, the scheme of interaction between the leaders of various levels and their followers tends to keep the same general pyramidical form.* Yet the modification is more apparent than real. If the conflict between the two rules distresses us, we can readily reconcile them. The pyramid scheme of interaction seems to make possible the supervision of the activities of a large number of persons, through two-way interaction between them and leaders of different levels. Whenever, therefore, this particular activity, supervision, remains largely the same from organization to organization, then the scheme of interaction—the pyramid—through which supervision is exercised remains largely the same too. Our rule stated that if the scheme of activity changed, the scheme of interaction changed too. But the rule also implies that if the activity does not change—and the job of supervision is

much the same from group to group—the interaction does not change either. The first rule holds after all, the second rule being merely one of its special cases.

The relation between the scheme of activities and the scheme of interaction in an organization is usually represented by the familiar organization chart, which shows the organization divided into departments and subdepartments, the various officers and subofficers occupying boxes, connected by lines to show which persons are subordinate to what other ones. Every such chart is too neat; it tells what the channels of interaction ought to be but not always what they are. The pyramid-type chart is particularly misleading because it shows only the interaction between superiors and subordinates, the kind of interaction that we shall call, following Barnard, *scalar*.[8] It does not show the interaction that goes on between two or more persons at about the same level of the organization, for instance, between two department heads or, in the Bank Wiring Room, between a wireman and an inspector. This kind of interaction we shall call *lateral* interaction, though we must remember there are borderline cases where the distinction between scalar and lateral interaction disappears. The conventional organization chart represents the scalar but not the lateral interaction. If it were not for the unhappy association with predatory spiders, the facts would be much better represented by a web, the top leader at the center, spokes radiating from him, and concentric circles linking the spokes. Interaction takes place along the concentric circles as well as along the spokes. But even the web is too neat a picture.

It is a mistake to think of the pyramid—or the web—scheme of interaction as always created by conscious planning. It is so created in only a few instances, for example, the large formal organizations of modern Western society, and these, in their origins, modeled themselves on previously existing patterns. The pyramid occurs not only where it is planned, as in the Western Electric Company, but also where it is not planned, as in a street gang or primitive tribe. Sometimes the pyramid is imposed on a group, as supervision was imposed on the Bank Wiremen; sometimes, as we shall see, a group spontaneously creates its own pyramid. Sometimes a group, if it is to operate successfully on the environment, needs the pyramid; sometimes a group does not need the pyramid but creates it anyhow. In any event, the fact that a pyramid of interaction may be a practical necessity of effective operations on the environment is no guarantee that the pyramid will appear. As we mentioned earlier, the possibility of coincidence between the practically necessary and the spontaneously produced is one of the fascinating discoveries that comes from the study of groups as of other organisms, but we shall never explain the existence of the pyramid of interaction or any other such item of group behavior by pointing out that it helps the group to survive in an environment. Even if we assume for the moment that it does help the group to survive, we shall sooner or later go on to examine in detail the mechanisms by which the item in question is produced. We shall study what the philosopers call efficient, rather than final, causes. But we are again running ahead of our argument. The immediate point is that the principles of organization are universal; they are not an invention of the Prussian general staff or of American big business.

The relationship between the scheme of activities and the scheme of interaction is the problem of *organization*, in the narrow sense of that word. When the leaders of military, industrial, and other concerns speak of organization, this is what they mean. For us the word has a much broader meaning, but the narrow one will do no harm so long as we know

what it is. Since our concern is with the small group, we had better not try to attain the higher reaches of organization theory, which apply only to large concerns. But one last point should be made. The complexity of organization does not end with the appearance of the hierarchy of leadership. In big concerns, several different hierarchies arise and intersect one another. The pyramid, from being two-dimensional, becomes three- and multi-dimensional, with several different chains of interaction between the followers and the upper leaders. In the jargon of the experts, a line-and-staff form of organization develops, and we shall have something to say about it in a later chapter, where the subject comes in naturally. For the moment we can summarize in the words of Eliot Chapple and Carleton Coon: "The coordination needed in any complex technique is impossible without interaction. As we have seen, most complex techniques involve the activities of more than one person, and, in fact, where people practice a number of complex techniques, extensive interactions must take place to coordinate the work of manufacturing, to secure raw materials, and to exchange the goods produced. In other words, the growth of complexity in technical processes goes hand in hand with an increase in the amount of interaction and in the complexity of the interaction pattern."[9]

CONCLUSION

Logically, of course, a third relationship of mutual dependence exists: the mutual dependence of interaction and sentiment, but we shall choose to consider this a part of the internal system, to which we turn in the next chapter. The two aspects of group life that we call the external and the internal systems are continuous with one another. The line between them can be drawn where we choose, arbitrarily, and we choose to draw it here. The only reason for drawing a line at all is to save words: we now can talk about the external system without repeating everything we have said in this chapter.

What goes into the external system is what we have shown goes in: the best definition is a process of pointing. If we must have a definition in words, we can say that the mutual dependence between the work done in a group and the motives for work, between the division of labor and the scheme of interaction, so far as these relationships meet the condition that the group survives in an environment—this we shall regularly speak of as the external system. But remember that when we talk of a group's survival in an environment we always deceive ourselves to some degree. The group is not passive before the environment; it reacts. It even defines what its environment shall be. Its purposes make different aspects of the environment important.

The relationship between group and environment is never a one-way matter. But we are weak creatures, and our tools of language and analysis are soft. We ought to say everything at once, yet in our desperation we find we have to start somewhere. We have chosen to begin with the environment and its influence on the group. We shall then show how the group, on the foundation of the relationships thus established, elaborates further tendencies of its own, which react so as to modify the adaptation to the environment. This again is not the truth, but a manner of speaking. Yet it is forced on us. What we need now is a willing and provisional suspension of disbelief. Until we have said everything, we shall have said nothing. We shall have to keep many balls in the air at the same time. Regard all our statements as partial truths until the last word and the last modification are in.

NOTES

1. This is an example from actual field research: see A. Davis, B. Gardner, and M. R. Gardner, *Deep South*, 147–151. Fig. 1 is reproduced, with modifications, from this book, by permission of The University of Chicago Press, the publishers.

2. For the logic of this method, see E. Forsyth and L. Katz, "A Matrix Approach to the Analysis of Sociometry Data," *Sociometry*, IX (November, 1946), 340–347.

3. See E. D. Chapple and C. S. Coon, *Principles of Anthropology*, 287.

4. A. N. Whitehead, *Science and the Modern World*, 68.

5. E. Mayo, *The Political Problem of Industrial Civilization*, 21.

6. In this and the following discussion, much reliance is placed on C. I. Barnard, *The Functions of the Executive*, chap. VIII.

7. P. F. Drucker, "The Way to Industrial Peace," *Harper's Magazine*, Vol. 193 (November, 1946), 390.

8. C. I. Barnard, *Organization and Management*, 150.

9. E. D. Chapple and C. S. Coon, *Principles of Anthropology*, 250.

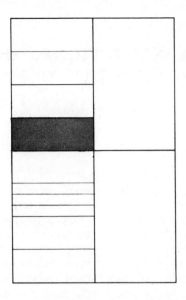

4. PSYCHOLOGISM

The psychologistic viewpoint typically defines the social in terms of objective behavior relations and seeks to explain it by referring to phenomena imposed on the social through the psychological characteristics of the participants themselves. George Homans' more recent work illustrates this viewpoint, as his earlier work illustrates the materialistic one. The excerpt that follows is the summary chapter of Social Behavior: Its Elementary Forms, *a book that came eleven years after* The Human Group. *Here Homans defines elementary social behavior and shows how it depends essentially on certain psychological dispositions to identify, pursue, and exchange rewards.*

THE INSTITUTIONAL AND
THE SUBINSTITUTIONAL

GEORGE C. HOMANS

According to my lights, a last chapter should resemble a primitive orgy after harvest. The work may have come to an end, but the worker cannot let go all at once. He is still full of energy that will fester if it cannot find an outlet. Accordingly he is allowed a time of license, when he may say all sorts of things he would think twice before saying in more sober moments, when he is no longer bound by logic and evidence but free to speculate about what he has done.

I propose to take my orgy out in putting a frame around this book. In this last chapter I shall return to a question I raised in the first, when I tried to set up some sort of definition of elementary social behavior. It is an exchange of rewards (or punishments) between at least two persons; the exchange is direct rather than indirect; and it is actual behavior and not just a norm specifying what behavior ought to be. Granted that they grade into one another by degrees, and that nothing more than an arbitrary line can be drawn between the two, what are the relations between the elementary and the more complex forms of social behavior, between the informal and the formal, between the subinstitutional and the institutional?

THE GROUP AS A MICROCOSM

In their private speculations, some sociologists were once inclined to think of the

From *Social Behavior: Its Elementary Forms* by George C. Homans, copyright © 1961 by Harcourt, Brace & World, Inc., and reprinted with their permission.

small, informal group as a microcosm of society at large: they felt that the same phenomena appeared in the former as in the latter but on a vastly reduced scale—a scale that, incidentally, made detailed investigation possible. And no doubt there are striking resemblances between the two. We have seen how members roughly equal in status within a small group are apt to associate with one another on "social" occasions more often than with either their superiors or inferiors in status; and their behavior has obvious points of resemblance with the more salient features of class and stratification systems—where members of families equal in status as recognized in the larger society are especially apt to visit, go to parties with, and even marry one another. No doubt the resemblances are not fortuitous: some of the same processes are at work in both cases. But to say that the two phenomena have points in common is not to say that one is a microcosm of the other, that the one is simply the other writ small. The two are not alike, if only because in an informal group a man wins status through his direct exchanges with the other members, while he gets status in the larger society by inheritance, wealth, occupation, office, legal authority—in every case by his position in some institutional scheme, often one with a long history behind it.

When to take another example, a number of followers get help from an informal leader, to whom they yield some power to control their behavior, the situation does look a lot like that of an appointed supervisor whose designated subordinates report to him and to whom in return he gives orders. Perhaps in the distant past, when formal organizations were first deliberately designed, the span of control—the number of men put under the command of a single officer—may have been modeled on what is apt to spring up spontaneously in a small group. But of course the situations are not really the same. The fact that higher authority has appointed the formal leader, that he is responsible to it, and that the punishments he inflicts are made possible by its support, makes all the difference, as anyone who has been both an informal and a formal leader knows. In the formal situation, moreover, both leader and followers get some of their rewards, not from exchange with one another, but from the exchange of work for pay with the organization of which they are a part. Both parties are more independent of one another than they are in the small, informal group. It is true that a formal leader may be more successful in his own job if he has something of the informal leader about him too—but this only adds to the evidence that the two are not the same.

THE COMPLEXITY OF REWARDS

If the informal group, like elementary social behavior in general, is not a true microcosm of society at large, the reason is not that the fundamental processes of behavior—the way the emission of an activity is governed by its pay-offs and its stimuli—are different in the two cases: far from being different, they are identical. The reason lies rather in the fact that, in the institutions of society at large, the relations between the fundamental processes are more complex. The increased complexity seems to take two main forms, which are themselves related to one another. First, a particular activity gets to be maintained not just by what I shall call its natural or primary reward but also by other, contrived rewards, particularly by generalized reinforcers like money and social approval. For instance, a man cuts wood, not because he needs it for his fire, but because a firm will pay him for cutting it. Second, the process of exchange by which an activity gets rewarded comes to be roundabout rather than direct. For instance, the man gets his pay at the end of the week, not from his own supervisor or somebody else he cut the wood for, but from a clerk who is himself rewarded by still another member of the firm. What the two processes have in common, compared with elementary social behavior, is an increased reliance on explicitly stated norms and orders: the man is told that he is to cut wood, and he is told how he will get his pay at the end of the week. These and other differences between institutional and subinstitutional behavior are differences in degree only. If we like, we may consider the differences in degree to be so great as to amount to differences in kind, so long as we do not observe—but it is always open to us to observe—how the one kind of behavior is forever growing out of the other. Then the continuity of the two is borne in on us.

Consider the first process as it must go on at the lowest level; consider, for instance, the expression of grief. In every society some people, not all, must find it rewarding to make some kind of outcry when a beloved companion dies. If this were not a common human trait, but simply something accepted as a convention by the members of particular societies, we should hardly find mourning at death as widely distributed among mankind as in fact it is. Cultures cannot pick up any old sorts of behavior and hope without more ado to carry them on generation after generation. What they pick up must be compatible with some fundamental repertory of human nature, though the compatibility may, of course, be complex.

Once a number of people have cried a number of times at a number of deaths, they begin to make a norm of it—to say that it is the thing one does or ought to do—and the verbal statement of a rule is the first step in the making of an institution. Then other members of their group, whose eyes would otherwise have been dry, may find themselves crying too, because other rewards and punishments have come to sanction the behavior. If they do not cry, they fail in showing respect for the dead, and so lose the esteem of people who are sincere in weeping. Since they do not feel much themselves, they will be ready to adopt as a convention any idiom of mourning the others offer them. And the first thing you know, the formal expression of grief at a bereavement has become an institution, taught to younger members of the society as part of their manners.

No doubt the origin of many institutions is of this sort. The behavior once reinforced for some people in one way, which I call primary, is maintained in a larger number of people by other sorts of reinforcement, in particular by such general reinforcers as social approval. Since the behavior does not come naturally to these others, they must be told how they are to behave—hence the verbal description of behavior, the norm.

Indeed we can see the process taking place before our eyes, and we have touched on it in the earlier part of the book—though only just touched because our main business was not with institutions. Restriction of output in an industrial group undoubtedly arose in the beginning because some members found its results rewarding. But restriction gets its results only if a rather large number of members conform to the output norm, and therefore nonconformists deprive the rest of a reward. Accordingly the members who would have been indifferent to the primary reward are nevertheless apt to conform, for fear of losing the esteem of their fellows; and then restriction of output is well on its way to becoming an institution, taught to new members and even to new generations as one of the laws of life in the factory. Such combinatory processes can snowball into immense institutional piles. Indeed the secondary sanctions of an institution can become so many and so marked that the people following the norms may cease to be conscious of the primary reward, which continues to do its work, but out of sight.

In moments of unguarded talk, some anthropologists have sounded to me as if they thought that the members of a society or some section of it maintained an institutional rule simply because it is a rule, taught them in their youth as something they must obey, and sanctioned by social approval. Were this really the case, I think we should observe far less change in human society than we observe in fact. For social approval does not operate alone: its power as a sanction depends on the continuing vigor of the primary reward. Social approval can come in to reinforce obedience to a rule only so long as some members of the group continue to find obedience rewarding for reasons other than the approval it gets them. As soon as they cease to find it rewarding, a member who disobeys is not depriving them of anything, and so does not forfeit their esteem. No doubt a norm may govern behavior for a while after its primary reward has lost its power, if only because each conformist is a victim of a conspiracy of silence. No one, for instance, dares admit he feels no grief, for fear of offending others who, for reasons like his own, give him no hint they are insincere.

But an institution that has reached this stage is vulnerable and apt to collapse if alternative behavior with a new primary reward presents itself as a possibility. Then someone of very high status or very low, who has little to gain by conformity or little to lose by its opposite, breaks away, and then the hollowness of the belief that disobedience will bring overwhelming social disapproval is soon exposed. The alternative, to be sure, may for a long period of time fail to present itself, because for one reason or another the society has remained shielded from change in the physical or social environment. The first point I should like to make about the relations between institutions and elementary social behavior is that institutions, as explicit rules governing the behavior of many people, are obeyed because rewards other than the primary ones come to be gotten by obeying them, but that these other rewards cannot do the work alone. Sooner or later the primary rewards must be provided. Institutions do not keep on going forever of their own momentum.

When asked to explain why the institutions of a society are what they are, some anthropologists seem reluctant to point to the primary rewards of behaving in accordance with institutional rules. Instead they are apt, as I have suggested, to point to the fact that the rules are taught to new members of society as they come along. When asked why these rules are taught rather than others, the anthropologists then point to the relations between one rule and another. If in a matrilineal society—to take one thoroughly hypothetical case—the rule is that a man's goods are inherited by his sister's son, then a rule of marriage specifying that a sister's son should marry his mother's brother's daughter might mean, if obeyed, that the man's daughter would get some benefit from her father's goods. The first rule, the rule of inheritance, provides a reward for obedience to the second rule, the rule of marriage. But this argument, sound as far as it goes, leaves something tacitly unexplained. Why does the father find it rewarding that his daughter should get some of his goods, or even the daughter find it rewarding that she should get the

benefit of her father's goods? This kind of question the anthropologists have a harder time answering. They may argue, as before, that the society—actually specific members of it—has taught a man that he must love and care for his daughter, but this is no explanation and only another description of what happens. Again we have a right to ask why the society has taught the man that rather than something else.

The fact is that some anthropologists have become so obsessed by the cultural uniqueness of particular societies that they have lost sight of what men have in common. If the anthropologists' reasoning is not to become circular, I think they must admit that they cannot fully explain their own findings unless they make certain assumptions about what men find rewarding, not just as members of a particular society but as members of a species. For instance, I do not think anyone can explain why so many societies in which legal authority over the family is vested in the father are also societies in which a boy develops a close relation with his mother's brother, unless he assumes that men, as men, react to authority in some such way as we have described in this book.[1] Of course the societies in question teach their youngsters how they ought to behave toward mother's brothers, but why do they teach them "closeness" rather than something else? Because "closeness" is rewarding under the circumstances, and rewarding for many men even apart from the norm and the sanctions attached to it. Otherwise, how did the norm itself come into existence?

It does not follow from my argument that social scientists should be particularly interested in "cultural universals," if this means actual institutions that appear in all societies, as marriage and the incest taboo are said to appear, though in fact they vary greatly in form from one society to another. But it does follow that they should be much interested in the underlying mechanisms of human behavior, like those we described in Chapter 4, for the underlying mechanisms can work themselves out in a wide variety of actual institutions. Human nature is the only true "cultural universal."

We social scientists talk as if "society" were the big thing. But an institution is functional for society only because it is functional for men. There is no functional prerequisite for the survival of a society except that the society provide sufficient rewards for its individual members to keep them contributing activities to its maintenance, and that it reward them not just as members of that society but as men.[2] Even when we talk as if "society" provided the rewards, we always, ultimately, mean that men provide them. No doubt they are men whose ancestors have learned, and who have learned themselves, to find specific kinds of behavior rewarding in specific historical circumstances, some of them long past; and they may have continued to find some of the behavior rewarding right up to the present. Since their historical experience may have been different from that of the members of another society, their present institutions may well be different from those of the other. But whatever they learned, they learned because they were men as well as members; and therefore the institutional differences, or similarities, are to be explained by the conjuncture between the nature of man and the nature of the circumstances. This is easy to say but not, of course, easy to do.

If you look long enough for the secret of society you will find it in plain sight: the secret of society is that it was made by men, and there is nothing in society but what men put there.

THE COMPLEXITY OF EXCHANGES

Let me now look at the second of the two processes by which institutions develop out of elementary social behavior—the increasing roundaboutness of the exchange of rewards, which is sometimes called the increasing division of labor. Some primitive societies seem to have developed a complexity of organization that hardly goes beyond what appears, for instance, in a street gang in our own society. The same simple types of transactions stand clearly revealed in both. The society is so hard up, physically or socially, that it has not been able to afford any very elaborate institutional development. One of the reasons why students of elementary social behavior are charmed with the very primitive societies is that they reveal mankind stripped down socially to its fundamentals. In the words of the anthropologist Lévi-Strauss, returning from the Nambikwara of central Brazil: "I had been looking for a society reduced to its simplest expression. That of the Nambikwara was so far reduced that all I found there was men."[3]

At the origin of even the most modern industrial society lies a social unit of much the same sort. Look back, for instance, at the earliest description of the society that, in my view, should count more than any other—more than Greece, Rome, and Israel—as the principal ancestor of our own: look back at Tacitus' description of the tiny Germanic tribal kingdoms of the first century A.D.[4] Of course the society is already highly institutionalized, governed to a high degree by rules inherited from the past, perhaps from a remote past. But the rules outline an organization that is closer to what naturally and spontaneously appears in any small group than anything we have known in more modern times. Consider the kingship itself. It is already in theory something a man inherits and does not acquire by his own actions—though if he is incompetent his high birth is unlikely to save him. But the relation between the king and his "companions" (gesiths, comites), who drink in his hall in peace and follow him in war, and whom he rewards with food, with jewelry, and finally with land, much more resembles the relation between the informal leader of a group and his followers than do most political systems that we have known in our society since that time. At the back, historically, of any of the great modern societies we shall find some such society as this—institutionalized indeed, but institutionalized in a pattern that betrays its kinship with the primeval small group.

Now suppose such a society has created a capital of some sort. By capital I mean anything that allows it to postpone actions leading to some immediate reward in order to undertake others whose rewards, though potentially greater, are both uncertain and deferred. The capital may take the form of unusually well-disciplined soldiers; it may take the form of a surplus of food or money; most important of all it may take the form of a moral code, especially a code supporting trust and confidence between men: a true belief that they will not always let you down in favor of short-term gains.

Without some capital no institutional elaboration can get off the ground. But given the capital, the society—really some man or group of men within the society, perhaps always ultimately a single man—is apt to invest it by trying out some set of activities that departs from the original or primeval institutional pattern. The new pattern envisages an inter-meshing of the behavior of a larger number of persons in a more complicated or roundabout manner than has hitherto been the custom. Having, for instance, conquered new territory with the help of his companions, the king may try to maintain permanent control over it, and to do so he will have to rely, since he now has more people under his rule, not just on his own ties with his companions but on his companions' ties with companions under them. That is, he may have to encourage the development of some sort of feudal system, and in doing so he will

have to spell out, to make a matter of explicit norms, the behavior toward one another of the people now made interdependent. He will have to do so for the same reason that makes a modern factory, when it has grown beyond a certain size, begin to spell out its organizational chart. But the question always remains whether the new arrangement will pay off before the capital runs out. Probably most such attempts by most human societies have failed.

Instead of handling his own finances and dispensing his own justice, the king may appoint a full-time treasurer and full-time judges. These institutions may ultimately increase the efficiency of his administration, attract to his rule, by the prospects of speedy justice, men who might otherwise have been drawn elsewhere, and maintain the peace on which his ability to levy increasing taxes finally depends. They may even set him free of his exclusive, and therefore dangerous, dependence on the loyalty of his companions. But these rewards take time to come in; and while he waits for them, he must invest capital to pay the treasurer and the judges enough to make up, and more than make up, for the time they take from other affairs. He must arrange that the rewards they get from doing their duty are greater than those they would get from appropriating the king's funds to their own uses or selling the king's justice for money in their own pockets. But to do all these things the king must have the capital; he must, for instance, be able to spare enough land from other uses so that his officers can be paid out of the rent, and this means that he must have effective control over the land. In all these undertakings the king is a risk-taker just as surely as is any venture-capitalist today: the institution of royal judges, for instance, may not pay off. Indeed the risks the king takes are greater, for they include his life.

Once the king has succeeded in maintaining his peace so that common men feel that mere anarchy is no danger to their enterprises, other kinds of things may happen at a lower level of society. A man who once made woolen cloth by performing every operation from the original carding and spinning to the final retail sale may decide to specialize on one operation, let us say the weaving itself. In so doing he may gain advantages in applying a more specialized skill to a larger volume of work, but he can get these advantages only if he is sure of his suppliers, the spinners, and of his outlets, the finishers, who must now become specialists too. Unless the whole chain of transactions can be maintained, so that the consumer gets his cloth in the end, every single specialization collapses. The volume of business may finally become great enough to provide a pay-off for a man whose specialization is the coordination of specialists—in the medieval cloth trade they called him a draper or clothier—and then we are at the threshold of modern society. We are also at the point where increased taxes on cloth may help pay off the king for his maintenance of the peace.

Of course I cannot go into all the details, nor are they the point. All of these innovations, whether political or economic, whether at the top of society or at the bottom, have the following characteristics. They require some form of capital to be attempted at all, for their payoffs are not immediate but deferred. And the capital must increasingly take the form of generalized reinforcers like money and social approval. But note that even the ability of a society to provide rewards of this sort depends on the previous accumulation of some little capital. Money is no use unless people are confident that it can be converted into goods, and a man who is worrying about where his next meal is coming from is unlikely to find social approval particularly rewarding.

The innovations are apt to require a longer chain of transactions before the ultimate reward is achieved—before, for instance, the customer gets his cloth—than did the systems that immediately preceded them. And the chain is more roundabout: if a man is to walk from one place to another he just starts straight out, but if he is to ride on a subway, someone has to build a steel mill first. The length and roundaboutness of the chain of transactions mean that the innovations link a larger number of people together than were linked hitherto: a customer once depended on a single weaver for his cloth; now he depends on a whole team of cloth-workers. But the innovations imply increased specialization, and as the number of people tied together increases, the richness of any particular tie is apt to decrease. After the Industrial Revolution people were apt to complain that the relationship between master and man had been impoverished, reduced to a mere cash nexus. The larger, finally, the number of persons concerned and the more complicated their interdependence, the less it is possible to leave their mutual adjustments to the rough and tumble of face-to-face contact. They must go by the rule, work by the book, which also means that institutional behavior tends to become impersonal. Although all recurrent behavior tends, sooner or later, to get described and consecrated in explicit norms, now the process is hastened. Indeed one of the institutional innovations without which the others cannot get very far must be an organization that specializes in the sanctioning of norms, that is, a legal system.

Except for a few recent economic historians who specialize in the study of economic development, scholars seldom, it seems to me, examine in detail the processes of institutional growth. Above all, they do not explain them. They tell us, for instance, that Henry II was the first king of England to send royal judges regularly on circuit throughout the country. They never ask what capital, social or economic, enabled him to undertake the innovation, what risks it ran, or what returns replaced the capital and allowed the institution to persist. But only answers to these questions would explain the most important developments in human history. After all, there are other entrepreneurs than economic ones, nor are the economic ones always the most important. Given the capital, every society tries institutional innovations. If they turn out to pay off—and a great deal of capital may be spent before they do—they persist. They may even replace the capital, and allow the society to go on to another innovation. But there must be a pay-off; it is never automatic and always problematical; and it may not continue. External circumstances may change; other parts of the social organization may fail and bring the institution down in their ruin; and the institution itself may exhaust the sources of its own reward—as when an advanced agriculture works out the soil available to it.

All history is there to remind us how precarious is the process of civilization. The decline of the Roman Empire is there to remind us of it, for the first large-scale experiment in Western civilization. But even the recovery of the West from the Roman collapse has been far from uninterrupted. Feudalism in northwestern Europe was in trouble from the beginning; indeed it could never have corresponded in the least to what doctrine said it ought to be, had it not been supported by sources outside itself: by national loyalties transcending the feudal tie and by a kingship that only just managed to remain something more than the top rung on the feudal ladder. The expansion of the twelfth and thirteenth centuries was followed by the stagnation of the fourteenth, as if the very success of medieval institutions in eliciting some kinds of reward had used

up the supply available. And in the sixteenth century English industry made tentative approaches to factory organization, which could not be maintained in the face of a market collapse and which were not revived until the eighteenth, when the application of steam power gave factory organization a pay-off that no other form of industrial production could match. The same refrain repeats itself over and over: institutions do not keep going just because they are enshrined in norms, and it seems extraordinary that anyone should ever talk as if they did. They keep going because they have pay-offs, ultimately pay-offs for individuals. Nor is society a perpetual-motion machine, supplying its own fuel. It cannot keep itself going by planting in the young a desire for those goods and only those goods that it happens to be in shape to provide. It must provide goods that men find rewarding not simply because they are sharers in a particular culture but because they are men.

THE PERSISTENCE OF ELEMENTARY SOCIAL BEHAVIOR

As the institutions of civilization depart further and further from elementary social behavior, the latter does not disappear in proportion. Far from it, it persists obviously and everywhere, ready to take its revenge. It may persist in its most elaborate form in areas where institutional arrangements have broken down and left gaps. I have argued that street gangs show an elaboration of informal pattern not unworthy to rank with that of a primitive hunting band. If street gangs included girls and allowed marriage the resemblance would be even closer. And the characteristics of elementary social behavior reassert themselves the more fully the further the institutional breakdown goes, in disaster, revolution, or defeat in war.

But I am not much interested in the elementary social behavior that lies outside the institutional system, as the street gang does. Much more important is the behavior that lies within the system. It sprouts in the "grapevine"; it is as well developed in the personal loyalties of some executives and political leaders as it is in the group of workers who will not let the exuberant production of one of their number show up the deficiencies of the rest. It appears in the invention of, and concern for, outward and visible signs of rank and status never warranted by the formal organization itself. Sometimes the activities exchanged in elementary social behavior get their value from the rules of the institution. Thus the help people exchanged for esteem in the Federal agency I have described so often would have had no value if the men concerned had not been employed at a certain kind of organized work. But though the institution gave value to the help, the process of exchange itself remained just as elementary, just as subinstitutional, as anything seen in a street gang. Elementary social behavior does not grow just in the gaps between institutions; it clings to institutions as to a trellis. It grows everywhere—if only because the norms established as institutions and the orders given in instituted organizations can never prescribe human behavior to the last detail, even if they were obeyed to the letter, which they are not. Indeed the elementary behavior helps explain how and why they are disobeyed.

We should not look on the subinstitutional as necessarily a kind of friction holding the institutional back, to be gotten rid of only to the advantage of the latter. On the contrary, the motives characteristic of elementary social behavior often mobilize solid support behind institutional aims. An obvious example is the way in which the soldiers' determination not to let their comrades down contributes more than anything else to the fighting power of an infantry outfit. Of course this is an instance of the phenomenon I started this chapter with—how institutions are maintained by other rewards than the one each is primarily set to achieve. Infantry combat is meant to defeat the enemy; this is undoubtedly a reward, though often one long in coming, but effective combat may also be rewarded, and more immediately, by the approval of your fellow soldiers whom you have covered as they have you. And sometimes elementary social behavior manages to support an institution in the institution's spite. The help exchanged in the Federal agency may well have made the work of the agency more effective than it would have been otherwise—but it was exchanged only by disregarding an official rule against helping.

THE CONFLICT OF THE INSTITUTIONAL AND THE SUBINSTITUTIONAL

Elementary social behavior, then, is not driven out by institutionalization but survives alongside it, acquiring new reasons for existence from it. Sometimes it contributes to the support of the institution. But sometimes, as we also know, the two work against each other. Since the relatively bad situations are the ones we are most interested in, because we might want to do something about them, I shall spend the rest of my time on the conditions in which the two are at odds.

Consider then a working group in an American office or factory—a group like those we have studied so often in this book. Exchange—it has been our main theme—is the basis, acknowledged or unacknowledged, of much human behavior, and each member of the group has obviously entered into exchange with the company. But the exchange as institutionalized, as subject to explicit rules, is a limited exchange: each member has agreed, in return for a money wage, to contribute his labor as directed by the company. To be sure he may get many rewards from his labor besides money: a pleasant place to work, a job that ranks high in the community, and sometimes interesting work to do. But the most fully institutionalized aspect of the exchange is that of labor for money: the company is not legally bound, as part of its bargain, to provide the other things. Industrialization has specialized exchanges. As it has advanced, it has ceased to recognize many of the sorts of things that entered into the exchange between superior and subordinate at a time when society had moved less far away from elementary social behavior. No transaction engages as much of the man as it used to.

What happens, we may then ask, to the behavior that has been simplified and rationalized away, that goes unrecognized institutionally? Has it really disappeared, or has it only been swept under the rug? As the worker gets down to his job in his department, he encounters many activities in his fellow workers that reward or punish him, and he learns activities that reward or punish his fellow workers. Though their nature may depend on arrangements made by the firm, they are treated as institutionally irrelevant to the exchange of labor for money. Thus the ledger clerks in the Eastern Utilities Co. found that their job was more skilled and more responsible than that of the cash posters, but it got the same pay and was allowed less autonomy. By the standards of elementary social behavior, justice had not been done them, and their status was threatened in consequence. But none of this was institutionally relevant to the bargain between them and the company.

I do not mean in the least to imply that the management of the Eastern Utilities Co. was unconcerned with justice. Just as much as the union did, it believed in

"a fair day's work for a fair day's wage," though the two might have disagreed about the exact value either term of the equation should take. But the notion of fair exchange, so far as it was institutionalized, took little into account besides work and money, and treated as outside its scope many of the aspects of justice that elementary social behavior in fact brings up. This may easily be seen in the replies the supervisors made when the ledger clerks complained. In effect they pointed out that the clerks had made a bargain to do what they were told in the way of work, in return for a fair wage. So long as management stuck to its part of the bargain, what call did the clerks have to ask for more than theirs? Institutionalization makes more complex the chains of transactions between men, but achieves it at the price of simplifying any one link. Elementary social behavior may compensate for the simplification, as it does at times in military units, but it may also find the simplification intolerable, as it did here. The ledger clerks expected the company to maintain justice in general and not justice in particular. Incorrigibly, and against the whole tendency of human history, they expected the management to behave like men, and not like actors playing an institutionalized role. Thank God they did; but at points like this elementary social behavior begins to break in on institutionalization and, instead of supporting it, does it damage. This is only one example of the way the two can fall at odds.

Let us recognize that the ledger clerks and others like them might not have found their status so threatened or trying to do something to improve it so rewarding had they not already enjoyed other sorts of reward in relative abundance. There is a hierarchy of values, and not till the lower ones have been met do the higher ones attract: it is a rich man who can afford to worry about his status. Only in a few places like America are wages so high that workers can begin to interest themselves in the finer points of distributive justice; and this has consequences for both management and organized labor. Business has been so successful in providing money that other values have risen in relative importance; its old assumption, child of past penury, that money would be enough to enlist the full energy of labor no longer works quite as well as it did, and business cannot make it work at all without creating a demand for new products to be bought with money. As for organized labor, the more successful it is in getting the general level of wages raised, the more likely it is to undermine its own unity; for then workers can begin to interest themselves not just in the absolute amount of wages but in wage differentials, and wage differentials are obviously apt to set one group of workers against another. A working class is perhaps most unified when its members have gotten enough above mere subsistence so that the bosses cannot buy them off one by one—they can wait out a strike together—but not so far above that wage differentials rise in value relative to the general level of wages. The nineteenth century reformers, by the way, must have founded their demand for universal suffrage on the assumption, which was true then, that the poorest class was also the largest: if all these people got the vote, they would be able to get their other deserts. But now that the curve of income distribution has changed in shape, and so many families have moved up that the middle-income levels have become the largest, we Americans may be able to oppress the poor by perfectly democratic methods: the poor have got the vote but they no longer have the votes. What I am suggesting here is that the very success of the specialized exchange of money for wages is one of the conditions that allows subinstitutional behavior to break in on

the institutional. We are at last rich enough to indulge our full humanity.

But let me get back to the office. The ledger clerks complained to their supervisor of the injustice of their position over against the cash posters, expecting him to take the matter up with the officer above him in the managerial pyramid. When he did little or nothing, they added his behavior to their complaints: "He doesn't stand up for us." They were expecting from him the sort of action that would have indeed been natural in an informal leader: in return for the loyalty they would have given him, an informal leader would certainly have represented their interests against any outside party. Once more the assumptions of subinstitutional were coming up against those of institutional behavior: as the ledger clerks had demanded a less specialized justice from their company, so now they asked for a less specialized leadership. They were asking again for a man and not a supervisor. But how could their supervisor stand up for them? He too was trapped by the institutional rules. He might report to higher authority the disaffection of the ledger clerks, but he had no further power to do anything about it. Institutionally speaking, he too was paid to do as he was told. To do anything effective he might have had to use with higher authority his own informal ties rather than his formal ones.

At this point the story of the ledger clerks ends. Although they were thinking of going to the union and asking it to take the matter up, they had not in fact done so. Nor is their case particularly striking in itself: I use it only to illustrate what I believe to be a large class of cases. Suppose that the office were not unionized and that many groups were nursing grievances—not only grievances about the actual amount of wages, that is, about a matter the institutional bargain did take cognizance of, but also grievances, like the ledger clerks', about matters it did not. Certainly these groups would approach their supervisors first; when they found that many of the supervisors could not effectively stand up for them, they would cast about for something else to do. Many of the groups would have developed informal leadership, and if the complaint were at all deeply felt, the leaders, as a condition of keeping their positions, would have to try to bring the complaints home to the management. The first thing you know they would have gotten together and organized a strike; and if their followers had enough of what I have called social capital, material and nonmaterial, to keep the strike up, they would have forced the company to accept a union—collective bargaining, grievance procedure, and all. Some such event is often the origin of unionization in a plant.

Note what has happened: subinstitutional has come into conflict with institutional behavior. The result is not a collapse of the old institution and a return to the elementary, but the founding of a new institution, the union, of a peculiar sort—an institution designed to maintain subinstitutional values: to make the company take a less specialized view of justice—for the grievance procedure in some degree does this—and to recapture for the workers some control over their environment by giving them more effective representation than either their supervisors or their informal leaders could have done. Of course the new institution, once formed, may in time run into the same trouble with elementary social behavior as the old one did earlier.

I suspect that many of our institutions have the same kind of origin. Indeed in an earlier book I claimed this of the complex of institutions we call democracy.[5] In informal groups it is hard for government *not* to be carried on with the consent of the governed. Democracy aims at re-establishing this elementary value in a much more complicated institutional setting. It is an institution designed to make good the human deficiencies of other institutions.

The invention of new institutions is not the only way of coping with the conflict between subinstitutional and institutional behavior. The conflict may be resolved, and resolved for long periods of time, by "good administration"—the sort of thing the ledger clerks would have enjoyed if their supervisor had managed to bring their complaints home to his own boss, and he in turn had begun to consider what adjustments he might make. Good administration is intelligent behavior within a more or less unchanging institutional framework, and it can compensate for many defects in the latter. If it were not so, we should not see so many autocracies and tyrannies so successful for so long—and successful even apart from their use of terror in governing their subjects.

But the problem need not be solved at all, temporarily or permanently. The society may tear itself apart in conflict without ever creating a new institution that will stick. Still more often the problem may simply persist without issuing in overt conflict but without resolution either. New forms of behavior that might have proved rewarding enough to establish themselves are not invented; or no one is able to risk the social capital to try them out. The result is a society of people to some extent apathetic, of institutions to some extent "frozen" in an unnatural equilibrium—unnatural in the sense that out of the elements lying around here and there something better might conceivably have been made.

Something of this sort seems to some of us to have happened to American industry even with the unions.[6] The original institutional compact, of money for obedience to orders, has not encouraged management to turn the worker

into a slave of a machine—as the human-
ists would have it—but to turn him into
the machine itself, into something, that is,
which has the admirable property that if
you will only feed it the right materials
and power it will do just what you want
it to, no more no less. If you will only
feed the worker money, you should get
out of him just exactly what you want.
When you do not get it, and since
elementary social behavior is always
breaking in you never do, you never
conclude that your theory is inadequate
but only that you have not applied it
rigorously enough. You redesign the
controls on the machine so that now—
you hope—it simply cannot get off the
track. For this purpose the assembly line,
where manpower is machine-paced, is
the best thing yet devised. But it is so
unnatural that you must feed your human
machines still more money to get them
to work on it at all. And the more money
they get the more valuable to them
relatively becomes the elementary social
behavior you have done your best to
eliminate. The worker is left so apathetic,
so many activities in his repertory have
gone unrewarded, that management
seems justified in its thinking that he is
incapable of independent responsibility
and that he can only be treated as a
machine fueled up with money and
made to run on a track. And so the wheel
comes full circle.

What industry often lacks is what we
have seen to be characteristic of strong
and lively institutions: not one motive
alone but a wide variety of motives
held by the men whose activities the
institution coordinates is enlisted in
support of its aims and not left to work
against them or at best at cross-purposes.
Industry might consider joining the
forces it has so far shown itself unable to
lick. As usual, this is easier said than done.

Of course you are at liberty to take a
moral stand and approve the present
situation, though for reasons opposite to
the ones an industrialist might bring up.
You can argue that workers ought not
support the purposes of management,
which cannot help being utterly at odds
with their own. They ought to stick to
the original narrow bargain and make
it work for their interests. They ought to
get as much money, for doing as little
work, as they can. They will not behave
quite the way you think they ought to,
but the price a man pays for having high
moral standards is seldom seeing them
realized. And at least your moral stand
will allow you to disregard the immediate
problem: for all practical purposes you
will be just as conservative as the most
hardboiled businessman. But the general
problem you will have a harder time
disregarding. Sooner or later, in this
society or another, you will find an
institution whose purposes you approve
of, and then you will have to consider
how the many motives of many men
can be brought to support it.

The trouble with civilized men is that
they cannot live with the institutions
they have themselves invented. In rewarding some kinds of social behavior
better than savage society could ever
have done, the new institutions drive
other behavior underground. But it does
not stay there forever. Sometimes the
very success of the institutions gives an
opening to behavior that men could little
afford to indulge in while they were still
on the make. If a poor society must be
human because it has nothing else, and a
rich society can be human because it has
everything else, we moderns are *nouveaux
riches* trying to acquire aristocratic
tastes. Sometimes the great rebellions
and revolutions, cracking the institutional crust, bring out elementary social
behavior hot and straight from the
fissures. They always appeal, for instance, to the simplest principles of
distributive justice: When Adam delved
and Eve span, who was then the gentle-
man? To call them simple is not, of

course, to call them bad: the question of value comes later. For the institutions the rebels invent in the endeavour to realize justice on earth are just as apt to sacrifice something human as the institutions that preceded them: they come corrupted by the very anger that gave them birth. And then men wonder whether the struggle was worth its cost that left them still facing their old problem: how to reconcile their social institutions with their social nature. Yet men have invented one peculiar institution that may just conceivably help them get out of their rat race. To call it science is almost as embarrassing as calling your wife Mrs. Smith: the name is too formal for the bedroom. If men are to feel at home in the world of their making, they will come to understand better what it is their institutions are to be reconciled with—and "better" means in just those ways science has committed itself to. This is the only reason for studying the familiar chaos that is elementary social behavior—except, of course, the sheer pleasure of the thing.

NOTES

1. See G. C. Homans and D. M. Schneider, *Marriage, Authority, and Final Causes* (Glencoe, Ill., 1955).

2. For an opposing view see D. F. Aberle, A. K. Cohen, A. K. Davis, M. F. Levy, Jr., and F. X. Sutton, "The Functional Prerequisites of a Society," *Ethics*, Vol. 60 (1950), pp. 100–111.

3. C. Lévi-Strauss, *Tristes Tropiques* (Paris, 1955), p. 339.

4. P. Cornelius Tacitus, *Germania*.

5. G. C. Homans, *The Human Group* (New York, 1950), pp. 464–466.

6. See A. Zaleznik, C. R. Christensen, and F. J. Roethlisberger, *The Motivation, Productivity, and Satisfaction of Workers* (Boston, 1958), pp. 394–411.

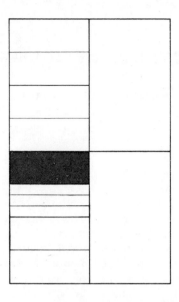

5. TECHNOLOGISM

The technologistic viewpoint typically defines the social in terms of objective behavior relations and seeks to explain it by referring to phenomena that are socially generated through technologically augmented characteristics of the participants' environments. Both William F. Ogburn and Fred Cottrell illustrate this viewpoint, but there is a secondary difference between them: Ogburn stresses cultural lag, while Cottrell stresses technological lead. More precisely, Ogburn notes that the development of "adaptive culture" (i.e., nontechnological social phenomena) lags behind technology and can thereby produce "social maladjustment," while Cottrell notes that the development of technology precedes the development of other social phenomena and thus facilitates the latter. It is as though the pessimistic rider in a horse-drawn carriage were to notice that his progress is less than the maximum because of the carriage's resistance to the horse's pull, while the optimistic rider notices that his progress is more than the minimum because of the horse's greater pull than the carriage's resistance.

THE HYPOTHESIS OF CULTURAL LAG

That this is an age of change is an expression frequently heard to-day. Never before in the history of mankind have so many and so frequent changes occurred. These changes, it should be observed, are in the cultural conditions. The climate is changing no more rapidly, and the geological processes affecting land and water distribution and altitude are going on with their usual slowness. Nor apparently is the biological nature of man undergoing more rapid changes than formerly. We know that biological man changes through mutations which occur very rarely indeed and we have no biological evidence to show and little reason to think that mutations in mental or physical man are occurring more frequently now than in the past. These changes that we see taking place all about us are in that great cultural accumulation which is man's social heritage. It has already been shown that these cultural changes were in early times rather infrequent, but that in modern times they have been occurring faster and faster until to-day mankind is almost bewildered in his effort to keep adjusted to these ever-increasing social changes. This rapidity of social change may be due to the increase in inventions which in turn is made possible by the accumulative nature of material culture. These conclusions follow from the preceding analyses.

I. THE HYPOTHESIS OF CULTURAL LAG

This rapidity of change in modern times raises the very important question of social adjustment. Problems of social adjustment are of two sorts. One concerns the adaptation of man to culture or perhaps preferably the adapting of culture to man. This subject is considered in Part V. The other problem is the question of adjustments, occasioned as a result of these rapid social changes, between the different parts of culture, which no doubt means ultimately the adaptation of culture to man. This second problem of adjustment between the different parts of culture is the immediate subject of our inquiry.

The thesis is that the various parts of modern culture are not changing at the same rate, some parts are changing much more rapidly than others; and that since there is a correlation and interdependence of parts, a rapid change in one part of our culture requires readjustments through other changes in the various correlated parts of culture. For instance, industry and education are correlated, hence a change in industry makes adjustments necessary through changes in the educational system. Industry and education are two variables, and if the change in industry occurs first and the adjustment through education follows, industry may be referred to as the independent variable and education as the dependent variable. Where one part of culture changes first, through some discovery or invention, and occasions changes in some part of culture dependent upon it, there frequently is a delay in the changes occasioned in the dependent part of culture. The extent of this lag will vary according to the nature of the cultural material, but may exist for a considerable number of years, during which time there may be said to be a maladjustment. It is desirable to reduce the period of maladjustment, to make the cultural adjustments as quickly as possible.

The foregoing account sets forth a problem that occurs when there is a rapid change in a culture of interdependent parts and when the rates of change in the parts are unequal. The discussion will be presented according to the following outlines. First the hypothesis will be presented, then examined and tested by a rather full consideration of the facts of a single instance, to be followed by several illustrations. Next the nature and cause of the phenomenon of cultural maladjustment in general will be analyzed. The extent of such cultural lags will be estimated, and finally the significance for society will be set forth.

A first simple statement of the hypothesis we wish to investigate now follows. A large part of our environment consists of the material conditions of life and a large part of our social heritage is our material culture. These material things consist of houses, factories, machines, raw materials, manufactured products, foodstuffs and other material objects. In using these material things we employ certain methods. Some of these methods are as simple as the technique of handling a tool. But a good many of the ways of using the material objects of culture involve rather larger usages and adjustments, such as customs, beliefs, philosophies, laws, governments. One important function of government, for instance, is the adjustment of the population to the material conditions of life, although there are other governmental functions. Sumner has called many of

these processes of adjustments, mores. The cultural adjustments to material conditions, however, include a larger body of processes than the mores; certainly they include the folk ways and social institutions. These ways of adjustment may be called, for purposes of this particular analysis, the adaptive culture. The adaptive culture is therefore that portion of the non-material culture which is adjusted or adapted to the material conditions. Some parts of the non-material culture are thoroughly adaptive culture such as certain rules involved in handling technical appliances, and some parts are only indirectly or partially so, as for instance, religion. The family makes some adjustments to fit changed material conditions, while some of its functions remain constant. The family, therefore, under the terminology used here is a part of the non-material culture that is only partly adaptive. When the material conditions change, changes are occasioned in the adaptive culture. But these changes in the adaptive culture do not synchronize exactly with the change in the material culture. There is a lag which may last for varying lengths of time, sometimes indeed, for many years.

An illustration will serve to make the hypothesis more clearly understood. One class of material objects to which we adjust ourselves is the forests. The material conditions of forestry have changed a good deal in the United States during the past century. At one time the forests were quite plentiful for the needs of the small population. There was plenty of wood easily accessible for fuel, building and manufacture. The forests were sufficiently extensive to prevent in many large areas the washing of the soil, and the streams were clear. In fact, at one time the forests seemed to be too plentiful, from the point of view of the needs of the people. Food and agricultural products were at one time the first need of the people and the clearing of land of trees and stumps was a common undertaking of the community in the days of the early settlers. In some places, the quickest procedure was to kill and burn the trees and plant between the stumps. When the material conditions were like these, the method of adjustment to the forests was characterized by a policy which has been called exploitation. Exploitation in regard to the forests was indeed a part of the mores of the time, and describes a part of the adaptive culture in relation to forests.

As time went on, however, the population grew, manufacturing became highly developed, and the need for forests increased. But the forests were being destroyed. This was particularly true in the Appalachian, Great Lakes and Gulf regions. The policy of exploitation continued. Then rather suddenly it began to be realized in certain centres of thought that if the policy of cutting timber continued at the same rate and in the same manner the forests would in a short time be gone and very soon indeed they would be inadequate to supply the needs of the population. It was realized that the custom in regard to using the forests must be changed and a policy of conservation was advocated. The new policy of conservation means not only a restriction in the amount of cutting down of trees, but it means a more scientific method of cutting, and also reforestation. Forests may be cut in such a way, by selecting trees according to their size, age and location, as to yield a large quantity of timber and yet not diminish the forest area. Also by the proper distribution of cutting plots in a particular area, the cutting can be so timed that by the time the last plot is cut the young trees on the plot first cut will be grown. Some areas when cut leave a land which is well adapted to farming, whereas such sections as mountainous regions when denuded of forests are poorly suited to agriculture. There of course are many

other methods of conservation of forests. The science of forestry is, indeed, fairly highly developed in principle, though not in practice in the United States. A new adaptive culture, one of conservation, is therefore suited to the changed material conditions.

That the conservation of forests in the United States should have been begun earlier is quite generally admitted. We may say, therefore, that the old policy of exploitation has hung over longer than it should before the institution of the new policy. In other words, the material conditions in regard to our forests have changed but the old customs of the use of forests which once fitted the material conditions very well have hung over into a period of changed conditions. These old customs are not only not satisfactorily adapted, but are really socially harmful. These customs of course have a utility, since they meet certain human needs; but methods of greater utility are needed. There seems to be a lag in the mores in regard to forestry after the material conditions have changed. Or translated into the general terms of the previous analysis, the material conditions have changed first; and there has been a lag in the adaptive culture, that is, that culture which is adapted to forests. The material conditions changed before the adaptive culture was changed to fit the new material conditions. This situation may be illustrated by Figure 1. Line 1 represents the material conditions, in regard to forests in the United States. Line 2 represents the adaptive culture,

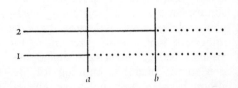

FIGURE 1

the policy of using the forests. The continuous lines represent the plentiful forests, with the sparse population and the mores of exploitation, the dotted lines, the new conditions of forests which are small in relation to the population and the new policy of conservation. The space between *a* and *b* represents the period when the old adaptive culture or mores exists with the changed material conditions, and is a period of maladjustment.

It is difficult to locate exactly the points *a* and *b*. Consider first the location of point *b*, or the time of the change from the policy of exploitation to the policy of conservation. The policy of conservation of forests certainly did not begin prior to 1904, when the first National Conservation Congress met. It was during Roosevelt's administration that many active steps in the direction of conservation were taken. Large areas of national forest lands were withdrawn from public entry. Gifford Pinchot was very active in spreading the gospel of conservation, and the House of Governors called by President Roosevelt was in large measure concerned with programmes of conservation. About this time many books and articles in magazines and periodicals were written on the subject. The conservation movement can hardly be said to have started in any extensive manner before this time. It is true that, earlier, papers had been read on the subject before scientific societies and there had been some teaching of scientific forestry, but prior to this time the idea of forest conservation was little known and the movement was certainly not extensive. Nor had the government taken any significant steps in a genuine policy of conservation. Indeed it might be argued with some success that we have not yet adopted fully a policy of conservation. For a great many of the private holdings are still exploited in very much the same old way. Reforestation is still largely a matter of theory in the United States. It is true that the government has taken a number of steps to preserve the forests but the conservationists are far from being satisfied with the progress of the movement to date. Certainly we have not attained the high mark maintained in western Europe.

It is also difficult to locate point *a*, that is, to determine when we should have started the conservation movement. Some features of conservation probably should have been instituted perhaps early in the last century. Thus the allotment of permanent forest areas might very well have been done coincidently with the extension of our domain; and the destruction of forests on land little suited to agriculture might have been prevented as the population spread to these new regions. At the time of the Civil War the population had become quite large, and shortly afterward the era of railroad-building set in followed by a great development of industry, insuring large population and concentration. It was at this time that the wonderful forests of the Great Lakes region were cut down, and the cuttings in the Appalachian regions increased greatly. Some close observers saw at that time what development of population and industry would take place, but the relation of the forests to such a condition was not appreciated. If scientific forestry had been applied then, many of the unnecessarily wasted forests would still exist and now be furnishing lumber. There would not have been such a washing of soil and the danger of floods would have been less. While some methods of forest conservation might have been applied to advantage shortly after colonial days, the proper time for more extensive developments of conservation was probably in the era following the Civil War. The population was becoming large; the west was being settled; the Pacific coast had been reached; the territorial boundaries had been fixed; industries, railroads, factories, corporations, trusts were all growing with rapidity. The east was in greater need of conservation of forests than the Pacific Northwest or Alaska; nevertheless very probably for the whole country, though its stages of development were unequal, an extensive conservation movement should have been instituted about the middle of the last half of the nineteenth century. It would seem, therefore, that there has been a lag of at least a quarter of a century in changing our forestry policy.

The foregoing discussion of forestry illustrates the hypothesis which it is proposed to discuss. It is desirable to state more clearly and fully the points involved in the analysis. The first point concerns the degree of adjustment or correlation between the material conditions and the adaptive non-material culture. The degree of this adjustment may be only more or less perfect or satisfactory; but we do adjust ourselves to the material conditions through some form of culture; that is, we live, we get along, through this adjustment. The particular culture which is adjusted to the material conditions may be very complex, and, indeed, quite a number of widely different parts of culture may be adjusted to a fairly homogeneous material condition. Of a particular cultural form, such as the family or government, relationship to a particular material culture is only one of its purposes or functions. Not all functions of family organization, as, for instance, the affectional function, are primarily adaptive to material conditions.

Another point to observe is that the changes in the material culture precede changes in the adaptive culture. This statement is not in the form of a universal dictum. Conceivably, forms of adaptation might be worked out prior to a change in the material situation and the adaptation might be applied practically at the same time as the change in the material conditions. But such a situation presumes a very high degree of planning, prediction and control. The collection of data, it is thought, will show that at the present time there are a very large number of cases where the material conditions change and the changes in the adaptive culture follow later. There are certain general theoretical reasons why this is so; but it is not desirable to discuss these until later. For the present, the analysis will only concern those cases where changes in the adaptive culture do not precede changes in the material culture. Furthermore, it is not implied that changes may not occur in non-material culture while the material culture remains the same. Art or education, for instance, may undergo many changes with a constant material culture.

Still another point in the analysis is that the old, unchanged, adaptive culture is not adjusted to the new, changed, material conditions. It may be true that the old adaptive culture is never wholly unadjusted to the new conditions. There may be some degree of adjustment. But the thesis is that the unchanged adaptive culture was more harmoniously related to the old than to the new material conditions and that a new adaptive culture will be better suited to the new material conditions than was the old adaptive culture. Adjustment is therefore a relative term, and perhaps only in a few cases would there be a situation which might be called perfect adjustment or perfect lack of adjustment.

ORGANIC ENERGY AND THE
LOW-ENERGY SOCIETY

FRED COTTRELL

With only insignificant exceptions, such as the limited amount of energy available on earth from lunar gravitation and from cosmic rays, the energy that is available to man has come, or currently comes, from the sun. Uranium and other possible sources of atomic energy were created as the gases from which the earth was derived combined to form solids. Coal and oil, peat and gas are accumulations stored in the earth's crust from past operations of plant and animal life that have converted the radiant energy of the sun into energy-laden substances. We shall treat these resources as if they were of a different type from those that make use of the recurring presence of the sun. While they represent only a tiny accretion as compared with their original source, they currently provide man with his major sources of energy. This is primarily due to the fact that one of the still unsolved problems of science is how to take full advantage of the sun's energy.

It is obvious that it is not lack of a source of energy which limits man's activities. The amount of sunlight falling upon the earth's surface is so great that it is almost incomprehensible.[1] An acre receives about 20 million Calories per day, and the amount of solar heat that falls on only 1½ square miles in a day is equivalent to that generated by an atom bomb such as that used at Hiroshima. Thus the amount of radiant energy is so far in excess of man's present ability to

convert it that it cannot be considered to limit human behavior. Energy-imposed limits stem from the particular means by which energy is converted into the particular forms desired by man at a particular time and place.

PLANTS AS CONVERTERS

Man has learned to convert radiant energy into other forms in only tiny amounts at a relatively high cost.[2] He has depended upon the action of plants to make the original synthesis and has proceeded from there to convert the resultant energy for his own purposes. His simplest method has been to eat plants, thus making some of their energy available to him. This system requires only a knowledge of what is edible. The converters automatically divert energy in sufficient quantities to ensure their own reproduction. This plant-man system is the prototype of all the systems of converters man uses; however, since man very early undoubtedly also ate animals, the plant-animal-man system is not much newer.

Plants vary in their capacity to survive in various soils and climates, and we can through the study of plant and animal ecology discover the limits within which the survival of various plants is possible. Plants also vary in their capacity to convert the energy of the sun into plant structure; Willcox[3] has shown that "the fixation of the calorific energy of the sun is variable with the species." The limits of the use of radiant energy by plants are fixed by the nature of photosynthesis itself.[4] It has been well established that only a small fraction of sunlight can ever be converted into other forms of energy by plant life. For example, it is estimated that only about $3\frac{1}{3}$ per cent of the sunlight falling on the United States as a whole could be so converted. As a matter of fact, no crop grown in this country even approaches such a figure. Here corn is the crop that probably yields the largest heat-energy return, and a bumper corn crop returns only about 0.3 per cent of the radiant energy falling upon the land on which it is grown. This return includes the heat which can be obtained by using the cobs, stalks, and leaves as well as the edible kernels. Such a return is exceptional. "Corn belt" corn is the product of extremely favorable geographic conditions, aided by scientific agriculture. In areas where the land is poorer and farming practices are less efficient the returns are very much smaller.

The amount of energy each plant can convert is specific to that plant. Willcox[5] gives the simple formula worked out by acrobiologic science for ascertaining what it is: "Divide 318 by the normal percentage nitrogen content of whatever agrotype is being considered; the quotient is the theoretical absolute maximum number of pounds of dry vegetable substance which that agrotype can yield on one acre of ground in one crop cycle." Now since a plant also consistently yields a given quantity of energy per pound of dry weight, it is possible to discover the limits that are self-imposed on a people who choose a given crop as their basic diet. Rice apparently comes closest to yielding the various food elements in the proportion required by the human body; but Indian corn, soya beans, millet, rye, and wheat have become the basic diet in some areas, as have potatoes, sweet potatoes, and other crops in other areas. The particular crop which would provide the largest energy return in a given area is not necessarily the one used there.

Factors other than energy efficiency affect the choice of foods made by man, and in a given instance the preference may be for a food that is less efficient than some other known and available food source. The total energy available to the people of a given area is thus determined by the inherent efficiency of the particular plant they have chosen to make their basic source of food.

Plants have in addition to their inherent efficiency another characteristic of great social significance. With few exceptions they are rooted in one place; thus the field in which a plant can act as a converter is the area which the plant itself occupies. Concentration of the energy which they produce involves the energy costs of harvesting them. Moreover, any mechanical energy which is derived from using them must involve another converter.

Where the only converters available consist of plants, animals used solely for food, and man, not only is man the controller and director of available energy, but his muscles provide all the mechanical energy he commands. And all operations which require the use of mechanical energy are limited to such as can be carried out by human beings.

Although man is a chemical-energy machine, his efficiency can be measured in terms of the heat value of the food he consumes as contrasted with the heat value of the mechanical energy he can deliver. Part of what a man consumes is utilized in such functions as respiration and the circulation of the blood. Part is given off as heat, and part is indigestible and leaves the body as waste product. Some energy is lost during sleep, and some is converted in the activity of the nervous system. So, as in the case of other engines, the total heat value of the fuel consumed can never be recovered in the form of mechanical energy. The average efficiency of the human being is about 20 per cent. This means that for each 100

Calories consumed as food the average man can deliver mechanical energy equivalent to 20 Calories of heat.

Physiologists are generally agreed that to maintain efficiency the average daily consumption of food should not be less than about 2,600 Calories per person per day. It is improbable that any population with a normal number of children and old people in it could consume more than 3,000 Calories per day per capita without producing excessive fat, which actually reduces the capacity to work. Three thousand Calories average intake and 20 per cent average efficiency provide mechanical energy equivalent to 600 Calories per person per day. This is a little less than one horsepower-hour (about 641.56 Calories).

No society keeps its members steadily employed at converting food into economically productive mechanical energy, and many societies have never supplied their members with as much as 3,000 Calories per day. Thus in many societies there is available considerably less than 1 horsepower-hour per day of mechanical energy per capita. Part of this mechanical energy must be used to produce or gather food. The remainder may be used for other pursuits. But no matter how little is used in procuring food the sum of the two cannot exceed the very modest total set by man's capacity as a mechanical-energy converter. Thus, regardless of the food supply, the difference per capita between the most and the least fortunate of societies, both using only men as mechanical energy converters, is not very great. The average consumption cannot fall very much below 2,000 Calories per day per person and, as we have seen, it cannot rise much above 3,000 Calories. So even taking the maximum difference in food consumption between the lowest and the highest to be as much as 1,000 Calories, at an efficiency of 20 per cent there is a difference in total mechanical energy available equivalent to about $\frac{1}{3}$

horsepower-hour per day per person. Nor is this fact significantly affected by the use of animals rather than, or in addition to, plants for food.

ANIMALS AS CONVERTERS

The differences between those who consume plants only and those who make use of animals as well as plants for food are probably significant rather for the pattern than for the limits of the field generated. Man usually adds meat to his diet if he can, and under some circumstances his chances for survival may be tremendously affected by his ability and willingness to provide himself with animal food. The chief significance of the use of animals lies in the fact that some edible animals can assimilate plants—and parts of plants, such as bark—which man cannot directly digest. Many of the grasses which are not directly consumable grow in areas where it is not possible for man unaided by other sources of energy to replace them with edible plants. Since sheep, goats, and cattle on the hoof can be driven over distances much greater than it is possible for a man to carry or drag the meat of their carcasses, man is able by following or driving livestock to consume the plant products of an area enormously more extensive than he could otherwise make use of. Similarly, man is able to live in climates where plants are not available the year round, partly by using the energy of plants stored in the form of animal products during the months when no plant food is available. Occasionally even carnivores are used to promote man's survival. The Plains Indians sometimes lived through a hard winter by eating the dogs which had shared their kill during the summer months.

The use of animals for food is subject to the limitation that the animals so used are in competition with men for plants. The number of plants in an area sets the limit on the food available both for man and for other animals. If man permits animals to eat plants which he otherwise might himself eat, or permits land to be used to raise plants for feed which could be used to raise plants for human food, he limits the number of men who can be fed from that land. Wheat, which is very widely used as a foodstuff, will serve as an illustration of this relationship. The amounts of energy made available to man through the use of wheat in the form of bread and in the form of animal products are shown in the table.

Since other feed crops can usually be grown more advantageously, wheat is only rarely raised to feed animals. However, other plants edible by human beings

100 lb. of Wheat Consumed as	Yield in Calories
Bread	120,000
Chicken	9,625
Eggs	30,000
Pork	38,700
Milk	25,230
Beef	11,500

exhibit the same pattern of loss as does wheat. Man gains through eating animals only a fraction of the energy contained in the plants eaten by those animals.

Nevertheless, in many areas people permit animals to survive even though this results in reducing the number of human beings who can live there. The case of the sacred cattle of India, which are permitted to eat food which would lengthen the life span of a large part of the population, is an example. Elsewhere animals are kept for the enjoyment of a particular class, as were the deer of the English forests. Sometimes, too, an inefficient use of animals is required by religious belief, as in the case of the Jews and the Mohammedans, who are prohibited from eating the flesh of swine, which happen to be more efficient converters of plants than are cattle. But

in certain large areas such as China, in some parts of Eastern Europe, and in Southeast Asia, men are unable to eat meat simply because the plants which animals might consume go directly to human consumption. In these areas a return to the consumption of meat could come about only with widespread reduction of the population or enormous increase in the available plant food supply, or both. In 1940 about 55 per cent of the world's population had a daily intake of 2,000 Calories or less; 30 per cent had 3,000 or more, and 15 per cent had about 2,500. The world average was about 2,400 Calories per day.[6] Asia, where the population presses most closely on the food supply, produces about 49 per cent of the plant foods but only about 16 per cent of the meat, dairy, and poultry products. With the world's population increasing steadily, it is unlikely that in most areas there will be any large general increase in the use of animals for food.

The domestication of *draft* animals greatly increases the *mechanical energy* available to those who possess them. There are many varieties of animals used for draft, and in order to be exact it would be necessary to calculate the costs and output of each kind. However, since the horse is so widely used it will serve to illustrate the energy gains to be made through the use of draft animals. As we have already indicated, Watt found that the horses in use in England in his day produced the energy equivalent to about $\frac{2}{3}$ horsepower, or about 6 horsepower-hours per 9-hour day. Morrison[7] says that a modern horse weighing 1,500 to 1,600 pounds can convert about 1 horsepower steadily for 10 hours a day, and that the average horse is about 20 to 25 per cent efficient. However, since horses in the United States today work only 800 to 1,000 hours a year, they deliver only 6 or 7 per cent of the heat value of their average annual food consumption. A man working 50 hours a week for 50 weeks a year delivers, then, only $\frac{1}{4}$ as much energy as a horse, but the heat energy consumed by the horse is 10 times as great as that consumed by the man. Compared strictly on the basis of energy, under these conditions man is $2\frac{1}{2}$ times as efficient as the horse.

The great value of the horse lies in the rate at which it is able to deliver energy. During a limited plowing season, for example, a man and a team can prepare a very much larger area for planting than can a man alone. Outside the tropics only a limited number of days can be spent in preparing the seedbed and planting. Crops require a minimum growing season, and the total planting time is the difference between the length of the growing season and the interval from the time when the ground can be worked to the time when frost sets in. Where the limit on the size of the crop that can be raised is found in the length of the period during which land can be prepared, the horse, by permitting a great increase in the amount of land plowed, may more than compensate for the days when it is idle.

It must not be forgotten, however, that the efficient use of draft animals takes place within distinct limits. In the first place, arable land is not always available in such quantities that plowing or harvesting is the limiting factor on the crop raised. Frequently the number of persons who have a right to share in the product of the land is great enough to make it possible for them to plant and harvest all the available land in the time permitted by the growing season. In such cases the net cost of using the horse would be greater than the increase in the energy returned. Furthermore, in many cases land that cannot be cultivated by the use of the horse exists interspersed with land fit for horse cultivation and land fit only for pasture. Where this is so, an economy that made use of the hoe could support a larger population than could an economy

that used only such land as could be cultivated by horses.

Because man's skill, intelligence, and dexterity enable him to do many things not possible to a horse, man can be employed many more hours of the year than the horse can. His efficiency rises proportionately. Thus those who control the method of cultivation may choose to rid themselves of horses in order to employ men. This might take place in an area dominated by the family as an economic unit because it would obligate family members to work for the food they had a right to share anyway. In a feudal or slave system the value of men as a source of military power and prestige or as contributors to the bodily comfort of the landlord or slaveowner often resulted in the displacement of horses by men. Where other values and social structures prevail, the relative efficiency of men as compared with draft animals in securing the desired results has determined the choice as to which would be permitted to survive.

One of the early evidences of population pressure is the reduction in the number of food animals, followed by the reduction of draft-and-food animals, such as cows and horses, in favor of those draft animals, such as the water buffalo, which can survive on the plant product of land which will not yield nearly as much energy in the form of humanly edible food. Thus many areas which once supported draft animals and food animals now make use of almost none. This tendency to regress has frequently been checked. The failure of a society to utilize its land in such a way that the land provides sufficient energy in the requisite form to maintain the population has often resulted in the society's being overrun by outsiders. If a society uses its land in such a way that it passes the point of diminishing energy returns, it may be conquered by a neighbor with greater surplus, who then may ruthlessly restore that land-to-population ratio which will yield maximum surplus. Feudal landlords who permitted the population to grow to the point where they had no horses were often defeated in battle by their horse-riding neighbors. The exploits in India and China of such horse-riding herders as Genghis Khan give evidence of some of the dangers of overpopulation.

The difference between the maximum and minimum mechanical-energy surplus available to those using only plant and animal converters is by modern standards very small. But in the absence of other energy sources these differences have been very significant.

Today all but the more primitive societies supplement plants and animals with other sources of energy; and it is therefore necessary to turn to the data on such primitive societies provided by anthropologists, archaeologists, and historians to ascertain the relation between plant and animal use and social life. These data have not, however, been presented in terms of the analytical concepts used here, and ideally they should be re-examined in terms of these concepts. Practical considerations preclude our doing this, and what follows is based upon summaries of anthropological and other research into primitive peoples. The result is the use of analytical categories that are not entirely germane to the problems here under consideration, but no better alternative is at present available.

FOOD–GATHERING SOCIETIES

One method of classifying societies is that developed by Forde in his classic work *Habitat, Economy and Society*. He groups the societies he discusses in three categories: food gatherers, cultivators, and pastoral nomads. We have found it expedient to lump the two latter types under one heading, "food raisers." The data that Forde worked with were collected by men using various field categories that could conveniently be subsumed under his types. All the societies studied are primarily dependent upon the use of plants, men, and animals as converters. The differences that they exhibit give some evidence of the range of social relationships possible within the limits imposed by these energy sources; they also give evidence of the social consequences of even slight variations, by today's standards, in sources and amounts of available energy.

As Forde points out, food gatherers are for the most part without the accouterments of "civilized" man. The surplus energy gained under this system is very small on an annual basis, though it might temporarily be enormous during berry-picking time or the salmon run or after a buffalo hunt. The total energy annually available does not permit any great expansion of population, and thus food gatherers have frequently fallen victim to the more numerous and powerful food raisers. In point of fact, once domestication of plants and animals has developed, the food gatherer has tended to be driven away from the areas in which food raising was possible. As a result, he currently exists chiefly where food gathering actually yields a higher return from existing resources than would an available alternative land use. The precarious existence of such contemporary food gatherers as the Eskimo, the Athabascan hunter, and the Indians of the Orinoco suggests why food gatherers often fail to survive in the face of more effective systems of energy exploitation.

Since food rarely grows in such abundance that a group can long remain in one place, everything that food gatherers use must be transported. Their means of transportation are, characteristically, limited to human portage or sledge dogs. Consequently, tools must be simple and light in weight. Housing must either be improvised at many different sites or be very easily transportable. Clothing must be light and simple. No great energy can be devoted to the erection of shrines or otherwise expended in placating or worshiping the gods. The size of the social unit is necessarily small, for if any great number of people gather together, they soon exhaust the local supply of most of their energy sources and have to range far afield in the search for new sources. The resulting expenditure of time and energy in gathering and dispersing endangers rather than contributes to survival. At best the division of labor is limited, for almost everyone must spend a great deal of time and energy in the pursuit of food. Priests and other social functionaries who gather no food cannot contribute enough to food-gathering groups to offset the energy lost in supporting them. The kinship groups among food gatherers may carry on economic, political, and religious functions, but such small units are incapable of creating or transmitting any very large culture base; consequently tradition, law, and religion remain relatively simple,* providing only a limited number of controls for the guidance of the head of the household.

The Paiute of the American West provides an example of the social simplicity of the life of the food gatherer. He lived principally upon a few types of seeds, such as the pine nut and acorn, upon lizards and snakes, grasshoppers and grubs, and the rabbits and the rare deer which he could kill. To get the latter, as Forde[8] puts it, "the deer hunter usually went out alone with his dog. Finding his quarry, he then had to run it down relentlessly, perhaps for several days, until he could get close enough to shoot it; he would then have to carry it painfully home on his back." And we may

add that unless he was unusually lucky a good deal of the meat would spoil before it could be eaten. The Paiute clothed himself after a fashion in rabbit skins, piled up brush in a wickiup to shield himself from the storm, and usually died before he was twenty-five years old. Although he lived in an extremely adverse environment, which today does not support one person per square mile, he probably is more typical of the food gatherer than the romantic cares to admit. Bilby's account of the Eskimo in *Nanook of the North* describes another food-gathering people living under adverse conditions. The fact that Nanook, his chief informant and the central character of the book and the film, later died of starvation puts a fitting conclusion to the account.

The Horse and the Plains Indians

The Plains Indians, like some other food gatherers, lived in a more favorable environment. But because they had no draft animals they were unable to cultivate the land extensively and raise crops that could compete successfully with the buffalo grass. In those few areas where trees killed off the grass the Indian could in turn kill the trees and for a few years get a crop from the land so cleared. In most of the prairie such cultivation methods supported only small groups of food raisers. The chief source of energy was the buffalo, which was hunted afoot with the aid of the long bow and arrow. During the summer the Plains Indians gathered into large groups for the purpose of staging a drive in which the buffalo were driven to their deaths over a bluff or into a trap. Only thus could these Indians survive in groups larger than a few households. Continuous hunting would have disturbed the grazing herds; this would have meant continuous movement of the tribe, which in turn would have led to further disturbance of the

---

* Simple, that is, if the culture as a whole is compared with that of the large social units of urban society. Some single aspect, such as the kinship system itself, may be relatively complex, as in the case of the aborigines of Australia.

buffalo. Hence the social, economic, and political units had to be small. The physical accouterments of life were few, though more numerous than in the case of the Paiute. The "man of distinction" was the hunter. The ritual connected with coming of age was designed both to teach the arts, skills, and attitudes necessary for effective hunting and to glorify or even sanctify them.

This pattern was changed whenever these Indians captured and redomesticated the horses which had escaped from the early Spanish expeditions. The introduction of the horse into these cultures serves as an excellent illustration of the effects which the adoption of a new converter may have. It also shows how the existing culture limits the use to which a new converter will be put. Forde[9] says that "the introduction of the horse did not basically change the culture of the western Plains, but it widened the range of activities, greatly increased success in hunting and provided a wealth of food and leisure...." It was also a "form of personal property which gave impetus to a wide range of modifications." As he points out, "the horse gave the ascendancy to the western nomadic hunting peoples, and the cultivators were either driven out or abandoned their more settled life and more advanced culture for the rich rewards of buffalo hunting."

Mishkin[10] goes further to show how the introduction of the horse changed what was regarded as the ideal man from one having those qualities of stoicism, patience, and skill which had characterized the hunter afoot with the long bow to one with the qualities of the daredevil rider, wielding a lance to hamstring his kill or using the short bow from horseback. In time the skilled horse thief and warrior was elevated to a position equal if not superior to that of the hunter. The size of the effective social unit changed as the advantage of the large group for

protection in warfare more than offset any residual value which the small group originally had in hunting. Social organization became necessary to control these larger groups. Picked hunters frequently brought in game for the whole community. Unskilled, slow, or crippled heads of households were denied the right to hunt lest they endanger the source of food for the whole group. The relationship between responsibility for the family and ability to meet that responsibility was altered by social fiat. One squaw could not preserve all the meat or dress the hides of all the game killed by one horse-borne hunter. Since there was no change in the division of labor between the sexes, polygyny became the rule, and the accumulation of women, particularly by stealing, became a source of power and prestige.

Many of the pre-Columbian food-gathering tribes were confined to areas in which food raisers were unable to operate. As the Plains Indians acquired the horse, the energy available to them increased sufficiently to permit them to drive back the cultivators and thus extend their hunting grounds. The gain was, however, temporary. As the European settlers moved westward, bringing the harness and the plow, which enabled them to turn under the buffalo grass of the plains and replace it with crops that yielded a larger surplus, they relentlessly drove the food-gathering Indians from their ancestral homeland into less and less satisfactory areas. Here their culture was destroyed by their inability to get at the buffalo, whose energy had sustained it, and they survive today only as a colorful anachronism.

Most other food gatherers have met a like fate. Some have been able to maintain their existence by attaching themselves to agricultural regions, by gathering a product of desert, mountain, or forest to exchange for the products of a culture yielding more surplus energy.

Some exist on sufferance, in areas unfitted for incorporation into dominant civilizations, as do the Seminoles of Florida, the Eskimo and isolated tribes in Alaska, Canada, and Greenland, and various native peoples in Africa, Asia, and South America. While anthropologists have discovered enormous differences among food gatherers, they have also shown that they operate within the limits which have been discussed above. These limits differ in some degree from those which characterize societies that Forde classifies as food gatherers. An unsatisfactory aspect of Forde's classification is that the transition from one to another means of securing food is in fact gradual. Many food gatherers raised some food or at least returned annually to the same areas where it grew naturally. Some promoted the growth of the edible plants by cutting down or killing trees whose shade reduced their fruitfulness, or by pulling weeds; these were in a limited sense food raisers. But even though what Forde called the food gatherer may not exactly typify any actual society, the "type" may serve to summarize the characteristics of those societies which modally resemble it.

FOOD–RAISING SOCIETIES

Forde's classifications apply not only to primitive or prehistoric peoples but also to modern farmers. For present purposes the category "food raiser" has most analytical significance when it is restricted to those people who are or have been almost completely dependent upon cultivated plants and/or domesticated animals for energy and those who, primarily dependent upon such sources, have secured supplementary energy through hunting wild animals and occasionally using wind or water power. Even when so restricted, "food raiser" is sometimes less useful than terms based upon other distinctions. For example, it is probable that there are more significant differences

between people who are dependent primarily upon cereals grown on irrigated soil and nomadic herdsmen (who are also food raisers) than there are between those herdsmen and some of the hunters who occupy country where game is plentiful. Nevertheless, the significance of the domestication of plants and animals as contrasted with the use of these converters in the wild state is very great. Food raising represents an advance in the means regularly to provide and secure energy surpluses.

In his work *Social Evolution*, Childe takes the position that all civilizations derive from "the cultivation of the same cereals and the breeding of the same species of animals." Curwen has traced the use of some of the existing food plants back to very early man and has shown how the appearance of new plants causes new social relationships to emerge. We shall not here attempt either to review or to criticize the whole of the theories propounded, but the facts adduced will show both how greatly surplus can be increased through the introduction of a new plant and how greatly surplus can vary among food raisers who use the same plant.

Curwen[11] estimates that the yield in Norman England was only 6 bushels per acre from 2 bushels of seed, with a total production per person of only 15 bushels per year. On the other hand, Thurnwald[12] found that in ancient Sumeria the yield was 80 to 100 times the seed. The total amounted to "2,800 litres per hectare," or nearly 32 bushels per acre, which is not a bad yield by today's standards. It is apparent that such great variability in yield at least established great differences in the energy limits under which men lived, however they may have used the surpluses so established. The variations in environment to which cultivated plants are subjected are easily observable even in old and well–established agrarian societies. The yield from the same seed on various parts of the same field frequently varies greatly; between farmers, or more particularly between regions, there is even greater variation. The usual adverse factors take their toll in differing degrees: there may be a shortage of some of the nutrients required for optimum growth; during the growing season there may be either too little or too much total precipitation, or precipitation may come at the wrong time; there may be other organisms to contend with, both plant and animal; the very processes of cultivation may be such as to reduce rather than to increase yield. Recently it has been discovered that the presence or absence of tiny traces of such minerals as cobalt and copper result in huge differences in plant yield. Where low yields are a consequence of a deficiency in minerals, that fact can now be determined and corrected; but a people dependent solely upon the energy of plants and animals could never develop the scientific knowledge necessary for the correction of such soil deficiency.

It is evident, then, that the limits imposed by the nature of the plants rarely constitute the actual and effective limits confronting those who depend upon those plants for daily living. In the first place, the land available sets limits to the amount of plant life that can be developed, whatever the character of the plants used. That plant life, in turn, sets limits upon the size of the possible population. It is comparatively easy to show, for example, that when population increases much beyond 3 persons per acre the energy derivable from most plants will not provide the means to carry out the intensive cultivation and restorative fertilization which are the only methods by which so little land can be made to provide sufficient energy to ensure the survival of its cultivators. The highest average energy yields produced anywhere in the world are secured from the intense cultivation of rice by the Japanese. They produce about 2,200 pounds of rice per acre. This yields roughly 9,000 Calories per acre per day the year round. Thus, $\frac{1}{3}$ acre would yield an average of 3,000 Calories, about what an active 150-pound man requires the year round for an adequate diet. During the period of intense cultivation he will, of course, demand more than this, but he can conserve his strength at other times. The average return from rice in India is only 829 pounds (1931–1936 average) as compared with the 2,200-pound Japanese yield. Therefore, in India a reduction of the amount of land per person below $\frac{2}{3}$ acre reduces the energy available to a point below that necessary for survival. Soya beans or sugar beets produce more than this per acre under specified conditions, but they require supplementation by other crops and do not yield more than rice does when all the necessary factors are taken into account.

For a long time economists have been pointing to the law of diminishing returns, which sets an outer limit on the amount of food that can be produced in a given area. While they have sometimes confused the physical product of plant life with the "economic" value thereof, and have sometimes extended the meaning of the law to cover all the economic effects of limited land, no matter what its use, in essence the argument really stems from the facts to which we have just alluded. It is true that after a given point is reached a specific plant on a given piece of land will yield only so much plant product, no matter what increases in expenditure of labor or what additions to it in the form of nutrient are made. Moreover, as that limit is approached it is highly probable that a great deal of what is done is not what is required to permit the plant to reach its maximum output. Therefore, most of what is done will not yield a commensurate return or even any return whatsoever in increased energy to compensate for the energy expended. This is true even where soil is fertile and good management and plant science are used extensively. Where magic and religion and other practices interfere, the loss of energy is no doubt excessive.

In dealing with food raisers it is, therefore, necessary to distinguish between the total energy surplus which might be achieved under optimum food-raising conditions and what is actually secured under the existing conditions of man-land ratio, cultivation techniques, etc. These existing conditions can usually be improved only by the adoption of some new energy converter. The probability that a food-raising people will adopt a new converter seems to depend in considerable part upon their current ability to produce an energy surplus. In other words, the presence of an energy surplus is favorable to the adoption of a converter that will enlarge that surplus.

As Forde[13] indicates, "the range of economic and social variation among cultivators is greater than among food-gatherers, and this variability is not related in any simple way with the physical conditions." As will be shown, it is generally true that as the energy available to man increases, the variety of his activities increases. Where the energy available is only slightly in excess of that required for survival, any very great variation in behavior among those situated in any one place is impossible. Thus, whereas the variability of food raisers is very great as compared with that of food gatherers, it is small as compared with the variability of those who have larger energy surpluses. Food raising permits variability, but it also imposes limits which are reflected in some generally predictable results. Food raising decreases the time and energy spent securing food and thus permits men to do other things, but the mechanical energy available each day is still no greater than that of the human beings and the domesticated draft animals present. Food raising permits an increase in the number of persons who can be supported from a given piece of land and thus permits an increase in the surplus locally available. The increased surplus may be used in a variety of ways. It may be widely dispersed and result only in a general increase in leisure. (However, such dispersal may, and often does, lead to an increase in population, so that the land available per person is decreased to the point where each unit of land is supporting all the population that it can; when this point has been reached, there is no surplus.) The increased surplus may be used merely to increase the amount of waste. Or it may be concentrated, and the concentrated product, too, may be used in a variety of ways. It may be sacrificed to the gods. It may be buried in a tomb or destroyed at the death of a landlord or other ruler. It may be expended in the military conquest of areas which themselves yield lower surpluses. It may create a leisure class that is devoted to the cultivation of knowledge and the arts or that simply demands the continuous use of surplus in the creation of goods and services that are not productive of new arts, or knowledge, or new fixed structures. But there must be a surplus before it can be devoted to any such use.

SURPLUS AND CIVILIZATION

Civilization waited on the appearance of such energy surpluses. As Childe[14] says, civilization meant "the aggregation of large populations in cities; the differentiation within these of primary producers . . . , full-time specialist artizans, merchants, officials, priests, and rulers; an effective concentration of economic and political power; the use of conventional symbols for recording and transmitting information (writing), and equally conventional standards of weights and of measures of time and space leading to some mathematical and calendrical science." All of which are impossible except where surplus energy exists in considerable quantity. As we have already indicated, Childe holds that in every case civilization grew out of the cultivation of the same plants and the breeding of the same animals. Thurnwald[15] emphasized the same general propositions. He was, however, primarily concerned with showing how such institutions as slavery and serfdom served to concentrate the surpluses of food-raising cultures in such manner as to permit the military protection of the land and the development of a class of skilled artisans and specialists, neither of which is possible where men must remain dispersed in order to gather the fruits of field and chase.

While there is considerable variation among food-raising peoples, there are also numerous likenesses among them as a consequence of the limits inherent in food raising. Among all food raisers the family is the basic consumption unit, and to a large extent it is also the production unit for much of the goods and services produced. Division of labor is limited and is primarily based on differences in skill and learning, sex, and size and muscular power. Since so large a part of what must be done requires merely brute strength, there are also likely to appear status differences which assign whole sections of the population to physical tasks without regard for the potential skill, intelligence, strength, or sex of individuals. If the emergence of complex institutions depends upon the development of a surplus, so too the development of a surplus depends upon the existence of such institutions. Once a balance is attained, however, it is difficult to upset.

The Egyptians: An Example

The Egypt of the age of the Pharaohs provide a good demonstration of the working of a balanced system in which a comparatively small energy surplus is utilized in such a way that there is no disturbance to the energy-producing pro-

cedures. The Egyptians left a durable record of their accomplishments, and these records have been subjected to a great deal of study. The Egyptian system operated, moreover, under unique physical circumstances which precluded a disturbance of the balance through soil exhaustion. The Nile regularly replaced the soil, and continuous cropping caused no depletion. The deserts, sea, and river cataracts formed barriers which could be crossed by an invader bent on conquest and plunder only with great expenditure of energy surpluses. The Egyptians were, under these favorable conditions, able to push food raising to a climactic* stage.

During long periods of its history the surpluses of Egypt were absorbed by the burial mounds or pyramids. These contain both direct and symbolic evidence of Egyptian accomplishments. During the reign of some of the Pharaohs almost the total surplus of the people was concentrated in the erecting and furnishing of the pyramid which was to honor the ruler upon his death. The ruling class was small and consumed no great amount of wealth, for the chief objective of its way of life was to accumulate surpluses to be taken into death. The population was held constant or even diminished, since men were worked to death about as fast as they could be brought to maturity. Even so, the surpluses were never great. The Cheops pyramid, together with its furnishings, absorbed all the surplus energy produced during the lifetime of about 3 million people. During a 20-year period 100,000 slaves are said to have worked to produce the tomb. This was about $\frac{1}{25}$ of the total population. We can calculate, then, that those who supplied

* This word is applied here in much the same way that it is used by ecologists. It indicates the culminating stage of the possible development in a region, given a limited set of plants and animals to begin with and assuming no major alteration in geographic conditions. We imply that given sufficient time the use of low-energy converters results in a type of persistent equilibrium between men and their environment.

FRED COTTRELL *Organic Energy and the Low-Energy Society* 157

the food to keep the pyramid builders alive each contributed only about 100 to 150 Calories a day. Thus, although the Egyptians enjoyed most favorable geographic circumstances, the total energy available to them was by modern standards extremely low, however high it may have been in comparison with the energy production of other societies of the time.

At other periods in its history the surpluses enabled Egypt to engage in conquest of all its neighbors. At still other times the surplus was exhausted in conspicuous expenditure and display among the living; at those times when controls over population broke down, the surplus was completely exhausted in civil war or by the increase in the number of mouths to be fed from the land.

It is possible to calculate the distance from their base on the Nile that the Egyptians could have advanced had they been willing to devote all their surpluses to conquest of neighboring peoples. The size of the surplus was one limiting factor: the surplus had to be carried or pulled from Egypt by men or asses. At some distance from the Nile the energy cost of transportation would have reduced the surplus derived from Egypt to a point below that available to the people being invaded, and Egyptian expansion would at this point have been checked. The topography and the resources of the region invaded, the will to resist and the military technology, strategy, and leadership of its inhabitants also would have been involved in fixing the ultimate limit to which the Egyptians could have advanced. Similarly, the possible spread of Egyptian culture was limited by its capacity to yield surplus under the very different conditions that prevailed outside Egypt. Egyptian culture was adopted elsewhere only with great difficulty. When Egypt did conquer a people, it was seldom able to assimilate them. And when conditions in Egypt led to disor-

ganization, the conquered people usually broke away and resumed their previous way of life. Such a resumption is reported in the Biblical story of the exodus of the Jews from Egypt.

The peoples of the Fertile Crescent contributed much to what we now regard as civilization. But the extent of their political holdings, the range over which they were able to secure and maintain cultural homogeneity, and the diversity of their skills and knowledge were slight by present standards. Their history shows cyclical variations within constant limits. The abuses of one system gave rise to another system, which in turn was defeated by its own weaknesses. None of these systems could, however, exceed the limits imposed by the basic converters, that is, plants and animals. And these same basic converters are depended upon by the greater portion of the people of the world today. Moreover, the cultures of the rest of the peoples of the modern world were developed in considerable part under the limitations imposed by the plant-animal-man system.

CURRENT LOW-ENERGY SOCIETIES

Societies such as those that now exist in India, Africa, and China have been greatly modified by the introduction of new converters but are still closely restricted by the limited energy which they have available. The population is in many of these areas so great that local resources will not supply an adequate diet. In Yünnan,[16] for example, about 100 families (500 to 600 people) share 150 acres. This is about all the people that plant life will support if the plants are eaten directly. Buck[17] found that in the 1930's nearly 90 per cent of the potential farm area of China was in crops, while only 1.1 per cent was in pasture. By comparison, in the United States 42 per cent is in crops and 47 per cent is being used to pasture animals. Moreover, in the United States much of the crop land is used for feed rather than for food. The energy available from animal power in China was and probably still is close to zero, and the limits on the mechanical energy available in many Chinese villages might be ascertained simply by multiplying the number of persons by 20 per cent of the heat value of the per capita food intake.

Under these circumstances the energy costs of transportation between village and field would cut deeply into the available surplus if the distances were great. Consequently villages are very small and located at frequent intervals. When the small surpluses available have been used to support centralization of control, the effect of that control on energy production has rarely been equivalent to its cost. Even the introduction of new sources of supply has tended to affect the old system adversely. For example, many Chinese villages had long paid their taxes and bought necessary imports by converting the leaves of the mulberry trees along the canal banks into silk. When the Central Government was forced by foreign powers to protect trade in Japanese silk, American cotton, and British Commonwealth wool, many villages lost this source of income and were confronted by a great change in their way of life. Often the land was sold to pay taxes, and city people gained control over it. The consequence here was a great increase in tension between town and country, absentee owner and tenant, and an intense effort to restore the earlier balance. The present turmoil in China evidences both the efforts of the Communists to achieve greater centralization, which upset the balance still further, and their efforts to restore to the peasant control over the land he cultivates and to the village the self-subsistent economy which trade upset.

India shows many of the same characteristics. The average net cultivated area per capita of agricultural population in Bengal in 1939 was less than 1 acre, and 46 per cent of farming families had less than 2 acres each.[18] The tillable land of India is supporting the maximum number of people which it can maintain with the energy that is obtainable from it with existing practices. If higher demands are made on the soil, it will pass the point of diminishing returns. Here also the village community serves as the predominant spatial and functional unit. It supplies almost no surplus beyond that required for the local institutions themselves. The energy costs of national government or more extensive social organization must be provided by other energy sources. In the past much of the energy used for these purposes was imported from Britain in the form of goods produced with British coal and water power.

In some areas that have used only organic sources for energy the population has been limited at a point short of that which characterizes the "overpopulated" parts of China and India. However, as land becomes scarce in relation to the population, the tendency has been for more and more intensive cultivation to be undertaken. This has frequently resulted in an effort on the part of each farmer to increase the only productive factor over which he himself has control, namely, children. As a consequence, even greater pressure has been put upon the soil and even less energy has been available to devote to the development of new agricultural techniques or the enlargement of the area under cultivation.

Among the Bantu in Africa[19] it is the labor of clearing the land that sets limits on cultivation. Every child thus becomes an economic asset, and there is continuous emphasis on increasing the size of the family. However, life is there so precariously balanced that a crop failure is likely to result in starvation and a reduction in the working population in the next crop cycle. This is also the case in at least some parts of China. In a village in Yünnan, Fei and Chiang found that the size of farm that can be worked by a man and his wife alone is too small to support a family. As a result children must work; in the absence of children the older adults will starve.

Economic reciprocity between parents and children tends to become a necessity in societies that are dependent on organic converters. Children supply in these areas what is secured in industrial societies through unemployment, health, and disability insurance, and old-age allowances. Parents develop in the child values that will ensure their own survival, and the commandment "Honour thy father and thy mother: that thy days may be long upon the land . . ." is a statement of a functional relationship.

Their Conservatism

Since the limits within which low-energy societies operate are so narrow, extensive conflict and its concomitant wastes cannot long be tolerated. Hence institutions develop which tend to reinforce rather than to weaken each other. The introduction of any new element is likely to be disastrous to one or more of the parts making up the web of the culture. When this happens, the traditional allocation of scarce resources is threatened, since men then no longer learn from all the sources of authority the same design for the "good life." As a consequence, resistance to change frequently mounts as the ramifications of change appear. Moreover, change is often introduced into low-energy societies by "outsiders" who have their own reasons for inducing it. Frequently such change provides a more satisfactory way of life for only a few of the "natives," while others are forced to bear costs which they consider totally disproportionate to any foreseeable gains. Those members of the society who value very highly certain of the gains to be made through the introduction of new converters, welcome change and encourage it. For others, whose pastoral and agricultural values are thereby destroyed, the "material benefits" which accompany the use of the new converters are not adequate compensation for the values lost, and they struggle to preserve the system that is jeopardized by the introduction of the new converters. Even in the highly industrialized United States of today there is great respect for the virtues of the husbandman and for the rural institutions which support and are supported by many American ideals. For example, the "family-sized farm" is widely held to be necessary to democracy, Christianity, and individualism.

Thus low-energy societies offer more barriers to change than just those imposed by the costs of securing the new converters needed to effect change. Added to these are the costs of social disorganization and of purposeful resistance. If these barriers are to be overcome, there must be considerable energy in the hands of those who seek to bring about change. Since, as we have indicated, most of the energy available in low-energy societies rests in the hands of those with traditional social claims to it—for example, peasants, landlords, and others who will not want such change—a great increase in energy is necessary in order to provide a surplus adequate to secure the introduction and use of new converters. In a low-energy society change must come slowly, for the range between the most and the least effective use is not, by modern standards, great. Therefore the conquest of users of low-energy converters has frequently meant that the surplus produced merely passed from the hands of one group to another, its size remaining relatively constant and the culture remaining basically unchanged. Such drastic changes as the engulfment of the Plains Indians in the United States have been possible only with the extensive use of converters that were far more effective in delivering surplus energy than those that existed prior to the conquest.

In the main, then, the low-energy system of a people dependent wholly on food raising is inherently self-perpetuating. It develops a balance between population numbers, social institutions, energy usages, and energy production which is exceedingly difficult to disturb and which, if disturbed, tends to reassert itself. As a consequence, the impact of modern industrial technology on peasant societies is far weaker than is generally assumed, and those who have endeavored to introduce new converters to such peoples have had limited success.

NOTES

1. Farrington Daniels, "Solar Energy," *Science*, vol. 109, no. 2821, p. 51, January 21, 1949.

2. Daniels, *cited*, p. 52.

3. O. W. Willcox, *Nations Can Live at Home*, p. 119, New York: W. W. Norton & Company, Inc., 1935.

Willcox sets out to prove that it is easily possible to feed a very much larger population than that found in the world today through selection of the proper plants and their cultivation in approved ways. To my knowledge no large area has as yet succeeded in producing even a considerable fraction of what Willcox holds to be theoretically possible.

4. Daniels, *cited*, p. 55.

5. Willcox, *cited*, p. 98.

6. Howard Ross Tolley, "Population and Food Supply," *Chronica Botanica*, vol. 11, no. 4, p. 219, Summer, 1948.

7. F. B. Morrison, *Feeds and Feeding*, 21st ed., p. 909, Ithaca, N.Y.: Morrison Publishing Co., 1950.

8. C. Daryll Forde, *Habitat, Economy and Society: A Geographical Introduction to Ethnology*, 5th ed., p. 38, New York: E. P. Dutton & Co., Inc., 1946.

9. Forde, *cited*, pp. 46f.

10. Bernard Mishkin, *Rank and Warfare among the Plains Indians*, chap. 2, American Ethnological Society Monograph 3, New York: J. J. Augustin, 1940.

11. E. Cecil Curwen, *Plough and Pasture*, p. 76, London: Cobbett Press, 1946.

An expanded version of this book, containing a section by Gudmund Hatt, has been published in this country (New York: Abelard Press. Inc., 1953).

12. Richard Thurnwald, *Economics in Primitive Communities*, p. 95, International Institute of African Languages and Cultures, London: Oxford University Press, 1932.

13. Forde, *cited*, p. 378.

14. V. Gordon Childe, *Social Evolution*, p. 161, New York: Abelard Press, Inc., 1951.

15. Thurnwald, *cited*. This is a general theme repeated at various points.

16. Hsiao-tung Fei, and Chih-i Chiang, *Earthbound China: A Study of Rural Economy in Yunnan*, p. 11, Chicago: University of Chicago Press, 1945.

17. John Lossing Buck, *Land Utilization in China*, p. 6, Chicago: University of Chicago Press, 1937.

Some of the findings in this work are criticized in the later book by Fei and Chiang cited just above. Because of this lack of agreement, no extensive use has here been made of figures on Chinese productivity.

18. D. Ghosh, *Pressure of Population and Economic Efficiency in India*, p. 43, Indian Council of World Affairs, London: Oxford University Press, 1946.

19. D. M. Goodfellow, *Principles of Economic Sociology*, p. 76, New York: McGraw–Hill Book Company, Inc., Blakiston Division, 1939.

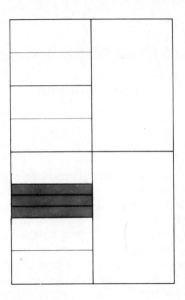

6. FUNCTIONAL STRUCTURALISM

The structuralist viewpoints in general define the social in terms of objective behavior relations and seek to explain it by referring to phenomena that are socially generated through characteristics of the participants' environments. In the structuralisms, these latter characteristics are constituted by the behavior of social participants occupying established positions relative to each other. Three related structuralist viewpoints may be distinguished: functional structuralism, exchange structuralism, and conflict structuralism.

Functional structuralism seeks to explain the social as being a consequence of the behavior of at least one participant (individual or group) toward others. Merton's paper on social deviance and conformity is an example of the utility of this viewpoint in devising a middle-range theory.

SOCIAL STRUCTURE AND ANOMIE

ROBERT K. MERTON

A decade ago, and all the more so before then, one could speak of a marked tendency in psychological and sociological theory to attribute the faulty operation of social structures to failures of social control over man's imperious biological drives. The imagery of the relations between man and society implied by this doctrine is as clear as it is questionable. In the beginning, there are man's biological impulses which seek full expression. And then, there is the social order, essentially an apparatus for the management of impulses, for the social processing of tensions, for the "renunciation of instinctual gratifications," in the words of Freud. Nonconformity with the demands of a social structure is thus assumed to be anchored in original nature.[1] It is the biologically rooted impulses which from time to time break through social control. And by implication, conformity is the result of an utilitarian calculus or of unreasoned conditioning.

With the more recent advancement of social science, this set of conceptions has undergone basic modification. For one thing, it no longer appears so obvious that man is set against society in an unceasing war between biological impulse and social restraint. The image of man as an untamed bundle of impulses begins to look more like a caricature than a portrait. For another, sociological perspectives have increasingly entered into the analysis of behavior deviating from prescribed patterns of conduct. For what-

Reprinted from the *American Sociological Review*, 1938, vol. 3, pp. 672–682, by permission of the American Sociological Association and the author.

ever the role of biological impulses, there still remains the further question of why it is that the frequency of deviant behavior varies within different social structures and how it happens that the deviations have different shapes and patterns in different social structures. Today, as a decade ago, we have still much to learn about the processes through which social structures generate the circumstances in which infringement of social codes constitutes a "normal" (that is to say, an expectable) response.[2] This paper is an essay seeking clarification of the problem.

The framework set out in this essay is designed to provide one systematic approach to the analysis of social and cultural sources of deviant behavior. Our primary aim is to discover how some *social structures exert a definite pressure upon certain persons in the society to engage in nonconformist rather than conformist conduct.* If we can locate groups peculiarly subject to such pressures, we should expect to find fairly high rates of deviant behavior in these groups, not because the human beings comprising them are compounded of distinctive biological tendencies but because they are responding normally to the social situation in which they find themselves. Our perspective is sociological. We look at variations in the *rates* of deviant behavior, not at its incidence.[3] Should our quest be at all successful, some forms of deviant behavior will be found to be as psychologically normal as conformist behavior, and the equation of deviation and abnormality will be put in question.

PATTERNS OF CULTURAL GOALS AND INSTITUTIONAL NORMS

Among the several elements of social and cultural structures, two are of immediate importance. These are analytically separable although they merge in concrete situations. The first consists of culturally defined goals, purposes and interests, held out as legitimate objectives for all or for diversely located members of the society. The goals are more or less integrated—the degree is a question of empirical fact—and roughly ordered in some hierarchy of value. Involving various degrees of sentiment and significance, the prevailing goals comprise a frame of aspirational reference. They are the things "worth striving for." They are a basic, though not the exclusive, component of what Linton has called "designs for group living." And though some, not all, of these cultural goals are directly related to the biological drives of man, they are not determined by them.

A second element of the cultural structure defines, regulates and controls the acceptable modes of reaching out for these goals. Every social group invariably couples its cultural objectives with regulations, rooted in the mores or institutions, of allowable procedures for moving toward these objectives. These regulatory norms are not necessarily identical with technical or efficiency norms. Many procedures which from the standpoint of particular individuals would be most efficient in securing desired values—the exercise of force, fraud, power—are ruled out of the institutional area of permitted conduct. At times, the disallowed procedures include some which would be efficient for the group itself—e.g., historic taboos on vivisection, on medical experimentation, on the sociological analysis of "sacred" norms—since the criterion of acceptability is not technical efficiency but value-laden sentiments (supported by most members of

the group or by those able to promote these sentiments through the composite use of power and propaganda). In all instances, the choice of expedients for striving toward cultural goals is limited by institutionalized norms.

Sociologists often speak of these controls as being "in the mores" or as operating through social institutions. Such elliptical statements are true enough, but they obscure the fact that culturally standardized practices are not all of a piece. They are subject to a wide gamut of control. They may represent definitely prescribed or preferential or permissive or proscribed patterns of behavior. In assessing the operation of social controls, these variations—roughly indicated by the terms *prescription, preference, permission* and *proscription*—must of course be taken into account.

To say, moreover, that cultural goals and institutionalized norms operate jointly to shape prevailing practices is not to say that they bear a constant relation to one another. The cultural emphasis placed upon certain goals varies independently of the degree of emphasis upon institutionalized means. There may develop a very heavy, at times a virtually exclusive, stress upon the value of given goals, involving comparatively little concern with the institutionally prescribed means of striving toward these goals. The limiting case of this type is reached when the range of alternative procedures is governed only by technical rather than by institutional norms. Any and all procedures which promise attainment of the all-important goal would be permitted in this hypothetical polar case. This constitutes one type of malintegrated culture. A second polar type is found in groups where activities originally conceived as instrumental are transmuted into self-contained practices, lacking further objectives. The original purposes are forgotten and close adherence to institutionally prescribed conduct becomes a matter of ritual.[4] Sheer conformity becomes a central value. For a time, social stability is ensured—at the expense of flexibility. Since the range of alternative behaviors permitted by the culture is severely limited, there is little basis for adapting to new conditions. There develops a tradition-bound, "sacred" society marked by neophobia. Between these extreme types are societies which maintain a rough balance between emphases upon cultural goals and institutionalized practices, and these constitute the integrated and relatively stable, though changing, societies.

An effective equilibrium between these two phases of the social structure is maintained so long as satisfactions accrue to individuals conforming to both cultural constraints, viz., satisfactions from the achievement of goals and satisfactions emerging directly from the institutionally canalized modes of striving to attain them. It is reckoned in terms of the product and in terms of the process, in terms of the outcome and in terms of the activities. Thus continuing satisfactions must derive from sheer participation in a competitive order as well as from eclipsing one's competitors if the order itself is to be sustained. If concern shifts exclusively to the outcome of competition, then those who perennially suffer defeat will, understandably enough, work for a change in the rules of the game. The sacrifices occasionally—not, as Freud assumed, invariably—entailed by conformity to institutional norms must be compensated by socialized rewards. The distribution of statuses through competition must be so organized that positive incentives for adherence to status obligations are provided for every position within the distributive order. Otherwise, as will soon become plain, aberrant behavior ensues. It is, indeed, my central hypothesis that aberrant behavior may be regarded sociologically as a symptom of dissociation between culturally prescribed aspirations and socially structured avenues for realizing these aspirations.

Of the types of societies which result from independent variation of cultural goals and institutionalized means, we shall be primarily concerned with the first—a society in which there is an exceptionally strong emphasis upon specific goals without a corresponding emphasis upon institutional procedures. If it is not to be misunderstood, this statement must be elaborated. No society lacks norms governing conduct. But societies do differ in the degree to which the folkways, mores and institutional controls are effectively integrated with the goals which stand high in the hierarchy of cultural values. The culture may be such as to lead individuals to center their emotional convictions about the complex of culturally acclaimed ends, with far less emotional support for prescribed methods of reaching out for these ends. With such differential emphases upon goals and institutional procedures, the latter may be so vitiated by the stress on goals as to have the behavior of many individuals limited only by considerations of technical expediency. In this context, the sole significant question becomes: Which of the available procedures is most efficient in netting the culturally approved value?[5] The technically most effective procedure, whether culturally legitimate or not, becomes typically preferred to institutionally prescribed conduct. As this process of attenuation continues, the society becomes unstable and there develops what Durkheim called "anomie" (or normlessness).[6]

The working of this process eventuating in anomie can be easily glimpsed in a series of familiar and instructive, though perhaps trivial, episodes. Thus, in competitive athletics, when the aim of victory is shorn of its institutional trappings and success becomes construed as "winning the game" rather than "winning under the rules of the game," a premium is implicitly set upon the use of illegitimate but technically efficient means. The star of the opposing football team is surreptitiously slugged; the wrestler incapacitates his opponent through ingenious but illicit techniques; university alumni covertly subsidize "students" whose talents are confined to the athletic field. The emphasis on the goal has so attenuated the satisfactions deriving from sheer participation in the competitive activity that only a successful outcome provides gratification. Through the same process, tension generated by the desire to win in a poker game is relieved by successfully dealing one's self four aces or, when the cult of success has truly flowered, by sagaciously shuffling the cards in a game of solitaire. The faint twinge of uneasiness in the last instance and the surreptitious nature of public delicts indicate clearly that the institutional rules of the game are *known* to those who evade them. But cultural (or idiosyncratic) exaggeration of the success-goal leads men to withdraw emotional support from the rules.[7]

This process is of course not restricted to the realm of competitive sport, which has simply provided us with microcosmic images of the social macrocosm. The process whereby exaltation of the end generates a literal *demoralization*, i.e., a de-institutionalization, of the means occurs in many[8] groups where the two components of the social structure are not highly integrated.

Contemporary American culture appears to approximate the polar type in which great emphasis upon certain success-goals occurs without equivalent emphasis upon institutional means. It would of course be fanciful to assert that accumulated wealth stands alone as a symbol of success just as it would be fanciful to deny that Americans assign it a place high in their scale of values. In some large measure, money has been consecrated as a value in itself, over and

above its expenditure for articles of consumption or its use for the enhancement of power. "Money" is peculiarly well adapted to become a symbol of prestige. As Simmel emphasized, money is highly abstract and impersonal. However acquired, fraudulently or institutionally, it can be used to purchase the same goods and services. The anonymity of an urban society, in conjunction with these peculiarities of money, permits wealth, the sources of which may be unknown to the community in which the plutocrat lives or, if known, to become purified in the course of time, to serve as a symbol of high status. Moreover, in the American Dream there is no final stopping point. The measure of "monetary success" is conveniently indefinite and relative. At each income level, as H. F. Clark has found, Americans want just about twenty-five per cent more (but of course this "just a bit more" continues to operate once it is obtained). In this flux of shifting standards, there is no stable resting point, or rather, it is the point which manages always to be "just ahead." An observer of a community in which annual salaries in six figures are not uncommon reports the anguished words of one victim of the American Dream: "In this town, I'm snubbed socially because I only get a thousand a week. That hurts."[9]

To say that the goal of monetary success is entrenched in American culture is only to say that Americans are bombarded on every side by precepts which affirm the right or, often, the duty of retaining the goal even in the face of repeated frustration. Prestigeful representatives of the society reinforce the cultural emphasis. The family, the school and the workplace—the major agencies shaping the personality structure and goal formation of Americans—join to provide the intensive disciplining required if an individual is to retain intact a goal that remains elusively beyond reach, if he is to be motivated by the promise of a gratification which is not redeemed. As we shall presently see, parents serve as a transmission belt for the values and goals of the groups of which they are a part—above all, of their social class or of the class with which they identify themselves. And the schools are of course the official agency for the passing on of the prevailing values, with a large proportion of the textbooks used in city schools implying or stating explicitly "that education leads to intelligence and consequently to job

and money success."[10] Central to this process of discipling people to maintain their unfulfilled aspirations are the cultural prototypes of success, the living documents testifying that the American Dream can be realized if one but has the requisite abilities. Consider in this connection the following excerpt from the business journal, Nation's Business, drawn from a large mass of comparable materials found in mass communications setting forth the values of business class culture.

The Document (*Nation's Business* Vol. 27, No. 8, p. 7)	*Its Sociological Implications*
" 'You have to be born to those jobs, buddy, or else have a good pull.'	Here is an heretical opinion, possibly born of continued frustration, which rejects the worth of retaining an apparently unrealizable goal and, moreover, questions the legitimacy of a social structure which provides differential access to this goal.
"That's an old sedative to ambition.	The counter-attack, explicitly asserting the cultural value of retaining one's aspirations intact, of not losing "ambition."
"Before listening to its seduction, ask these men:	A clear statement of the function to be served by the ensuing list of "successes." These men are living testimony that the social structure is such as to permit these aspirations to be achieved, *if one is worthy*. And correlatively, failure to reach these goals testifies only to one's own personal shortcomings. Aggression provoked by failure should therefore be directed inward and not outward, against oneself and not against a social structure which provides free and equal access to opportunity.
"Elmer R. Jones, president of Wells-Fargo and Co., who began life as a poor boy and left school at the fifth grade to take his first job.	Success prototype I: *All* may properly have the *same* lofty ambitions, for however lowly the starting-point, true talent can reach the very heights. Aspirations must be retained intact.

"Frank C. Ball, the Mason fruit jar king of America, who rode from Buffalo to Muncie, Indiana, in a boxcar along with his brother George's horse, to start a little business in Muncie that became the biggest of its kind.

"J. L. Bevan, president of the Illinois Central Railroad, who at twelve was a messenger boy in the freight office at New Orleans."

Success prototype II: Whatever the present results of one's strivings, the future is large with promise; for the common man may yet become a king. Gratifications may seem forever deferred, but they will finally be realized as one's enterprise becomes "the biggest of its kind."

Success prototype III: If the secular trends of our economy seem to give little scope to small business, then one may rise within the giant bureaucracies of private enterprise. If one can no longer be a "king" in a realm of his own creation, he may at least become a "president" in one of the economic democracies. No matter what one's present station, messenger boy or clerk, one's gaze should be fixed at the top.

From divers sources there flows a continuing pressure to retain high ambition. The exhortational literature is immense, and one can choose only at the risk of seeming invidious. Consider only these: The Reverend Russell H. Conwell, with his *Acres of Diamonds* address heard and read by hundreds of thousands and his subsequent book, *The New Day*, or *Fresh Opportunities: A Book for Young Men*; Elbert Hubbard, who delivered the famous *Message to Garcia* at Chautauqua forums throughout the land; Orison Swett Marden, who, in a stream of books, first set forth *The Secret of Achievement*, praised by college presidents, then explained the process of *Pushing to the Front*, eulogized by President McKinley and finally, these democratic testimonials notwithstanding, mapped the road to make *Every Man a King*. The symbolism of a commoner rising to the estate of economic royalty is woven deep in the texture of the American culture pattern, finding what is perhaps its ultimate expression in the words of one who knew whereof he spoke, Andrew Carnegie: "Be a king in your dreams. Say to yourself, 'My place is at the top.' "[11]

Coupled with this positive emphasis upon the obligation to maintain lofty goals is a correlative emphasis upon the penalizing of those who draw in their ambitions. Americans are admonished "not to be a quitter" for in the dictionary of American culture, as in the lexicon of youth, "there is no such word as 'fail.' " The cultural manifesto is clear: one must not quit, must not cease striving, must not lessen his goals, for "not failure, but low aim, is crime."

Thus the culture enjoins the acceptance of three cultural axioms: First, all should strive for the same lofty goals since these are open to all; second, present seeming failure is but a way-station to ultimate success; and third, genuine failure consists only in the lessening or withdrawal of ambition.

In rough psychological paraphrase, these axioms represent, first, a symbolic "secondary reinforcement" of incentive; second, curbing the threatened extinction of a response through an associated stimulus; third, increasing the motive-strength to evoke continued responses despite the continued absence of reward.

In sociological paraphrase, these axioms represent, first, the deflection of criticism of the social structure onto one's self among those so situated in the society that they do not have full and equal access to opportunity; second, the preservation of a given structure of social power by having individuals in the lower strata identify themselves, not with their compeers, but with those at the top (whom they will ultimately join); and third, providing pressures for conformity with the cultural dictates of unslackened ambition by the threat of less than full membership in the society for those who fail to conform.

It is in these terms and through these processes that contemporary American culture continues to be characterized by a heavy emphasis on wealth as a basic symbol of success, without a corresponding emphasis upon the legitimate avenues on which to march toward this goal. How do individuals living in this cultural context respond? And how do our observations bear upon the doctrine that deviant behavior typically derives from biological impulses breaking through the restraints imposed by culture? What, in short, are the consequences for the behavior of people variously situated in a social structure of a culture in which the emphasis on dominant success-goals has become increasingly separated from an equivalent emphasis on institutionalized procedures for seeking these goals?

TYPES OF INDIVIDUAL ADAPTATION

Turning from these *culture patterns*, we now examine types of adaptation by individuals within the culture-bearing society. Though our focus is still the cultural and social genesis of varying rates and types of deviant behavior, our perspective shifts from the plane of patterns of cultural values to the plane of types of adaptation to these values among those occupying different positions in the social structure.

We here consider five types of adaptation, as these are schematically set out in the following table, where (+) signifies "acceptance," (−) signifies "rejection," and (±) signifies "rejection of prevailing values and substitution of new values."

A TYPOLOGY OF MODES OF INDIVIDUAL ADAPTATION[12]

Modes of Adaptation	Culture Goals	Institutionalized Means
I. Conformity	+	+
II. Innovation	+	−
III. Ritualism	−	+
IV. Retreatism	−	−
V. Rebellion[13]	±	±

Examination of how the social structure operates to exert pressure upon individuals for one or another of these alternative modes of behavior must be prefaced by the observation that people may shift from one alternative to another as they engage in different spheres of social activities. These categories refer to role behavior in specific types of situations, not to personality. They are types of more or less enduring response, not types of personality organization. To consider these types of adaptation in several spheres of conduct would introduce a complexity unmanageable within the confines of this paper. For this reason, we shall be primarily concerned with economic activity in the broad sense of "the production, exchange, distribution and consumption of goods and services" in our competitive society, where wealth has taken on a highly symbolic cast.

I. Conformity

To the extent that a society is stable, adaptation type I—conformity to both cultural goals and institutionalized means

—is the most common and widely diffused. Were this not so, the stability and continuity of the society could not be maintained. The mesh of expectancies constituting every social order is sustained by the modal behavior of its members representing conformity to the established, though perhaps secularly changing, culture patterns. It is, in fact, only because behavior is typically oriented toward the basic values of the society that permits us to speak of a human aggregate as comprising a society. Unless there is a deposit of values shared by interacting individuals, there exist social relations, if the disorderly interactions may be so called, but no society. It is thus that, in 1948, one may refer to a Society of Nations primarily as a figure of speech or as an imagined objective, but not as a sociological reality.

Since our primary interest centers on the sources of *deviant* behavior, and since we have briefly examined the mechanisms making for conformity as the modal response in American society, little more need be said regarding this type of adaptation, at this point.

II. Innovation

Great cultural emphasis upon the success-goal invites this mode of adaptation through the use of institutionally proscribed but often effective means of attaining at least the simulacrum of success—wealth and power. This response occurs when the individual has assimilated the cultural emphasis upon the goal without equally internalizing the institutional norms governing ways and means for its attainment.

From the standpoint of psychology, great emotional investment in an objective may be expected to produce a readiness to take risks, and this attitude may be adopted by people in all social strata. From the standpoint of sociology, the question arises, which features of our social structure predispose toward this type of adaptation, thus producing greater frequencies of deviant behavior in one social stratum than in another?

On the top economic levels, the pressure toward innovation not infrequently erases the distinction between business-like strivings this side of the mores and sharp practices beyond the mores. As Veblen observed, "It is not easy in any given case—indeed it is at times impossible until the courts have spoken—to say whether it is an instance of praiseworthy salesmanship or a penitentiary offense." The history of the great American fortunes is threaded with strains toward institutionally dubious innovation as is attested by many tributes to the Robber Barons. The reluctant admiration often expressed privately, and not seldom publicly, of these "shrewd, smart and successful" men is a product of a cultural structure in which the sacrosanct goal virtually consecrates the means. This is no new phenomenon. Without assuming that Charles Dickens was a wholly accurate observer of the American scene and with full knowledge that he was anything but impartial, we cite his perceptive remarks on the American love of "smart" dealing: which gilds over many a swindle and gross breach of trust; many a defalcation, public and private; and enables many a knave to hold his head up with the best, who well deserves a halter.... The merits of a broken speculation, or a bankruptcy, or of a successful scoundrel, are not gauged by its or his observance of the golden rule, "Do as you would be done by," but are considered with reference to their smartness.... The following dialogue I have held a hundred times: "Is it not a very disgraceful circumstance that such a man as So-and-so should be acquiring a large property by the most infamous and odious means, and notwithstanding all the crimes of which he has been guilty, should be tolerated and abetted by your Citizens? He is a public nuisance, is he not?" "Yes, sir." "A convicted liar?" "Yes, sir." "He has been kicked and cuffed, and caned?" "Yes, sir." "And he is utterly dishonorable, debased, and profligate?" "Yes, sir." "In the name of wonder, then, what is his merit?" "Well, sir, he is a smart man."[14]

Not all of these large and dramatic departures from institutional norms in the top economic strata are known, and possibly fewer deviations among the lesser middle classes come to light. Sutherland has repeatedly documented the prevalence of "white-collar criminality" among business men. He notes, further, that many of these crimes were not prosecuted because they were not detected or, if detected, because of "the status of the business man, the trend away from punishment, and the relatively unorganized resentment of the public against white-collar criminals."[15] A study of some 1,700 prevalently middle-class individuals found that "off the record crimes" were common among wholly "respectable" members of society. Ninety-nine per cent of those questioned confessed to having committed one or more of 49 offenses under the penal law of the State of New York, each of these offenses being sufficiently serious to draw a maximum sentence of not less than one year. The mean number of offenses in adult years—this exludes all offenses committed before the age of sixteen—was 18 for men and 11 for women. Fully 64% of the men and 29% of the women acknowledged their guilt on one or more counts of felony which, under the laws of New York is ground for depriving them of all rights of citizenship. One keynote of these findings is expressed by a minister, referring to false statements he made about a commodity he sold, "I tried truth first, but it's not always successful." On the basis of these results, the authors modestly conclude that "the number of acts legally constituting crimes are far in excess of those officially reported. Unlawful behavior, far from being an abnormal social or psychological manifestation, is in truth a very common phenomenon."[16]

But whatever the differential rates of deviant behavior in the several social strata, and we know from many sources that the official crime statistics uniformly showing higher rates in the lower strata are far from complete or reliable, it appears from our analysis that the greatest pressures toward deviation are exerted upon the lower strata. Cases in point permit us to detect the sociological mechanisms involved in producing these pressures. Several researches have shown that specialized areas of vice and crime constitute a "normal" response to a situation where the cultural emphasis upon pecuniary success has been absorbed, but where there is little access to conventional and legitimate means for becoming successful. The occupational opportunities of people in these areas are largely confined to manual labor and the lesser white-collar jobs. Given the American stigmatization of manual labor *which has been found to hold rather uniformly in all social classes,*[17] and the absence of realistic opportunities for advancement beyond this level, the result is a marked tendency toward deviant behavior. The status of unskilled labor and the consequent low income cannot readily compete *in terms of established standards of worth* with the promises of power and high income from organized vice, rackets and crime.[18]

For our purposes, these situations exhibit two salient features. First, incentives for success are provided by the established values of the culture; *and* second, the avenues available for moving toward this goal are largely limited by the class structure to those of deviant behavior. It is the *combination* of the cultural emphasis and the social structure which produces intense pressure for deviation. Recourse to legitimate channels for "getting in the money" is limited by a class structure which is not fully open at each level to men of good capacity.[19] Despite our persisting open-class-ideology,[20] advance toward the success-goal is relatively rare and notably difficult for those armed with little formal education and few economic resources. The dominant pressure leads toward the gradual attenuation of legitimate, but by and large ineffectual, strivings and the increasing use of illegitimate, but more or less effective, expedients.

Of those located in the lower reaches of the social structure, the culture makes incompatible demands. On the one hand, they are asked to orient their conduct toward the prospect of large wealth— "Every man a king," said Marden and Carnegie and Long—and on the other, they are largely denied effective opportunities to do so institutionally. The consequence of this structural inconsistency is a high rate of deviant behavior. The equilibrium between culturally designated ends and means becomes highly unstable with progressive emphasis on attaining the prestige-laden ends by any means whatsoever. Within this context, Al Capone represents the triumph of amoral intelligence over morally prescribed "failure," when the channels of vertical mobility are closed or narrowed *in a society which places a high premium on economic affluence and social ascent for all its members.*[21]

This last qualification is of central importance. It implies that other aspects of the social structure, besides the extreme emphasis on pecuniary success, must be considered if we are to understand the social sources of deviant behavior. A high frequency of deviant behavior is not generated merely by lack of opportunity or by this exaggerated pecuniary emphasis. A comparatively rigidified class structure, a feudalistic caste order, may limit opportunities far beyond the point which obtains in American society today. It is only when a system of cultural values extols, virtually above all else, certain *common* success-goals *for the population at large* while the social structure rigorously restricts or completely closes access to approved modes of reaching these goals *for a considerable part of the same population,* that deviant behavior ensues on a large scale. Otherwise said, our egalitarian ideology denies by implication the existence of non-competing individuals and groups in the pursuit of pecuniary success. Instead, the same body of success-symbols is held to apply for all. Goals are held to transcend class lines, not to be bounded by them, yet the actual social organization is such that there exist class differentials in accessibility of the goals. In this setting, a cardinal American virtue, "ambition," promotes a cardinal American vice, "deviant behavior."

This theoretical analysis may help explain the varying correlations between crime and poverty.[22] "Poverty" is not an isolated variable which operates in precisely the same fashion wherever found; it is only one in a complex of identifiably interdependent social and cultural variables. Poverty as such and consequent limitation of opportunity are not enough to produce a conspicuously high rate of criminal behavior. Even the notorious "poverty in the midst of plenty" will not necessarily lead to this result. But when poverty and associated disadvantages in competing for the culture values approved for *all* members of the society are linked with a cultural emphasis on pecuniary success as a dominant goal, high rates of criminal behavior are the "normal" outcome. Thus, crude (and not necessarily reliable) crime statistics suggest that poverty is less highly correlated with crime in southeastern Europe than in the United States. The economic life-chances of the poor in these European areas would seem to be even less promising than in this country, so that neither poverty nor its association with limited opportunity is sufficient to account for the varying correlations. However, when we consider the full configuration—

poverty, limited opportunity and the assignment of cultural goals—there appears some basis for explaining the higher correlation between poverty and crime in our society than in others where rigidified class structure is coupled with *differential class symbols of success.*

The victims of this contradiction between the cultural emphasis on pecuniary ambition and the social bars to full opportunity are not always aware of the structural sources of their thwarted aspirations. To be sure, they are typically aware of a discrepancy between individual worth and social rewards. But they do not necessarily see how this comes about. Those who do find its source in the social structure may become alienated from that structure and become ready candidates for Adaptation V (rebellion). But others, and this appears to include the great majority, may attribute their difficulties to more mystical and less sociological sources. For as the distinguished classicist and sociologist-in-spite-of-himself, Gilbert Murray, has remarked in this general connection. "The best seed-ground for superstition is a society in which the fortunes of men seem to bear practically no relation to their merits and efforts. A stable and well-governed society does tend, speaking roughly, to ensure that the Virtuous and Industrious Apprentice shall succeed in life, while the Wicked and Idle Apprentice fails. And in such a society people tend to lay stress on the reasonable or visible chains of causation. But in [a society suffering from anomie] . . ., the ordinary virtues of diligence, honesty, and kindliness seem to be of little avail."[23] And in such a society people tend to put stress on mysticism: the workings of Fortune, Chance, Luck.

In point of fact, both the eminently "successful" and the eminently "unsuccessful" in our society not infrequently attribute the outcome to "luck." Thus, the prosperous man of business, Julius

Rosenwald, declared that 95 per cent of the great fortunes were "due to luck."[24] And a leading business journal, in an editorial explaining the social benefits of great individual wealth, finds it necessary to supplement wisdom with luck as the factors accounting for great fortunes: "When one man through wise investments—aided, we'll grant, by good luck in many cases—accumulates a few millions, he doesn't thereby take something from the rest of us."[25] In much the same fashion, the worker often explains economic status in terms of chance. "The worker sees all about him experienced and skilled men with no work to do. If he is in work, he feel lucky. If he is out of work, he is the victim of hard luck. *He can see little relation between worth and consequences.*"[26]

But these references to the workings of chance and luck serve distinctive functions according to whether they are made by those who have reached or those who have not reached the culturally emphasized goals. For the successful, it is in psychological terms, a disarming expression of modesty. It is far removed from any semblance of conceit to say, in effect, that one was lucky rather than altogether deserving of one's good fortune. In sociological terms, the doctrine of luck as expounded by the successful serves the dual function of explaining the frequent discrepancy between merit and reward while keeping immune from criticism a social structure which allows this discrepancy to become frequent. For if success is primarily a matter of luck, if it is just in the blind nature of things, if it bloweth where it listeth and thou canst not tell whence it cometh or whither it goeth, then surely it is beyond control and will occur in the same measure *whatever the social structure.*

For the unsuccessful and particularly for those among the unsuccessful who find little reward for their merit and their effort, the doctrine of luck serves the psychological function of enabling them to preserve their self-esteem in the face of failure. It may also entail the dysfunction of curbing motivation for sustained endeavor.[27] Sociologically, as implied by Bakke,[28] the doctrine may reflect a failure to comprehend the workings of the social and economic system, and may be dysfunctional inasmuch as it eliminates the rationale of working for structural changes making for greater equities in opportunity and reward.

This orientation toward chance and risk-taking, accentuated by the strain of frustrated aspirations, may help explain the marked interest in gambling—an institutionally proscribed or at best permissive rather than preferred or prescribed mode of activity—within certain social strata.[29]

Among those who do not apply the doctrine of luck to the gulf between merit, effort and reward there may develop an individuated and cynical attitude toward the social structure, best exemplified in the cultural cliché that "it's not what you know, but whom you know, that counts."

In societies such as our own, then, the great cultural emphasis on pecuniary success for all and a social structure which unduly limits practical recourse to approved means for many set up a tension toward innovative practices which depart from institutional norms. But this form of adaptation presupposes that individuals have been imperfectly socialized so that they abandon institutional means while retaining the success-aspiration. Among those who have fully internalized the institutional values, however, a comparable situation is more likely to lead to an alternative response in which the goal is abandoned but conformity to the mores persists. This type of response calls for further examination.

III. Ritualism

The ritualistic type of adaptation can be readily identified. It involves the abandoning or scaling down of the lofty cultural goals of great pecuniary success and rapid social mobility to the point where one's aspirations can be satisfied. But though one rejects the cultural obligation to attempt "to get ahead in the world," though one draws in one's horizons, one continues to abide almost compulsively by institutional norms.

It is something of a terminological quibble to ask whether this genuinely represents "genuinely deviant behavior." Since the adaptation is, in effect, an internal decision and since the overt behavior is institutionally permissive, though not culturally preferred, it is not generally considered to represent a "social problem." Intimates of individuals making this adaptation may pass judgment in terms of prevailing cultural emphases and may "feel sorry for them," they may, in the individual case, feel that "old Jonesy is certainly in a rut." Whether this is described as deviant behavior or no, it clearly represents a departure from the cultural model in which men are obliged to strive actively, preferably through institutionalized procedures, to move onward and upward in the social hierarchy.

We should expect this type of adaptation to be fairly frequent in a society which makes one's social status largely dependent upon one's achievements. For, as has so often been observed,[30] this ceaseless competitive struggle produces acute status anxiety. One device for allaying these anxieties is to lower one's level of aspiration—permanently. Fear produces inaction, or more accurately, routinized action.[31]

The syndrome of the social ritualist is both familiar and instructive. His implicit life-philosophy finds expression in a series of cultural clichés: "I'm not sticking *my* neck out;" "I'm playing safe;" "I'm satisfied with what I've got;" "Don't aim high and you won't be disappointed." The theme threaded through these attitudes is that high ambitions invite frustration and danger whereas lower aspirations produce satisfaction and security. It is a response to a situation which appears threatening and excites distrust. It is the attitude implicit among workers who carefully regulate their output to a constant quota in an industrial organization where they have occasion to fear that they will "be noticed" by managerial personnel and "something will happen" if their output rises and falls.[32] It is the perspective of the frightened employee, the zealously conformist bureaucrat in the teller's cage of the private banking enterprise or in the front office of the public works enterprise.[33] It is, in short, the mode of adaptation of individually seeking a *private* escape from the dangers and frustrations which seem to them inherent in the competition for major cultural goals by abandoning these goals and clinging all the more closely to the safe routines and the institutional norms.

If we should expect *lower-class* Americans to exhibit Adaptation II—"innovation"—to the frustrations enjoined by the prevailing emphasis on large cultural goals and the fact of small social opportunities, we should expect *lower-middle class* Americans to be heavily represented among those making Adaptation III, "ritualism." For it is in the lower middle class that parents typically exert continuous pressure upon children to abide by the moral mandates of the society, and where the social climb upward is less likely to meet with success than among the upper middle class. The strong disciplining for conformity with mores reduces the likelihood of Adaptation II and promotes the likelihood of Adaptation III. The severe training leads many to carry a heavy burden of anxiety. The socialization patterns of the lower middle class thus promote the very character structure most predisposed toward ritualism,[34] and it is in this stratum,

accordingly, that the adaptive pattern III should most often occur.[35]

But we should note again, as at the outset of this paper, that we are here examining *modes of adaptation* to contradictions in the cultural and social structure: we are not focussing on character or personality types. Individuals caught up in these contradictions can and do move from one type of adaptation to another. Thus it may be conjectured that some ritualists, conforming meticulously to the institutional rules, are so steeped in the regulations that they become bureaucratic virtuosos, that they over-conform precisely because they are subject to guilt engendered by previous nonconformity with the rules (*i.e.*, Adaptation II). And the occasional passage from ritualistic adaptation to dramatic kinds of illicit adaptation is well-documented in clinical case-histories and often set forth in insightful fiction. Defiant outbreaks not infrequently follow upon prolonged periods of over-compliance.[36] But though the psychodynamic mechanisms of this type of adaptation have been fairly well identified and linked with patterns of discipline and socialization in the family, much sociological research is still required to explain why these patterns are presumably more frequent in certain social strata and groups than in others. Our own discussion has merely set out one analytical framework for sociological research focussed on this problem.

IV. Retreatism

Just as Adaptation I (conformity) remains the most frequent, Adaptation IV (the rejection of cultural goals and institutional means) is probably the least common. People who "adapt" (or maladapt) in this fashion are, strictly speaking, *in* the society but not *of* it. Sociologically, these constitute the true "aliens." Not sharing the common frame of values, they can be included as members of the

society (in distinction from the *population*) only in a fictional sense.

In this category fall some of the adaptive activities of psychotics, autists, pariahs, outcasts, vagrants, vagabonds, tramps, chronic drunkards and drug addicts.[37] They have relinquished culturally prescribed goals and their behavior does not accord with institutional norms. This is not to say that in some cases the source of their mode of adaptation is not the very social structure which they have in effect repudiated nor that their very existence within an area does not constitute a "problem" for members of the society.

From the standpoint of its sources in the social structure, this mode of adaptation is most likely to occur when *both* the culture goals and the institutional practices have been thoroughly assimilated by the individual and imbued with affect and high value, but accessible institutional avenues are not productive of success. There results a twofold conflict: the interiorized moral obligation for adopting institutional means conflicts with pressures to resort to illicit means (which may attain the goal) and the individual is shut off from means which are both legitimate and effective. The competitive order is maintained but the frustrated and handicapped individual who cannot cope with this order drops out. Defeatism, quietism and resignation are manifested in escape mechanisms which ultimately lead him to "escape" from the requirements of the society. It is thus an expedient which arises from continued failure to near the goal by legitimate measures and from an inability to use the illegitimate route because of internalized prohibitions, *this process occurring while the supreme value of the success-goal has not yet been renounced.* The conflict is resolved by abandoning *both* precipitating elements, the goals and the means. The escape is complete, the conflict is eliminated and the individual is asocialized.

In public and ceremonial life, this type of deviant behavior is most heartily condemned by conventional representatives of the society. In contrast to the conformist, who keeps the wheels of society running, this deviant is a nonproductive liability; in contrast to the innovator who is at least "smart" and actively striving, he sees no value in the success-goal which the culture prizes so highly; in contrast to the ritualist who conforms at least to the mores, he pays scant attention to the institutional practices.

Nor does the society lightly accept these repudiations of its values. To do so would be to put these values into question. Those who have abandoned the quest for success are relentlessly pursued to their haunts by a society insistent upon having all its members orient themselves to success-striving. Thus, in the heart of Chicago's Hobohemia are the book stalls filled with wares designed to revitalize dead aspirations.

The Gold Coast Book Store is in the basement of an old residence, built back from the street, and now sandwiched between two business blocks. The space in front is filled with stalls, and striking placards and posters.

These posters advertise such books as will arrest the attention of the down-and-out. One reads: ". . . Men in thousands pass this spot daily, but the majority of them are not financially successful. They are never more than two jumps ahead of the rent men. Instead of that, they should be more bold and daring," "Getting Ahead of the Game," before old age withers them and casts them on the junk heap of human wrecks. If you want to escape this evil fate—the fate of the vast majority of men —come in and get a copy of *The Law of Financial Success.* It will put some new ideas in your head, and put you on the highroad to success. 35 cent.

There are always men loitering before its stalls. But they seldom buy. Success comes high, even at 35 cents, to the hobo.[38]

But if this deviant is condemned in real life, he may become a source of gratification in fantasy-life. Thus Kardiner has advanced the speculation that such figures in contemporary folklore and popular culture bolster "morale and self-esteem by the spectacle of man rejecting current ideals and expressing contempt for them." The prototype in the films is of course Charlie Chaplin's bum.

He is Mr. Nobody and is very much aware of his own insignificance. He is always the butt of a crazy and bewildering world in which he has no place and from which he constantly runs away into a contented do-nothingness. *He is free from conflict because he has abandoned the quest for security and prestige, and is resigned to the lack of any claim to virtue or distinction.* [A precise characterological portrait of Adaptation IV.] He always becomes involved in the world by accident. There he encounters evil and aggression against the weak and helpless which he has no power to combat. Yet always, in spite of himself, he becomes the champion of the wronged and oppressed, not by virtue of his great organizing ability but by virtue of homely and insolent trickiness by which he seeks out the weakness of the wrongdoer. He always remains humble, poor, and lonely, but is contemptuous of the incomprehensible world and its values. He therefore represents the character of our time who is *perplexed by the dilemma either of being crushed in the struggle to achieve the socially approved goals of success and power* (he achieves it only once—in *The Gold Rush*) or of *succumbing to a hopeless resignation and flight from them.* Charlie's bum is a great comfort in that he gloats in his ability to outwit the pernicious forces aligned against him if he chooses to do so and affords every man the satisfaction of feeling that the ultimate flight from social goals to loneliness is an act of *choice* and not a symptom of his defeat. Mickey Mouse is a continuation of the Chaplin saga.[39]

This fourth mode of adaptation, then, is that of the socially disinherited who if they have none of the rewards held out by society also have few of the frustrations attendant upon continuing to seek these rewards. It is, moreover, a "privatized" rather than a collective mode of adaptation. Although people exhibiting this deviant behavior may gravitate toward centers where they come into contact with other deviants and although they may come to share in the subculture of these deviant groups, their adaptations were largely private and isolated rather than unified under the ægis of a new cultural code. The type of collective adaptation remains to be considered.

V. Rebellion

This adaptation leads men outside the environing social structure to envisage and seek to bring into being a new, that is to say, a greatly modified social structure. It presupposes alienation from reigning goals and standards. These come to be regarded as purely "arbitrary." And the arbitrary is precisely that which can neither exact allegiance nor possess legitimacy, for it might as well be otherwise. In our society, organized movements for rebellion apparently aim to introduce a social structure in which the cultural standards of success would be sharply modified and provision would be made for a closer correspondence between merit, effort and reward.

But before examining "rebellion" as a mode of adaptation, we must distinguish it from a superficially similar but essentially different type, "*ressentiment*." Introduced in a special technical sense, by Nietzsche, the concept of *ressentiment* was taken up and developed sociologically by Max Scheler.[40] This complex sentiment has three interlocking elements. First, diffuse feelings of hate, envy and hostility; second, a sense of being powerless to express these feelings actively against the person or social stratum evoking them; and third, a continual re-experiencing of this impotent hostility.[41] The essential point distinguishing *ressentiment* from rebellion is that the former does not involve a genuine change in values.

Ressentiment involves a sour-grapes pattern which asserts merely that desired but unattainable objectives do not actually embody the prized values—after all, the fox in the fable does not say that he abandons all taste for sweet grapes; he says only that these particular grapes are not sweet. Rebellion, on the other hand, involves a genuine transvaluation, where the direct or vicarious experience of frustration leads to full denunciation of previously prized values—the rebellious fox simply renounces the prevailing taste for sweet grapes. In *ressentiment*, one condemns what one secretly craves; in rebellion, one condemns the craving itself. But though the two are distinct, organized rebellion may draw upon a vast reservoir of the resentful and discontented as institutional dislocations become acute.

When the institutional system is regarded as the barrier to the satisfaction of legitimized goals, the stage is set for rebellion as an adaptive response. To pass into organized political action, allegiance must not only be withdrawn from the prevailing social structure but must be transferred to new groups possessed of a new myth.[42] The dual function of the myth is to locate the source of large-scale frustrations in the social structure and to portray an alternative structure which would not, presumably, give rise to frustration of the deserving. It is a charter for action. In this context, the functions of the counter-myth of the conservatives —briefly sketched in an earlier section of this paper—become further clarified: whatever the source of mass frustration, it is not to be found in the basic structure of the society. The conservative myth may thus assert that these frustrations are in the nature of things and would occur in *any* social system: "Periodic mass unemployment and business depressions can't be legislated out of existence; it's just like a person who feels good one day and bad the next."[43] Or, if not the doc-

trine of inevitability, then the doctrine of gradual and slight adjustment: "A few changes here and there, and we'll have things running as ship-shape as they can possibly be." Or, the doctrine which deflects hostility from the social structure onto the individual who is a "failure" since "every man really gets what's coming to him in this country."

The myths of rebellion and of conservatism both work toward a "monopoly of the imagination" seeking to define the situation in such terms as to move the frustrate toward or away from Adaptation V. It is above all the "renegade" who, though himself "successful," renounces the prevailing values that becomes the target of greatest hostility among those in rebellion. For he not only puts the values in question, as does the out-group, but he signifies that the unity of the group is broken.[44] Yet, as has so often been noted, it is typically a rising class rather than the most depressed strata which organizes the resentful and the rebellious into a revolutionary group.

THE STRAIN TOWARD ANOMIE

The social structure we have examined produces a strain toward anomie and deviant behavior. The pressure of such a social order is upon outdoing one's competitors. So long as the sentiments supporting this competitive system are distributed throughout the entire range of activities and are not confined to the final result of "success," the choice of means will remain largely within the ambit of institutional control. When, however, the cultural emphasis shifts from the satisfactions deriving from competition itself to almost exclusive concern with the outcome, the resultant stress makes for the breakdown of the regulatory structure. With this attenuation of institutional controls, there occurs an approximation to the situation erroneously held by the utilitarian philosophers to be typical of society, a situation in which calculations of personal advantage and fear of punishment are the only regulating agencies.

This strain toward anomie does not operate evenly throughout the society. Some effort has been made in the present analysis to suggest the strata most vulnerable to the pressures for deviant behavior and to set forth some of the mechanisms operating to produce those pressures. For purposes of simplifying the problem, monetary success was taken as the major cultural goal, although there are, of course, alternative goals in the repository of common values. The realms of intellectual and artistic achievement, for example, provide alternative career patterns which may not entail large pecuniary rewards. To the extent that the cultural structure attaches prestige to these alternatives and the social structure permits access to them, the system is somewhat stabilized. Potential deviants may still conform in terms of these auxiliary sets of values.

But the central tendencies toward anomie remain, and it is to these that the analytical scheme here set forth calls particular attention.

THE ROLE OF THE FAMILY

Since this symposium centers about the social institution of the family, a final word should be said drawing together the implications scattered throughout the foregoing discussion concerning the role of the family in these patterns of deviant behavior.

It is the family, of course, which is a major transmission belt for the diffusion of cultural standards to the oncoming generation. But what has until lately been overlooked is that the family largely transmits that portion of the culture accessible to the social stratum and groups in which the parents find themselves. It is, therefore, a mechanism for disciplining the child in terms of the cultural goals and mores characteristic of this narrow range of groups. Nor is the socialization confined to direct training and disciplining. The process is, at least in part, inadvertent. Quite apart from direct admonitions, rewards and punishments, the child is exposed to social prototypes in the witnessed daily behavior and casual conversations of parents. Not infrequently, *children detect and incorporate cultural uniformities even when these remain implicit and have not been reduced to rules.*

Language patterns provide the most impressive evidence, readily observable in clinical fashion, that children, in the process of socialization, detect uniformities which have not been explicitly formulated for them by elders or contemporaries and which are not formulated by the children themselves. Persistent errors of language among children are most instructive. Thus, the child will spontaneously use such words as "mouses" or "moneys," *even though he has never heard such terms or been taught "the rule for forming plurals."* Or he will create such words as "falled," "runned," "singed," "hitted," "bested" though he has not been taught, at the age of three, "rules" of conjugation. Or, he will refer to a choice morsel as "gooder" than another less favored, or perhaps through a logical extension, he may describe it as "goodest" of all. Obviously, he has detected the implicit paradigms for the expression of plurality, for the conjugation of verbs, and the inflection of adjectives. The very nature of his error and misapplication of the paradigm testifies to this.[45]

It may be tentatively inferred, therefore, that he is also busily engaged in *detecting and acting upon the implicit paradigms of cultural evaluation, and categorization of people and things, and the formation of estimable goals* as well as assimilating the explicit cultural orientation set forth in an endless stream of commands, explanations and exhortations by parents. It would appear that in addition to the important researches of the depth psychologies on the socialization process, there is need for supplementary types of direct observation of culture diffusion within the family. It may well be that the child retains the implicit paradigm of cultural values detected in the day-by-day behavior of his parents even when this conflicts with their explicit advice and exhortations.

It is, however, *the projection of parental ambitions* onto the child which is more centrally relevant to this paper. As is well known, many parents confronted with personal "failure" or limited "success" may mute their original goal-emphasis and may defer further efforts to reach the goal, attempting to reach it vicariously through their children. "The influence may come through the mother or the father. Often it is the case of a parent who hopes that the child will attain heights that he or she failed to attain."[46] In a research now in process on the social organization of public housing developments, we have found among both Negroes and Whites that the lower the occupational level of the parent, the larger the proportion having aspirations for a professional career for their children.[47] Should this finding be confirmed by further research it will have large bearing upon the problem in hand. For if compensatory projection of parental ambition onto children is typical, then it is precisely those parents least able to provide free access to opportunity for their children— the "failures" and "frustrates"—who exert greatest pressure upon their children for high achievement. And this syndrome of lofty aspirations and limited realistic opportunities, as we have seen, is precisely the pattern which invites deviant behavior. This clearly points to the need for investigation focussed upon occupational goal-formation in the several social strata

if the inadvertent role of family disciplining in deviant behavior is to be understood from the perspectives of our analytical scheme.

CONCLUDING REMARKS

It should be apparent that the foregoing discussion is not pitched on a moralistic plane. Whatever the sentiments of the reader concerning the moral desirability of coördinating the goals-and-means phases of the social structure, it is clear that imperfect coördination of the two leads to anomie. Insofar as one of the most general functions of social structure is to provide a basis for predictability and regularity of social behavior, it becomes increasingly limited in effectiveness as these elements of the social structure become dissociated. At the extreme, predictability is minimized and what may be properly called anomie or cultural chaos supervenes.

This essay on the structural sources of deviant behavior remains but a brief prelude. It has not included a detailed treatment of the structural elements which predispose towards one rather than another of the alternative responses open to individuals living in an ill-balanced social structure; it has largely neglected but not denied the relevance of the social-psychological processes determining the specific incidence of these responses; it has only briefly considered the social functions fulfilled by deviant behavior; it has not put the explanatory power of the analytical scheme to full empirical test by determining group variations in deviant and conformist behavior; it has only touched upon rebellious behavior which seeks to refashion the social framework.

It is suggested that these and related problems may be advantageously analyzed by use of this scheme.

NOTES

1. See, for example, S. Freud, *Civilization and Its Discontents* (*passim*, and esp. at p. 63); Ernest Jones, *Social Aspects of Psychoanalysis* (London, 1924), p. 28. If the Freudian notion is a variety of the "original sin" doctrine, then the interpretation advanced in this paper is a doctrine of "socially derived sin".

2. "Normal" in the sense of the psychologically expectable, if not culturally approved, response to determinate social conditions. This statement does not, of course, deny the role of biological and personality differences in fixing the *incidence* of deviant behavior. It is simply that *this* is not the problem considered here. It is in the same sense as our own, I take it, that James S. Plant speaks of the "normal reaction of normal people to abnormal conditions." See his *Personality and the Cultural Pattern* (New York, 1937), p. 248.

3. The position taken here has been perceptively described by Edward Sapir: ". . . problems of social science differ from problems of individual behavior in degree of specificity, not in kind. Every statement about behavior which throws the emphasis, explicitly or implicitly, on the actual, integral experiences of defined personalities or types of personalities is a datum of psychology or psychiatry rather than of social science. Every statement about behavior which aims, not to be accurate about the behavior of an actual individual or individuals or about the expected behavior of a physically and psychologically defined type of individual, but which abstracts from such behavior in order to bring out in clear relief certain expectancies with regard to those aspects of individual behavior which various people share, as an interpersonal or 'social' pattern, is a datum, however crudely expressed, of social science." I have here chosen the second perspective; although I shall have occasion to speak of attitudes, values and function, it will be from the standpoint of how the social structure promotes or inhibits their appearance in specified types of situations. See Sapir, "Why Cultural Anthropology Needs the Psychiatrist," *Psychiatry*, 1938, 1, 7–12.

4. This ritualism ·may be associated with a mythology which rationalizes these practices so that they appear to retain their status as means, but the dominant pressure is toward strict ritualistic conformity, irrespective of the mythology. Ritualism is thus most complete when such rationalizations are not even called forth.

5. In this connection, one sees the relevance of Elton Mayo's paraphrase of the title of Tawney's well-known book. "Actually the problem is *not that of the sickness of an acquisitive society; it is that of the acquisitiveness of a sick society.*" *Human Problems of an Industrial Civilization* (New York, 1933), p. 153. Mayo deals with the process through which wealth comes to be the basic symbol of social achievement and sees this as arising from a state of anomie. My major concern here is with the social consequences of a heavy emphasis upon monetary success as a goal in a society which has not adapted its structure to the implications of this emphasis. A complete analysis would require the simultaneous examination of both processes.

6. Durkheim's resurrection of the term "anomie" which, so far as I know, first appears in approximately the same sense in the late sixteenth century, might well become the object of an investigation by a student interested in the historical filiation of ideas. Like the term "climate of opinion" brought into academic and political popularity by A. N. Whitehead three centuries after it was coined by Joseph Glanvill, the word "anomie" (or anomy or anomia) has lately come into frequent use, once it was re-introduced by Durkheim. Why the resonance in contemporary society? For a magnificent model of the type of research required by questions of this order, see Leo Spitzer, "*Milieu* and *Ambiance*: An Essay in Historical Semantics," *Philosophy and Phenomenological Research*, 1942, 3, 1–42, 169–218.

7. It appears unlikely that cultural norms, once interiorized, are wholly eliminated. Whatever residuum persists will induce personality tensions and conflict, with some measure of ambivalence. A manifest rejection of the once-incorporated institutional norms will be coupled with some latent retention of their emotional correlates. "Guilt feelings", "a sense of sin", "pangs of conscience" are diverse terms referring to this unrelieved tension. Symbolic adherence to the nominally repudiated values or rationalizations for the rejection of these values constitute a more subtle expression of these tensions.

8. "Many," not all, unintegrated groups, for the reason mentioned earlier. In groups where the primary emphasis shifts to institutional means, the outcome is normally a type of ritualism rather than anomie.

9. Leo C. Rosten, *Hollywood* (New York, 1940), p. 40.

10. Malcolm S. MacLean, *Scholars, Workers and Gentlemen* (Harvard University Press, 1938), p. 29.

11. *Cf.* A. W. Griswold, *The American Cult of Success* (Yale University doctoral dissertation, 1933); R. O. Carlson, "*Personality Schools*": *A Sociological Analysis* (Columbia University Master's Essay, 1948).

12. There is no lack of typologies of alternative modes of response to frustrating conditions. Freud, in his *Civilization and Its Discontents* (p. 30 ff.) supplies one; derivative typologies, often differing in basic details, will be found in Karen Horney, *Neurotic Personality of Our Time* (New York, 1937); S. Rozenzweig, "The experimental measurement of types of reaction to frustration," in H. A. Murray et al., *Explorations in Personality* (New York, 1938), 585–599; and in the work of John Dollard, Harold Lasswell, Abram Kardiner, Erich Fromm. But particularly in the strictly Freudian typology, the perspective is that of types of individual responses, quite apart from the place of the individual within the social structure. Despite her consistent concern with "culture," for example, Horney does not explore differences in the impact of this culture upon farmer, worker and businessman, upon lower-, middle-, and upper-class individuals, upon members of various ethnic and racial groups, *etc.* As a result, the role of "inconsistencies in culture" is *not* located in its differential impact upon diversely situated

groups. Culture becomes a kind of blanket covering all members of the society equally, apart from their idiosyncratic differences in life-history. It is a primary assumption of our typology that these responses occur with different frequency within various sub-groups in our society precisely because members of these groups or strata are differentially subject to cultural stimulation and social restraints. This sociological orientation will be found in the writings of Dollard and, less systematically, in the work of Fromm, Kardiner and Lasswell. On the general point, see note 3 of this paper.

13. This fifth alternative is on a plane clearly different from that of the others. It represents a transitional response seeking to *institutionalize* new goals and new procedures to be shared by other members of the society. It thus refers to efforts to *change* the existing cultural and social structure rather than to accommodate efforts *within* this structure.

14. Charles Dickens, *American Notes* (Boston: Books, Inc., 1940), p. 218.

15. E. H. Sutherland, "White Collar Criminality," *American Sociological Review*, 1940, 5, 1–12; "Crime and Business," *Annals, American Academy of Political and Social Science*, 1941, 217, 112–118: "Is 'White Collar Crime' Crime?" *American Sociological Review*, 1945, 10, 132–139.

16. James S. Wallertsein and Clement J. Wyle, "Our Law-Abiding Law-Breakers," *Probation*, April, 1947.

17. National Opinion Research Center, *National Opinion on Occupations*, April, 1947. This research on the ranking and evaluation of ninety occupations by a nation-wide sample presents a series of important empirical data. Of great significance is their finding that, despite a slight tendency for people to rank their own and related occupations higher than do other groups, there is a substantial agreement in ranking of occupations among all occupational strata. More researches of this kind are needed to map the cultural topography of contemporary societies.

18. See Joseph D. Lohman, "The Participant Observer in Community Studies," *American Sociological Review*, 1937, 2, 890–898 and William F. Whyte, *Street Corner Society* (Chicago, 1943). Note Whyte's conclusions: "It is difficult for the Cornerville man to get onto the ladder [of success], even on the bottom rung. ... He is an Italian, and the Italians are looked upon by upper-class people as among the least desirable of the immigrant peoples ... the society holds out attractive rewards in terms of money and material possessions to the 'successful' man. For most Cornerville people these rewards are available only through advancement in the world of rackets and politics." (Pp. 273–274.)

19. Numerous studies have found that the educational pyramid operates to keep a large proportion of unquestionably able but economically disadvantaged youth from obtaining higher formal education. This fact about our class structure has been noted with dismay, for example, by Vannevar Bush in his governmental report, *Science: The Endless Frontier*. For a recent study, see W. L. Warner, R. J. Havighurst and M. B. Loeb, *Who Shall Be Educated?* (New York, 1944).

20. The shifting historical role of this ideology is a profitable subject for exploration. The "office-boy-to-president" imagery was once in approximate accord with the facts, in the loose sense that vertical mobility was probably more common then than now. The ideology persists however, possibly because it still performs an important function for motivating members of the society to work within the social framework. It probably operates to increase the probability of Adaptation I and to lessen the probability of Adaptation V. In short, the role of this doctrine has changed from that of roughly valid theorem to that of an ideology.

21. The role of the Negro in this connection raises almost as many theoretical as practical questions. It has been reported that large segments of the Negro population have assimilated the dominant caste's values of pecuniary success and social advancement, but have "realistically adjusted" themselves to the "fact" that social ascent is presently confined almost entirely to movement within the caste. See John Dollard, *Caste and Class in a Southern Town* (New Haven, 1936), 66 ff.; Donald Young, *American Minority Peoples* (New York, 1932), 581; Robert A. Warner, *New Haven Negroes* (New Haven, 1940), 234. See also the subsequent discussion in this paper.

22. This analytical scheme may serve to resolve some of the apparent inconsistencies in the relation between crime and economic status mentioned by P. A. Sorokin. For example, he notes that "not everywhere nor always do the poor show a greater proportion of crime . . . many poorer countries have had less crime than the richer countries. . . . The economic improvement in the second half of the nineteenth century, and the beginning of the twentieth, has not been followed by a decrease of crime." See his *Contemporary Sociological Theories* (New York, 1928), 560–561. The crucial point is, however, that low economic status plays a different dynamic role in different social and cultural structures, as is set out in the text. One should not, therefore, expect a linear correlation between crime and poverty.

23. Gilbert Murray, *Five Stages of Greek Religion* (New York, 1925), 164–165. Professor Murray's chapter on "The Failure of Nerve," from which I have taken this excerpt, must surely be ranked among the most civilized and perceptive sociological analyses in our time.

24. See the quotation from an interview cited in Gustavus Meyers, *History of the Great American Fortunes* (New York, 1937), 706.

25. *Nation's Business*, Vol. 27, No. 9, pp. 8–9.

26. E. W. Bakke, *The Unemployed Man* (New York, 1934), p. 14 (I have supplied the emphasis). Bakke hints at the structural sources making for a belief in luck among workers. "There is a measure of hopelessness in the situation when a man knows that *most of his good or ill fortune is out of his own control and depends on luck.*" (Emphasis supplied.) Insofar as he is forced to accommodate himself to occasionally unpredictable decisions of management, the worker is subject to job insecurities and anxieties: another "seed-ground" for belief in destiny, fate, chance. It would be instructive to learn if such beliefs become lessened where workers' organizations reduce the

probability that their occupational fate will be out
of their own hands. See R. K. Merton, "The
Machine, the Worker, and the Engineer," *Science*,
24 January, 1947, 105, 79–84 (esp. at 79–80).

27. At its extreme, it may invite resignation and
routinized activity (Adaptation III) or a fatalistic
passivism (Adaptation IV), of which more presently.

28. Bakke, *op. cit.*, 14, where he suggests that "the
worker knows less about the processes which cause
him to succeed or have no chance to succeed than
business or professional people. There are more
points, therefore, at which events appear to have
their incidence in good or ill luck."

29. Cf. R. A. Warner, *New Haven Negroes* and
Harold F. Gosnell, *Negro Politicians* (Chicago, 1935),
123–125, both of whom comment in this general
connection on the great interest in "playing the
numbers" among less-advantaged Negroes.

30. See, for example, H. S. Sullivan, "Modern
Conceptions of Psychiatry," *Psychiatry*, 1940, 3,
111–112; Margaret Mead, *And Keep Your Powder
Dry* (New York, 1942), Chapter VII; R. K. Merton,
M. Fiske and A. Curtis, *Mass Persuasion* (New York,
1946), 159–160.

31. P. Janet, "The Fear of Action," *Journal of
Abnormal Psychology*, 1921, 16, 150–160, and the
extraordinary discussion by F. L. Wells, "Social
Maladjustments: Adaptive Regression," in Clark
Murchison, Ed., *Handbook of Social Psychology* (1935),
which bears closely on the type of adaptation
examined here.

32. F. J. Roethlisberger and W. J. Dickson,
Management and the Worker (Cambridge, 1939),
Chapter 18 and pp. 531 ff.; and on the more general
theme, the typically perspicacious remarks of
Gilbert Murray, *op. cit.*, 138–139.

33. R. K. Merton, "Bureaucratic Structure and
Personality," *Social Forces*, 1940, 18, 560–568; "Role
of the Intellectual in Public Bureaucracy," *Ibid.*,
1945, 23, 405–415.

34. See, for example, Allison Davis and John
Dollard, *Children of Bondage* (Washington, 1940),
Chapter 12 ("Child Training and Class"), which,
though it deals with the lower- and lower-middle
class patterns of socialization among Negroes in the
Far South, appears applicable, with slight modification, to the white population as well. On this, see
further M. C. Erickson, "Child-rearing and Social
Status," *American Journal of Sociology*, 1946, 53,
190–192; Allison Davis and R. J. Havighurst, "Social
Class and Color Differences in Child-rearing,"
American Sociological Review, 1946, 11, 698–710:
". . . *the pivotal meaning of social class* to students of
human development is that it defines and systema-
tizes different learning environments for children of
different classes." "Generalizing from the evidence
presented in the tables, we would say that middle-
class children [the authors do not distinguish between
lower-middle and upper-middle strata] are subjected earlier and more consistently to the influences
which make a child an orderly, conscientious,
responsible, and tame person. In the course of this
training middle-class children probably suffer more
frustration of their impulses."

35. This hypothesis still awaits empirical test.
Beginnings in this direction have been made with
the "level of aspiration" experiments which explore

the determinants of goal-formation and modification
in specific, experimentally devised activities. There
is, however, a major obstacle, not yet surmounted,
in drawing inferences from the laboratory situation,
with its relatively slight ego-involvement with the
casual task—pencil-and-paper mazes, ring-throwing,
arithmetical problems, etc.—applicable to the strong
emotional investment with success-goals in the
routines of everyday life. Nor have these experiments, with their *ad hoc* group formations, been able
to reproduce the acute social pressures obtaining in
daily life. (What laboratory experiment reproduces,
for example, the querulous nagging of a modern
Xantippe: "The trouble with you is, you've got no
ambition; a real man would go out and do things"?)
Among studies with a definite though limited
relevance, see especially R. Gould, "Some Sociological Determinants of Goal Strivings," *Journal of
Social Psychology*, 1941, 13, 461–473; L. Festinger,
"Wish, expectation and Group Standards as Factors
Influencing Level of Aspiration," *Journal of Abnormal
and Social Psychology*, 1942, 37, 184–200. For a
resume of researches to the present, see Kurt Lewin
et al., "Level of Aspiration," in J. McV. Hunt, Ed.,
Personality and the Behavior Disorders (New York,
1944), I, Chap. 10.

The conception of "success" as a ratio between
"aspiration" and "achievement" pursued systematically in the level-of-aspiration experiments has,
of course, a long prehistory. Gilbert Murray (*op. cit.*,
138–139) notes the prevalence of this conception
among the thinkers of fourth century Greece. And
in *Sartor Resartus*, Carlyle observes that "happiness"
(gratification) can be represented by a fraction in
which the numerator represents achievement and
the denominator, aspiration. Much the same notion
is examined by William James (*The Principles of
Psychology* [New York, 1902], I, 310). See also F. L.
Wells, *op. cit.*, 879, and P. A. Sorokin, *Social and
Cultural Dynamics* (New York, 1937), III, 161–164.
The critical question is whether this familiar insight
can be subjected to rigorous experimentation in
which the contrived laboratory situation adequately
reproduces the salient aspects of the real-life situation
or whether disciplined observation of routines of
behavior in everyday life will prove the more
productive method of inquiry.

36. In her novel, *The Bitter Box* (New York, 1946),
Eleanor Clark has portrayed this process with great
sensitivity. The discussion by Erich Fromm, *Escape
from Freedom* (New York, 1941), 185–206, may be
cited, without implying acceptance of his concept of
"spontaneity" and "man's inherent tendency toward
self-development." For an example of a sound
sociological formulation: "As long as we assume . . .
that the anal character, as it is typical of the European
lower middle class, is caused by certain early
experiences in connection with defecation, we have
hardly any data that lead us to understand why a
specific class should have an anal social character.
However, if we understand it as one form of
relatedness to others, rooted in the character
structure and resulting from the experiences with the
outside world, we have a key for understanding why
the whole mode of life of the lower middle class, its
narrowness, isolation, and hostility, made for the
development of this kind of character structure"

(pp. 293–294). For an example of a formulation stemming from a kind of latter-day benevolent anarchism here judged as dubious: ". . . there are also certain psychological qualities inherent in man that need to be satisfied. . . . The most important seems to be the tendency to grow, to develop and realize potentialities which man has developed in the course of history—as, for instance, the faculty of creative and critical thinking. . . . It also seems that this general tendency to grow—which is the psychological equivalent of the identical biological tendency—results in such specific tendencies as the desire for freedom and the hatred against oppression, since freedom is the fundamental condition for any growth" (pp. 287–288).

37. Obviously, this is an elliptical statement. These individuals may retain some orientation to the values of their own groupings within the larger society or, occasionally, to the values of the conventional society itself. They may, in other words, shift to other modes of adaptation. But Adaptation IV can be easily detected. Nels Anderson's account of the behavior and attitudes of the bum, for example, can readily be recast in terms of our analytical scheme. See *The Hobo* (Chicago, 1923), 93–98, *et passim.*

38. H. W. Zorbaugh, *The Gold Coast and the Slum* (Chicago, 1929), 108.

39. Abram Kardiner, *The Psychological Frontiers of Society* (New York, 1945), 369–370. (Emphases supplied.) One cannot here pursue the digression of setting out methodological models for putting these hypotheses to stringent empirical test.

40. Max Scheler, *L'homme du ressentiment* (Paris, n.d.). This essay first appeared in 1912; revised and completed, it was included in Scheler's *Abhandlungen und Aufsätze*; appearing thereafter in his *Vom Umsturz der Werte* (1919). The last text was used for the French translation. It has had considerable influence in varied intellectual circles. For an excellent and well-balanced discussion of Scheler's essay, indicating some of its limitations and biasses, the respects in which it prefigured Nazi conceptions, its anti-democratic orientation and, withal, its occasionally brilliant insights, see V. J. McGill, "Scheler's Theory of Sympathy and Love," *Philosophy and Phenomenological Research*, 1942, 2, 273–291. For another critical account which properly criticizes Scheler's view that social structure plays only a secondary role in *ressentiment*, see Svend Ranulf, *Moral Indignation and Middle-Class Psychology: A Sociological Study* (Copenhagen, 1938), 199–204.

41. Scheler, *op. cit.*, 55–56. No English word fully reproduces the complex of elements implied by the word *ressentiment*; its nearest approximation in German would appear to be *Groll*.

42. George S. Pettee, *The Process of Revolution* (New York, 1938), pp. 8–24; see particularly his account of "monopoly of the imagination."

43. R. S. and H. M. Lynd, *Middletown in Transition* (New York, 1937), p. 408, for a series of cultural clichés exemplifying the conservative myth.

44. See the acute observations by George Simmel, *Soziologie* (Leipzig, 1908), 276–277.

45. W. Stern, *Psychology of Early Childhood* (New York, 1924), 166, notes the *fact* of such errors (*e.g.*, "drinked" for "drank"), but does not draw the inferences regarding the detection of implicit paradigms.

46. H. A. Murray *et al.*, *Explorations in Personality*, 307.

47. From a research into the social organization of planned communities by R. K. Merton and Patricia J. Salter, under a grant from the Lavanburg Foundation. The details of patterns of vocational aspiration for children will be set out in a forthcoming publication.

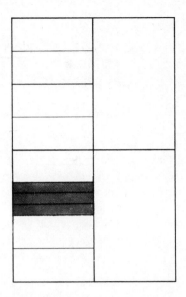

7. EXCHANGE STRUCTURALISM

Exchange structuralism seeks to explain the social as an exchange of behavior between two or more participants—no matter what combination of beneficial and injurious behavior is involved in the exchange. The opening chapter of Blau's book sets forth the basic premises, concepts, and propositions on which his exchange structuralist theory is built.

THE STRUCTURE OF SOCIAL ASSOCIATIONS

PETER M. BLAU

*Of course the elementary qualities of which the social fact consists are
present in germ in individual minds. But the social fact emerges from
them only when they have been transformed by association since it is
only then that it appears. Association itself is also an active factor
productive of special effects. In itself it is therefore something new.
When the consciousness of individuals, instead of remaining isolated,
becomes grouped and combined, something in the world has been altered.*

EMILE DURKHEIM, *Suicide*

To speak of social life is to speak of the
associations between people—their associating together in work and in play,
in love and in war, to trade or to worship,
to help or to hinder. It is in the social
relations men establish that their interests
find expression and their desires become
realized. As Simmel put it: "Social
association refers to the widely varying
forms that are generated as the diverse
interests of individuals prompt them to
develop social units in which they realize
these—sensual or ideal, lasting or fleeting,
conscious or unconscious, casually im-
pelling or teleologically inducing—interests."[1] Simmel's fundamental postulate,
and also that of this book, is that the
analysis of social associations, of the
processes governing them, and of the
forms they assume is the central task of
sociology. The title of this first chapter
can be considered a free translation of
Simmel's basic concept, "Die Formen
der Vergesellschaftung."

People's associations proliferate
through social space and time. Social

relations unite not only individuals in
groups but also groups in communities
and societies. The associations between
individuals tend to become organized
into complex social structures, and they
often become institutionalized to per-
petuate the form of organization far
beyond the life span of human beings.
The main sociological purpose of studying processes of face-to-face interaction
is to lay the foundation for an understanding of the social structures that
evolve and the emergent social forces
that characterize their development.

The objectives of our investigation are
to analyze social associations, the processes that sustain them and the forms
they attain, and to proceed to inquire into
the complex social forces and structures to
which they give rise. Broad as this topic
is, it is intended to provide a specific
focus that explicitly excludes many
sociological problems from consideration.
Sociology is defined by Weber as "a
science which attempts the interpretative
understanding of social action in order
thereby to arrive at a causal explanation
of its course and effects.... Action is
social insofar as, by virtue of the subjective meaning attached to it by the

acting individual (or individuals), it takes account of the behavior of others and is thereby oriented in its course."[2] A concern with social action, broadly conceived as any conduct that derives its impetus and meaning from social values, has characterized contemporary theory in sociology for some years. The resulting preoccupation with value orientations has diverted theoretical attention from the study of the actual associations between people and the structures of their associations. While structures of social relations are, of course, profoundly influenced by common values, these structures have a significance of their own, which is ignored if concern is exclusively with the underlying values and norms. Exchange transactions and power relations, in particular, constitute social forces that must be investigated in their own right, not merely in terms of the norms that limit and the values that reinforce them, to arrive at an understanding of the dynamics of social structures. If one purpose of the title of this chapter is to indicate a link with the theoretical tradition of Simmel, another purpose is to distinguish the theoretical orientation in this monograph from that of Weber and Parsons; not "the structure of social action"[3] but the structure of social associations is the focal point of the present inquiry.

After illustrating the concept of social exchange and its manifestations in various social relations, this chapter presents the main theme of how more complex processes of social association evolve out of simpler ones. Forces of social attraction stimulate exchange transactions. Social exchange, in turn, tends to give rise to differentiation of status and power. Further processes emerge in a differentiated status structure that lead to legitimation and organization, on the one hand, and to opposition and change, on the other. Whereas the conception of reciprocity in exchange implies the existence of balancing forces that create a strain toward equilibrium, the simultaneous operations of diverse balancing forces recurrently produce imbalances in social life, and the resulting dialectic between reciprocity and imbalance gives social structures their distinctive nature and dynamics.

THE EXCHANGE OF SOCIAL REWARDS

By Honour, in its proper and genuine Signification, we mean nothing else but the good Opinion of others. . . .

The Reason why there are so few Men of real Virtue, and so many of real Honour, is, because all the Recompence a Man has of a virtuous Action, is the Pleasure of doing it, which most People reckon but poor Pay; but the Self-denial a Man of Honour submits to in one Appetite, is immediately rewarded by the Satisfaction he receives from another, and what he abates of his Avarice, or any other Passion, is doubly repaid to his Pride. . . .

MANDEVILLE, *The Fable of the Bees*

Most human pleasures have their roots in social life. Whether we think of love or power, professional recognition or sociable companionship, the comforts of family life or the challenge of competitive sports, the gratifications experienced by individuals are contingent on actions of others. The same is true for the most selfless and spiritual satisfactions. To work effectively for a good cause requires making converts to it. Even the religious experience is much enriched by communal worship. Physical pleasures that can be experienced in solitude pale in significance by comparison. Enjoyable as a good dinner is, it is the social occasion that gives it its luster. Indeed, there is something pathetic about the person who derives his major gratification from food or drink as such, since it reveals either excessive need or excessive greed; the pauper illustrates the former, the glutton, the latter. To be sure, there are profound solitary enjoyments—reading a good book, creating a piece of art, producing a scholarly work. Yet these, too, derive much of their significance from being later communicated to and shared with others. The lack of such anticipation makes the solitary activity again somewhat pathetic: the recluse who has nobody to talk to about what he reads; the artist or scholar whose works are completely ignored, not only by his contemporaries but also by posterity.

Much of human suffering as well as much of human happiness has its source in the actions of other human beings. One follows from the other, given the facts of group life, where pairs do not exist in complete isolation from other social relations. The same human acts that cause pleasure to some typically cause displeasure to others. For one boy to enjoy the love of a girl who has committed herself to be his steady date, other boys who had gone out with her must suffer the pain of having been rejected. The satisfaction a man derives from exercising power over others requires that they endure the deprivation of being subject to his power. For a professional to command an outstanding reputation in his field, most of his colleagues must get along without such pleasant recognition, since it is the lesser professional esteem of the majority that defines his as outstanding. The joy the victorious team members experience has its counterpart in the disappointment of the losers. In short, the rewards individuals obtain in social associations tend to entail a cost to other individuals. This does not mean that most social associations involve zero-sum games in which the gains of some rest on the losses of others. Quite the contrary, individuals associate with one another because they all profit from their association. But they do not necessarily all profit equally, nor do they share the cost of providing the benefits equally, and even if there are no direct costs to participants, there are often indirect costs born by those excluded from the association, as the case of the rejected suitors illustrates.

Some social associations are intrinsically rewarding. Friends find pleasure in associating with one another, and the enjoyment of whatever they do together —climbing a mountain, watching a football game—is enhanced by the gratification that inheres in the association itself. The mutual affection between lovers or family members has the same result. It is not what lovers do together but their doing it *together* that is the distinctive source of their special satisfaction—not seeing a play but sharing the experience of seeing it. Social interaction in less intimate relations than those of lovers, family members, or friends, however, may also be inherently rewarding. The sociability at a party or among neighbors or in a work group involves experiences that are not especially profound but are intrinsically gratifying. In these cases, all associates benefit simultaneously from their social interaction, and the only cost they incur is the indirect one of giving up alternative opportunities by devoting time to the association.

Social associations may also be rewarding for a different reason. Individuals often derive specific benefits from social relations because their associates deliberately go to some trouble to provide these benefits for them. Most people like helping others and doing favors for them —to assist not only their friends but also their acquaintances and occasionally even strangers, as the motorist who stops to aid another with his stalled car illustrates. Favors make us grateful, and our expressions of gratitude are social rewards that tend to make doing favors enjoyable, particularly if we express our appreciation and indebtedness publicly and thereby help establish a person's reputation as a generous and competent helper. Besides, one good deed deserves another. If we feel grateful and obligated to an associate for favors received, we shall seek to reciprocate his kindness by doing things for him. He in turn is likely to reciprocate, and the resulting mutual exchange of favors strengthens, often without explicit intent, the social bond between us.

A person who fails to reciprocate favors is accused of ingratitude. This very accusation indicates that reciprocation is expected, and it serves as a social sanction that discourages individuals from forgetting their obligations to associates. Generally, people are grateful for favors and repay their social debts, and both their gratitude and their repayment are social rewards for the associate who has done them favors.[4] The fact that furnishing benefits to others tends to produce these social rewards is, of course, a major reason why people often go to great trouble to help their associates and enjoy doing so. We would not be human if these advantageous consequences of our good deeds were not important inducements for our doing them.[5] There are, to be sure, some individuals who selflessly work for others without any thought of reward and even without expecting gratitude, but these are virtually saints, and saints are rare. The rest of us also act unselfishly sometimes, but we require some incentive for doing so, if it is only the social acknowledgment that we are unselfish.

An apparent "altruism" pervades social life; people are anxious to benefit one another and to reciprocate for the benefits they receive. But beneath this seeming selflessness an underlying "egoism" can be discovered; the tendency to help others is frequently motivated by the expectation that doing so will bring social rewards. Beyond this self-interested concern with profiting from social associations, however, there is again an "altruistic" element or, at least, one that removes social transactions from simple egoism or psychological hedonism. A

basic reward people seek in their associations is social approval, and selfish disregard for others makes it impossible to obtain this important reward.[6]

The social approval of those whose opinions we value is of great significance to us, but its significance depends on its being genuine. We cannot force others to give us their approval, regardless of how much power we have over them, because coercing them to express their admiration or praise would make these expressions worthless. "Action can be coerced, but a coerced show of feeling is only a show."[7] Simulation robs approval of its significance, but its very importance makes associates reluctant to withold approval from one another and, in particular, to express disapproval, thus introducing an element of simulation and dissimulation into their communications. As a matter of fact, etiquette prescribes that approval be simulated in disregard of actual opinions under certain circumstances. One does not generally tell a hostess, "Your party was boring," or a neighbor, "What you say is stupid." Since social conventions require complimentary remarks on many occasions, these are habitually discounted as not reflecting genuine approbation, and other evidence that does reflect it is looked for, such as whether guests accept future invitations or whether neighbors draw one into further conversations.

In matters of morality, however, individuals have strong convictions that constrain them to voice their actual judgments more freely. They usually do not hesitate to express disapproval of or, at least, withhold approval from associates who have violated socially accepted standards of conduct. Antisocial disregard for the welfare of the ingroup meets universally with disapprobation regardless of how immoral, in terms of the mores of the wider community, the norms of a particular group may be. The significance of social approval, therefore, discourages conduct that is utterly and crudely selfish. A more profound morality must rest not merely on group pressure and long-run advantage but primarily on internalized normative standards. In the ideal case, an individual unerringly follows the moral commands of his conscience whatever the consequences. While such complete morality is attained only by the saint and the fool, and most men make some compromises,[8] moral standards clearly do guide and restrain human conduct. Within the rather broad limits these norms impose on social relations, however, human beings tend to be governed in their associations with one another by the desire to obtain social rewards of various sorts, and the resulting exchanges of benefits shape the structure of social relations.

The question that arises is whether a rationalistic conception of human behavior underlies this principle that individuals pursue social rewards in their social associations. The only assumption made is that human beings choose between alternative potential associates or courses of action by evaluating the experiences or expected experiences with each in terms of a preference ranking and then selecting the best alternative. Irrational as well as rational behavior is governed by these considerations, as Boulding has pointed out:

All behavior, in so far as the very concept of behavior implies doing one thing rather than another, falls into the above pattern, even the behavior of the lunatic and the irrational or irresponsible or erratic person. The distinction between rational and irrational behavior lies in the degree of self-consciousness and the stability of the images involved rather than in any distinction of the principle of optimum.[9]

What is explicitly *not* assumed here is that men have complete information, that they have no social commitments restricting their alternatives, that their preferences are entirely consistent or remain constant, or that they pursue one specific ultimate goal to the exclusion of all others. These more restrictive assumptions, which are not made in the present analysis, characterize rationalistic models of human conduct, such as that of game theory.[10] Of particular importance is the fact that men strive to achieve diverse objectives. The statement that men select the most preferred among available alternatives does not imply that they always choose the one that yields them the greatest material profit.[11] They may, and often do, choose the alternative that requires them to make material sacrifices but contributes the most to the attainment of some lofty ideal, for *this* may be their objective. Even in this choice they may err and select an alternative that actually is not the best means to realize their goal. Indeed, the need to anticipate in advance the social rewards with which others will reciprocate for favors in exchange relations inevitably introduces uncertainty and recurrent errors of judgment that make perfectly rational calculations impossible. Granted these qualifications, the assumption that men seek to adjust social conditions to achieve their ends seems to be quite realistic, indeed inescapable.

BASIC PROCESSES

To reward, is to recompense, to remunerate, to return good for good received. To punish, too, is to recompense, to remunerate, though in a different manner; it is to return evil for evil that has been done.

ADAM SMITH, *The Theory of Moral Sentiments*

The basic social processes that govern associations among men have their roots in primitive psychological processes, such as those underlying the feelings of attraction between individuals and their desires for various kinds of rewards. These psychological tendencies are primitive only in respect to our subject matter, that is, they are taken as given without further inquiry into the motivating forces that produce them, for our concern is with the social forces that emanate from them.

The simpler social processes that can be observed in interpersonal associations and that rest directly on psychological dispositions give rise to the more complex social processes that govern structures of interconnected social associations, such as the social organization of a factory or the political relations in a community. New social forces emerge in the increasingly complex social structures that develop in societies, and these dynamic forces are quite removed from the ultimate psychological base of all social life. Although complex social systems have their foundation in simpler ones, they have their own dynamics with emergent properties. In this section, the basic processes of social associations will be presented in broad strokes, to be analyzed subsequently in greater detail, with special attention to their wider implications.

Social attraction is the force that induces human beings to establish social associations on their own initiative and to expand the scope of their associations once they have been formed. Reference here is to social relations into which men enter of their own free will rather than to either those into which they are born (such as kinship groups) or those imposed on them by forces beyond their control (such as the combat teams to which soldiers are assigned), although even in these involuntary relations the extent and intensity of the association depend on the degree of mutual attraction. An individual is attracted to another if he expects associating with him to be in some way rewarding for himself, and his interest in the expected social rewards draws him to the other. The psychological needs and dispositions of individuals determine which rewards are particularly salient for them and thus to whom they will be attracted. Whatever the specific motives, there is an important difference between the expectation that the association will be an intrinsically rewarding experience and the expectation that it will furnish extrinsic benefits, for example, advice. This difference calls attention to two distinct meanings of the term "attraction" and its derivatives. In its narrower sense, social attraction refers to liking another person *intrinsically* and having positive feelings toward him; in the broader sense, in which the term is now used, social attraction refers to being drawn to another person for any reason whatsoever. The customer is attracted in this broader sense to the merchant who sells goods of a given quality at the lowest price, but he has no intrinsic feelings of attraction for him, unless they happen to be friends.

A person who is attracted to others is interested in proving himself attractive to them, for his ability to associate with them and reap the benefits expected from the association is contingent on their finding him an attractive associate and thus wanting to interact with him. Their attraction to him, just as his to them, depends on the anticipation that the association will be rewarding. To arouse this anticipation, a person tries to impress others. Attempts to appear impressive are pervasive in the early stages of acquaintance and group formation. Impressive qualities make a person attractive and promise that associating with him will be rewarding. Mutual attraction prompts people to establish an association, and the rewards they provide each other in the course of their social interaction, unless their expectations are disappointed, maintain their mutual attraction and the continuing association.

Processes of social attraction, therefore, lead to processes of social exchange. The nature of the exchange in an association experienced as intrinsically rewarding, such as a love relationship, differs from that between associates primarily concerned with extrinsic benefits, such as neighbors who help one another with various chores, but exchanges do occur in either case. A person who furnishes needed assistance to associates, often at some cost to himself, obligates them to reciprocate his kindness. Whether reference is to instrumental services or to such intangibles as social approval, the benefits each supplies to the others are rewards that serve as inducements to continue to supply benefits, and the integrative bonds created in the process fortify the social relationship.

A situation frequently arises, however, in which one person needs something another has to offer, for example, help from the other in his work, but has nothing the other needs to reciprocate for the help. While the other may be sufficiently rewarded by expressions of gratitude to help him a few times, he can hardly be expected regularly to devote time and effort to providing help without receiving any return to compensate him for his troubles. (In the case of intrinsic attraction, the only return expected is the willingness to continue the association.) The person in need of recurrent services from an associate to whom he has nothing to offer has several alternatives. First, he may force the other to give him help. Second, he may obtain the help he needs from another source. Third, he may find ways to get along without such help.[12] If he is unable or unwilling to choose any of these alternatives, however, there is only one other course of action left for him; he must subordinate himself to the other and comply with his wishes, thereby rewarding the other with power over himself as an inducement for furnishing the needed help. Willingness to comply with another's demands is a generic social reward, since the power it gives him is a generalized means, parallel to money, which can be used to attain a variety of ends. The power to command compliance is equivalent to credit, which

a man can draw on in the future to obtain various benefits at the disposal of those obligated to him.[13] The unilateral supply of important services establishes this kind of credit and thus is a source of power.

Exchange processes, then, give rise to differentiation of power. A person who commands services others need, and who is independent of any at their command, attains power over others by making the satisfaction of their need contingent on their compliance. This principle is held to apply to the most intimate as well as the most distant social relations. The girl with whom a boy is in love has power over him, since his eagerness to spend much time with her prompts him to make their time together especially pleasant for her by acceding to her wishes. The employer can make workers comply with his directives because they are dependent on his wages. To be sure, the superior's power wanes if subordinates can resort to coercion, have equally good alternatives, or are able to do without the benefits at his disposal. But given these limiting conditions, unilateral services that meet basic needs are the penultimate source of power. Its ultimate source, of course, is physical coercion. While the power that rests on coercion is more absolute, however, it is also more limited in scope than the power that derives from met needs.

A person on whom others are dependent for vital benefits has the power to enforce his demands. He may make demands on them that they consider fair and just in relation to the benefits they receive for submitting to his power. On the other hand, he may lack such restraint and make demands that appear excessive to them, arousing feelings of exploitation for having to render more compliance than the rewards received justify. Social norms define the expectations of subordinates and their evaluations of the superior's demands. The fair exercise of power gives rise to approval of the superior, whereas unfair exploitation promotes disapproval. The greater the resources of a person on which his power rests, the easier it is for him to refrain from exploiting subordinates by making excessive demands, and consequently the better are the chances that subordinates will approve of the fairness of his rule rather than disapprove of its unfairness.

There are fundamental differences between the dynamics of power in a collective situation and the power of one individual over another. The weakness of the isolated subordinate limits the significance of his approval or disapproval of the superior. The agreement that emerges in a collectivity of subordinates concerning their judgment of the superior, on the other hand, has far-reaching implications for developments in the social structure.

Collective approval of power legitimates that power. People who consider that the advantages they gain from a superior's exercise of power outweigh the hardships that compliance with his demands imposes on them tend to communicate to each other their approval of the ruler and their feelings of obligation to him. The consensus that develops as the result of these communications finds expression in group pressures that promote compliance with the ruler's directives, thereby strengthening his power of control and legitimating his authority. "A feeling of obligation to obey the commands of the established public authority is found, varying in liveliness and effectiveness from one individual to another, among the members of any political society."[14] Legitimate authority is the basis of organization. It makes it possible to organize collective effort to further the achievement of various objectives, some of which could not be attained by individuals separately at all and others that can be attained more effectively by coordinating efforts. Al-

though power that is not legitimated by the approval of subordinates can also be used to organize them, the stability of such an organization is highly precarious.

Collective disapproval of power engenders opposition. People who share the experience of being exploited by the unfair demands of those in positions of power, and by the insufficient rewards they receive for their contributions, are likely to communicate their feelings of anger, frustration, and aggression to each other. There tends to arise a wish to retaliate by striking down the existing powers. "As every man doth, so shall it be done to him, and retaliation seems to be the great law that is dictated to us by nature."[15] The social support the oppressed give each other in the course of discussing their common grievances and feelings of hostility justifies and reinforces their aggressive opposition against those in power. It is out of such shared discontent that opposition ideologies and movements develop—that men organize a union against their employer or a revolutionary party against their government.

In brief, differentiation of power in a collective situation evokes contrasting dynamic forces: legitimating processes that foster the organization of individuals and groups in common endeavors; and countervailing forces that deny legitimacy to existing powers and promote opposition and cleavage. Under the influence of these forces, the scope of legitimate organization expands to include ever larger collectivities, but opposition and conflict recurrently redivide these collectivities and stimulate reorganization along different lines.

The distinctive characteristic of complex social structures is that their constituent elements are also social structures. We may call these structures of interrelated groups "macrostructures" and those composed of interacting individuals "microstructures." There are some parallels between the social processes in microstructures and macrostructures. Processes of social attraction create integrative bonds between associates, and integrative processes also unite various groups in a community. Exchange processes between individuals give rise to differentiation among them, and intergroup exchanges further differentiation among groups. Individuals become incorporated in legitimate organizations, and these in turn become part of broader bodies of legitimate authority. Opposition and conflict occur not only within collectivities but also between them. These parallels, however, must not conceal the fundamental differences between the processes that govern the interpersonal associations in microstructures and the forces characteristic of the wider and more complex social relations in macrostructures.

First, value consensus is of crucial significance for social processes that pervade complex social structures, because standards commonly agreed upon serve as mediating links for social transactions between individuals and groups without any direct contact. Sharing basic values creates integrative bonds and social solidarity among millions of people in a society, most of whom have never met, and serves as functional equivalent for the feelings of personal attraction that unite pairs of associates and small groups. Common standards of valuation produce media of exchange—money being the prototype but not the only one—which alone make it possible to transcend personal transactions and develop complex networks of indirect exchange. Legitimating values expand the scope of centralized control far beyond the reach of personal influence, as exemplified by the authority of a legitimate government. Opposition ideals serve as rallying points to draw together strangers from widely dispersed places and unite them in a common cause. The study of these

problems requires an analysis of the significance of social values and norms that must complement the analysis of exchange transactions and power relations but must not become a substitute for it.

A second emergent property of macrostructures is the complex interplay between the internal forces within substructures and the forces that connect the diverse substructures, some of which may be microstructures composed of individuals while others may themselves be macrostructures composed of subgroups. The processes of integration, differentiation, organization, and opposition formation in the various substructures, which often vary greatly among the substructures, and the corresponding processes in the macrostructure all have repercussions for each other. A systematic analysis of these intricate patterns, which will only be adumbrated in chapters ten and eleven, would have to constitute the core of a general theory of social structures.

Finally, enduring institutions typically develop in macrostructures. Established systems of legitimation raise the question of their perpetuation through time. The strong identification of men with the highest ideals and most sacred beliefs they share makes them desirous to preserve these basic values for succeeding generations. The investments made in establishing and expanding a legitimate organization create an interest in stabilizing it and assuring its survival in the face of opposition attacks. For this purpose, formalized procedures are instituted that make the organization independent of any individual member and permit it to persist beyond the life span or period of tenure of its members. Institutionalization refers to the emergence of social mechanisms through which social values and norms, organizing principles, and knowledge and skills are transmitted from generation to generation. A society's institutions constitute the social matrix in which individuals grow up and are socialized, with the result that some aspects of institutions are reflected in their own personalities, and others appear to them as the inevitable external conditions of human existence. Traditional institutions stabilize social life but also introduce rigidities that make adjustment to changing conditions difficult. Opposition movements may arise to promote such adjustment, yet these movements themselves tend to become institutionalized and rigid in the course of time, creating needs for fresh oppositions.

RECIPROCITY AND IMBALANCE

Now in these unequal friendships the benefits that one party receives and is entitled to claim from the other are not the same on either side; . . . the better of the two parties, for instance, or the more useful or otherwise superior as the case may be, should receive more affection than he bestows; since when the affection rendered is proportionate to desert, this produces equality in a sense between the parties, and equality is felt to be an essential element of friendship.

ARISTOTLE, *The Nicomachean Ethics*

There is a strain toward imbalance as well as toward reciprocity in social associations. The term "balance" itself is ambiguous inasmuch as we speak not only of balancing our books but also of a balance in our favor, which refers, of course, to a lack of equality between inputs and outputs. As a matter of fact, the balance of the accounting sheet merely rests, in the typical case, on an underlying imbalance between income and outlays, and so do apparent balances in social life. Individuals and groups are interested in, at least, maintaining a balance between inputs and outputs and staying out of debt in their social transactions; hence the strain toward reciprocity. Their aspirations, however, are to achieve a balance in their favor and accumulate credit that makes their status superior to that of others; hence the strain toward imbalance.

Arguments about equilibrium—that all scientific theories must be conceived in terms of equilibrium models or that any equilibrium model neglects the dynamics of real life—ignore the important point that the forces sustaining equilibrium on one level of social life constitute disequilibrating forces on other levels. For supply and demand to remain in equilibrium in a market, for example, forces must exist that continually disturb the established patterns of exchange. Similarly, the circulation of the elite, an equilibrium model, rests on the operation of forces that create imbalances and disturbances in the various segments of society. The principle suggested is that balanced social states depend on imbalances in other social states; forces that restore equilibrium in one respect do so by creating disequilibrium in others. The processes of association described illustrate this principle.

A person who is attracted to another will seek to prove himself attractive to the other. Thus a boy who is very much attracted to a girl, more so than she is to him, is anxious to make himself more attractive to her. To do so, he will try to impress her and, particularly, go out of his way to make associating with him an especially rewarding experience for her. He may devote a lot of thought to finding ways to please her, spend much money on her, and do the things she likes on their dates rather than those he would prefer. Let us assume that he is successful and she becomes as attracted to him as he is to her, that is, she finds associating with him as rewarding as he finds associating with her, as indicated by the fact that both are equally eager to spend time together.

Attraction is now reciprocal, but the reciprocity has been established by an imbalance in the exchange. To be sure, both obtain satisfactory rewards from the association at this stage, the boy as the result of her willingness to spend as much time with him as he wants, and the girl as the result of his readiness to make their dates enjoyable for her. These reciprocal rewards are the sources of their mutual attraction. The contributions made, however, are in imbalance. Both devote time to the association, which involves giving up alternative opportunities, but the boy contributes in addition special efforts to please her. Her company is sufficient reward by itself, while his is not, which makes her "the more useful or otherwise superior" in terms of their own evaluations, and he must furnish supplementary rewards to produce "equality in a sense between the parties." Although two lovers may, of course, be equally anxious to spend time together and to please one another, it is rare for a perfect balance of mutual affection to develop spontaneously. The reciprocal attraction in most intimate relations—marriages and lasting friendships as well as more temporary attachments—is the result of some imbalance of contributions that compensate for inequalities in spontaneous affection, notably in the form of one partner's greater willingness to defer to the other's wishes.

The relationship between this conception and balance theory in psychology may be briefly indicated. Thus, Newcomb's ABX scheme is concerned with an individual A, who is attracted to another individual B, has a certain attitude toward an object X, and perceives B to have a certain attitude toward X.[16] Discrepancies between any of these elements produce a strain toward balance both in individual systems, that is, internal psychological states, and in collective systems, that is, interpersonal relations. For example, if A prefers the Democrats and B the Republicans, there are several ways for A to restore balance: he may become more favorable toward the Republicans; he may misperceive B's attitude as being really not Republican; he may lose interest in politics,

making the disagreement inconsequential; or he may cease to associate with B and search for other associates whose opinions he finds more congenial. The focus here is on the implications that imbalances in interpersonal relations have for psychological processes that restore balance in the mental states of individuals,[17] on the one hand, and for changes in interpersonal relations on the other. Initially, however, individuals tend to cope with impending imbalances of attraction by seeking to prove themselves attractive to associates they find attractive in order to establish friendly relations and become integrated among them. These processes, rather than those to which Newcomb calls attention, are the main concern of the preceding discussion and of the more extensive one in the next chapter.

The theoretical principle that has been advanced is that a given balance in social associations is produced by imbalances in the same associations in other respects. This principle, which has been illustrated with the imbalances that underlie reciprocal attraction, also applies to the process of social differentiation. A person who supplies services in demand to others obligates them to reciprocate. If some fail to reciprocate, he has strong inducements to withhold the needed assistance from them in order to supply it to others who do repay him for his troubles in some form. Those who have nothing else to offer him that would be a satisfactory return for his services, therefore, are under pressure to defer to his wishes and comply with his requests in repayment for his assistance. Their compliance with his demands gives him the power to utilize their resources at his discretion to further his own ends. By providing unilateral benefits to others, a person accumulates a capital of willing compliance on which he can draw whenever it is to his interest to impose his will upon others, within the limits of the significance the continuing supply of his benefits has for them. The general advantages of power enable men who cannot otherwise repay for services they need to obtain them in return for their compliance; although in the extreme case of the person who has much power and whose benefits are in great demand, even an offer of compliance may not suffice to obtain them.

Here, an imbalance of power establishes reciprocity in the exchange. Unilateral services give rise to a differentiation of power that equilibrates the exchange. The exchange balance, in fact, rests on two imbalances: unilateral services and unilateral power. Although these two imbalances make up a balance or equilibrium in terms of one perspective, in terms of another, which is equally valid, the exchange equilibrium reinforces and perpetuates the imbalances of dependence and power that sustain it. Power differences not only are an imbalance by definition but also are actually experienced as such, as indicated by the tendency of men to escape from domination if they can. Indeed, a major impetus for the eagerness of individuals to discharge their obligations and reciprocate for services they receive, by providing services in return, is the threat of becoming otherwise subject to the power of the supplier of the services. While reciprocal services create an interdependence that balances power, unilateral dependence on services maintains an imbalance of power.

Differentiation of power evidently constitutes an imbalance in the sense of an inequality of power; but the question must be raised whether differentiation of power also necessarily constitutes an imbalance in the sense of a strain toward change in the structure of social relations. Power differences as such, analytically conceived and abstracted from other considerations, create such a pressure toward change, because it can be assumed that men experience having to submit to power as a hardship from which they would prefer to escape. The advantages men derive from their ruler or government, however, may outweigh the hardships entailed in submitting to his or its power, with the result that the analytical imbalance or disturbance introduced by power differences is neutralized. The significance of power imbalances for social change depends, therefore, on the reactions of the governed to the exercise of power.

Social reactions to the exercise of power reflect once more the principle of reciprocity and imbalance, although in a new form. Power over others makes it possible to direct and organize their activities. Sufficient resources to command power over large numbers enable a person or group to establish a large organization. The members recruited to the organization receive benefits, such as financial remuneration, in exchange for complying with the directives of superiors and making various contributions to the organization. The leadership exercises power within the organization, and it derives power from the organization for use in relation with other organizations or groups. The clearest illustration of this double power of organizational leadership is the army commander's power over his own soldiers and, through the force of their arms, over the enemy. Another example is the power business management exercises over its own employees and, through the strength of the concern, in the market. The greater the external power of an organization, the greater are its chances of accumulating resources that put rewards at the disposal of the leadership for possible distribution among the members.

The normative expectations of those subject to the exercise of power, which are rooted in their social experience, govern their reactions to it. In terms of these standards, the benefits derived from being part of an organization or political society may outweigh the investments required to obtain them, or the demands made on members may exceed the returns they receive for fulfilling these demands. The exercise of power, therefore, may produce two different kinds of imbalance, a positive imbalance of benefits for subordinates or a negative imbalance of exploitation and oppression.

If the members of an organization, or generally those subject to a governing leadership, commonly agree that the demands made on them are only fair and just in view of the ample rewards the leadership delivers, joint feelings of obligation and loyalty to superiors will arise and bestow legitimating approval on their authority. A positive imbalance of benefits generates legitimate authority for the leadership and thereby strengthens and extends its controlling influence. By expressing legitimating approval of, and loyalty to, those who govern them subordinates reciprocate for the benefits their leadership provides, but they simultaneously fortify the imbalance of power in the social structure.

If the demands of the men who exercise power are experienced by those subject to it as exploitative and oppressive, and particularly if these subordinates have been unsuccessful in obtaining redress for their grievances, their frustrations tend to promote disapproval of existing powers and antagonism toward them. As the oppressed communicate their anger and aggression to each other, provided there are opportunities for doing so, their mutual support and approval socially justify and reinforce the negative orientation toward the oppressors, and their collective hostility may inspire them to organize an opposition. The exploitative use of coercive power that arouses active opposition is more prevalent in the relations between organizations and groups than within organizations. Two reasons for this are that the advantages of legitimating approval restrain organizational superiors and that the effectiveness

of legitimate authority, once established, obviates the need for coercive measures. But the exploitative use of power also occurs within organizations, as unions organized in opposition to exploitative employers show. A negative imbalance for the subjects of power stimulates opposition. The opposition negatively reciprocates, or retaliates, for excessive demands in an attempt to even the score, but it simultaneously creates conflict, disequilibrium, and imbalance in the social structure.[18]

Even in the relatively simple structures of social association considered here, balances in one respect entail imbalances in others. The interplay between equilibrating and disequilibrating forces is still more evident, if less easy to unravel, in complex macrostructures with their cross-cutting substructures, where forces that sustain reciprocity and balance have disequilibrating and imbalancing repercussions not only on other levels of the same substructure but also on other substructures. As we shall see, disequilibrating and re-equilibrating forces generate a dialectical pattern of change in social structures.

CONCLUSIONS

In this chapter the basic processes underlying the structure of social associations were outlined, and some of the emergent forces characteristic of complex social structures were briefly indicated. The principles presented in simplified form to convey an overall impression of the theoretical scheme in this book will be elaborated and refined in subsequent chapters. After discussing processes of social integration, support, and exchange in interpersonal associations in some detail, various aspects of social differentiation in groups will be analyzed, and finally attention will be centered on the implication of these social forces as well as of newly emergent ones for organization and change in complex social structures.

The discussion will proceed, therefore, from the basic processes that govern the social interaction between individuals in microstructures to the increasingly complex processes in macrostructures composed of several layers of intersecting substructures. We shall be concerned with the changes in social processes that occur as one moves from simpler to more complex social structures and with the new social forces that emerge in the latter. Entire countries, for example, cannot rely for social control primarily on social approval and personal obligations, as small groups of friends can, and must consequently give formalized procedures and coercive powers, such as law courts and police forces, a more prominent role. While progressing from the simpler to the more complex seems to be the only logical sequence, it does pose some problems in the study of social life.

The pattern of association between two individuals is, of course, strongly influenced by the social context in which it occurs. Even the analysis of social interaction in dyads, therefore, must not treat these pairs as if they existed in isolation from other social relations. The mutual attraction of two persons and the exchanges between them, for example, are affected by the alternative opportunities of each, with the result that competitive processes arise that include wider circles and that complement and modify the processes of exchange and attraction in this pair and in other pairs. The power of an individual over another depends entirely on the social alternatives or lack of alternatives of the subjected individual, and this fact, as well as some others, makes it mandatory to examine power relations in a wider context than the isolated pair. Simmel's perceptive dis-

cussion of the dyad and the triad is instructive in this connection.[19]

Simmel's analysis of the dyad seems to be conceived as a polar case that highlights, by contrast, the distinctive characteristics of group life. To cite only one example, the death or withdrawal of one individual destroys the dyad, whereas groups are not completely dependent on any single member. His discussion of the triad is explicitly concerned with the significance of a multiplicity of social relations in social life, and his use of the triad for this purpose is apparently intended to emphasize the crucial distinction between a pair and any group of more than two.[20] Power can be strengthened by dividing the opposition (*divide et impera*); it can be resisted by forming coalitions (*tertius gaudens*); and power conflicts can be mediated by third parties. All these distinctive processes of the dynamics of power cannot be manifest in a dyad. The legitimation of the power of a superior and the mobilization of opposition to him also do not occur in dyads but only if a superior is confronted by a group of subordinates in communication with each other.

It is essential, in the light of these considerations, to conceptualize processes of social association between individuals realistically as finding expression in networks of social relations in groups and not to abstract artificially isolated pairs from this group context. Crusoe and Friday were a dyad that existed in isolation, but most associations are part of a broad matrix of social relations. Although the analysis of complex structures will be postponed until after interpersonal processes have been examined, the group structures within which the associations between individuals occur will be taken into account from the very beginning.

NOTES

1. Georg Simmel, *Soziologie*, Leipzig: Duncker und Humblot, 1908, p. 6 (my translation).
2. Max Weber, *The Theory of Social and Economic Organization*, New York: Oxford University Press, 1947, p. 88.
3. The title of Talcott Parsons' first major work, *The Structure of Social Action*, New York: McGraw-Hill, 1937, would also be appropriate for some of his later theoretical writings, as he himself has noted in *The Social System*, Glencoe: Free Press, 1951, p. ix.
4. "We rarely meet with ingratitude, so long as we are in a position to confer favors." François La Rochefoucauld, *The Maxims*, London: Oxford University Press, 1940, p. 101 (#306).
5. Once a person has become emotionally committed to a relationship, his identification with the other and his interest in continuing the association provide new independent incentives for supplying benefits to the other. Similarly, firm commitments to an organization lead members to make recurrent contributions to it without expecting reciprocal benefits in every instance. The significance of these social attachments is further elaborated in subsequent chapters.
6. Bernard Mandeville's central theme is that private vices produce public benefits because the importance of social approval prompts men to contribute to the welfare of others in their own self-interest. As he put it tersely at one point, "Moral Virtues are the Political Offspring which Flattery begot upon Pride." *The Fable of the Bees*, Oxford: Claredon, 1924, Vol. I, 51; see also pp. 63–80.
7. Erving Goffman, *Asylums*, Chicago: Aldine, 1962, p. 115.
8. Heinrich von Kleist's story "Michael Kohlhaas" is a pathetic illustration of the foolishness inherent in the insistence on rigid conformity with moral standards in complete disregard of consequences.
9. Kenneth Boulding, *Conflict and Defense*, New York: Harper, 1962, p. 151.
10. For a discussion of game theory which calls attention to its limitations, see R. Duncan Luce and Howard Raiffa, *Games and Decisions*, New York: Wiley, 1957, esp. chapters iii and vii. For other criticisms of game theory, notably its failure to utilize empirical research, and an attempt to incorporate some of its principles into a substantive theory of conflict, see Thomas C. Schelling, *The Strategy of Conflict*, Cambridge: Harvard University Press, 1960, esp. chapters iv and vi.
11. See on this point George C. Homans, *Social Behavior*, New York: Harcourt, Brace and World, 1961, pp. 79–80; and Anatol Rapoport, *Fights, Games, and Debates*, Ann Arbor: University of Michigan Press, 1960, p. 122.
12. The last two of these alternatives are noted by Parsons (*op. cit.*, p. 252) in his discussion of a person's reactions to having his expectations frustrated by another.
13. See Parsons, "On the Concept of Influence," *Public Opinion Quarterly*, 27 (1963), 37–62, esp. pp. 59–60.
14. Bertrand de Jouvenel, *Sovereignty*, University of Chicago Press, 1957, p. 87.
15. Adam Smith, *The Theory of Moral Sentiments* (2nd ed.), London: A. Millar, 1761, p. 139.
16. Theodore M. Newcomb, *The Acquaintance Process*, New York: Holt, Rinehart and Winston, 1961, esp. chapter ii. See also Fritz Heider, *The Psychology of Interpersonal Relations*, New York: Wiley, 1958.
17. Processes that restore the psychological balance of individuals by reducing dissonance, that is, by decreasing the significance of an unattainable object or person, are the central focus in Leon Festinger, *A Theory of Cognitive Dissonance*, Evanston: Row, Peterson, 1957.
18. Organized opposition gives expression to latent conflicts and makes them manifest.
19. Georg Simmel, *The Sociology of Georg Simmel*, Glencoe: Free Press, 1950, chapters iii and iv.
20. See *ibid.*, pp. 138–139, 141, 145.

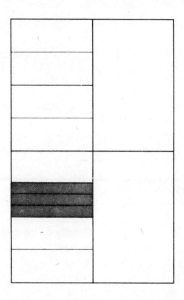

8. CONFLICT STRUCTURALISM

Conflict structuralism seeks to explain the social as an exchange of behavior between two or more participants—given that the exchange involves some injurious *behavior. The article by van den Berghe shows how conflict structuralism and functional structuralism complement each other. Dahrendorf's discussion of the former includes a critique of functionalism and states some of the social phenomena that he believes an adequate theory of conflict must explain.*

DIALECTIC AND FUNCTIONALISM:
TOWARD A THEORETICAL SYNTHESIS

PIERRE L. VAN DEN BERGHE

Functionalism and the Hegelian-Marxian dialectic each stress one of two essential aspects of social reality, and are thus complementary to one another. My procedure will be to examine in turn the basic postulates of functionalism and the Hegelian-Marxian dialectic, show the limitations of each theory as a complete model of society, examine some of Dahrendorf's[1] reformulations, and, finally, by retaining and modifying elements of the two approaches, search for a unified theory.

FUNCTIONALISM

With the rapidly growing body of literature on functionalism,[2] that theoretical position has become both more sophisticated and more elusive of definition. Davis even goes so far as to argue that, irrespective of what they call themselves, all sociologists use much the same analytical framework.[3] Adherence to Davis' viewpoint can result in either optimism or dismay. I shall try to show, however, that functionalism is not a myth, but an important though fragmentary approach to social reality.

One must reject at the outset facile criticisms based on beating the dead horse of extreme Malinowskian functionalism. Such criticisms as that societies are never perfectly integrated, that not every element of a social system is functional or essential, and that functionalism cannot

account for change have been satisfactorily answered and shown to be untrue or irrelevant by leading exponents of the "school," notably by Merton.[4]

Our concern, then, is with the more recent brand of functionalism in its most sophisticated and cautious form, and as represented by Parsons, Merton and Davis. Reduced to its common denominator, the functionalist or "structure-function" approach seems to involve the following postulates or elements:

1) Societies must be looked at holistically as systems of interrelated parts.

2) Hence, causation is multiple and reciprocal.

3) Although integration is never perfect, social systems are fundamentally in a state of dynamic equilibrium, i.e. adjustive responses to outside changes tend to minimize the final amount of change within the system. The dominant tendency is thus towards stability and inertia, as maintained through built-in mechanisms of adjustment and social control.

4) As a corollary of 3), dysfunctions, tensions and "deviance" do exist and can persist for a long time, but they tend to resolve themselves or to be "institutionalized" in the long run. In other words, while perfect equilibrium or integration is never reached, it is the limit towards which social systems tend.

5) Change generally occurs in a gradual, adjustive fashion, and not in a sudden, revolutionary way. Changes which appear to be drastic, in fact affect mostly the social superstructure while leaving the core elements of the social

Reprinted from the *American Sociological Review* (October 1963), pp. 695–705, by permission of the American Sociological Association and the author.

and cultural structure largely unchanged.

6) Change comes from basically three sources: adjustment of the system to exogenous (or extra-systemic) change; growth through structural and functional differentiation; and inventions or innovations by members or groups within society.

7) The most important and basic factor making for social integration is value consensus, i.e., underlying the whole social and cultural structure, there are broad aims or principles which most members of a given social system consider desirable and agree on. Not only is the value system (or ethos) the deepest and most important source of integration, but it is also the stablest element of socio-cultural systems.

The first two postulates are useful and provisionally acceptable, although we shall formulate reservations about the first one later. Any wholesale rejection of the holistic approach leads to sterile classification of cultural items torn out of context (as represented for example by diffusionism in anthropology). A rejection of the model of multiple and reciprocal causation entails all the pitfalls of the many different brands of one-sided determinism.

The other five elements of functionalism outlined above are further reducible to two basic postulates, those of consensus and of dynamic equilibrium or integration. Both of these assumptions can be traced back to Comte, and have permeated much of British and American sociology and anthropology via Durkheim, acquiring the sanctity of tradition. The two postulates lead to a self-created *impasse* by making certain problems insoluble and by presenting a partially valid but slanted concept of social reality.

In a nutshell my argument is that, while societies do indeed show a tendency towards stability, equilibrium, and consensus, they simultaneously generate within themselves the opposites of these.

Let us begin with the assumption that value consensus constitutes the most basic focus of social integration. Consensus is certainly an important basis for integration, but it is also true that societies (except perhaps the least differentiated ones) fall far short of complete consensus, and often exhibit considerable dissension[5] about basic values. To generalize from the Trobrianders and the Arunta to complex, stratified and culturally pluralistic societies is clearly unsound. Numerous societies (e.g. colonial countries) integrate widely different cultures possessing quite different value systems. Even in culturally homogeneous societies, various social groups such as classes can hold antithetical political and economic values (as shown by class conflicts in nineteenth century Europe). Conversely, consensus such as is found in charismatic movements of a revivalistic or messianistic type can precipitate the disintegration of a society, as we shall see later.

What remains then of the consensus assumption? Clearly, to make value consensus a prerequisite to the existence of a social system (as Parsons does, for example) is untenable.[6] Granting that consensus is often an important (but not a necessary) basis of social integration, one has to accept that consensus can also have disintegrative consequences, that most complex societies show considerable dissension, and that there are alternative bases of integration to consensus (e.g. economic interdependence and political coercion). Consensus, then, is a major dimension of social reality, but so are dissension and conflict. Furthermore, there is no necessary direct relation between consensus and equilibrium or integration.

The postulate of consensus, however, is logically gratuitous to functionalist theory, i.e. one could logically retain a functionalist model of integration while rejecting the consensus assumption. We must therefore examine separately the postulate of dynamic equilibrium, the real logical cornerstone of the "structure-function" approach. Here a common confusion must be dispelled at once. The concepts of equilibrium or integration are distinctly different from those of stability and inertia. Relatively integrated societies can change faster than societies in a state of strain and conflict. The model of dynamic equilibrium has change built into it, albeit a minimization thereof. Adjustive change of the social system, in response either to exogenous change, or to endogenous change in one of its parts, is a condition to the maintenance of equilibrium. Conversely, increasing disequilibrium or malintegration can result from stability and inertia in certain elements of a society (e.g. the political systems) which fail to adjust to changes in other parts of the society. However, a simple inverse relation between equilibrium and stability is likewise untenable, as not all change is adjustive. We shall return to this point later.

The usefulness of the integration or equilibrium model (in its sophisticated and minimal form) suggests that it must be salvaged, at least in part. A minimum of integration must certainly be maintained for any social system to subsist. Furthermore, far from making the analysis of change impossible, functionalism has proven a powerful intrument in dealing with at least two major types of change: growth in complexity through differentiation, and adjustment to extra-systemic changes (e.g. problems of acculturation). At the same time, the equilibrium model cannot account for certain phenomena, and, hence, cannot be accepted as a complete and satisfactory representation of society.

More specifically, a dynamic equilibrium model cannot account for the irreducible facts that:

1) reaction to extra-systemic change is not always adjustive,

2) social systems can, for long periods,

go through a vicious circle of ever deepening malintegration,

3) change can be revolutionary, i.e. both sudden and profound,

4) the social structure itself generates change through internal conflicts and contradictions.

The fourth shortcoming of functionalism results from looking at social structure as the static "backbone" of society, and considering structural analysis in social science as analogous to anatomy or morphology in biology. More than anybody else, Radcliffe-Brown is responsible for this one-sided outlook which has blinded functionalism to the conflicts and contradictions inherent in social structure.[7] In short, through its incomplete emancipation from organicism, functionalism has systematically overlooked one of the crucial sources of endogenous change. Insofar as functionalists have had to take cognizance of problems of conflict and dissension, they have done so in terms of "deviance," or "variance," i.e. an unaccountable aberration from, or modification of, the "dominant pattern" which somehow tends to resolve itself through "institutionalization." To account for endogenous change through conflict and contradiction, the dialectic must be introduced to complement functionalism. We shall return to that point later.

Related to, but analytically distinguishable from, the problem of endogenous change are the difficulties arising from the functionalist assumption that social systems adjust gradually to changes from outside, and uniformly tend towards equilibrium or integration. Basically, I believe that it is correct to speak of a long-range tendency towards integration. Functionalism is slanted in that it underrates conflict and disequilibrium, and assumes too much continuity, gradualness and uniformity in the process of change. Rather than scrapping the equilibrium model, however, we must try to modify it.

An expanded model of equilibrium has to allow for at least two alternative sequences of change. A social system can, and often does, gradually adjust to external changes, and hence, tend fairly uniformly towards integration. But a social system can also resist exogenous change and fail to adapt, either by remaining static or by introducing reactionary change. In this case, a cycle of cumulative dysfunction and increasing malintegration is initiated, which beyond a certain point, becomes irreversible, and makes drastic revolutionary change inevitable. This second alternative is compatible with a postulate of long-range tendency towards equilibrium. Indeed, revolution is fundamentally a process whereby accumulated imbalances between major elements of society (e.g. the political and the economic system) are eliminated, and a new state of relative integration achieved. This expanded equilibrium model meets the first three objections to the "classical" functionalist position: it allows the possibility of maladjustive change, of vicious circles of malintegration, and of abrupt "social mutations" through revolution.

At the same time, the revised model raises new problems which must be answered if it is to be heuristic. What forces "push" a society towards either the adjustive or the maladjustive alternative? In the latter case, what are the symptoms that the vicious circle is irreversible, short of revolution? What is the empirical range of variation on the dimension of integration (i.e. how closely can a system approximate perfect equilibrium), and, conversely, how much disequilibrium can it tolerate?

I can only suggest tentative answers. As regards the first question, we may hypothesize that the probability of entering a maladaptive cycle increases to the extent that the *status quo* is rewarding (or, conversely, that innovation is perceived as threatening) either to the society as a

whole, or to its ruling group or groups (i.e. those who have the power to determine and enforce policy). While this statement appears tautological, I must stress that the notions of "reward" and "threat" are much broader and less mechanistic than the Marxian concept of "class interests," and include such diverse things as prestige, emotional or physical security, power, wealth and values. Likewise, I make no assumption that a single ruling class automatically acts in conformity with its "objective interests."

As symptoms of the inevitability of revolution (by which I do not necessarily imply physical violence), I would suggest lack of communication, unwillingness to compromise, disagreement about the "rules of the game," and reciprocal denial of legitimacy between the opposing groups. Finally, concerning societal tolerance for disequilibrium, the limits appear much wider than a functionalist position would lead one to expect. For many different reasons (such as efficient repression, strong ties of economic interdependence, or a complex crisscrossing of lines of conflict and cleavage), social systems can show great resilience to malintegration.

THE HEGELIAN-MARXIAN DIALECTIC

Let us now turn to the dialectic and see what it can offer social theory. Facile rejection of the dialectic method based either on vulgar Marxism, or, at a more sophisticated level, on the failure of Marxian orthodoxy to explain certain facts and predict certain developments has led many sociologists to throw out the baby with the bath. A detailed critical examination of dialectical materialism and Hegelian idealism is plainly out of place here: first, because there is no point in beating the dead horse of orthodoxy; second, because the task has been successfully accomplished by countless people.[8]

What can usefully be salvaged of the

dialectic? Marx himself shows us the way here by rejecting Hegelian idealism and retaining the dialectic outlook. The irony is that Marx then fell into the dialectic trap by advancing his own brand of one-sided determinism as an antithesis to Hegel's idealism. Clearly, Marx's economic determinism (and hence much of the complex theoretical edifice built upon it) is as untenable as the idealism of Hegel which Marx ridiculed with ponderous sarcasm. There is no logical reason, however, why the dialectic method or outlook should be tied to any one-sided determinism, and why discarding the latter should entail a rejection of the former.

Hegel's great insight consisted in conceiving of change as inherent in the nature of ideas. Marx, in turn, showed the applicability of the thesis-antithesis-synthesis sequence to social structure. Two important limitations to the dialectic suggest themselves at this point. First, any claim that the dialectical process is the *only* source of change is untenable. The dialectical analysis of change complements and does not supplant the functionalist view of change through differentiation and adaption to external conditions. Any approximation to a satisfactory model of social dynamics requires at least these three distinct sources of change (not to mention individual invention or innovation which is at a different level of analysis because of its psychological dimension, and which is difficult to integrate into either the dialectic or the functionalist model).

The second limitation of the dialectic is its dualistic view of social reality. The difficulty seems to be that Hegel and Marx confused an empirical tendency for contradictions and conflicts to polarize into pairs of opposites, with a logical necessity to do so. In the realm of ideas, a thesis can give rise to several different antitheses and syntheses. Similarly, Marx ran into insuperable, self-created *impasses* by trying to cling to his binary class model, and, in fact, he often was forced to speak of "intermediate" classes (e.g. the petty bourgeoisie), or remnants from pre-capitalistic classes (e.g. the feudal nobility). As to the peasantry, it still remains the *Poltergeist* of Marxian class analysis.

What is left of the dialectic, one may legitimately ask, if one accepts all the above restrictions? Admittedly not very much, but the residual core is of great importance. As a reformulation of a "minimum" dialectic, the following elements appear both useful and valid:

1) Change is not only ubiquitous, but an important share of it is generated within the system; i.e. the social structure must be looked at, not only as the static framework of society, but also as the source of a crucial type of change.

2) Change of intra-systemic or endogenous origin often arises from contradiction and conflict between two or more opposing factors. These "factors" can be values, ideologies, roles, institutions or groups.

This minimum dialectic approach (if it can still be called that) seems applicable at three different levels of analysis. The first level, that of values or ideas, corresponds to Hegel's use of the dialectic, and includes the study of contradictions and conflicts between values, political or religious ideologies, and scientific or philosophical theories. In short, it is concerned with all conflicts involving abstract but explicitly formulated cultural concepts, viewed in isolation from concrete participants.

The other two levels of dialectic analysis are intertwined in Marx's writings, but it is essential to distinguish between them. One of them deals with institutionalized principles or forces arising out of the social structure, or, in different words, with the internal contradictions (generally latent, i.e. unrecognized and unintended) growing out of institutionalized processes of interaction. For example, the principle of authority is essential to the maintenance of structural stability and functional efficiency of practically all human groups; but, at the same time, authority generates conflicts and tensions which can threaten the disruption of groups. Finally, the third level of analysis concerns group conflicts. In any society, different groups (defined by sex, age, "race," culture, education, relation to the means of production, wealth, power, prestige, descent, etc.) have, by virtue of their differing roles and statuses, interests which often are conflicting.

Obviously, a binary model of group opposition based on the relation to the means of production (as advanced by Marx) or on the exercise of power (Mosca), or on any other single factor, is untenable. While some oppositions are inherently dualistic (e.g. those based on sex), and while conflict often favors polarization into two camps, there is no magic in the number two. Conflicts arising from differences between age groups, for example, often follow a three-fold division (young, adult, old). Furthermore, societies invariably have several lines of cleavages which may, but often do not, overlap. Neither is it permissible to assume that groups in different positions *necessarily* have conflicting interests, or that they are always *conscious* of "objectively" antagonistic interests, or that, if groups have *some* conflicting interests, they cannot simultaneously share interests that override differences.

A CRITIQUE OF DAHRENDORF

Having sketched the main lines of theoretical house-cleaning in relation to functionalism and the dialectic, and indicated which elements of both should be retained, we can turn to Dahrendorf's work. While Dahrendorf's central concern is much the same as ours, and while he reaches a number of similar conclusions, his reformulations are slanted more in favor of the dialectic and against functionalism.[9] After criticizing functionalism and Marxian orthodoxy, Dahrendorf pleads for a development of conflict theory. He considers the two theoretical approaches valid and complementary (with many of the same limitations dealt with here), but leaves open the question whether the thesis and the antithesis can be integrated into a grand theoretical synthesis. Dahrendorf then assigns himself the task of developing one circumscribed aspect of conflict theory, namely class conflict as a special case of group conflict, which, in turn, is a special case of an all-encompassing conflict model.

Within present space limitations, I could not do justice to Dahrendorf's valuable contributions. Suffice it to say that he rejects Marx's definition of class as determined by the relation to the means of production, and Marx's notion that complex societies can be analyzed in terms of a basic dichotomy.[10] Dahrendorf then substitutes his own definition of class as determined by the unequal distribution of authority.[11] From that concept of class, he derives a binary model of class conflict, but unlike Marx, he does not apply it to total societies. Each "imperatively coordinated association" (Weber's *Herrschaftsverband*), which can be anything from a chess club or a nuclear family, to an industrial organization or a state, has its own dichotomous class structure; those who exercise authority, and those who are excluded from it. A total society thus has a multiplicity of "class-pairs" which may or may not overlap.[12] The distribution of authority within a given association is always dichotomous, different positions in relation to authority necessarily involve conflicting interests, and class conflict revolves around the struggle for authority.[13]

Dahrendorf then refines his analysis by introducing several variables (such as intensity and violence of conflict, and suddenness and radicalness of change) from which he derives a set of testable propositions.[14] Many of the latter withstand the test of my South African evidence and prove quite useful, while others call for refinement and modification. But a detailed examination of them would be out of place here. Instead, I want to question two of Dahrendorf's most basic notions, namely his concept of class and his postulate of the dichotomous nature of conflict.

The central importance that Dahrendorf assigns to authority in his analysis of class is open to question. He reverses the Marxian chain of causation and considers economic factors as derivative from the unequal distribution of authority.[15] To be sure, Dahrendorf's political determinism is more cautious than Marx's economic determinism, insofar as Dahrendorf admits the existence of many other types of conflict group besides "classes." But he neither demonstrates why authority is prior to the relation to the means of production, nor convincingly shows how "classes" are different from other conflict groups, and, hence, why they should constitute a special analytical category. I would therefore suggest a more general theory of group conflict, where authority would not occupy a privileged position, but would rather be one of many desirable "goods" (along with material rewards, control of the means of production, power, prestige, spheres of cultural, linguistic, ideological, intellectual or religious influence, etc.).

As concerns the dichotomous nature of conflict, Dahrendorf's reformulation is certainly a major improvement over Marx's society-wide two-class model. However, Dahrendorf does not strike at the core of the difficulty. Reducing every conflict situation to a dualistic opposition involves straining the facts. Dahrendorf experiences the same difficulties as Marx in handling "intermediate groups." For example, he divides the "middle-class" into bureaucrats holding delegated auth-

ority, and clerical or white-collar workers who are excluded from authority; he is forced to recognize that some groups (such as staff specialists) are in an "ambiguous" position; and he acknowledges that modern enterprises have a "diffuse" authority structure resulting from functional differentiation.[16]

In short, authority, while an important dimension of conflict, is not necessarily an overriding one, nor is it logically or empirically prior to other sources of conflict. As to polarization, it is an empirical tendency rather than a necessary condition of conflict. A pluralistic model thus seems to impose itself. If one argues that dualism is intrinsic to dialectical thinking, I am prepared to abandon the term "dialectic," though not the elements thereof which are essential to a balanced view of social reality.

TOWARD A SYNTHESIS

So far we have reduced two theories that are generally considered antithetical to a minimum form. The most ambitious task that remains is to reach a synthesis between the two. The desirability of achieving a unitary approach seems obvious. It is not enough to say that two theories are complementary and can be used *ad hoc* for different purposes; one must also show that they are reconcilable. While such an endeavor is beyond that scope of this paper, I hope to show that an attempt at synthesis offers some promise by stressing four important points of convergence and overlap.

First, both approaches are holistic, i.e. look at societies as systems of interrelated parts. On first sight, this point seems to offer little comfort, because the types of interrelation on which each theory is based seem antithetical. Functionalists have adhered to a model of multiple and reciprocal causation; they have conceived of interdependence of parts as resulting mostly from functional specialization and complementarity, and as making for equilibrium. Hegelian-Marxian analysts, on the other hand, have generally leaned toward single-factor and unidirectional causation, and viewed interdependence as a conflictual relation. Furthermore, both theories can be criticized on the ground that they tend to represent societies as *more* holistic than they are in fact. Sophisticated functionalism accepts, of course, that different parts of a social system can have varying degrees of autonomy from one another, and that their relationship can be segmental. Indeed, the interdependence of differentiated parts in a system necessarily call forth the antithetical notion of relative autonomy without which the system could not be internally structured. Nevertheless, functionalists have, like Marxian theorists, tended to stress interrelationship, and, conversely, to underrate the extent of "compartmentalization" possible in a social system.

Different elements of a society can simply coexist without being significantly complementary, interdependent or in opposition to one another. For example, a subsistence economy can independently coexist with a money economy, even though the same persons participate in both, and even though they may both produce some of the same commodities. In plural societies, two or more unrelated legal systems with overlapping jurisdictions may function side by side. Persons can move back and forth from one cultural system to another, alternately assuming different values and roles. Thus anthropologists have frequently been confronted with the apparent paradox of rapid acculturation and great conservatism and cultural resilience to outside influences.[17]

The coexistence of largely autonomous and disparate elements in a plural society can be treated in a conventional functionalist framework as a limiting case of a social system. This evasion by definition is not very helpful because such plural societies do "hang together" in spite of conflict and compartmentization. These remarks suggest that social systems can consist, at least in part, of sub-systems which are functionally unrelated and structurally discrete and disparate, but which are interlocked because they share certain elements in common. For example, in a "developing" country, the labor forces engaged in two largely unrelated economic sectors (money and subsistence) typically show considerable overlap. Similarly, the same person can occupy widely different statuses in two stratification systems (e.g. a traditional caste system and an imported Western-type class system) that are juxtaposed but unrelated except through common personnel.

While both bodies of theory overstress interdependence and present an unsatisfactory model thereof, they also show enough overlap to point toward a more workable view of intra-systemic relations.[18] In three different ways the principle of interdependence contains its own dialectic. First, the functionalist notion of differentiated systems consisting of interrelated parts logically implies the opposite concept of relative autonomy. Secondly, parts can be interdependent in that they *adjust to* one another, or *react against* one another. In other words, interdependence and equilibrium are independently variable. Finally, tensions within a social system can arise from conflicting tendencies for the parts to seek more autonomy, and for the whole to maintain centralized control. This latter source of tension is characteristic, for example, of political systems stressing "mechanical" (as opposed to "organic") solidarity, such as those based on segmentary lineages.

A second major overlap concerns the dual role of both conflict and consensus. Whereas functionalism regards concensus as a major focus of stability and integration, and the dialectic views conflict as the source of disintegration and revolutionary change, each of those factors can have the opposite effect. Several authors, notably Coser, have stressed the integrative and stabilizing aspects of conflict.[19] For example, interdependent conflict groups and the crisscrossing of conflict lines can "sew the social system together" by cancelling each other out and preventing disintegration along one primary line of cleavage. Furthermore, in a number of societies, conflict is institutionalized and ritualized in ways that seem conducive to integration.[20] Gluckman goes so far as to argue that ritualized conflict evidences the absence of basic dissension. Such rituals, according to Gluckman, are most prominent in societies where there are rebels (who oppose the incumbents of social roles without rejecting social values), but not revolutionaries.[21]

Not only can conflict contribute to integration. Reciprocally, consensus can prevent adaptation to change and lead to maladjustive inertia, or precipitate the disintegration of a group. The high degree of consensus typical of "utopian" or "other-worldly" reform movements is related to their ephemeral character. Strict adherence to "impractical" norms (e.g. celibacy, or the destruction of means of subsistence in expectation of the coming of the messiah) can obviously be disastrous. This type of phenomenon is analogous at the social level to Durkheim's altruistic suicide, brought about by "excess" of social solidarity. In a different way, consensus on such norms as extreme competition and individualistic laissez-faire, or suspiciousness and treachery as reported of the Dobu,[22] or malevolence and resort to witchcraft is hardly conducive to social solidarity and integration.

At yet another level of analysis, consensus can be disintegrative. In complex and stratified societies, consensus within groups is, in part, a function of dissension between groups. In other words, ingroup unity is reinforced by inter-group conflict, leading to an increasing polarization of opinion. Thus ideological polarization is a process in which growing dissension between sub-groups in a social system is intimately linked with growing consensus within the various groups. In different words, consensus is defined not only in terms of the norms of a particular group as the functionalist approach conceives of it, but also in terms of dissension with the norms of other groups. A total conception of consensus must include a dialectic of normative opposition among the constituent groups of a society.

If both conflict and consensus, as central concepts of the dialectic and functionalism, play a role opposite to that assigned to them by the respective theories, our main contention receives strong confirmation. Not only does each theory emphasize one of two aspects of social reality which are complementary and inextricably intertwined, but some of the analytical concepts are applicable to both approaches.

Thirdly, functionalism and the dialectic share an evolutionary notion of social change. For both Hegel and Marx, the dialectic process is an ascensional spiral towards progress. The functionalist concept of differentiation postulates an evolutionary growth in structural complexity and functional specificity analogous to biological evolution. Admittedly, these two evolutionary views are different, and each presents serious difficulties. We are all aware of the pitfalls of organicism, the teleological implications of "progress," and the untenability of assuming that evolution is unilinear or has an endpoint (e.g. Marx's Communism or Comte's "positive stage"). Nevertheless, the convergence of the two theories on some form of evolutionism suggests that the concept of social evolution (in the minimal sense of change in discernable directions) may be inescapable, however ridden with problems existing brands thereof might be. More specifically, the dialectical and functionalist notions of evolution, while dissimiliar, have at least one important point in common: both theories hold that a given state of the social system presupposes all previous states, and, hence, contains them, if only in residual or modified form.

Finally, (and herein probably lies the major area of *rapprochement*) both theories are fundamentally based on an equilibrium model. In the case of functionalism, this is obvious. But the dialectic sequence of thesis-antithesis-synthesis also involves a notion of equilibrium. Indeed, synthesis is the resolution of the contradiction between thesis and antithesis. The dialectic conceives of society as going through alternating phases equilibrium and disequilibrium: the thesis is the initial equilibrated stage of the cycle; the emergence of the antithesis leads to the intermediate disequilibrated phase; finally, as the contradiction resolves itself in the synthesis, one enters the terminal, balanced stage of the cycle, which then starts anew.[23] While this model is different from the classical notion of dynamic equilibrium, the two views are not contradictory nor incompatible with a postulate of long-range tendency towards integration.

Interestingly, this theoretical convergence on equilibrium also leads to an empirical overlap in dealing with the different sources of change. Earlier, when we dealt with the inability of functionalism to account for lack of adaptation to external change and the consequences thereof, we suggested a reformulation of the dynamic equilibrium model which is very close to the dialectic. Cumulative imbalances and abrupt qualitative changes (which are dialectic notions) were found to result from lack of adjustment to exogenous change. The traditional dialectic approach is not concerned with reactions of social systems to changes

from outside, and conceives of societies as being closed systems. Conversely, the problems of interrelations between systems, exogenous change, boundary-maintenance, etc. have been dealt with by functionalism. Yet, only by introducing dialectical concepts into classical functionalist theory can one satisfactorily account for systemic reactions to outside changes.

We saw that functionalism and the dialectic converge on an equilibrium model which is compatible with an assumption of long-range tendency towards integration. So far, we have used the terms "equilibrium" and "integration" interchangeably. The functionalist concept of dynamic equilibrium does imply integration, i.e. interdependence and compatibility between the parts of a system. The dialectic, while stating that incompatibilities inevitably emerge, also stresses that they resolve themselves in the synthesis. But integration and its corollaries do not exhaust the functionalist definition of dynamic equilibrium. The latter is also defined by minimization of change, a notion outwardly alien to the dialectic which treats change as axiomatic and stability as problematical.

Empirically, one can argue as strongly for the ubiquity of inertia as for that of change. Also, as we already stressed, the amount or rate of change bears no simple relation to the degree of equilibrium. However the facts are not at issue here, but rather the way facts have been treated by the two bodies of theory under consideration. Once more, there are similarities in outlook between functionalism and the dialectic in spite of differences in emphasis. There is, for example, little in acculturation theory (an outgrowth of anthropological functionalism) to suggest minimization of change. The concept of inertia on the other hand is not alien to Marxian class analysis. Marx considers the ruling class as inherently unwilling and unable to adjust to the forces it unleashes, and views the class struggle as a fight between the "progressive" and "reactionary" elements of society. Insofar as reaction implies action, however, the bourgeoisie under capitalism is not, according to Marx, a truly inert element, but Marx considers the petty bourgeoisie and the peasantry as largely passive and inert in the class struggle.

Inertia is thus no more alien to a dialectic approach than change is to functionalism. The maintenance or reestablishment of equilibrium implies adjustive change in both bodies of thought. If one abandons the unnecessary assumption of minimization of change, as indeed many funcionalists have done, there remains no fundamental difference in the dialectical and functionalist concepts of equilibrium and disequilibrium.

CONCLUSION

Because of its scope, this paper is sketchy and leaves many problems unanswered. Our central contention is that the two major approaches which have dominated much of social science present partial but complementary views of reality. Each body of theory raises difficulties which can be resolved, either by rejecting certain unnecessary postulates, or by introducing concepts borrowed from the other approach. As functionalism and the dialectic show, besides important differences, some points of convergence and overlap, there is hope of transcending *ad hoc* eclecticism and of reaching a balanced theoretical synthesis.

NOTES

1. Ralf Dahrendorf, *Class and Class Conflict in Industrial Society*, Stanford: Stanford University Press, 1959; "Toward a Theory of Social Conflict," *Journal of Conflict Resolution*, 2 (June, 1958), pp. 170–183; "Out of Utopia: Toward a Reorientation of Sociological Analysis," *American Journal of Sociology*, 64 (September, 1958), pp. 115–127.

2. For a sample of titles covering the last two decades see: Bernard Barber, "Structural-Functional Analysis: Some Problems and Misunderstandings," *American Sociological Review*, 21 (April, 1956), pp. 129–135; Harry C. Bredemeier, "The Methodology of Functionalism," *American Sociological Review*, 20 (April, 1955), pp. 173–180; Walter Buckley, "Social Stratification and the Functional Theory of Social Differentiation," *American Sociological Review*, 23 (August, 1958), pp. 369–375; Francesca Cancian, "Functional Analysis of Change," *American Sociological Review*, 24 (December, 1960), pp. 818–827; Kingsley Davis, "The Myth of Functional Analysis as a Special Method in Sociology and Anthropology," *American Sociological Review*, 24 (December, 1959), pp. 752–772; Kingsley Davis and Wilbert E. Moore, "Some Principles of Stratification," *American Sociological Review*, 10 (April, 1945), pp. 242–249; Ronald Philip Dore, "Function and Cause," *American Sociological Review*, 26 (December, 1961), pp. 843–853; Harold Fallding, "Functional Analysis in Sociology," *American Sociological Review*, 28 (February, 1963), pp. 5–13; Dorothy Gregg and Elgin Williams, "The Dismal Science of Functionalism," *American Anthropologist*, 50 (October–December, 1948), pp. 594–611; Carl G. Hempel, "The Logic of Functional Analysis," in Llewellyn Gross (Ed.), *Symposium on Sociological Theory*, Evanston, Ill.: Row, Peterson and Co., 1959, pp. 271–307; Wayne Hield, "The Study of Change in Social Science," *British Journal of Sociology*, 5 (March, 1954), pp. 1–10; David Lockwood, "Some Remarks on the 'Social System,'" *British Journal of Sociology*, 7 (June, 1956), pp. 134–146; Wilbert E. Moore, "But Some Are More Equal than Others," *American Sociological Review*, 28 (February, 1963), pp. 13–18; Richard L. Simpson, "A Modification of the Functional Theory of Stratification," *Social Forces*, 35 (December, 1956), pp. 132–137; Melvin Tumin, "On Inequality," *American Sociological Review*, 28 (February, 1963), pp. 19–26; Melvin Tumin, "Some Principles of Stratification: A Critical Analysis," *American Sociological Review*, 18 (August, 1953), pp. 387–394; Dennis H. Wrong, "The Functional Theory of Stratification: Some Neglected Considerations," *American Sociological Review*, 24 (December, 1959), pp. 772–782.

3. Davis, *op. cit.*

4. Robert K. Merton, *Social Theory and Social Structure*, Glencoe, Ill.: The Free Press, 1949, Chapter I.

5. In the absence of an exact antonym for "consensus," we shall use "dissension" rather than coin "dissensus."

6. The central importance of "patterns of value-orientations" for social integration is a recurrent theme in Parsons' work. Not only must there be a substantial amount of cognitive acceptance of values by actors in a social system, but actors must internalize these values, and be motivated to act in accordance with them. Cf. Talcott Parsons, *The Social System*, Glencoe, Ill.: The Free Press, 1951, pp. 36–37, 326, 350–351; *Structure and Process in Modern Societies*, Glencoe, Ill.: The Free Press, 1960, pp. 172–176; and Max Black (Ed.), *The Social Theories*

of Talcott Parsons, Englewood Cliffs: Prentice-Hall, 1961, pp. 342-343.

7. Cf. A. R. Radcliffe-Brown, *Structure and Function in Primitive Society*, Glencoe, Ill.: The Free Press, 1952, p. 180.

8. See, for example, Dahrendorf's critique of Marx from the point of view of sociological theory in his *Class and Class Conflict in Industrial Society*.

9. In the following discussion, references will be mostly to his *Class and Class Conflict in Industrial Society*.

10. *Op. cit.*, pp. 136-137, 171.

11. *Op. cit.*, pp. 136-139.

12. *Op. cit.*, pp. 141-142.

13. *Op. cit.*, pp. 165, 173-174.

14. *Op. cit.*, pp. 211-239.

15. *Op. cit.*, pp. 136-137.

16. *Op. cit.*, pp. 52-56, 251, 300-303.

17. For a treatment of problems of cultural coexistence in plural societies, see J. C. Mitchell, *Tribalism and the Plural Society*, London: Oxford University Press, 1960.

18. For a detailed and useful discussion of functional autonomy and interdependence, and their relations to equilibrium, see Alvin W. Gouldner, "Reciprocity and Autonomy in Functional Theory," in Llewellyn Gross, *op. cit.*, pp. 241-270.

19. Lewis A. Coser, *The Functions of Social Conflict*, Glencoe, Ill.: The Free Press, 1956. Others have stressed that "variant" values are found side by side with "dominant" values, that these "variant" values can be integrative, and that different sub-cultures within a society adhere to different values. See Florence R. Kluckhohn and Fred L. Strodtbeck, *Variations in Value Orientations*, Evanston, Ill.: Row, Peterson, 1961; Florence R. Kluckhohn, "Dominant and Substitute Profiles of Cultural Orientations," *Social Forces*, 28 (May, 1950), pp. 376-394; Herman Turk, "Social Cohesion Through Variant Values," *American Sociological Review*, 28 (February, 1963), pp. 28-37.

20. See Max Gluckman, *Custom and Conflict in Africa*, Oxford: Blackwell, 1955, and *Rituals of Rebellion in South-East Africa*, Manchester: University of Manchester Press, 1954; and Pierre L. van den Berghe, "Institutionalized Licence and Normative Stability," *Cahiers d'Etudes Africaines*, 11 (1963), pp. 413-423.

21. *Custom and Conflict in Africa*, p. 134.

22. Reo F. Fortune, *The Sorcerers of Dobu*. London: G. Routledge and Sons, 1932.

23. The term "cycle," insofar as it implies repetitiveness is, of course, somewhat misleading in reference to the dialectic process, since both Hegel and Marx conceived of social change as an ascensional spiral.

TOWARD A THEORY OF SOCIAL CONFLICT

RALF DAHRENDORF

I

After an interval of almost fifty years, a theme has reappeared in sociology which has determined the origin of that discipline more than any other subject area. From Marx and Comte to Simmel and Sorel, social conflict, especially revolutions, was one of the central themes in social research. The same is true of many early Anglo-Saxon sociologists (although in their work the problem of revolution has been characteristically somewhat

Reprinted from *The Journal of Conflict Resolution*, 2:170-183, by permission of the author and the Center for Research in Conflict Resolution. Copyright 1958; the University of Michigan.

neglected), for example, the Webbs in England, Sumner in the United States. However, when Talcott Parsons in 1937 established a certain convergence in the sociological theories of Alfred Marshall, Émile Durkheim, Vilfredo Pareto, and Max Weber,[2] he no longer had in mind an analysis of social conflict; his was an attempt to solve the problem of integration of so-called "social systems" by an organon of interrelated categories. The new question was now "What holds societies together?"—no longer "What drives them on?" The influence of the Parsonian posing of the question on the more recent sociology (and by no means only an American sociology) can hardly be overrated. Thus it is possible that the revival of the study of social conflict in the last decades appears to many not so much a continuation of traditional research paths as a new thematic discovery —an instance of dialectic irony in the development of science.

At this time, approaches toward a systematic study of social conflict are still relatively isolated, compared with the innumerable works on social gratification or on structure and function of specific institutions, organizations, and societies. Still the thesis of a revival of the study of social conflict can be justified with regard to the works of Aron, Philip, Brinton, Kerr, Coser, Brinkmann, Geiger, Gluckmann, and others,[3] as well as an attempt to determine a systematic locus and a specific framework for a theory of conflict in sociological analysis.

Types and Varieties of Social Conflict

To begin with a commonplace observation: The problem of conflict is no less complex than that of integration of societies. We now know that the attempt to reduce all actually occurring conflicts among social groups to a common principle, say that of classes, is sterile. It leads either to empty generalizations (such as "Every society experiences social conflicts") or to empirically unjustifiable oversimplifications (such as "The history of all societies so far has been a history of class struggles"). It seems advisable, first, to sort out and to classify the problems which are conceived under the general heading of "social conflict." Even a superficial reflection leads to the distinction of a series of types.

There are wars, and there are conflicts among political parties—evidently two different kinds of struggle. With regard to a given society, A, one could say there are *exogenous* conflicts brought upon or into A from the outside, and there are

endogenous conflicts generated within A. Of these two categories, which, at least analytically, can be relatively precisely distinguished, there are again several types. Let us confine our attention for the moment—for reasons which will presently be given—to endogenous conflicts. Then further subdivisions are directly perceived: slaves versus freemen in Rome, Negroes versus whites in the United States, Protestants versus Catholics in the Netherlands, Flemings versus Walloons in Belgium, Conservatives versus Laborites in England, unions versus employers in many countries. All these are opposing groups in well-known conflicts. Perhaps each of these examples does not fall into a separate category; but certainly they cannot all be subsumed under a single type of social conflict. Whatever criterion one chooses for classification—for example, the objects of contention, the structural origin of the conflicting groups, the forms of conflict —several distinct types result.

The Limits and Goals of a Theory of Social Conflict

An ideal sociology cannot, in principle, exclude any of these categories and types of conflict from analysis. Nevertheless, the types mentioned do not all have the same importance for sociological analysis. A brief recollection of the intent of a sociological theory of conflict reveals that the contribution of sociology to the understanding of conflict (as well as the contribution of conflict to the social process) is in specific instances greater in some cases than in others.

The intent of a sociological theory of conflict is to overcome the predominatingly arbitrary nature of unexplained historical events by deriving these events from social structural elements—in other words, to explain certain processes by prognostic connections. Certainly it is important to describe the conflict between workers and employers purely as such; but it is more important to produce a proof that such a conflict is based on certain social structural arrangements and hence is bound to arise wherever such structural arrangements are given. Thus it is the task of sociology to derive conflicts from specific social structures and not to relegate these conflicts to psychological variables ("aggressiveness") or to descriptive-historical ones (the influx of Negroes into the United States) or to chance.

In the sense of strict sociological analysis, conflicts can be considered explained if they can be shown to arise from the structure of social positions independently of the orientation of populations and of historical *dei ex machina*. This is necessarily a very abstract formulation; instead of elaborating it, it may be advisable to illustrate its meaning by the following treatment of a form of social conflict. First, however, let us draw a consequence of this formulation which will help to make our problem more precise.

Since the recognition of the inadequacy of the Marxist-Leninist theory of imperialism, the explanation of exogenous conflicts on the basis of the structure of a given society is once again an open problem, the treatment of which has scarcely begun. It seems, moreover, that the explanation of exogenous conflicts[4] by the tools of sociological structure analysis is possible only in a metaphorical sense— namely, only in case the entire societies (or less comprehensive "social systems") are taken to be the units of a new structure,[5] that is, when C is analyzed in terms of the structure of its elements A and B without consideration of the inner structure of A and B. On these grounds it seems sensible to exclude exogenous conflict for the time being from a theory of social conflicts.

On the other hand, the above-mentioned examples of endogenous conflict, if considered from the point of view of their structural significance, fall into two groups. On the one hand, they point to conflicts which arise only in specific societies on the basis of special historical conditions (Negroes or whites in the United States, Protestants versus Catholics in the Netherlands; Flemings versus Walloons in Belgium); on the other hand, however, there are conflicts which can be understood as expressions of general structural features of societies, or of societies in the same stage of development (Conservatives versus Laborites in England, unions versus employers' associations).[6] Certainly in both cases an analysis leading to generalization is possible: a theory of minority or religious conflict is as meaningful as that of class conflict. Nevertheless, their respective weights within a general theory of society are evidently distinguishable. It is not surprising that the "classical" theory of conflict —I mean here primarily the class theory of conflict—has, above all, called attention to such social frictions which can be derived from the structure of societies independently of structurally incidental historical data.

The following approaches toward a theory of conflict also relate themselves to conflicts based on structure. So far, we are by no means considering a general theory of social conflict, although I would undertake to defend the assertion that we are dealing here with one of the most important, if not the most important, type of social conflict. However important as problems of social conflict St. Bartholomew's Night, Crystal Night, and Little Rock may be, the French Revolution and the British General Strike of 1926 and June 17, 1953, seem to me more germane for structural analysis. To put it less dramatically, the sociological theory of conflict would do well to confine itself for the time being to an explanation of the frictions between the rulers and the ruled in given social structural organizations.

II

The explanation of motion requires two separate attacks. We must know the point of departure and the direction of motion or, better yet, the moving force. No theory of social change or of conflict can forego the description of the structural entity which undergoes change or within which conflicts occur. Such a description is offered by the integration theory of society. However, it is erroneous to assume that a description of how the elements of a structure are put together into a stable whole offers, as such, a point of departure for a structural analysis of conflict and change. So far, the claim of the so-called "structural-functional" theory of modern sociology to the status of a general theory of society is demonstrably unjustified.

Toward a Critique of a Structural-Functional Theory

This critique has been led in recent times repeatedly, most effectively by D. Lockwood.[7] It is based on a relatively simple argument. As long as we orient our analysis toward the question as to how the elements of a society are combined into a co-ordinated functioning whole, then the representation of society as a social system is the last point of reference. We are therefore faced with the task of determining certain associations, institutions, or processes within this balanced whole, that is—in Merton's definition—of determining the intentional or unintentional consequences of these associations for the functioning and the preservation of the system. In this way, we come to contentions such as "the educational system functions as a mechanism of assigning social positions," or "religion functions as an agent of integrating dominant values." The majority of sociological investigations in the last years moves in this area of analysis.

However, such an approach leads to difficulties, if we put a question of a different sort. What was the function of the English trade unions in the General Strike of 1926? What was the function of the construction worker in Stalin Allee on June 17, 1953? Without doubt, it can be argued in many cases that militant trade unions or opposition political groups and parties also contribute to the functioning of the existing system.[8] But even when this is the case—and in the two cases cited it would be difficult to establish this—such a conclusion would say little about the role of the group in question. Moreover, it is clear that the intentional, as well as the unintentional, effects of such oppositional groups are in the contribution toward an abolition or destruction of the existing system. The structural-functional position has a comfortable label for such cases: they are "dysfunctional" organizations, institutions, or processes. But this designation again tells us less than nothing. It not only fails to explain the place of these things in the process but actually hinders such explanation by a terminology which seems to be congruent with the system but which, upon closer examination, reveals itself as a residual category. Whatever does not fit is conjured out of the world by word magic.

In every science, residual categories are a fruitful point of departure for new developments. It seems to me that a careful analysis of problems which the term "dysfunction" hides in the structural-functional theory automatically puts us on the trace of a meaningful sociological theory of conflict. At the same time, it offers a remarkable vantage point associated with an attempt of a scientific analysis of society.

Two Models of Society

If we extrapolate the analytical approaches of the structural-functional theory somewhat beyond their boundaries and investigate their implicit postulates, we can construct a model of society which lies at the base of this theory and determines its perspectives. The essential elements of this societal model are these:

1. Every society is a relatively persisting configuration of elements.[9]

2. Every society is a well-integrated configuration of elements.

3. Every element in a society contributes to its functioning.

4. Every society rests on the consensus of its members.

It should be clear that a theory based on this model does not lend itself to the explanation, not even the description, of the phenomena of social conflict and change. For this purpose, one needs a model which takes the diametrically opposite position on all the four points above:

1. Every society is subjected at every moment to change: social change is ubiquitous.

2. Every society experiences at every moment social conflict: social conflict is ubiquitous.

3. Every element in a society contributes to its change.

4. Every society rests on constraint of some of its members by others.

The remarkable nature of our vantage point becomes evident when we examine the two groups of postulates with respect to their truth content, that is, if we ask ourselves which of the two models promises greater utility for cognition of reality. It appears that the juxtaposed pairs of postulates are in no way mutually exclusive with respect to social reality. It is impossible to decide by an empirical investigation which of the two models is more nearly correct; the postulates are not hypotheses. Moreover, it seems meaningful to say that both models are in a certain sense valid and analytically fruitful. Stability and change, integration and conflict, function and "dysfunction,"

consensus and constraint are, it would seem, two equally valid aspects of every imaginable society. They are dialectically separated and are exhaustive only in combination as a description of the social problems. Possibly a more general theory of society may be thought of which lifts the equivalidity of both models, the coexistence of the uncombinable, onto a higher level of generality. As long as we do not have such a theory, we must content ourselves with the finding that society presents a double aspect to the sociological understanding, each no better, no more valid, than the other. It follows that the criticism of the unapplicability of the structural-functional theory for the analysis of conflict is directed only against a claim of generality of this theory but leaves untouched its competence with respect to the problem of integration. It follows, on the other hand, also that the theory of conflict and change is not a general theory. Comparisons between natural and social sciences always carry the danger of misunderstanding. However, it may be maintained, without attributing to this analogy more than a logical meaning, that the situation of the sociologists is not unlike that of the physicists with respect to the theory of light. Just as the physicists can solve certain problems only by assuming the wave character of light and others, on the contrary, only by assuming a corpuscular or quantum theory, so there are problems of sociology which can be adequately attacked only with an integration theory and others which require a conflict theory for a meaningful analysis. Both theories can work extensively with the same categories, but they emphasize different aspects. While the integration theory likens a society to an ellipse, a rounded entity which incloses all of its elements, conflict theory sees society rather as a hyperbola which, it is true, has the same foci but is open in many directions and appears as a tension field of the determining forces.

The Tasks of a Theory of Social Conflict

The double aspect of society and the dialectics of the two types of sociological theory are in themselves a most fruitful object of reflection. Nevertheless, another problem seems to be more urgent. The theory of social integration has recently developed to a flourishing state as the structural-functional approach in ethnology and sociology. Our theory of conflict, however, is still in a very rudimentary state. It is an approach based on postulating ubiquitous social change and social conflict, the "dysfunctionality" of all the elements of social structure, and the constraining character of social unity. Our considerations put us in a position to formulate some requirements of such a theory:

1. It should be a scientific theory (as is the theory of social integration), that is, it should be formulated with reference to a plausible and demonstrable explanation of empirical phenomena.

2. The elements of the theory should not contradict the conflict model of society.

3. The categories employed should, whenever possible, agree with those of the integration theory or at least correspond to them.

4. A conflict theory should enable us to derive social conflicts from structural arrangements and thus show these conflicts systematically generated.

5. It should account both for the multiplicity of forms of conflict and for their degrees of intensity.

The last goal of a social theory is the explanation of social change. The integration theory gives us a tool for determining the point of departure of the process. To find the locus of the forces which drive the process and social change is the task of a theory of conflict.

It must develop a model which makes understandable the structural origin of social conflict. This seems possible only if we understand conflicts as struggles among social groups, that is, if we make our task precise to the extent that it reduces to the structural analysis of conflicting groups. Under this supposition three questions come especially to the forefront, which conflict theory must answer:

1. How do conflicting groups arise from the structure of society?

2. What forms can the struggles among such groups assume?

3. How does the conflict among such groups effect a change in the social structures?

III

Wherever men live together and lay foundations of forms of social organization, there are positions whose occupants have powers of command in certain contexts and over certain positions, and there are other positions whose occupants are subjected to such commands. The distinction between "up" and "down"—or, as the English say, "Them" and "Us"—is one of the fundamental experiences of most men in society,[10] and, moreover, it appears that this distinction is intimately connected with unequal distribution of power. The main thesis of the following attempt to construct a model for the structural analysis of conflict is that we should seek the structural origin of social conflict in the dominance relations which prevail within certain units of social organization. For these units I will use Max Weber's concept of "imperatively co-ordinated group." The thesis is not new; it is found (however often with important modifications) in the formulation of many social scientists before and after Marx. But we shall make no attempt to trace the history of this thesis.

Authority and Authority Structures

The concepts of power and authority are very complex ones. Whoever uses them is likely to be accused of lack of precision and of clarity to the extent that he tries to define them "exhaustively." Is the influence of a father on his children, the influence of an industrial combine on the government, or the influence of a demagogue on his followers an instance of an authority relation? Here, as in most other cases, it is basically not a question of a definition but rather a question of an "operational definition," as it is often called today: a method of determination which allows us to identify as such the state of affairs when we are actually confronted with it. However, for the purpose of analysis and identification, Weber's determination of authority is sufficient: "The likelihood that a command of a certain content will be obeyed by given persons."[11] This determination contains the following elements:

1. Authority denotes a relation of supra- and subordination.

2. The supra-ordinated side prescribes to the subordinated one certain behavior in the form of a command or a prohibition.

3. The supra-ordinated side has the right to make such prescriptions; authority is a legitimate relation of supra- and subordination; authority is not based on personal or situational chance effects but rather on an expectation associated with social position.

4. The right of authority is limited to certain contents and to specific persons.

5. Failure to obey the prescriptions is sanctioned; a legal system (or a system of quasi-legal customs) guards the effectiveness of authority.

This determination of authority makes possible the identification of a cabinet minister, an employer, and a party secretary as occupants of authority positions—in contrast to an industrial syndicate or a demagogue, neither of which satisfies condition 3 above.[13]

It is not the intention of our "definition" of authority to solve all analytical and empirical problems of this category.[13] In fact, the very first step of our model leads us deep into these problems: in each imperatively co-ordinated group, two aggregates can be distinguished: those which have only general ("civil") basic rights and those which have authority rights over the former. In contrast to prestige and income, a continuum of gradual transition cannot be constructed for the distribution of authority. Rather, there is a clear dichotomy. Every position in an imperatively co-ordinated group can be recognized as belonging to one who dominates or one who is dominated. Sometimes, in view of the bureaucratic large-scale organization of modern societies—under the influence of the state—this assumption may at first sight seem problematic. However, a sharper analysis leaves no doubt that here also the split into the dominating and dominated is valid, even though in reality a considerable measure of differentiation is discernible among those in the dominating group.[14]

The Conflict-Theory Model

The dichotomy of social roles within imperatively co-ordinated groups,[15] the division into positive and negative dominance roles, is a fact of social structure. If and insofar as social conflicts can be referred to this factual situation, they are structurally explained. The model of analysis of social conflict which is developed against a background of an assumption of such a dichotomy involves the following steps:

1. In every imperatively co-ordinated group, the carriers of positive and negative dominance roles determine two quasi-groups with opposite latent interests. We call them "quasi-groups"

because we have to do here with mere aggregates, not organized units; we speak of "latent interests," because the opposition of outlook need not be conscious on this level; it may exist only in the form of expectations associated with certain positions. The opposition of interests has here a quite formal meaning, namely, the expectation that an interest in the preservation of the status quo is associated with the positive dominance roles and an interest in the change of the status quo is associated with the negative dominance roles.

2. The bearers of positive and negative dominance roles, that is, the members of the opposing quasi-groups, organize themselves into groups with manifest interests, unless certain empirically variable conditions (the condition of organization) intervene. Interest groups, in contrast to quasi-groups, are organized entities, such as parties, trade unions; the manifest interests are formulated programs and ideologies.

3. Interest groups which originate in this manner are in constant conflict concerned with the preservation or change in the status quo. The form and the intensity of the conflict are determined by empirically variable conditions (the conditions of conflict).

4. The conflict among interest groups in the sense of this model leads to changes in the structure of the social relations in question through changes·in the dominance relations. The kind, the speed, and the depth of this development depend on empirically variable conditions (the conditions of structural change).

The intent of such a model is to delimit a problem area, to identify the factors pertinent to it, to put them into order— that is, to propose fruitful questions— and at the same time to fix precisely their analytical focus. We have delimited our problem area by viewing social conflict as a conflict among groups which emerge from the authority structure of social organizations. We have identified pertinent factors in the conditions of organization, of conflict, and of change. Their order, however, can be expressed on the basis of the model in three functions: interest groups (for example, parties) are a function of conditions of organization if an imperatively co-ordinated group is given; specific forms of conflict (e.g., parliamentary debates) are a function of the conditions of conflict if the interest groups are given; specific forms of change (e.g., revolutions) are a function of the conditions of change if the conflict among interest groups is given. Thus the task of the theory of conflict turns out to be to identify the three sets of conditions and to determine as sharply as possible their respective weight—ideally, by quantitative measure.[16] The following remarks are hardly more than a tentative indication of the sorts of variables in question.

Empirical Conditions of Social Conflict

As far as the conditions of organization are concerned, three groups of factors come to mind. First, we have certain effective social conditions: for example, the possibility of communication among the members of the quasi-group and a certain method of recruitment into the quasi-groups. Next there are certain political conditions which must be fulfilled if interest groups are to emerge. Here, above all, a guaranty of freedom of coalition is important. Finally, certain technical conditions must be fulfilled: an organization must have material means, a founder, a leader, and an ideology.

Under conditions of conflict, two kinds are immediately conspicuous: the degree of social mobility of individuals (or of families) and the presence of effective mechanisms for regulating social conflicts. If we imagine a continuum of intensity of social conflict among interest groups, ranging from democratic debate to civil war, we may conjecture that the presence or absence of social mobility and of regulating mechanisms has considerable influence on the position of specific given conflicts on this continuum. Here, as with the other conditions, the determination of the exact weights of the factors is a task of empirical investigation.

Finally, a third group of conditions or variables determines the form and the extent of social structural changes which arise from the conflict of interest groups. Probably a relatively intimate connection exists between the intensity of the conflict and the change, that is, also between the conditions of conflict and of the structural changes. However, additional factors come into play, such as the capacity of the rulers to stay in power and the pressure potential of the dominated interest group. The sociology of revolutions and especially the unwritten sociology of uncompleted revolutions should contribute considerably to making these factors precise.

It need hardly be re-emphasized that these unsystematic observations can, as such, hardly lay a foundation of a theory of conflict. Nevertheless, we put ourselves in a position to ask meaningful questions both on the theoretical level and with respect to empirical problems. Each of the conditions mentioned offers a fruitful object of theoretically oriented investigations. And in the empirical sphere, the systematic association of factors in such an investigation redirects our questions from a haphazard search for *ad hoc* relations in the world of coincidences to a meaningful study of specific interdependencies, whose locus and meaning are fixed by a general perspective. By the nature of the subject, our exposition up to this point had to remain somewhat abstract in form.

In spite of the tentative nature of the above-mentioned frame of reference, it is nevertheless possible to test its resolving power on some empirical problems.

IV

Strictly speaking, every form of differentiated social organization may also be described as an imperatively co-ordinated group—a state and an industrial enterprise, a chess club and a university, a party and a church. Thus, strictly speaking, the theory of conflict is applicable to all these cases. Our decision to single out two of these imperatively co-ordinated groups—the state and the industrial enterprise—for purposes of analysis is, in principle, arbitrary, although the special empirical meaning of these two forms of social organization in so-called industrialized society certainly needs no justification. In its application to the analysis of industrial and political conflict, the theory of conflict comes very near to the positions of the traditional, especially Marxist, theory of classes. At the same time, it becomes evident that the theory of classes is only a special case of the theory of conflict.

Social Conflict in Industrial Enterprise

The approach to a theory of social conflict taken here can be tellingly illustrated in the example of an industrial enterprise. An industrial enterprise is, among other things,[17] an imperatively co-ordinated group. It contains positions with which are associated an expectation and a right of exercising authority and other positions whose occupants are subjected to authority. There are managers of many grades, and there are workers. The authority of managers is institutionalized and legitimate. It is guaranteed by legalistic and quasi-legalistic sanctions (disciplinary fines, demotion, dismissal, etc.). A conflict of (latent) interests between managers and workers is thus structurally unavoidable. Therefore, we can formulate the assumption that, from these quasi-groups, interest groups emerge as soon as the conditions of organization (communication within the quasi-groups, regulated recruiting into the quasi-groups, freedom of coalition, leaders and ideologies, technical means) are on hand. The emerging interest groups are employers' associations and trade unions. The conflict between these interest groups varies in its intensity in direct relation to the conditions of conflict, especially to the degree of mobility from one group to another and to the presence of effective mechanisms for regulating conflicts (channels for collective bargaining, arbitration institutions, etc.). This conflict leads—either through negotiations or through strikes—finally to changes in the structure of industrial organizations and in the position of the involved groups.

This sort of analysis evidently tells us little that we already do not know; it seems, after decades of industrial conflict, almost trivial. Therefore, I have expressly designated it as an illustration of conflict theory. Nevertheless, even this illustration is not entirely trivial when we realize two of its implications: if conflict theory is useful, then it follows that industrial conflict exists regardless of whether the managers are owners-entrepreneurs or whether they are agents elected by bodies of stockholders, or whether they are government officials; that is, relationships of ownership in principle do not affect either the existence or the intensity of industrial conflicts. Furthermore, it follows that industrial conflict is present even if the complete system of its regulation has been realized. Regulation influences, it is true, the intensity of the conflict, but no mechanism is imaginable which abolishes conflicts altogether. Consequences of this sort suggested by applications of conflict theory are by no means trivial. In the face of two burning problems of sociological analysis, this assertion should be justified, at least in outline.

THE PROBLEM OF CO-DETERMINATION

It is now evident that co-determination in the German coal and steel industry has not led to the abolition, not even to alleviation, of industrial conflict. On the other hand, it is not to be doubted that all the involved groups expected that co-determination would bring such a result about. How can we explain this discrepancy? Under the assumptions and in the light of conflict theory, an explanation is indeed possible: industrial organization is an imperatively co-ordinated group. Social conflicts between the bearers of positive and negative dominance roles are unavoidable in it. Co-determination means, above all, the elevation of workers' representatives into management positions, that is, a change of certain persons from negative to positive dominance positions (*Aufsichtsrat, Arbeitsdirektor*). These changes leave the authority structure of industrial organization as a structure of positions with command functions unchanged. Co-determination has created a new authority position, that of the *Arbeitsdirektor*; but it has not abolished the contrast between up and down, nor could it abolish it. It bypasses the possibilities of effective regulation of social contradictions and thus has neither annihilated industrial conflict nor contributed to its regulation.

Conflict theory allows us to go a step farther and to formulate the assumption that co-determination not only is useless as an instrument for regulating industrial conflicts but also, in the long run, threatens to lead to a sharpening of such conflicts. In this connection, I do not have in mind the much-discussed problem of "loyalty conflict" with which the *Arbeitsdirektor* is faced.[18] Structurally, another fact is more important. The *Arbeitsdirektor* and the *Aufsichtsratsvertreter* in the industries affected by the right of co-determination are defined as the representatives of the employees. Their rise to responsible positions appears, therefore, as a rise of a new group to authority. However, this group consists not of the totality of workers but of workers' representatives. Thus a situation results that those whose task it is to represent the interests of the occupants of negative dominant positions in an industrial enterprise have themselves become occupants of positive dominance positions and, as such, stand, as a result of structural necessity, on the other side of the barrier that separates up from down. Somewhat pointedly expressed: not only has co-determination failed to make industrial conflict milder, but it has at the same time robbed the occupants of the negative dominance positions of their representation, that is, it has blocked a channel of expression of the conflict. There is thus the danger that the existing latent conflict will create new, completely unregulated, forms of expression and will assume more radical forms when the representatives of the workers perceive their task as representatives of interests in an unambiguous and radical manner.[19]

The above analysis, because of its almost superficial brevity, is wide open to many kinds of critical objections. Therefore, we shall break it off at this point, with the assertion that a strict and detailed application of conflict theory to the problem of co-determination enables us to make the indicated assumptions sufficiently precise that they can be subjected to empirical tests. The same holds for a second problem of outstanding actual importance, which will be briefly analyzed here from the perspective of conflict theory: the problem of conflict and of change in totalitarian states.

The Problem of the Totalitarian State

Since June 17, 1953, and with greater certainty since the events in Hungary and Poland in the autumn of 1956, we know that social conflict (and social change!) have by no means disappeared in the totalitarian states. Conflict theory raises this knowledge to the status of law. The state, that is, society in its political aspect, is an imperatively co-ordinated group. There are in it mere citizens (voters) and occupants of positions equipped with command opportunities. Therefore, political conflict is a structural fact of society under every imaginable condition. This conflict can assume mild or severe forms; it can even disappear for limited periods from the field of vision of a superficial observer; but it cannot be abolished. Now one of the aspects of a totalitarian state is an attempt to suppress the opposition, that is, to suppress social conflict. The question then arises, against the background of conflict theory, In which way do social frictions become manifest under such circumstances? We can analyze totalitarian states from the point of view of conditions of organization of interest groups—that of conflict and of structural change—and hope to arrive in this way at meaningful explanations of historical events and to testable predictions. Again it is possible here to make only a few indications.

Let us begin—for reasons which will soon become evident—with the conditions of conflict. The intensity of social conflicts depends on the measure of social mobility and on the presence of mechanisms for regulating the conflicts. Both mobility and regulation can be present in totalitarian states. One could argue that the regular "purges" in Communist states —that is, a replacement of the bearers of authority—function as a guaranty of stability (in the sense of alleviating social conflicts). In the same way the systematic requirement of discussion with the aim of deciding the political "platforms" within and outside the state party may be an effective mechanism of regulation.[20]

Still there seems to be an inherent tendency in most totalitarian states to isolate socially the leadership layer and to prevent discussions, that is, to disregard the mechanisms for regulating conflicts. If this is the case, social conflicts threaten to increase in potential intensity and to take on a revolutionary character.

From the point of view of conditions of structural change, this means that political conflicts in totalitarian states aim more and more at sudden replacement of the ruling class. The important variable which determines the probability of realizing a radical change is the resistance of the rulers to the pressures making for change. Perhaps it is meaningful to make the empirical generalization that this resistance does increase to a certain degree with increasing pressure, but then gives way to a relatively speedy dissolution and so promotes change.

Central for the analysis of conflicts in totalitarian states, however, is our third set of conditions (first, as listed in the theory): the condition of organization. It follows in a way from the "definition" of a totalitarian state that there are no conditions in it for the organization of opposing interest groups. More specifically, although the social and technical conditions are often present, the political conditions are lacking;[21] there is no freedom of coalition. At this point, the resistance of the German Eastern Zone government to free elections becomes clear, as does the general threat of violent, possibly revolutionary, conflict in totali-

tarian states. When—as expressly in Hungary or virtually on June 17, 1953 in Berlin—an opportunity for organization occurs to latent conflict groups, the total edifice of the totalitarian state collapses. Moreover, it seems very probable that this possibility can become realized at any moment in every totalitarian state.[22] In modern totalitarian societies founded on ideological state parties, there is a constant danger from the point of view of the rulers that a permitted organization, even the state party itself, may become the root of an opposition movement and of revolutionary conflict.

Again our analysis will be broken off at the point where it promises testable results. It was not the intent of this discussion to treat exhaustively some empirical problem. Rather, we wanted to show that conflict theory puts us in a position to formulate more sharply urgent problems of empirical investigation, to bring within our grasp unexplained events, to see what is known from additional points of view, and to transform tentative questions into a systematic search—that is, to do precisely what a scientific theory should accomplish. It needs hardly to be said explicitly that conflict theory in the form here presented is almost as incomplete as the two empirical analyses indicated in this section. In spite of all progress, the theory of social conflict is still more a challenge to the sociologist than a result of his researches.

NOTES

1. This paper was translated by Anatol Rapaport, Mental Health Research Unit, University of Michigan.

The following presentation is an attempt to depict in a systematic form the fundamental ideas of my book *Soziale Klassen und Klassenconflikt in der industriellen Gesellschaft* (Stuttgart, 1957). However, the presentation departs significantly in its organization and thematic scope from that given in my book: (1) whereas the book binds together theoretical considerations and empirical analysis, the present

exposition is essentially limited to the theoretical aspects; (2) whereas in the book I have developed the theoretical orientations in a critical dialogue with other authors, particularly with Marx, the presentation in the following exposition is systematic. It need hardly be elaborated that much of what is expressly developed in the book could be only formally treated here and often with dogmatic brevity. Nevertheless, it may be noted that the present exposition, especially in the first and fourth sections, contains in certain respects formulations beyond the scope of the book.

2. Cf. *Structure of Social Action* (New York, 1937; 2nd ed., Glencoe, 1949).

3. Raymond Aron, "Social Structure and the Ruling Class," in *Class Status and Power*, Ed. Reinhard Bendix and Seymour Martin Lipset (London, 1954); André Philip, *Le Socialisme trahi* (Paris, 1957); Crane Brinton, *The Anatomy of Revolution* (2nd ed.; New York, 1952); Clark Kerr, "Industrial Conflict and Its Mediation," *American Journal of Sociology*, Vol. XL, No. 3 (November, 1954); Lewis Coser, *The Functions of Social Conflict* (London, 1956), and "Social Conflict and Social Change," *British Journal of Sociology*, Vol. VIII, No. 3 (September, 1957); Carl Brinkmann, *Soziologische Theorie der Revolution* (Tübingen, 1948); Theodor Geiger, *Klassengesellschaft in Schmelztiegel* (Köln-Hagen, 1949); Max Gluckmann, *Custom and Conflict in Africa* (London, 1957).

4. We recall here that a conflict which, from the point of view of Society A, appears as exogenous is represented from another point of view as a conflict between two societies or systems, A and B.

5. Talcott Parsons and the political scientist David Easton (*The Political System* [New York, 1953]) are currently working on an attempt to analyze international conflicts by means of a model in which entire societies, such as the United States and the U.S.S.R., appear as elements and are treated as if they had no inner structure. This procedure is methodologically entirely legitimate. It remains to be seen what results it can achieve and how it may be connected to the analysis of intrasocietal conflicts.

6. The conflict between free men and slaves in ancient Rome possibly belongs to this second group, although not on the same level of generality.

7. David Lockwood, "Some Notes on 'The Social System,' " *British Journal of Sociology*, Vol. VII, No. 2 (1956). Although Lockwood's argument leads to the same conclusion, it proceeds somewhat differently (cf. my *Social Classes and the Class Conflict*, pp. 159 ff.).

8. This aspect of social conflict is, in fact, central in the analysis of Lewis Coser (continuing that of Simmel) in his work on the functions of social conflict (cf. n. 3).

9. There is much controversy over this implication of the structural-functional approach. Most functionalists deny that they make such an assumption. Indeed, assertions to the contrary are found in the works of Parsons, Merton, and others. Nevertheless, it can be shown that these assertions are, from the point of view of structural-functional theory, mere declarations. The notion of equilibrium and the concept of a system would have little sense if they did not make the assumption of stability of societies. However, two limitations are to be observed: (1) we have to do here (also in the implications which follow) not with a metaphysical postulate but rather with an assumption made for the purpose of analysis; and (2) stability does not mean statics in the sense of complete absence of processes within the "system."

10. Empirical corroborations for these generalizations are found in two significant publications of last year: Heinrich Popitz *et al.*, *Das Gesellschaftsbild des Arbeiters* ("The Worker's Image of Society")

(Tübingen, 1957); Richard Hoggart, *The Uses of Literacy* (London, 1957).

11. Max Weber, "Wirtschaft und Gesellschaft," in *Grundriss der Sozialökonomik*, III (3rd ed.; Tübingen, 1947), 28.

12. This third condition, that of legitimacy, denotes the distinction between power (as an actual command relationship) and authority (cf. Weber's "Definitionen," *op. cit.*).

13. Thus it is clear that the phenomenon of authority is here deliberately treated unilaterally. The double aspect of society may be illustrated in this category, as in practically any other. Integration theory, too, treats of authority. However, this theory emphasizes not the polemical, conflict-generating aspect of this social relation but, on the contrary, the integrative, unifying aspect. Parsons is doubtless right when he says that authority "is the capacity to mobilize the resources of the society for the attainment of goals for which a general 'public' commitment has been made, or may be made. It is mobilization, above all, of the action of persons and groups, which is *binding* on them by virtue of their position in society" ("The Distribution of Power in American Society," *World Politics*, X, No. 1 [October, 1957], 140). However, in a way C. Wright Mills, who is criticized by Parsons, is also right when he emphasizes, as we do, the "presumptive illegitimacy" and "dysfunctionality" of all authority.

14. The position of authority of the bureaucrat was already of concern to Max Weber and to many sociologists since. Here there seems to be indeed a differentiation of authority. However, it is a differentiation of a special kind. In modern bureaucratic administration, the exercise of authority has undergone to a certain degree a division of labor; hence the multiplicity of positions, distinguishable by the number of "assignable persons" and the scope of "specific content" to which authority privileges are attached. In the sense of our analysis, there can be no doubt that the entire bureaucracy belongs (at times!) to the ruling side.

15. In what follows, I shall designate the roles to which the expectation of the exercise of authority is attached as "positive dominance roles" and, conversely, the roles without authority privileges as "negative dominance roles."

16. By this remark is meant (1) a mathematical formulation of the functions, (2) a development of measurement scales for each of the conditions, and (3) the adjustment of the combined scales to groups of conditions.

17. It should be recalled that the description of a social organization as an imperatively coordinated group is not exhaustive, nor should it be so. Rather, this description singles out for analysis one aspect of social organizations. For this reason, the statement "This social organization is an imperatively coordinated group" is not a tautology.

18. The social role of the *Arbeitsdirektor* is complex in the legal formulation of its rights and duties. The law prescribes that the *Arbeitsdirektor* (1) is a representative of the employees, or should not be appointed to the *Aufsichtsrat* (supervisory council) against the votes of the workers' representatives; (2) shall have equal rights and duties with the other members of the board of directors of the enterprise.

However, the conflict which results from the incompatible role expectations is less a sociological structural one than a psychological problem for the individual *Arbeitsdirektor*. For, structurally, only the latter expectation can hold realistically: the *Arbeitsdirektor* is, first and foremost, a member of the board of directors, that is, of the management.

19. The dogmatic brevity of the present analysis can give rise to misunderstandings. What is meant here is that conflict theory offers a conclusion to the effect that the intensity of social conflict is at a minimum where the conflict as such is taken seriously and is pursued most energetically, for example, in United States industry. Conversely, all attempts to erase the lines of conflict by institutions such as co-determination threaten, contrary to their intent, to sharpen conflicts. The oft repeated question of Sombart, "Why is there no socialism in the United States?" finds an answer not in the vague notion of the "American way of life" but in the generally positive value attached to conflict in the United States.

20. I would suspect the significant part of an explanation of the remarkable stability of the U.S.S.R. in arguments of this sort (and not in the assumption of the unlimited power of totalitarian leaders).

21. For certain technical conditions of organization, this is valid only within limits. Thus the liquidation of potential leaders of the opposition is a central component of totalitarian authority. In a way, both the East German and the Hungarian events can be taken as corroborations of the effectiveness of this policy.

22. Relevant here is the well-known slight decrease of pressure which seems to precede every revolution. Insofar, for example, as a certain relaxation of police control makes possible only an *ad hoc* organization, the emergence of open conflict becomes acute.

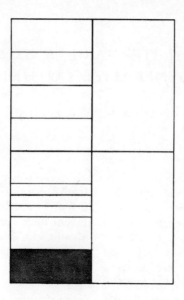

9. SYMBOLIC INTERACTIONISM

Symbolic interactionism typically defines the social in terms of objective behavior relations and seeks to explain it by referring to phenomena that are socially generated through characteristics of the social participants themselves. The selection from George Herbert Mead's writings presents some of his ideas about that set of social participant characteristics called "the self." The article by Herbert Blumer is a resumé of Mead's ideas that shows how symbolic interactionism would account for a wide variety of social phenomena.

PLAY, THE GAME, AND THE GENERALIZED OTHER

GEORGE HERBERT MEAD

We were speaking of the social conditions under which the self arises as an object. In addition to language we found two illustrations, one in play and the other in the game, and I wish to summarize and expand my account on these points. I have spoken of these from the point of view of children. We can, of course, refer also to the attitudes of more primitive people out of which our civilization has arisen. A striking illustration of play as distinct from the game is found in the myths and various of the plays which primitive people carry out, especially in religious pageants. The pure play attitude which we find in the case of little children may not be found here, since the participants are adults, and undoubtedly the relationship of these play processes to that which they interpret is more or less in the minds of even the most primitive people. In the process of interpretation of such rituals, there is an organization of play which perhaps might be compared to that which is taking place in the kindergarten in dealing with the plays of little children, where these are made into a set that will have a definite structure or relationship. At least something of the same sort is found in the play of primitive people. This type of activity belongs, of course, not to the everyday life of the people in their dealing with the objects about

them—there we have a more or less definitely developed self-consciousness—but in their attitudes toward the forces about them, the nature upon which they depend; in their attitude toward this nature which is vague and uncertain, there we have a much more primitive response; and that response finds its expression in taking the role of the other, playing at the expression of their gods and their heroes, going through certain rites which are the representation of what these individuals are supposed to be doing. The process is one which develops, to be sure, into a more or less definite technique and is controlled; and yet we can say that it has arisen out of situations similar to those in which little children play at being a parent, at being a teacher—vague personalities that are about them and which affect them and on which they depend. These are personalities which they take, roles they play, and in so far control the development of their own personality. This outcome is just what the kindergarten works toward. It takes the characters of these various vague beings and gets them into such an organized social relationship to each other that they build up the character of the little child.[1] The very introduction of organization from outside supposes a lack of organization at this period in the child's experience. Over against such a situation of the little child and primitive people, we have the game as such.

The fundamental difference between the game and play is that in the latter the child must have the attitude of all the others involved in that game. The attitudes of the other players which the participant assumes organize into a sort of unit, and it is that organization which controls the response of the individual. The illustration used was of a person playing baseball. Each one of his own acts is determined by his assumption of the action of the others who are playing the game. What he does is controlled by his being everyone else on that team, at least in so far as those attitudes affect his own particular response. We get then an "other" which is an organization of the attitudes of those involved in the same process.

The organized community or social group which gives to the individual his unity of self may be called "the generalized other." The attitude of the generalized other is the attitude of the whole community.² Thus, for example, in the case of such a social group as a ball team, the team is the generalized other in so far as it enters—as an organized process or social activity—into the experience of any one of the individual members of it.

If the given human individual is to develop a self in the fullest sense, it is not sufficient for him merely to take the attitudes of other human individuals toward himself and toward one another within the human social process, and to bring that social process as a whole into his individual experience merely in these terms: he must also, in the same way that he takes the attitudes of other individuals toward himself and toward one another, take their attitudes toward the various phases or aspects of the common social activity or set of social undertakings in which, as members of an organized society or social group, they are all engaged; and he must then, by generalizing these individual attitudes of that organized society or social group itself, as a whole, act toward different social projects which at any given time it is carrying out, or

toward the various larger phases of the general social process which constitutes its life and of which these projects are specific manifestations. This getting of the broad activities of any given social whole or organized society as such within the experiential field of any one of the individuals involved or included in that whole is, in other words, the essential basis and prerequisite of the fullest development of that individual's self: only in so far as he takes the attitudes of the organized social group to which he belongs toward the organized, co-operative social activity or set of such activities in which that group as such is engaged, does he develop a complete self or possess the sort of complete self he has developed. And on the other hand, the complex co-operative processes and activities and institutional functionings of organized human society are also possible only in so far as every individual involved in them or belonging to that society can take the general attitudes of all other such individuals with reference to these processes and activities and institutional functionings, and to the organized social whole of experiential relations and interactions thereby constituted—and can direct his own behavior accordingly.

It is in the form of the generalized other that the social process influences the behavior of the individuals involved in it and carrying it on, i.e., that the community exercises control over the conduct of its individual members; for it is in this form that the social process or community enters as a determining factor into the individual's thinking. In abstract thought the individual takes the attitude of the generalized other³ toward himself, without reference to its expression in any particular other individuals; and in concrete thought he takes that attitude in so far as it is expressed in the attitudes toward his behavior of those other individuals with whom he is involved in the given social situation or act. But only by taking the attitude of the generalized other toward himself, in one or another of these ways, can he think at all; for only thus can thinking—or the internalized conversation of gestures which constitutes thinking—occur. And only through the taking by individuals of the attitude or attitudes of the generalized other toward themselves is the existence of a universe of discourse, as that system of common or social meanings which thinking presupposes at its context, rendered possible.

The self-conscious human individual, then, takes or assumes the organized social attitudes of the given social group or community (or of some one section thereof) to which he belongs, toward the social problems of various kinds which confront that group or community at any given time, and which arise in connection with the correspondingly different social projects or organized co-operative enterprises in which that group or community as such is engaged; and as an individual participant in these social projects or co-operative enterprises, he governs his own conduct accordingly. In politics, for example, the individual identifies himself with an entire political party and takes the organized attitudes of that entire party toward the rest of the given social community and toward the problems which confront the party within the given social situation; and he consequently reacts or responds in terms of the organized attitudes of the party as a whole. He thus enters into a special set of social relations with all the other individuals who belong to that political party; and in the same way he enters into various other special sets of social relations, with various other classes of individuals respectively, the individuals of each of these classes being the other members of some one of the particular organized subgroups (determined in socially functional terms) of which he himself is a member within the entire given society or social community. In the most highly developed, organized, and complicated human social communities—those evolved by civilized man—these various socially functional classes or subgroups of individuals to which any given individual belongs (and with the other individual members of which he thus enters into a special set of social relations) are of two kinds. Some of them are concrete social classes or subgroups, such as political parties, clubs, corporations, which are all actually functional social units, in terms of which their individual members are directly related to one another. The others are abstract social classes or subgroups, such as the class of debtors and the class of creditors, in terms of which their individual members are related to one another only more or less indirectly, and which only more or less indirectly function as social units, but which afford or represent unlimited possibilities for the widening and ramifying and enriching of the social relations among all the individual members of the given society as an organized and unified whole. The given individual's membership in several of these abstract social classes or subgroups makes possible his entrance into definite social relations (however indirect) with an almost infinite number of other individuals who also belong to or are included within one or another of these abstract social classes or subgroups cutting across functional lines of demarcation which divide different human social communities from one another, and including individual members from several (in some cases from all) such communities. Of these abstract social classes or subgroups of human individuals the one which is most inclusive and extensive is, of course, the one defined by the logical universe of discourse (or system of universally significant symbols) determined by the participation and communicative interaction of individuals; for of all such classes or subgroups, it is the one which claims the largest number of individual members, and which enables the largest conceivable number of human individuals to enter into some sort of social relation, however indirect or abstract it may be, with one another—a relation arising from the universal functioning of gestures as significant symbols in the general human social process of communication.

I have pointed out, then, that there are two general stages in the full development of the self. At the first of these stages, the individual's self is constituted simply by an organization of the particular attitudes of other individuals toward himself and toward one another in the specific social acts in which he participates with them. But at the second stage in the full development of the individual's self, that self is constituted not only by an organization of these particular individual attitudes, but also by an organization of the social attitudes of the generalized other or the social group as a whole to which he belongs. These social or group attitudes are brought within the individual's field of direct experience, and are included as elements in the structure or constitution of his self, in the same way that the attitudes of particular other individuals are; and the individual arrives at them, or succeeds in taking them, by means of further organizing, and then generalizing, the attitudes of particular other individuals in terms of their organized social bearings and implications. So the self reaches its full development by organizing these individual attitudes of others into the organized social or group attitudes, and by thus becoming an individual reflection of the general systematic pattern of social or group behavior in which it and the others are all involved— a pattern which enters as a whole into the individual's experience in terms of these organized group attitudes which, through the mechanism of his central nervous system, he takes toward himself, just as he takes the individual attitudes of others.

The game has a logic, so that such an organization of the self gesture which tends to arouse in the individual the attitude which it arouses in others, and it is this perfecting of the self by the gesture which mediates the social activities that gives rise to the process of taking the role of the other. The latter phrase is a little unfortunate because it suggests an actor's attitude which is actually more sophisticated than that which is involved in our own experience. To this degree it does not correctly describe that which I have in mind. We see the process most definitely in a primitive form in those situations where the child's play takes different roles. Here the very fact that he is ready to pay out money, for instance, arouses the attitude of the person who receives money; the very process is calling out in him the corresponding activities of the other person involved. The individual stimulates himself to the response which he is calling out in the other person, and then acts in some degree in response to that situation. In play the child does not definitely act out the role which he himself has aroused in himself. It is that which gives, as I have said, a definite content in the individual which answers to the stimulus that affects him as it affects somebody else. The content of the other that enters into one personality is the response in the individual which his gesture calls out in the other.

We may illustrate our basic concept by a reference to the notion of property. If we say "This is my property, I shall control it," that affirmation calls out a certain set of responses which must be the same in any community in which property exists. It involves an organized attitude with reference to property which is common to all the members of the community. One must have a definite attitude of control of his own property and respect for the property of others. Those attitudes (as organized sets of responses) must be there on the part of all, so that when one says such a thing he calls out in himself the response of the others. He is calling out the response of what I have called a generalized other. That which makes society possible is such common responses, such organized attitudes, with reference to what we term property, the cults of religion, the process of education, and the relations of the family. Of course, the wider the society the more definitely universal these objects must be. In any case there must be a definite set of responses, which we may speak of as abstract, and which can belong to a very large group. Property is in itself a very abstract concept. It is that which the individual himself can control and nobody else can control. The attitude is different from that of a dog toward a bone. A dog will fight any other dog trying to take the bone. The dog is not taking the attitude of the other dog. A man who says "This is my property" is taking an attitude of the other person. The man is appealing to his rights because he is able to take the attitude which everybody else in the group has with reference to property, thus arousing in himself the attitude of others.

What goes to make up the organized self is the organization of the attitudes which are common to the group. A person is a personality because he belongs to a community, because he takes over the institutions of that community into his own conduct. He takes its language as a medium by which he gets his personality, and then through a process of taking the different roles that all the others furnish he comes to get the attitude of the members of the community. Such, in a certain sense, is the structure of a man's personality. There are certain common responses which each individual has toward certain common things, and in so far as those common responses are awakened in the individual when he is affecting other persons he arouses his own self. The structure, then, on which the self is built is this response which is common to all, for one has to be a member of a community to be a self. Such responses are abstract attitudes, but they constitute just what we term a man's character. They give him what we term his principles, the acknowledged attitudes of all members of the community toward what are the values of that community. He is putting himself in the place of the generalized other, which represents the organized responses of all the members of the group. It is that which guides conduct controlled by principles, and a person who has such an organized group of responses is a man whom we say has character, in the moral sense.

It is a structure of attitudes, then, which goes to make up a self, as distinct from a group of habits. We all of us have, for example, certain groups of habits, such as the particular intonations which a person uses in his speech. This is a set of habits of vocal expression which one has but which one does not know about. The sets of habits which we have of that sort mean nothing to us; we do not hear the intonations of our speech that others hear unless we are paying particular attention to them. The habits of emotional expression which belong to our speech are of the same sort. We may know that we have expressed ourselves in a joyous fashion but the detailed process is one which does not come back to our conscious selves. There are whole bundles of such habits which do not enter into a conscious self, but which help to make up what is termed the unconscious self.

After all, what we mean by self-consciousness is an awakening in ourselves of the group of attitudes which we are arousing in others, especially when it is an important set of responses which go to make up the members of the community. It is unfortunate to fuse or mix up consciousness, as we ordinarily use that term, and self-consciousness. Consciousness, as frequently used, simply has reference to the field of experience, but self-consciousness refers to the ability to call out in ourselves a set of definite responses which belong to the others of the group. Consciousness and self-consciousness are not on the same level. A man alone has, fortunately or unfortunately, access to his own toothache, but that is not what we mean by self-consciousnessness.

I have so far emphasized what I have called the structures upon which the self is constructed, the framework of the self, as it were. Of course we are not only what is common to all: each one of the selves is different from everyone else; but there has to be such a common structure as I have sketched in order that we may be members of a community at all. We cannot be ourselves unless we are also members in whom there is a community of attitudes which control the attitudes of all. We cannot have rights unless we have common attitudes. That which we have acquired as self-conscious persons makes us such members of society and gives us selves. Selves can only exist in definite relationships to other selves. No hard-and-fast line can be drawn between our own selves and the selves of others, since our own selves exist and enter as such into our experience only in so far as the selves of others exist and enter as such into our experience also. The individual possesses a self only in relation to the selves of the other members of his social group; and the structure of his self expresses or reflects the general behavior pattern of this social group to which he belongs, just as does the structure of the self of every other individual belonging to this social group.

NOTES

1. "The Relation of Play to Education," *University of Chicago Record*, I (1896–1897), 140 ff.

2. It is possible for inanimate objects, no less than for other human organisms, to form parts of the generalized and organized—the completely socialized—other for any given human individual, in so far as he responds to such objects socially or in a social fashion (by means of the mechanism of thought, the internalized conversation of gestures). Any thing—any object or set of objects, whether animate or inanimate, human or animal, or merely physical—toward which he acts, or to which he responds, socially, is an element in what for him is the generalized other; by taking the attitudes of which toward himself he becomes conscious of himself as an object or individual, and thus develops a self or personality. Thus, for example, the cult, in its primitive form, is merely the social embodiment of the relation between the given social group or community and its physical environment—an organized social means, adopted by the individual members of that group or community, of entering into social relations with that environment, or (in a sense) of carrying on conversations with it; and in this way that environment becomes part of the total generalized other for each of the individual members of the given social group or community.

3. We have said that the internal conversation of the individual with himself in terms of words or significant gestures—the conversation which constitutes the process or activity of thinking—is carried on by the individual from the standpoint of the "generalized other." And the more abstract that conversation is, the more abstract thinking happens to be, the further removed is the generalized other from any connection with particular individuals. It is especially in abstract thinking, that is to say, that the conversation involved is carried on by the individual with the generalized other, rather than with any particular individuals. Thus it is, for example, that abstract concepts are concepts stated in terms of the attitudes of the entire social group or community; they are stated on the basis of the individual's consciousness of the attitudes of the generalized other toward them, as a result of his taking these attitudes of the generalized other and then responding to them. And thus it is also that abstract propositions are stated in a form which anyone—any other intelligent individual—will accept.

SOCIOLOGICAL IMPLICATIONS OF
THE THOUGHT OF
GEORGE HERBERT MEAD

HERBERT BLUMER

My purpose is to depict the nature of human society when seen from the point of view of George Herbert Mead. While Mead gave human society a position of paramount importance in his scheme of thought he did little to outline its character. His central concern was with cardinal problems of philosophy. The development of his ideas of human society was largely limited to handling these problems. His treatment took the form of showing that human group life was the essential condition for the emergence of consciousness, the mind, a world of objects, human beings as organisms possessing selves, and human conduct in the form of constructed acts. He reversed the traditional assumptions underlying philosophical, psychological, and sociological thought to the effect that human beings possess minds and consciousness as original "givens," that they live in worlds of pre-existing and self-constituted objects, that their behavior consists of responses to such objects, and that group life consists of the association of such reacting human organisms. In making his brilliant contributions along this line he did not map out a theoretical scheme of human society. However, such a scheme is implicit in his work. It has to be constructed by tracing the implications of the central matters which he analyzed. This is what I propose to do. The central

Reprinted from the *American Journal of Sociology* (March 1966), pp. 535–548, by permission of the author and the University of Chicago Press.

matters I shall consider are (1) the self, (2) the act, (3) social interaction, (4) objects, and (5) joint action.

THE SELF

Mead's picture of the human being as an actor differs radically from the conception of man that dominates current psychological and social science. He saw the human being as an organism having a self. The possession of a self converts the human being into a special kind of actor, transforms his relation to the world, and gives his action a unique character. In asserting that the human being has a self, Mead simply meant that the human being is an object to himself. The human being may perceive himself, have conceptions of himself, communicate with himself, and act toward himself. As these types of behavior imply, the human being may become the object of his own action. This gives him the means of interacting with himself—addressing himself, responding to the address, and addressing himself anew. Such self-interaction takes the form of making indications to himself and meeting these indications by making further indications. The human being can designate things to himself—his wants, his pains, his goals, objects around him, the presence of others, their actions, their expected actions, or whatnot. Through further interaction with himself, he may judge, analyze, and evaluate the things he has designated to himself. And by continuing to interact with himself he may plan and organize his action with regard to what he has designated and evaluated. In short, the possession of a self provides the human being with a mechanism of self-interaction with which to meet the world—a mechanism that is used in forming and guiding his conduct.

I wish to stress that Mead saw the self as a process and not as a structure. Here Mead clearly parts company with the great bulk of students who seek to bring a self into the human being by identifying it with some kind of organization or structure. All of us are familiar with this practice because it is all around us in the literature. Thus, we see scholars who identify the self with the "ego," or who regard the self as an organized body of needs or motives, or who think of it as an organization of attitudes, or who treat it as a structure of internalized norms and values. Such schemes which seek to lodge the self in a structure make no sense since they miss the reflexive process which alone can yield and constitute a self. For any posited structure to be a self, it would have to act upon and respond to itself—otherwise, it is merely an organization awaiting activation and release without exercising any effect on itself or on its operation. This marks the crucial weakness or inadequacy of the many schemes such as referred to above, which misguidingly associate the self with some kind of psychological or personality structure. For example, the ego, as such, is not a self; it would be a self only by becoming reflexive, that is to say, acting toward or on itself. And the same thing is true of any other posited psychological structure. Yet, such reflexive action changes both the status and the character of the structure and elevates the process of self-interaction to the position of major importance.

We can see this in the case of the reflexive process that Mead has isolated in the human being. As mentioned, this reflexive process takes the form of the person making indications to himself, that is to say, noting things and determining their significance for this line of action. To indicate something is to stand over against it and to put oneself in the position of acting toward it instead of automatically responding to it. In the face of something which one indicates, one can withhold action toward it, inspect it, judge it, ascertain its meaning, determine its possibilities, and direct one's action with regard to it. With the mechanism of self-interaction the human being ceases to be a responding organism whose behavior is a product of what plays upon him from the outside, the inside, or both. Instead, he acts toward his world, interpreting what confronts him and organizing his action on the basis of the interpretation. To illustrate: a pain one identifies and interprets is very different from a mere organic feeling and lays the basis for doing something about it instead of merely responding organically to it; to note and interpret the activity of another person is very different from having a response released by that activity; to be aware that one is hungry is very different from merely being hungry; to perceive one's "ego" puts one in the position of doing something with regard to it instead of merely giving expression to the ego. As these illustrations show, the process of self-interaction puts the human being over against his world instead of merely in it, requires him to meet and handle his world through a defining process instead of merely responding to it, and forces him to construct his action instead of merely releasing it. This is the kind of acting organism that Mead sees man to be as a result of having a self.[1]

THE ACT

Human action requires a radically different character as a result of being formed through a process of self-interaction. Action is built up in coping with the world instead of merely being released from a pre-existing psychological structure by factors playing on that structure. By making indications to himself and by interpreting what he indicates, the human being has to forge or piece together a line of action. In order to act the individual has to identify what he wants, establish an objective or goal, map out a prospective line of behavior, note and interpret the actions of others, size up his situation, check himself at this or that point, figure out what to do at other points, and frequently spur himself on in the face of dragging dispositions or discouraging settings. The fact that the human act is self-directed or built up by means in no sense that the actor necessarily exercises excellence in its construction. Indeed, he may do a very poor job in constructing his act. He may fail to note things of which he should be aware, he may misinterpret things that he notes, he may exercise poor judgment, he may be faulty in mapping out prospective lines of conduct, and he may be half-hearted in contending with recalcitrant dispositions. Such deficiencies in the construction of his acts do not belie the fact that his acts are still constructed by him out of what he takes into account. What he takes into account are the things that he indicates to himself. They cover such matters as his wants, his feelings, his goals, the actions of others, the expectations and demands of others, the rules of his group, his situation, his conceptions of himself, his recollections, and his images of prospective lines of conduct. He is not in the mere recipient position of responding to such matters; he stands over against them and has to handle them. He has to organize or cut out his lines of conduct on the basis of how he does handle them.

This way of viewing human action is directly opposite to that which dominates psychological and social sciences. In these sciences human action is seen as a product of factors that play upon or through the human actor. Depending on the preference of the scholar, such determining factors may be physiological stimulations, organic drives, needs, feelings, unconscious motives, conscious motives, sentiments, ideas, attitudes, norms, values, role requirements, status demands, cultural prescriptions, institutional pressures, or social-system requirements. Regardless of which factors are chosen, either singly or in combination, action is regarded as their product and hence is explained in their terms. The formula is simple: Given factors play on the human being to produce given types of behavior. The formula is frequently amplified so as to read: Under specified conditions, given factors playing on a given organization of the human being will produce a given type of behavior. The formula, in either its simple or amplified form, represents the way in which human action is seen in theory and research. Under the formula the human being becomes a mere medium or forum for the operation of the factors that produce the behavior. Mead's scheme is fundamentally different from this formula. In place of being a mere medium for operation of determining factors that play upon him, the human being is seen as an active organism in his own right, facing, dealing with, and acting toward the objects he indicates. Action is seen as conduct which is constructed by the actor instead of response elicited from some kind of preformed organization in him. We can say that the traditional formula of human action fails to recognize that the human being is a self. Mead's scheme, in contrast, is based on this recognition.

SOCIAL INTERACTION

I can give here only a very brief sketch of Mead's highly illuminating analysis of social interaction. He identified two forms or levels—non-symbolic interaction and symbolic interaction. In non-symbolic interaction human beings respond directly to one another's gestures or actions; in symbolic interaction they interpret each other's gestures and act on the basis of the meaning yielded by the interpretation. An unwitting response to the tone of another's voice illustrates non-symbolic interaction. Interpreting the shaking of a fist as signifying that a person is preparing to attack illustrates symbolic interaction. Mead's concern was predominantly with symbolic interaction. Symbolic interaction involves *interpretation*, or ascertaining the meaning of the actions or remarks of the other person, and *definition*, or conveying indications to another person as to how he is to act. Human association consists of a process of such interpretation and definition. Through this process the participants fit their own acts to the ongoing acts of one another and guide others in doing so.

Several important matters need to be noted in the case of symbolic interaction. First, it is a formative process in its own right. The prevailing practice of psychology and sociology is to treat social interaction as a neutral medium, as a mere forum for the operation of outside factors. Thus psychologists are led to account for the behavior of people in interaction by resorting to elements of the psychological equipment of the participants—such elements as motives, feelings, attitudes, or personality organization. Sociologists do the same sort of thing by resorting to societal factors, such as cultural prescriptions, values, social roles, or structural pressures. Both miss the central point that human interaction is a positive shaping process in its own right. The participants in it have to build up their respective lines of conduct by constant interpretation of each other's ongoing lines of action. As participants take account of each other's ongoing acts, they have to arrest, reorganize, or adjust their own intentions, wishes, feelings, and attitudes; similarly, they have to judge the fitness of norms, values, and group prescriptions for the situation being formed by the acts of others. Factors of psychological equipment and social organization are not substitutes for the interpretative process; they are admissable only in terms of how they are handled in the interpretative process. Symbolic interaction has to be seen and studied in its own right.

Symbolic interaction is noteworthy in a second way. Because of it human group life takes on the character of an ongoing process—a continuing matter of fitting developing lines of conduct to one another. The fitting together of the lines of conduct is done through the dual process of definition and interpretation. This dual process operates both to sustain established patterns of joint conduct and to open them to transformation. Established patterns of group life exist and persist only through the continued use of the same schemes of interpretation; and such schemes of interpretation are maintained only through their continued confirmation by the defining acts of others. It is highly important to recognize that the established patterns of group life just do not carry on by themselves but are dependent for their continuity on recurrent affirmative definition. Let the interpretations that sustain them be undermined or disrupted by changed definitions from others and the patterns can quickly collapse. This dependency of interpretations on the defining acts of others also explains why symbolic interaction conduces so markedly to the transformation of the forms of joint activity that make up group life. In the flow of group life there are innumerable points at which the participants are *re*defining each other's acts. Such redefinition is very common in adversary relations, it is frequent in group discussion, and it is essentially intrinsic to dealing with problems. (And I may remark here that no human group is free of problems.) Redefinition imparts a formative character to human interaction, giving rise at this or that point to new objects, new conceptions, new relations, and new types of behavior. In short, the reliance on symbolic interaction makes human group life a developing process instead of a mere issue or product of psychological or social structure.

There is a third aspect of symbolic interaction which is important to note. In making the process of interpretation and definition of one another's acts central in human interaction, symbolic interaction is able to cover the full range of the generic forms of human association. It embraces equally well such relationships as cooperation, conflict, domination, exploitation, consensus, disagreement, closely knit identification, and indifferent concern for one another. The participants in each of such relations have the same common task of constructing their acts by interpreting and defining the acts of each other. The significance of this simple observation becomes evident in contrasting symbolic interaction with the various schemes of human interaction that are to be found in the literature. Almost always such schemes construct a general model of human interaction or society on the basis of a particular type of human relationship. An outstanding contemporary instance is Talcott Parsons' scheme which presumes and asserts that the primordial and generic form of human interaction is the "complementarity of expectations." Other schemes depict the basic and generic model of human interaction as being "conflict," others assert it to be "identity through common sentiments," and still others that it is agreement in the form of "consensus." Such schemes are parochial. Their great danger lies in imposing on the breadth of human interaction an image derived from the study of only one form of interaction. Thus, in different hands, human society is said to be fundamentally a sharing of common values; or, conversely, a struggle for power; or, still differently, the exercise of consensus; and so on. The simple point implicit in Mead's analysis of symbolic interaction is that human beings, in interpreting and defining one another's acts, can and do meet each other in the full range of human relations. Proposed schemes of human society should respect this simple point.

OBJECTS

The concept of object is another fundamental pillar in Mead's scheme of analysis. Human beings live in a world or environment of objects, and their activities are formed around objects. This bland statement becomes very significant when it is realized that for Mead objects are human constructs and not self-existing entities with intrinsic natures. Their nature is dependent on the orientation and action of people toward them. Let me spell this out. For Mead, an object is anything that can be designated or referred to. It may be physical as a chair or imaginary as a ghost, natural as a cloud in the sky or manmade as an automobile, material as the Empire State Building or abstract as the concept of liberty, animate as an elephant or inanimate as a vein of coal, inclusive of a class of people as politicians or restricted to a specific person as President de Gaulle, definite as a multiplication table or vague as a philosophical doctrine. In short, objects consist of whatever people indicate or refer to.

There are several important points in this analysis of objects. First, the nature of an object is constituted by the meaning it has for the person or persons for whom it is an object. Second, this meaning is not intrinsic to the object but arises from how the person is initially prepared to act toward it. Readiness to use a chair as something in which to sit gives it the meaning of a chair; to one with no experience with the use of chairs the object would appear with a different meaning, such as a strange weapon. It follows that objects vary in their meaning. A tree is not the same object to a lumberman, a botanist, or a poet; a star is a different object to a modern astronomer than it was to a sheepherder of antiquity; communism is a different object to a Soviet patriot than it is to a Wall Street broker. Third, objects—all objects—are social products in that they are formed and transformed by the defining process that takes place in social interaction. The meaning of the objects—chairs, trees, stars, prostitutes, saints, communism, public education, or whatnot—is formed from the ways in which others refer to such objects or act toward them. Fourth, people are prepared or set to act toward objects on the basis of the meaning of the objects for them. In a genuine sense the organization of a human being consists of his objects, that is, his tendencies to act on the basis of their meanings. Fifth, just because an object is something that is designated, one can organize one's action toward it instead of responding immediately to it; one can inspect the object, think about it, work out a plan of action toward it, or decide whether or not to act toward it. In standing over against the object in both a logical and psychological sense, one is freed from coercive response to it. In this profound sense an object is different from a stimulus as ordinarily conceived.

This analysis of objects puts human group life into a new and interesting perspective. Human beings are seen as living in a world of meaningful objects—not in an environment of stimuli or self-constituted entities. This world is socially produced in that the meanings are fabricated through the process of social interaction. Thus, different groups come to develop different worlds—and these worlds change as the objects that compose them change in meaning. Since people are set to act in terms of the meanings of their objects, the world of

objects of a group represents in a genuine sense its action organization. To identify and understand the life of a group it is necessary to identify its world of objects; this identification has to be in terms of the meanings objects have for the members of the group. Finally, people are not locked to their objects; they may check action toward objects and indeed work out new lines of conduct toward them. This condition introduces into human group life an indigenous source of transformation.

JOINT ACTION

I use the term "joint action" in place of Mead's term "social act." It refers to the larger collective form of action that is constituted by the fitting together of the lines of behavior of the separate participants. Illustrations of joint action are a trading transaction, a family dinner, a marriage ceremony, a shopping expedition, a game, a convivial party, a debate, a court trial, or a war. We note in each instance an identifiable and distinctive form of joint action, comprised by an articulation of the acts of the participants. Joint actions range from a simple collaboration of two individuals to a complex alignment of the acts of huge organizations or institutions. Everywhere we look in a human society we see people engaging in forms of joint action. Indeed, the totality of such instances—in all of their multitudinous variety, their variable connections, and their complex networks—constitutes the life of a society. It is easy to understand from these remarks why Mead saw joint action, or the social act, as the distinguishing characteristic of society. For him, the social act was the fundamental unit of society. Its analysis, accordingly, lays bare the generic nature of society.

To begin with, a joint action cannot be resolved into a common or same type of behavior on the part of the participants.

Each participant necessarily occupies a different position, acts from that position, and engages in a separate and distinctive act. It is the fitting together of these acts and not their commonality that constitutes joint action. How do these separate acts come to fit together in the case of human society? Their alignment does not occur through sheer mechanical juggling, as in the shaking of walnuts in a jar or through unwitting adaptation, as in an ecological arrangement in a plant community. Instead, the participants fit their acts together, first, by identifying the social act in which they are about to engage and, second, by interpreting and defining each other's acts in forming the joint act. By identifying the social act or joint action the participant is able to orient himself; he has a key to interpreting the acts of others and a guide for directing his action with regard to them. Thus, to act appropriately, the participant has to identify a marriage ceremony as a marriage ceremony, a holdup as a holdup, a debate as a debate, a war as a war, and so forth. But, even though this identification be made, the participants in the joint action that is being formed still find it necessary to interpret and define one another's ongoing acts. They have to ascertain what the others are doing and plan to do and make indications to one another of what to do.

This brief analysis of joint action enables us to note several matters of distinct importance. It calls attention, first, to the fact that the essence of society lies in an ongoing process of action—not in a posited structure of relations. Without action, any structure of relations between people is meaningless. To be understood, a society must be seen and grasped in terms of the action that comprises it. Next, such action has to be seen and treated, not by tracing the separate lines of action of the participants—whether the participants be single individuals, collectivities, or organizations—but in

terms of the joint action into which the separate lines of action fit and merge. Few students of human society have fully grasped this point or its implications. Third, just because it is built up over time by the fitting together of acts, each joint action must be seen as having a career or a history. In having a career, its course and fate are contingent on what happens during its formation. Fourth, this career is generally orderly, fixed and repetitious by virtue of a common identification or definition of the joint action that is made by its participants. The common definition supplies each participant with decisive guidance in directing his own act so as to fit into the acts of the others. Such common definitions serve, above everything else, to account for the regularity, stability, and repetitiveness of joint action in vast areas of group life; they are the source of the established and regulated social behavior that is envisioned in the concept of culture. Fifth, however, the career of joint actions also must be seen as open to many possibilities of uncertainty. Let me specify the more important of these possibilities. One, joint actions have to be initiated—and they may not be. Two, once started a joint action may be interrupted, abandoned, or transformed. Three, the participants may not make a common definition of the joint action into which they are thrown and hence may orient their acts on different premises. Four, a common definition of a joint action may still allow wide differences in the direction of the separate lines of action and hence in the course taken by the joint action; a war is a good example. Five, new situations may arise calling for hitherto unexisting types of joint action, leading to confused exploratory efforts to work out a fitting together of acts. And, six, even in the context of a commonly defined joint action, participants may be led to rely on other considerations in interpreting and defining each other's lines of action. Time does not allow me to spell out and illustrate the importance of these possibilities. To mention them should be sufficient, however, to show that uncertainty, contingency, and transformation are part and parcel of the process of joint action. To assume that the diversified joint actions which comprise a human society are set to follow fixed and established channels is a sheer gratuitous assumption.

From the foregoing discussion of the self, the act, social interaction, objects, and joint action we can sketch a picture of human society. The picture is composed in terms of action. A society is seen as people meeting the varietites of situations that are thrust on them by their conditions of life. These situations are met by working out joint actions in which participants have to align their acts to one another. Each participant does so by interpreting the acts of others and, in turn, by making indications to others as to how they should act. By virtue of this process of interpretation and definition joint actions are built up; they have careers. Usually, the course of a joint action is outlined in advance by the fact that the participants make a common identification of it; this makes for regularity, stability, and repetitiveness in the joint action. However, there are many joint actions that encounter obstructions, that have no pre-established pathways, and that have to be constructed along new lines. Mead saw human society in this way—as a diversified social process in which people were engaged in forming joint actions to deal with situations confronting them.

This picture of society stands in significant contrast to the dominant views of society in the social and psychological sciences—even to those that pretend to view society as action. To point out the major differences in the contrast is the best way of specifying the sociological implications of Mead's scheme of thought.

The chief difference is that the dominant views in sociology and psychology fail, alike, to see human beings as organisms having selves. Instead, they regard human beings as merely responding organisms and, accordingly, treat action as mere response to factors playing on human beings. This is exemplified in the efforts to account for human behavior by such factors as motives, ego demands, attitudes, role requirements, values, status expectations, and structural stresses. In such approaches the human being becomes a mere medium through which such initiating factors operate to produce given actions. From Mead's point of view such a conception grossly misrepresents the nature of human beings and human action. Mead's scheme interposes a process of self-interaction between initiating factors and the action that may follow in their wake. By virtue of self-interaction the human being becomes an acting organism coping with situations in place of being an organism merely responding to the play of factors. And his action becomes something he constructs and directs to meet the situations in place of an unrolling of reactions evoked from him. In introducing the self, Mead's position focuses on how human beings handle and fashion their world, not on disparate responses to imputed factors.

If human beings are, indeed, organisms with selves, and if their action is, indeed, an outcome of a process of self-interaction, schemes that purport to study and explain social action should respect and accommodate these features. To do so, current schemes in sociology and psychology would have to undergo radical revision. They would have to shift from a preoccupation with initiating factor and terminal result to a preoccupation with a process of formation. They would have to view actions as something constructed by the actor instead of something evoked from him. They would

THEY WOULD have to depict the milieu of action in terms of how the milieu appears to the actor in place of how it appears to the outside student. They would have to incorporate the interpretive process which at present they scarcely deign to touch. They would have to recognize that any given act has a career in which it is constructed but in which it may be interrupted, held in abeyance, abandoned, or recast.

On the methodological or research side the study of action would have to be made from the position of the actor. Since action is forged by the actor out of what he perceives, interprets, and judges, one would have to see the operating situation as the actor sees it, perceive objects as the actor perceives them, ascertain their meaning in terms of the meaning they have for the actor, and follow the actor's line of conduct as the actor organizes it—in short, one would have to take the role of the actor and see his world from his standpoint. This methodological approach stands in contrast to the so-called objective approach so dominant today, namely, that of viewing the actor and his action from the perspective of an outside, detached observer. The "objective" approach holds the danger of the observer substituting his view of the field of action for the view held by the actor. It is unnecessary to add that the actor acts toward his world on the basis of how he sees it and not on the basis of how that world appears to the outside observer.

In continuing the discussion of this matter, I wish to consider especially what we might term the structural conception of human society. This conception views society as established organization, familiar to us in the use of such terms as social structure, social system, status position, social role, social stratification, institutional structure, cultural pattern, social codes, social norms, and social values. The conception presumes that a human society is structured with regard to (a) the social positions occupied by the people in it and with regard to (b) the patterns of behavior in which they engage. It is presumed further that this interlinked structure of social positions and behavior patterns is the over-all determinant of social action; this is evidenced, of course, in the practice of explaining conduct by such structural concepts as role requirements, status demands, strata differences, cultural prescriptions, values, and norms. Social action falls into two general categories: conformity, marked by adherence to the structure, and deviance, marked by departure from it. Because of the central and determinative position into which it is elevated, structure becomes necessarily the encompassing object of sociological study and analysis—epitomized by the well-nigh universal assertion that a human group or society is a "social system." It is perhaps unnecessary to observe that the conception of human society as structure or organization is ingrained in the very marrow of contemporary sociology.

Mead's scheme definitely challenges this conception. It sees human society not as an established structure but as people meeting their conditions of life; it sees social action not as an emanation of societal structure but as a formation made by human actors; it sees this formation of action not as societal factors coming to expression through the medium of human organisms but as constructions made by actors out of what they take into account; it sees group life not as a release or expression of established structure but as a process of building up joint actions; it sees social actions as having variable careers and not as confined to the alternatives of conformity to or deviation from the dictates of established structure; it sees the so-called interaction between parts of a society not as a direct exercising of influence by one part on another but as mediated throughout by interpretations made by people; accordingly, it sees society not as a system, whether in the form of a static, moving or whatever kind of equilibrium, but as a vast number of occurring joint actions, many closely linked, many not linked at all, many prefigured and repetitious, others being carved out in new directions, and all being pursued to serve the purposes of the participants and not the requirements of a system. I have said enough, I think, to point out the drastic differences between the Meadian conception of society and the widespread sociological conceptions of it as structure.

The differences do not mean, incidentally, that Mead's view rejects the existence of structure in human society. Such a position would be ridiculous. There are such matters as social roles, status positions, rank orders, bureaucratic organizations, relations between institutions, differential authority arrangements, social codes, norms, values, and the like. And they are very important. But their importance does not lie in an alleged determination of action nor in an alleged existence as parts of a self-operating societal system. Instead, they are important only as they enter into the process of interpretation and definition out of which joint actions are formed. The manner and extent to which they enter may vary greatly from situation to situation, depending on what people take into account and how they aessss what they take account of. Let me give one brief illustration. It is ridiculous, for instance, to assert, as a number of eminent sociologists have done, that social interaction is an interaction between social roles. Social interaction is obviously an interaction between *people* and not between roles; the needs of the participants are to interpret and handle what confronts them—such as a topic of conversation or a problem—and not to give expression to their roles. It is only in highly ritualistic relations that the direction and content of conduct can be explained by roles. Usually, the direction and content are fashioned out of what people in interaction have to deal with. That roles affect in varying degree phases of the direction and content of action is true but is a matter of determination in given cases. This is a far cry from asserting action to be a product of roles. The observation I have made in this brief discussion of social roles applies with equal validity to all other structural matters.

Another significant implication of Mead's scheme of thought refers to the question of what holds a human society together. As we know, this question is converted by sociologists into a problem of unity, stability, and orderliness. And, as we know further, the typical answer given by sociologists is that unity, stability, and orderliness come from a sharing in common of certain basic matters, such as codes, sentiments, and, above all, values. Thus, the disposition is to regard common values as the glue that holds a society together, as the controlling regulator that brings and keeps the activities in a society in orderly relationship, and as the force that preserves stability in a society. Conversely, it is held that conflict between values or the disintegration of values creates disunity, disorder, and instability. This conception of human society becomes subject to great modification if we think of society as consisting of the fitting together of acts to form joint action. Such alignment may take place for any number of reasons, depending on the situations calling for joint action, and need not involve, or spring from, the sharing of common values. The participants may fit their acts to one another in orderly joint actions on the basis of compromise, out of duress, because they may use one another in achieving their respective ends, because it is the sensible thing to do, or out of sheer necessity. This is particularly likely to be true in our modern complex societies with their great diversity in composition, in lines of interest, and in their respective worlds of concern. In very large measure, society becomes the formation of workable relations. To seek to encompass, analyze, and understand the life of a society on the assumption that the existence of a society necessarily depends on the sharing of values can lead to strained treatment, gross misrepresentation, and faulty lines of interpretation. I believe that the Meadian perspective, in posing the question of how people are led to align their acts in different situations in place of presuming that this necessarily requires and stems from a sharing of common values, is a more salutary and realistic approach. *eg. EMPLOYMENT.*

There are many other significant sociological implications in Mead's scheme of thought which, under the limit of space, I can do no more than mention. Socialization shifts its character from being an effective internalization of norms and values to a cultivated capacity to take

the roles of others effectively. Social control becomes fundamentally and necessarily a matter of self-control. Social change becomes a continuous indigenous process in human group life instead of an episodic result of extraneous factors playing on established structure. Human group life is seen as always incomplete and undergoing development instead of jumping from one completed state to another. Social disorganization is seen not as a breakdown of existing structure but as an inability to mobilize action effectively in the face of a given situation. Social action, since it has a career, is recognized as having a historical dimension which has to be taken into account in order to be adequately understood.

In closing I wish to say that my presentation has necessarily skipped much in Mead's scheme that is of great significance. Further, I have not sought to demonstrate the validity of his analyses. However, I have tried to suggest the freshness, the fecundity, and the revolutionary implications of his point of view.

NOTES

1. The self, or indeed human being, is not brought into the picture merely by introducing psychological elements, such as motives and interests, alongside of societal elements. Such additions merely compound the error of the omission. This is the flaw in George Homan's presidential address on "Bringing Man Back In" (*American Sociological Review*, XXIX, No. 6, 809–818).

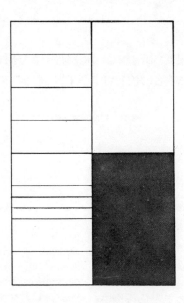

10. SOCIAL ACTIONISM

Social actionism typically defines the social in terms of subjective behavior relations and seeks to explain it by referring to phenomena generated by the social through characteristics of participants' environments and of the participants themselves. Scott details the history of social actionism (and the implicit beginnings of functional imperativism) in Parsons' work before and after World War II.

THE CHANGING FOUNDATIONS OF
THE PARSONIAN ACTION SCHEME

JOHN FINLEY SCOTT

Talcott Parsons' "action scheme" has undergone many changes. Although these have been widely discussed, there remains one revision on which little has been said. What has happened to the voluntaristic thesis?

In the prewar versions of the scheme, voluntarism was more than a polemic against what Parsons called "positivism"; it was also an argument for the causal efficacy of valuation. As introduced in "The Place of Ultimate Values in Sociological Theory" and developed in *The Structure of Social Action*,[1] the polemic was a depreciation of efforts to reduce human conduct to the explanatory framework of the natural sciences. Parsons also argued that a primordially creative element, independent of the natural world of "heredity and environment," was active in valuation and the choice of goals. Voluntarism thus involved the premises of philosophical idealism.

Things have changed remarkably in the postwar writings. The treatment of mentality shows the substantive influence of Freud and the methodological influence of Tolman, while a tone of naturalism prevails over much that before the war was held to be autonomous from nature. This is the position of Parsons' monograph, "Values, Motives, and Systems of Action,"[2] and of his related postwar papers.

Reprinted from the *American Sociological Review* (October 1963), pp. 716–735, by permission of the American Sociological Association and the author.

PRELIMINARY REMARKS

Robin Williams has noted that *The Structure of Social Action* is best understood in the light of doctrines current in the generation before it was written.[3] Edward Devereux has emphasized the polemical content of the book and its organization round a critique of "positivism."[4] This paper takes up the subjects of these eluciditory asides and makes them the start of its whole concern: it argues that *The Structure of Social Action* is really much more a book about the philosophy of science than its distinctively sociological title would suggest,[5] and attempts to account for much that has changed during the evolution of the action scheme by following up some of the philosophical issues with which it was originally concerned.

Among the many papers dealing with the action scheme, two in particular detail its relation to issues in the philosophy of science. The first is Howard Pinney's review essay, "The Structure of Social Action."[6] The second is Max Black's study in the Cornell symposium, *The Social Theories of Talcott Parsons*.[7] Both Black and Pinney consider the action scheme only at one point in time. This paper starts with the prewar texts and then goes on through to the postwar discussions. It deals with the changing foundations of the scheme insofar as those foundations are certain philosophical concerns which provided Parsons with criteria for delimiting the categories of the scheme and for defining its key terms. Perhaps most important are the concerns about valuation, which, though they themselves appear to have changed, are still reflected in Parsons' abiding emphasis on the "analytical independence" of values. The paper thus offers a partial answer to the question posed by Black: how are the basic categories of Parsons' theory obtained?

It will help to distinguish three aspects of the Parsonian texts. First, there is the "action scheme" in the narrow sense, including only the definitions of the general elements or categories of action. Second, there are theories or models of particular action systems, such as those of personality or social systems. Though these too are highly abstract, they do go beyond definitions and make empirically contingent assertions in ways that the "pure categories" of the action scheme (in the narrow sense) do not. Third, there are the "empirical" papers, treating, for example, of the kinship organization of a particular society, usually in the light of the action system models. While these three aspects often blend in Parsons' writing,[8] this paper deals only with the action scheme in the narrow sense.

Parsons' writings do not form a systematic whole in the sense that the "theorems" of social organization can be deduced from the "axioms" of the action scheme.[9] As a result it is entirely possible to say that Parsons has retreated from the metaphysical distinctiveness he attributed to certain ends and values in the first version of the action scheme at the same time that he has continued to defend their distinctive role and "analytical independence" in sociological theory. The immediate point is that the action scheme in this narrow sense is the best place to look for specific associations with epistemology and ontology, and begin the quest for foundations. Such foundations are relevant for sociology because philosophical beliefs have implications

for the interpretation of matters of fact. If one believes, for example, in the ubiquity of moral obligation—a belief fostered by the introspective method of idealistic epistemology—then it is not hard to locate this sense of obligation as the foundation of social control. Historically, idealists have emphasized the role of internalization in social control and have depreciated the role of sanctions.[10]

Two aspects of the action scheme are especially relevant here: its subjective reference, to "action from the point of view of the actor," and its normative orientation, the claim that action always involves a reference to or consideration of some normative element. No elaboration is necessary today to recall the importance of these two aspects to the scheme as a whole, especially in its earlier forms. These are also the parts of the scheme most closely connected with the traditional philosophical debate between "idealism" and "materialism." The scientific import of that debate in Parsons' early work was the choice between a non-natural and a natural interpretation of the phenomena of minded behavior. He thought natural interpretations rested on a materialistic metaphysic of physical determinism. Such interpretations, he judged, did not explain the mental phenomena of cognition, rationality, and evaluation so much as they explained them away, and the only alternative he saw was the introduction of non-natural factors of volition or "will"; hence the voluntaristic thesis. Since this paper argues that Parsons has moved from a non-natural position on this matter to a naturalistic one, it shows that the subjective and normative aspects of the action scheme have undergone parallel changes.[11]

There is also an important informal difference between the pre- and postwar expositions. The relation of this prewar action scheme to its philosophical premises can be seen very clearly if one reviews Parsons' singularly unnoticed essay, "The Place of Ultimate Values in Sociological Theory." But if one seeks the parallel relation in the postwar versions of the action scheme, Parsons is not so helpful. There is no paper in which Parsons sets forth his postwar premises on philosophy and the scope and limits of science as clearly as he did earlier in "The Place of Ultimate Values in Sociological Theory." Further, in those sections of the postwar texts most directly comparable to the prewar position, one finds that Parsons' terminology consistently has a double meaning with respect to topics on which he was once quite clear, such as whether the action scheme is "voluntaristic."

The consistency with which these double meanings are found is sufficiently pronounced to warrant referring to them as "crucial equivocations." It is as if Parsons were writing his postwar papers so as to maintain both a *terminological* continuity with his earlier work and a *programmatic* continuity with such "epistemological leftists" as Tolman, of whose methodology Parsons wrote after the war in terms of praise.[12] This interpretation is, to be sure, hypothetical, but it permits a consistent reading of what are otherwise perplexing passages in the later Parsonian texts. And the resolution of these equivocations is important; for if they are genuine then there are not one but two action schemes, different not only in their founding premises and motivating concerns, but also in the types of data they can encompass, in the hypotheses which can be subsumed under them, and in the character and scope of substantive theory that they are likely to inspire.

THE PREWAR FOUNDATIONS

The most complete exposition of the prewar action scheme is given in *The Structure of Social Action*. This book

essentially has two parts: the first is the exposition of Parsons' action scheme as it stood at the time; the second, the direct thesis of the book, attempts to show that the action scheme, or a "voluntaristic theory of action," emerges from the sociological parts of the writings of Marshall, Pareto, Durkheim and Weber. These two parts remain fairly separate, even though voluntarism is iterated in the second part, and the polemic against positivism is continued from beginning to end. Now whether the voluntaristic thesis really emerges from these writers, or whether it was a thesis that Parsons imputed to them when in fact it was pretty much his own original synthesis of idealism with empirical science, is an interesting question; but it need not be more than mentioned here.[13] The present concern is with Parsons' analysis of action and its components, as offered principally in the second and nineteenth chapters of the book.

Action in general terms is said to have the following characteristics: first, the smallest unit of analysis is called the "unit act," which is defined as "the least amount" of action that can be identified as possessing all of action's defining constituents. A unit act is composed of the following: first, it implies an *actor*, an agent of whom action is predicated. This agent is associated with, but is not identical to, a person or organism. Second, "for purposes of definition the act must have an 'end,' a future state of affairs to which the process of action is oriented."[14] Third, action is initiated in a *situation* which differs in one or more important respects from the future state of affairs anticipated in connection with the end.

Finally, "there is inherent in the conception of this unit, in its analytical uses, a certain mode of relation between these elements."[15] Where, in a given situation, different means exist to the same end, the selection between means is called "the normative orientation of action." Parsons' elaboration of this fourth property of action is especially relevant here:

[Means] cannot, in general, be conceived as chosen at random or as dependent exclusively on the conditions of action, but must in some sense be subject to the influence of an *independent, determinate selective factor*, a knowledge of which [presumably knowledge by the observer of action] is necessary to the understanding of a concrete course of action. What is essential to the concept of action is that there should be a normative orientation, not that it should be of any particular type.[16]

What differs from this is not action, at least so far as Parsons' scheme is concerned.

Parsons then discusses some of his scheme's more important implications, including its essentially subjective reference. The scheme ". . . deals with phenomena, with things and events, *as they appear from the point of view of the actor* whose action is being analyzed and considered."[17] Unlike the physical sciences, Parsons says, the action scheme studies phenomena that "have a scientifically relevant subjective aspect." This does not mean that the social scientist reviews the contents of his own mind, but that "he is very much interested in the minds of the persons whose action he studies."[18] This leads to a distinction between subjective and non-subjective points of view, which Parsons labels as those of the actor and observer respectively.

This subjective point of view means that the action scheme is not offered for use in the study of "whole organisms" as is done by biologists and behavioristic psychologists. Organisms in this sense, says Parsons, are "spatially distinguishable separate units." The unit of reference of the action scheme is not this physically isolable unit but an "ego" or "self." In this way physical properties which are intrinsic to inseparable components of the organism, such as prehensility, can serve as means to the course of action

selected by ego. Parsons feels that it would be paradoxical to speak so of action predicated of the whole organism, behaving in the context of "environment."[19]

This, briefly, is the action scheme as Parsons developed it in 1937. Action involves actors, goals, conditions, and means. Orientation to action necessarily involves a normative element and its components are distinguished as they are seen from the point of view of the actor, which is to say that action has a subjective reference.

Why does the action scheme require a subjective reference and normative orientation? What is it in the acts of men that cannot be got at through "objective" procedures, and yet which bears on their scientific study? Why is action always normative? Why must norms be specifically excluded from the natural conditions of action? To find Parsons' answers to these questions, the first place to look is in *The Structure of Social Action*; but its answers are incomplete. The basic reference there to the questions just raised is to the "independent determinate selective factor"; while in other passages Parsons stresses a creative element in action. It is ". . . a process in which the concrete human being plays an active, not merely an adaptive role."[20] But this critical "active" role is not elaborated in the book, even though, in the summary of each of the writers whom he reviews (except Pareto), Parsons stresses it as the essential problem that led them from their diverse starting points toward a common voluntaristic theory. It is only in the earlier paper, "The Place of Ultimate Values in Sociological Theory," that Parsons writes directly on the nature of valuation generally and on related questions of the "freedom" or autonomy of the will, together with his views on the extent to which what he calls "positive science" can ever come to know valuational elements. Most important of all, the paper throws much light on the intellectual concerns—concerns that presuppose an idealistic epistemology—which led Parsons to formulate the action scheme in the particular way he did.[21]

Compared with the labyrinthine exposition in *The Structure of Social Action*, "The Place of Ultimate Values" is a model of brevity. The opening sentence sets the issue directly:

The positivistic reaction against philosophy has, in its effect on the social sciences, manifested a strong tendency to obscure the fact that man is essentially an active, creative, evaluating creature.[22]

Positivism Parsons views as at bottom a metaphysical position. He believes that "positivistic social theory has evolved a genuinely materialistic metaphysics."[23] Such a metaphysical scheme, he holds, has no place in its frame of reference for volitional elements; the language of "space and time" account for all that there is, or can be. But action involves volition at its source.

Neither the knowledge of the relation of means and ends on which action is based nor the application of that knowledge comes automatically. Both are the result of effort, *the exercise of will*.[24]

Remarks further on in the paper indicate that by "automatic," Parsons means natural and material; "effort" and "will" correspondingly mean non-natural effort and a will at least partly free from natural constraints. For example:

It should be clear that the creative, voluntaristic element which we have found to be involved in the factor of ends precludes action ever being *completely* determined by modern scientific knowledge in the sense of the positive sciences.[25]

Because of the "creative character of the factor of ends," they cannot be fitted "into the category of acts of the external world." The result is a "negation of the positivistic view that the 'realities' which can be studied by empirical science are the sole realities significant for human action."[26]

This discussion from "The Place of Ultimate Values" provides a clue to what Parsons means when he speaks in *The Structure of Social Action* of "an independent determinate selective factor." If the paper can be read as an introduction to the book, then what these factors are independent of is what Parsons construes to be the natural world. They repose instead in the separate realm of ideas and value. They are determinate, not in terms of their own causes (for if any such causes were determinate, then the voluntary element would disappear) but in terms of their consequences for action as it occurs in the natural world. If this interpretation is correct, it follows that Parsons is not only arguing against the utility of theories of conduct that take no account of the effect of ends and values. He is also arguing that the ends that men do seem to choose can never be fully explained by a natural or empirical science. The implications of that argument for any substantive hypothesis on the sociology of norms and values are both plain and profound.

Parsons then goes on to give various arguments of why his non-naturalistic or dualistic position is correct and why a naturalistic monism is false; but these do not relate directly on the present topic. However, his summary does so relate:

If this [naturalistic] explanation is rejected, it seems to me that there is only one other avenue left open. The world of "empirical fact" must be only a part, only one aspect, of the universe so far as it is significant to man. The "external world," i.e., that of science, is as it were an island in a sea the character of which is something different from the island. Our relation to the other aspects of the universe is different from that of the scientist to empirical facts. . . . [The relation] is something transcending science. . . . The ultimate reason, then, for the causal independence of the ends of action, the fact that they are not determined by the facts of human nature and environment, is the fact that man stands in significant relations to aspects of reality other than those revealed by science.[27]

Thus Parsons' prewar concept of "action" bears a considerable burden of philosophy. The sections just quoted can be read as a testament to idealism. It is important to note that it is not an idealistic monism: in *The Structure of Social Action* Parsons cautions against "idealistic theories of action" which would reduce the material world to symbolic representations or sensations of it; an "idealistic reduction" would have all the faults of a parallel materialistic or "positivistic reduction."[28] But the action scheme is more than a spelling out of the implications of certain philosophical ideas for technical scientific application: it is also a philosophical statement in its own right. Asserting that human action participates in two metaphysical realms, that of ideas and values for its formation, and that of material fact for its realization, it gives a metaphysical dualism as the foundation for sociology as a science. As such it is subject to all the problems in any *a priori* specification of what may become empirically problematic; but the immediate concern is not so much to spell out these problems as to call attention to their presence.

Much of the remainder of "The Place of Ultimate Values" is taken up with mustering evidence for the doctrine that ultimate, non-natural ends, indeterminate with respect to "positive" factors, "exist and play a decisive role in human life."[29] But note a technique of exposition that can be encountered elsewhere in Parsons' essays in theory: spelling out in detail, and in the form of a putatively empirical discussion, what is, by virtue of Parsons' definitions, a tautology.[30] The putatively empirical claim here is that valuation involves primordial creativity;

actually, Parsons treats this as a matter of definition. Value is defined as "the creative element in action in general, the element which is causally independent of the positivistic factors of heredity and environment."[31] Value so defined has necessarily to be freely formed and not explainable by natural science. Thus there is no empirical question of whether values can be scientifically explained, since by Parsons' definition of value such an explanation would be impossible. The only empirical questions that can be raised are whether there is any such thing as value so conceived, or action in pursuit of such values.

To conclude this section, the following is essayed as the metaphysical foundations of the prewar action scheme. First, there are two realms of being: the world of material fact; and the world of ideas, from which comes value. Material facts relate to values as conditions of their realization, but there is an aspect of valuation which is distinct from the world of fact and is not reducible to it. Values are not completely describable in a natural determinate system, even though values have consequences in that system, because valuation involves creative and innovative factors which rest on "acts of will." The result is that the sciences of action are methodologically independent of the sciences of nature; the methods of natural science are perhaps instrcutive to the methods of the "sciences of action," but they definitely are not canons for them. Since human action involves a will which at bottom operates in mental autonomy and privacy, special methods —methods with a subjective reference— are needed to tap this mental content. *Verstehen* is suggested as such a method. The "rigid positivistic view of things" is thus mistaken when it prescribes a mechanical analogy or (more recently) a "physicalistic" scheme of scientific language reduction for the sciences of action, for such schemes and analogies rest on a notion of the unity of science which the fundamental distinction between the realms of fact and value makes conspicuously false. The failing common to all "positivistic" theories of action is that they ignore this distinction; by implicitly treating ends as if they were reducible to the conditions of action, they ultimately deny them the independent effect that they really do have. Only "radical behaviorism," which denies that statements about private mental events (and therefore about valuation) can be meaningful, contends with the fact-value distinction in an explicit and consistent way. Although consistent, radical behaviorism is false.[32]

There is a parallel risk in a rigidly idealistic theory of action: it too would unwarrantably bridge the basic distinction between the realms of fact and value. Although as consistent as radical behaviorism, radical idealism is equally untenable. Values would exist in such a scheme, but "action" itself, the *relation* between fact and value, would disappear.

The tenable position is voluntarism. It gives both the realms of determinate matter and creative mind their suitable places in the analysis of human affairs. A metaphysical dualism,[33] in which both the world of space and time and the world of ultimate value are equally and irreducibly real, where voluntary action is not a hypothesis but a premise, is the foundation on which *The Structure of Social Action* is built.[34]

THE POSTWAR FOUNDATIONS

The concept of "action" in 1937 was unmistakably distinguished from the concept of "behavior" by two points. The first of these was the inclusion in action of an element which, with respect to what Parsons then called heredity and environment, is creative and autonomous: the choice of ultimate values. The second derives from the autonomy of the first:

knowledge about the ends of action transcends the objective method of natural science, by which only the facts of heredity and environment can be known. The first of these points is, of course, the normative aspect of the action scheme; the second, its subjective reference. These two aspects were built into the scheme in deference to explicit metaphysical premises about the nature of mental events.

The concept of "action" in 1951—the next time Parsons gave a full and formal statement of the scheme—is by no means so sharply distinguished from behavior. The considerations on which Parsons so clearly based the autonomy of action from nature in 1937 are stated in the postwar version of the action scheme in a very different way. The postwar texts show crucial equivocations at every point where a comparison with the subjective and normative aspects of the prewar scheme could otherwise be directly made. Reviewing the postwar texts, it is therefore not at all clear what Parsons' position is today on those very matters which have been argued to be the foundations of an important part of the scheme of 1937.

Because of the crucial equivocations, two interpretations are possible. At one pole of interpretation, "action" (1952) is essentially a "naturalistic" concept (that is, one which claims no properties beyond the access of natural or empirical science) such as Tolman's concept of "purposive behavior."[35] As such it would not be consistent with the earlier concept. At the other pole of interpretation, however, "action" (1951) may be viewed as programmatically continuous with, if not identical to, the prewar position and its metaphysical dualism. Certainly there has been a change in tone, in terminology, and in emphasis: Parsons now speaks in his opening statements of the orientation of behavior rather than of action. Evaluation is now related to such natural-sounding notions as "need-dispositions," and it is held to be disciplined by psychodynamic factors that were never more than mentioned in passing before the war. But while Parsons has increased the scope of the natural elements in action, he has not made voluntarism impossible in principle. The postwar writing is still careful to make room for the postulate of voluntarism, if ever it might be needed.

This paper argues that the postwar ambiguity obtains because Parsons no longer believes that valuation involves a metaphysical autonomy. As a result of a new respect for psychoanalytical theory and other naturalistic persuasions, plainly at odds with his prewar doctrine, he has had to make the appropriate adjustments in the action scheme. At the same time he has stressed the continuity of his postwar work with what he did before. Since the subjective and normative aspects of action were the means by which voluntarism was given its salience and necessity in the action scheme of 1935 and 1937, they are the parts most changed in the scheme of 1951, where voluntarism has been obscured and reduced to a wholly hypothetical role.

Parsons makes only a few comments which directly compare the prewar and postwar versions of the action scheme on the matter of subjective and normative elements; these are discussed in due course. The first task is to review the action scheme in the postwar texts, attending to the subjective and normative aspects of action, and to see how both natural and non-natural poles of interpretation (as posed above) are almost always possible at the critical points: these are the "crucial equivocations." The principal sources for the postwar theory are Parsons' contributions to the volume edited by him and Edward Shils, *Toward a General Theory of Action*.[36]

The action scheme of 1951 still uses a means-ends framework, but its constituent elements are presented somewhat differently from the 1937 version. Following the order of presentation used in the prewar scheme (in *Structure*) the first element remains the actor. But where Parsons' prewar emphasis on subjective reference (and subsequently on first-person verbal reports) limited "actors" to humans, the postwar scheme is offered "for the analysis of the behavior of living organisms,"[37] as long as the other criteria of action are met. The second element, that action involves ends, is substantially unchanged in its formal terms: "behavior is oriented to ends or goals or other anticipated states of affairs." Nor are there important changes in the notion of the situation. But the normative orientation—which in the prewar scheme involved an "independent determinate selective factor" and was the point of entry for a non-natural concept of mind and will—is substantially reduced: the postwar scheme says only that "behavior is normatively regulated." While voluntarism would not be inconsistent with such a conception of action, it is not a necessary conclusion from it. The postwar scheme then uses a new term, "motivation": action involves the expenditure of energy or effort. The scheme is extended by the addition of the now celebrated three modes of orientation of action: cognition, cathexis, and evaluation. The last of these has an interesting relation to the special status in the prewar scheme of the sources of valuation: it is the means by which such references to the *possibility* of autonomous choice as do exist in the postwar scheme are introduced.

The evaluative mode reflects a possible plurality of means which may be used for the achievement of one end; action may also involve more than one end. In terms of the other modes of orientation this means that there is more than one "cathected object" in the action situation; "there are alternative opportunities for gratification."[38] Parsons' detailed discussion of the evaluative mode suggests both the naturalistic and non-naturalistic poles of interpretation. For example, the evaluative mode allocates energy among alternatives "in an attempt to optimize gratification."[39] This statement taken alone would suggest that evaluation really operates toward only one end, that of gratification generally, which other parts of the text suggest can be accounted for in the natural terms of "behavior psychology" and physiology; gratification thus would be a naturally reducible end.[40] So considered, evaluation becomes only a special type of cognition, that is, a way of appraising the gratificatory or deprivatory properties of objects only in those instances where "ordinary" cognitions cannot determine the difference in gratificatory potential among a plurality of objects. But the very next statement in the text moves away from this interpretation and inclines toward the notion of autonomous choice:

Evaluation is functionally necessary for the resolution of conflicts among interests and among cognitive interpretations which are not resolved automatically; and thus necessitate *choice:* or at least specific selective mechanisms.[41]

This is the first crucial equivocation. It equivocates on whether choice, which was explicitly stressed as autonomous before the war, is or is not now held to be autonomous. At the least, there may be specific selective mechanisms—a term which connotes a naturalistic reduction.[42] So far, the autonomy of choice has the status of a hypothesis. Parsons now does not say definitely, as he did before the war, that free choice is a *fact* of human life which the action scheme cannot afford to ignore.[43]

In this part of his exposition Parsons does make one statement which can be read as a comment on the relation between evaluation in the new scheme and in the old. But he does so without indicating the extent to which the doctrine of the

old scheme still applies: the hypothetical tenor is still there and with it another crucial equivocation.

These concepts [of selection or choice] all underline and define the voluntaristic or purposive aspect of systems of action as conceived by the present analytical scheme. Without this purposive aspect, most of the elements of the orientation of action under consideration here—and above all the elements of value-orientation—would become analytically superfluous epiphenomena.[44]

To modern readers the synonymy implied in the section quoted between "voluntaristic" and "purposive" aspects is misleading. For if by "voluntaristic" Parsons means essentially what he meant by it before the war—and by "purposive" (a term not used before the war) he means something in line with Tolman's concept of purposive behavior (as Parsons suggests elsewhere in the postwar texts)—then these terms are not synonyms at all: prewar "voluntarism" involves an important non-natural element, and Tolmanian "purposiveness" is wholly natural. The relation between the old and new versions of the scheme is still unclear.

Parsons then continues to comment on the hypothetical character of the autonomy of evaluation:

The *empirical* significance of selective or value standards as determinants of concrete action may be considered problematical and should not be prejudged. But the theory of action analyzes action in such a way as to leave the door open for attributing a major significance to these standards and their patterning. The older type of biological frame of reference did not leave this door open and thus prejudged the question.[45]

While Parsons would be right to say that metaphysical materialism (if that is what he means by "the older type of biological frame of reference") "prejudges" the significance of ends, the comparative point is that it does so only in a way parallel to the prejudgment found in voluntarism. If the statement, "the empirical significance of value standards is problematic and should not be prejudged," is regarded as a proper approach for the social sciences, then Parsons' prewar elevation of the explanatory power of norms and values is equally as improper as the reduction of that power by metaphysical materialism. If materialism constitutes a premature reduction, then voluntarism constitutes a premature non-reduction. Since neither position considers the effect of value selection to be problematic, both are inconsistent with this postwar recommendation. Although a "normative orientation" applies both to pre- and postwar schemes, the foundations of the status of norms—the role they are held to play in conduct and the reasons for action having a normative orientation at all—have apparently undergone a basic change.

Parsons next considers the status of "mind." Before the war the necessary independence of mind from material nature was the reason for the subjective reference of the action scheme. But now,

We do *not* postulate a substantive entity, a mind which is somehow dissociated from the organism and the object world. The organization of observational data in terms of the theory of action is quite possible and fruitful in modified behavioristic terms, and such a formulation avoids many of the difficult questions of introspection and empathy.[46]

By the use of Tolman's constructs from "rat psychology,"

. . . we have all the essential components of the analysis of action defined in Tolman's manner without raising further difficulties. What the actor thinks or feels can be treated as a system of intervening variables.[47]

Now before the war there definitely was a substantive entity involved in action which was somehow dissociated from the organism and the object world, or the world of "heredity and invironment" as Parsons called it then. What actors think or feel was not only independent, it was private; a subjective reference was essential and the method of *verstehen* was invoked. But Tolman's behavioristic position, in terms of which the elements of the action scheme can now be defined, was always opposed to the confirmatory use of such non-public data as those which *verstehen* would provide.[48] Here the case is similar to that of the normative orientation. The retreat from mind-body dualism has removed the need for a subjective reference. But Parsons does not comment on the implications of Tolmanian behaviorism for the subjective reference of prewar years; nor does he clarify the relation between "behaviorism" as he spoke of it then, and "modified behaviorism" as he speaks of it now.

To conclude the review of the postwar perspective as it stood in the early fifties,[49] some remarks may be considered from Parsons' book, *The Social System*. Far along in its pages will be found perhaps his most relevant comments on the relation between the pre- and post-war action schemes. Yet even here—where Parsons comes closest to acknowledging that a shift in foundations has actually occurred—he still seems unwilling to abandon the spirit of the mind-body dualism completely. Even as he allows that his postwar scheme "may now be considered to be a revision of the scheme presented . . . in *The Structure of Social Action*," he advances the qualification that it "constitutes a revision rather than a drastic repudiation of that scheme."[50]

In view of the sections discussed above, however, this revision cannot help but take on the character of such a repudiation. It is difficult for Parsons to defend the idea that his new scheme continues the tradition of the old; ironically, this is largely because of the clarity with which he rested his case for the old scheme on what is today a highly unfashionable metaphysic. It is therefore not surprising that his acknowledgement, when it gets to the heart of the matter, must involve still another crucial equivocation:

The question is that of the theoretical relevance and adequacy of the conceptual schemes of ... "the natural sciences" for full analysis of the phenomena of action. There is ample evidence of the inadequacy or inconvenience or both of these conceptual schemes for this purpose.[51]

This is not helpful because "inconvenience" and "inadequacy" can be very different things. A scheme which is adequate in terms of a capacity to include all of a given universe of data can still be inconvenient in, say, a heuristic sense. Perhaps this is the reason why so many behavioral scientists continue to use a "working vocabulary" suggestive of vitalism and primordial idealistic causation, when in fact they are describing nothing that could not be reduced to naturalistic terms; and when they have no objection to carrying out such a reduction—as they must (since the discrediting of introspection) in order to place any propositions phrased in that vocabulary in empirically contingent form. This is a different matter from a scheme which (though possibly convenient) is inadequate because it fails to provide for including all the data; and this latter sense is clearly what Parsons meant when he criticized as inadequate the schemes of the natural sciences before the war. In this respect, then, Parsons' connoted synonymy between inconvenience and inadequacy is equivocal in an important sense. It does not tell us whether the view now held of "the natural sciences" and their relation to the action scheme is the same as it was before the war.

In one sentence Parsons does acknowledge that the subjective reference, so essential to the old scheme, is not essential to the new:

Contrary to the point of view held by the author in *The Structure of Social Action*, it now appears that [the subjective point of view] is not essential to the frame of reference of the theory of action in its most elementary form.[52]

But even as subjectivism is abandoned as a general element, Parsons strives to save it for use in the important particular case of human action—thus saving it on "practical" rather than *a priori* grounds for the area of his prewar concern:

[Subjectivism] is, however, necessarily involved at the levels of elaboration of systems of action at which culture, that is shared symbolic patterns, become involved. It is, that is a consequence of the fact that action comes to be oriented in terms of symbols which serve also to communicate with other actors.[53]

Since man is the prototypical culture-bearing animal, subjectivism remains necessary for the study of human action. This is only a minor revision from the prewar framework, for it is clear that Parsons never intended to apply the prewar scheme to organisms other than humans.

So conceived, the difference between the pre- and postwar schemes is one of formal generality: the postwar scheme is applicable, along the lines of Tolman's concepts, to behaving agents generally;[54] while in the important special case of human action the scheme still has to include a subjective reference. Then, notwithstanding the conciliatory remarks about behaviorism in "Values, Motives, and Systems of Action," Parsons repairs to his prewar position. He poses a dilemma:

It is possible, of course, to remain a behavioristic purist and avoid this subjective reference, but only in one of two ways. The first is to repudiate the action frame of reference altogether and attempt to maintain a biological frame of reference. The other is to use the action frame of reference, but to keep the elaboration of the theory of action to pre-symbolic, that is, pre-cultural levels.[55]

Before the war subjectivism was necessary because of the inherent properties of mind. Now the defense of subjectivism has shifted to its use in the study of a particular type of behavior, but it is what Mead and others who sought a naturalistic account of mentality have called "minded behavior." In this last defense of the spirit, if not the letter, of the old metaphysical doctrine, Parsons raises more questions than he puts to rest.

First, if these remarks about "behavioristic purism" are taken to mean what they say, they are not consistent with the statements in "Values, Motives, and Systems of Action" that the action scheme can be expressed in "modified behavioristic terms," avoiding the "difficult questions of introspection and empathy" by treating "what the actor thinks or feels as a system of intervening variables." In these words Parsons professes that he too is pure. Nor do these remarks accord with the one other statement in which he directly mentions the relation of the new scheme to the old:

The present exposition of the theory of action [from "Values, Motives, and Systems of Action"] represents in one major respect a revision and extension of the position stated in Parsons, *The Structure of Social Action* (pp. 43–51, 732–733), particularly in the light of psychoanalytic theory, of developments in behavior psychology, and of developments in the anthropological analysis of culture. It has become possible to incorporate these elements effectively, largely because of the conception of a system of action in both the social and psychological spheres and their integration with systems of cultural patterns has been considerably refined and extended in the intervening years. [sic][56]

Yet it is clear that no plausible interpretation of Freudian theory, not any possible modification of "behavior psychology," could ever make them admissible to the prewar scheme, where they were only too forcefully ruled out on *a priori* grounds.

Second, Parsons has said that his postwar usage is substantially parallel to that of Tolman. But if so this leads to still more ambiguity on the status of subjectivism in the postwar scheme. For Tolman never had any use for subjective reports: "another organism's private mind, if he have any, can never be got at" was a maxim from which he never varied throughout the course of his writing.

If the "dilemma of the behavioristic purist" which Parsons poses in *The Social System* is to be clearly understood, some prior questions have to be answered. First, what is "behavioristic purism?" Parsons may mean it to be the accounting of behavior purely in the language of physiology. Tolman acknowledged this type of "muscle twitch" behaviorism and distinguished it from a behaviorism with a more liberal vocabulary of organism-environment arrangements and rearrangements.[57] But if this is what Parsons means, his remarks seem inconsistent with his favorable references to "modified behaviorism" in "Values, Motives, and Systems of Action." Or he may mean by "pure behaviorism" a strict adherence to what has become the doctrine's modern form—a program of scientific epistemology, for making scientific statements testable by use of intersubjectively verifiable or "public" data. Since the time of Tolman's programmatic papers, the influence of Bridgman's idea of "operationism," and the parallel influence of the doctrine variously called logical positivism or logical empiricism,[58] this epistemological interpretation has been the dominant connotation of "behaviorism." This interpretation of Parsons' idea of "behaviorism" in *The Social System* is consistent with his other postwar comments on the doctrine.

Second, must the behavioristic purist really contend with the dilemma Parsons poses for him? This depends on his position as distinguished above. The "muscle twitch" behaviorist very possibly must: Watson's reduction of all ratiocination to slight movements of the vocal chords was not very persuasive. The immediate point is that the epistemological behaviorist need not face the dilemma: Parsons' challenge, on which his whole remaining defense of subjectivism rests, is prematurely posed.

In posing it, Parsons invokes the unstated premise that there can be no behavioristic or naturalistic account of the meaning of symbols. But if instead there *can* be such an account, then the behaviorist has a third alternative to the two horns of the dilemma: he may retain the action scheme, and rely on a naturalistic reduction of the meaning of symbols so as to avoid the need for faith (which Parsons' version of subjectivism requires) in the indubitability of certain non-public data. Though there is not sufficient space to judge the success of such a reduction here, it certainly is worth mentioning that enough such reductions have been advanced for Parsons to have known of the quest. One of the first, if not the best, was Hume's theory of ideas and impressions developed in *A Treatise on Human Nature*. More recently several proposed reductions have been invented; most of them center on some version of the idea that meaning is the property a symbol has when in conventional occasions of usage it elicits consistent responses. Tolman has used related criteria himself.[59] The example best known to sociologists, the work of G. H. Mead, does somewhat the same thing with the notion of the "significant symbol."[60] Now if a naturalistic account of symbolic communication is possible, then publicly verifiable data can be used for all empirical applications of the concepts of the action scheme, and the need for a subjective reference is entirely removed. It is therefore important for the defense of subjectivism to contend directly with the naturalistic tradition. But Parsons writes as if the impossibility of a naturalistic reduction were a settled and closed matter.

The crucial equivocations make impossible any unequivocal statement of the philosophical and methodological foundations of the postwar action scheme. With that qualification the following summary is ventured: it is problematic whether the realm of values is separate from the realm of natural facts. Valuation has "fundamental significance" for the action scheme, but its autonomy from the natural settings of action is "problematic and should not be prejudged." Behaviorism is not wholly embraced, but "the categories developed by Tolman in his studies of animal behavior have brought these implications within reaching distance." And in any case the independence of mind from matter (or at least from organism) is no longer asserted; while subjectivism remains, it remains because of the refractory properties of symbolism rather than because of the metaphysically given autonomy of private mental states. The foundation of Parsons' postwar position is a cautious naturalism.

CONCLUSION AND COMMENT

The changes in the action scheme can be better understood and more fairly evaluated if its intellectual history is considered together with its formal content. *The Structure of Social Action* was addressed to American sociologists at a time when most of them were relatively unfamiliar with European social thought; indeed, its abiding influence owes less to the voluntaristic thesis than to its emphasis on Weber, Pareto, and Durkheim as theorists in their own right.[61] Then too the book appeared at a time when much of its audience was preoccupied with designs for the quick ascendence of sociology to the status of a science. To Parsons, the designs as he read them risked too great an involvement with the materialistic fallacies of "positive science."

Starting from appropriate—and contemporary—premises, such as the idea that "science" is a *method* of making empirical propositions known rather than the subject of such propositions, it is a simple matter to eviscerate the polemical parts of the voluntaristic thesis. As a polemic, the thesis is an argument against metaphysical monism and for a metaphysical dualism as the foundation of the behavioral sciences. But even aside from the shortcomings it shares with all metaphysical arguments, Parsons' exposition of voluntarism fails to cover vital points. *The Structure of Social Action*, with all respect for the monumental scholarship that went into its writing and for the exhaustive detail of its exposition, never advances its discussion beyond nineteenth century epistemology; and never answers the one question on which so much of its discussion turns: what is the nature of valuation? To get an answer to that question it is necessary to extrapolate from the discussion in "The Place of Ultimate Values in Sociological Theory," where valuation involves a will independent in critical ways from the world of nature. While this is not, to be sure, the only possible answer to the unanswered questions in *The Structure of Social Action*, it is the only one that can be found in the Parsonian texts.

Most important of all, if a book as long as *The Structure of Social Action* invokes the thesis that ends are non-natural, it ought to consider the best arguments for the thesis that ends *are* natural. *The Structure of Social Action* does this only through a straw man polemic against a metaphysical ghost. Though Parsons refers continually to "positivists," he almost never names any, nor gives examples of their work;[62] and one can search at length through the antecedent writings of Hume, Mach, Mead, Dewey, Russell, and Tolman, and never find the metaphysical materialism that Parsons was so concerned to reject. All these writers rested their case on an epistemological argument that would be as critical of Parsons' construction of "positivism" as it would have been of voluntarism. *The Structure of Social Action* is notable for the number of German idealists it cites and for the host of epistemological naturalists it ignores.[63]

This positivistic straw man, however, may have had more solid flesh in the sociology of the thirties.[64] The idea of "science" then was affected by the polemics in which it was used, and a review of programmatic papers of the time will show that they often did advance the unsophisticated positivism of which Parsons spoke. At least for some sociologists "science" was not so much a method as a body of knowledge, whose theories were more acceptable the more they had a semblance of analogy to nineteenth century physics.[65] Although Parsons opposed metaphysical materialism by presenting a contrary metaphysic, he also called attention to the value of considering minded behavior as sociological data; and that value obtains irrespective of whether the polemic which caught the attention can stand the test of time.

The postwar scheme had a different audience. Even if voluntarism had not been taken up noticeably, many ancillary goals of the prewar program had been achieved. Nearly a generation of work in substantive sociology by Parsons, his students, and many others on whom he had some influence had emphasized a purposive or "means-ends" approach, and had provided examples of the ability of variations in norms, as independent variables, to account for variations in social structure.[66] Thus there was less need to continue the old polemic.

The postwar papers also appeared at a time when they could play a role in the integration of several traditional disciplines in the emerging Harvard Department of Social Relations, of which Parsons was the chairman. A unified theory of action was an obvious analogue to such a unified department,[67] and it is to be noted that Parsons undertook to gain the assent of that department's faculty to as much as possible of the content of *Toward a General Theory of Action*. It is doubtful whether many who signed the "General Statement" in that volume would have assented to Parsons' prewar position, and in view of this the crucial equivocations in the postwar texts may be viewed as reflecting the dual requirement of gaining widespread assent to the action scheme while avoiding a flat contradiction of its earlier form. Thus the "General Statement" is even more naturalistic and further to the "epistemological left" in its treatment of mental phenomena than is "Values, Motives, and Systems of Action."

Finally, Devereux has acknowledged that Parsons' interest in Freudian psychology culminated in his undergoing a "didactic psychoanalysis."[68] It is entirely possible that the experience of analysis and the encounter with psychoanalytic theories may have provided Parsons with a persuasive naturalistic basis for many of the phenomena that he believed, in 1935, to be evidence for the existence of mental autonomy and free will.

In his most recent writings, however, Parsons often appears to be moving back toward the prewar position. In his response to the Cornell symposium, Parsons mentioned that Devereux was right in emphasizing the role of *verstehen*, for the subjective point of view has "always been essential to the scheme."[68] Then too he makes some puzzling remarks in rejoinder to Black's criticisms:

Broadly speaking, I take it that Professor Black expresses an attitude of skepticism toward the empirical status of the assumptions of action theory. In my opinion this would not be possible for a man immersed in the recent developments of social science. Many of these points have been historically controversial. But the radical denial of any of the basic ones I have just reviewed, seems to me to be out of court in the present state of the relevent disciplines. The position of the old fashioned behaviorist, for example, who denies the scientific legitimacy of "subjective" data, or of the mechanist who denies that any sort of "normative" control ever operates in the empirical world, are no longer strongly held. Indeed, in my opinion many of these questions are no longer controversial in any authentic sense.[69]

Since Tolman was one of the foremost "old fashioned behaviorists" who denied the scientific legitimacy of subjective data (at least insofar as they were supposed to be actual accounts of mental states) this passage refutes once more the commendation of Tolmanian behaviorism given in "Values, Motives, and Systems of Action." The passage as a whole raises many questions. What are the "recent developments of social science" by which he who is immersed in them is shown the truth of Parsons' theory? Does Parsons really mean to claim that within the variety of disciplines for which the action scheme is offered, that even within sociology itself, a radical denial of the scheme itself is out of court? That positions contrary to it are no longer strongly held? It is one thing to claim that the opposition is incorrect, unlettered, or unimportant; it is another to claim that it does not even exist. It is doubtful that Parsons could gain agreement to the passage just cited were it presented to the men who signed the "General Statement" in *Toward a General Theory of Action*. He tells of peace where there is no peace.

In another sense, however, it may be only too true that there has been little disagreeable response to the postwar action scheme. In order to maintain a terminological continuity with the old scheme and at the same time a programmatic continuity with the new epistemological left, Parsons is constrained to write in the most general and equivocal of terms. The ironic result is a position so uncommitted that there is little in it to disagree with. Perhaps this also explains why the action scheme in a broad sense—which Parsons once claimed was systematic, with the action scheme being the axiomatic base for his more concrete theories—actually is not systematic at all, as many commentators have noted. For if it were, it would be vastly easier to discern the discontinuities between the present version and its earlier form.

Finally, some mention may be made of the relation of the changing foundations of the action scheme to changes—or continuities—in Parsons' substantive theory. Some observers sense a trend in the latter which is, *prima facie*, contrary to the changes in the action scheme in the narrow sense. The trend involves the extent to which Parsons holds norms, especially internalized norms, to account for social order. This is not an easy matter to assess on the basis of the Parsonian texts. *The Structure of Social Action* was too concerned with voluntarism, the polemic against positivism, and secondary review, to say very much about the structure of social action, and thus about the *specific* structural role of normative elements in society. There are clues, as in Parsons' implicit rejection of Hobbes' claim that external sanctions, "a power to keep all men in awe," account for social order, but little more.[70] But in later writing the equilibrium of social systems appears to be increasingly explained on the basis of internalized commitment to common systems of norms,[71] while relatively little emphasis is given to the possibly independent distribution of power to enforce "external" sanctions. Other observers, however, are prepared to argue that for Parsons' substantive theories the emphasis on norms has been continuous, that although the tone and terminology have changed, the relative importance of norms and values has been maintained.

It is entirely possible that as a result of attending to different aspects of Parsons'

complex theories both of these interpretations are correct. The present point is that there is no *necessary* connection between changes in the action scheme and changes in the substantive theory, even though, through intellectual affinity, changes in one may inspire changes in the other. Parsons' work as a whole consists of many logically separate themes, unified by a common style and terminology rather than by derivation from a single set of axioms. There is no strict inconsistency between voluntarism and the assertion that ends and values, though independent, are actually of little or no importance in human affairs. Corollarily, there is no inconsistency between the thesis that norms are reducible to the conditions of action and the thesis that as purely natural intervening variables they are important to human social organization. Hence this paper's ultimate concern: what are the conditions under which norms can be variables in sociological theory?

Although he has abandoned a metaphysical basis for the independence of norms and values, Parsons has continually emphasized that norms, if they are to be important, must be at least "analytically independent." This emphasis has been the keystone of many cautionary remarks by himself and others. Norms, we are told, must not be "reducible to the conditions of action," nor explainable in terms of "biological categories"; they must instead be dealt with at "their own analytic level." To fail in this entails the fallacy of "reductionism."

Particular reductions stand or fall according to the test of evidence, and the behavioral sciences have seen many premature reductions fail. With respect for Parsons' early concerns, it is only fair to mention their persistence in the apparent differences between animate and inanimate nature and within the latter between symbolic and infra-symbolic behavior, with which any comprehensive naturalistic reduction will have to come to terms. But there is no *general* fallacy of reductionism. In his opposition to the reduction of norms, Parsons has consistently given an argument which, though offered as an account of the conditions necessary and sufficient if norms are to be variables in an explanatory system, is actually an argument for according them a certain ontological status—the status of the eternally independent variable. This is not required for norms to be explanatory variables.

Consider norms as factor "B." If B explains C, but A explains B, then A explains C; but this hardly implies, as the opponents of reduction so often assert, that all theories of the effect of B on C are otiose, or that B becomes "epiphenomenal." The explanation of B does not cause the effect of B on C to cease; that

effect becomes instead a special case of the effect of A. Sociologists already entertain a partial explanation of norms in the argument that, whatever their specific source, they have evolved in response to the requirements of viable social organization.[72] This hypothesis, a very general one, does not immediately account for much normative variation. Some day the behavioral sciences may be able to explain this remaining variation—the conditions under which men hold to one value rather than another and under which norms respecting these values prevail in particular groups. But such explanation does not obviate accounts of the effect of particular values on social institutions. Rather, it increases the range and precision of such accounts by subsuming them under a truly more general theory.

NOTES

Kingsley Davis and Neil Smelser, students of Parsons at different times, offered important criticisms of earlier drafts (1960) of this paper. I also want to acknowledge improvements wrought by Joan Holden in matters of prose style.

1. Talcott Parsons, "The Place of Ultimate Values in Sociological Theory," *International Journal of Ethics* (now *Ethics*), 45 (1934–1935), pp. 282–316. Hereafter this essay will be cited as "Ultimate Values." Talcott Parsons, *The Structure of Social Action*, New York: McGraw-Hill, 1937; reprinted unchanged, with a new introduction, Glencoe: The Free Press, 1949; and New York: The Free Press of Glencoe, 1961, will be cited as *Structure*.

2. The monograph bears the names of Parsons and of Edward Shils, in Parsons and Shils (Eds.), *Toward a General Theory of Action*, Cambridge: Harvard, 1951, pp. 47–275; hereafter cited as "Values, Motives, etc."

3. Robin Williams, "The Sociological Theory of Talcott Parsons," in Max Black (Ed.), *The Social Theories of Talcott Parsons*, Englewood Cliffs: Prentice-Hall, 1961, p. 67.

4. Edward C. Devereux, "Parsons' Sociological Theory," in Black, *op. cit.*, esp. pp. 7–16.

5. In this connection see also John Finley Scott, "The Impossible Theory of Action: Some Questions on Parsons' Prewar Classification of Action Theories," *Berkeley Journal of Sociology*, 7 (1962), pp. 51–62. The paper cited, which complements the present one and comes to related conclusions, goes more completely into the organization of *Structure* and the interpretation of some of its key concepts.

6. In *Ethics*, 50 (1940), pp. 164–192. Pinney's otherwise detailed review takes no account of

"Ultimate Values" (*op. cit.*). Had he done so he could have resolved many of the things he found perplexing in Parsons' book.

7. Max Black, "Some Questions About Parsons' Theories," in Black, *op. cit.*, pp. 268–288.

8. Neil Smelser uses the terms "action schema" and "theory of action" in this broader way. In his *Social Change in the Industrial Revolution*, Chicago: The University of Chicago, 1959, pp. 10 ff., the action scheme (following Parsons) as a set of concepts and the source of "some empty boxes" is merged with the somewhat more substantive propositions about the four imperatives of a social system. Then too Parsons' own title, *Toward a General Theory of Action*, suggests a broad reference to a substantive theory rather than solely to concepts. It would be helpful to distinguish "action schemes" as concepts and definitions and "action theories" as substantive theories which use these concepts, but this distinction is not made in Parsons' work.

9. Consider the following dialogue: Parsons and Shils, 1952: ". . . we carry deductive procedures further than is common in the social sciences (excluding economics). . . . We do feel we have carried the implications of our assumptions somewhat further than others have carried theirs" ("Values, Motives, etc.," pp. 49–50). Black, 1960–1961: "To anybody familiar with deductive procedures in mathematics and the natural sciences, Parsons' claim [just quoted] will seem surprising. There is very little strict deduction in Parsons' work" (Black, *op. cit.*, p. 271n). Parsons, replying to Black: "Notwithstanding some statements which I have made on occasion, my present considered opinion is that,

though it has moved in that direction, my approach is not yet a deductive system, but rather a [prolegomenon] to such a system" (Parsons, "The Point of View of the Author," in Black, *op. cit.*, p. 321).

There is also a curious paradox in the deductive status of at least one of the pattern-variables. Of these Parsons says that they derive, "in a sense," from the categories of the action scheme ("Values, Motives, etc.," p. 76). One is a dilemma between affectivity and affective neutrality. Now action always involves cognition and cathexis, and cathexis is defined as "affect plus object"; therefore action always involves affect. Yet the affectivity-affective neutrality dilemma is held to be one of orientation, presumably the orientation of action. Since action must always be affective by definition, it' follows either that affective neutrality is impossible or that the dilemma is one between action (which is affective) and non-action (which need not be affective).

This of course is a country mile from the real issue: what Parsons means by "affectivity-affective neutrality" when he really gets into the matter is the distinction between immediate and deferred gratification. One may ask why Parsons named one distinction and then talked about another. A possible answer is that he did so to make a place for a choice between evaluation and non-evaluation. Then one may ask why evaluation need be salient. The answer given below in this paper is that it needs to be in order to maintain a terminological continuity with the prewar writing. If the distinction had been put directly in terms of immediate and deferred gratification, with the naturalistic criterion of valuation that "gratification" often connotes, then the differences between the new scheme and the old could have been somewhat more plainly observed. (I owe to Howard Jolly the original suggestion that "affectively neutral action" might be paradoxical.)

10. The "idealist" and "empirical" traditions in the sociology of norms and conduct are considered further in John Finley Scott, "The Internalization of Norms" (Paper read at the 1963 convention of the American Sociological Association, Los Angeles).

11. Some remarks may be in order to clarify the meaning of the term "naturalism." Very generally it is the point of view of those opposed to "supernaturalism," not only theological but also epistemological. If Parsons has in fact advanced a non-natural thesis in his early work it is only supernatural in this epistemological sense.

Naturalism so conceived is a quite broad point of view. Its position in epistemology is that knowledge is only what the methods of science provide. "Logical Empiricism," the transplantation in America of Vienna positivism, has had logical and historical affinities with psychological naturalism even though its "verifiability theory" has been liberalized over the years. Most naturalists agree, however, that there is a unity of scientific method, whatever the method is. A critique of arguments for a plurality of methods is developed in Ernest Nagel, "Malicious Philosophies of Science" in Nagel, *Sovereign Reason*, Glencoe: The Free Press, 1954, pp. 22–27. Much of what Nagel says there would be applicable to Parsons' argument in "Ultimate Values" and in *Structure*, Ch. 19, although Nagel's opponents in

the essay cited are more extreme. A fairly radical naturalistic position is found in Moritz Schlick, "Philosophy of Organic Life," in Herbert Feigl and May Brodbeck (Eds.), *Readings in the Philosophy of Science*, New York: Appleton–Century–Crofts, 1953, pp. 523–536. See also several essays in Yervant H. Krikorian (Ed.), *Naturalism and the Human Spirit*, New York: Columbia, 1944, especially John Dewey's polemic in his "Antinaturalism in Extremis," pp. 1–13; and Thelma Z. Lavine, "Naturalism and the Sociological Analysis of Knowledge," pp. 183–209. Lavine offers one critical paragraph (p. 190) on Parsons' view of "non-empirical cognitions," as developed (in connection with Durkheim) in *Structure*, pp. 431 ff.

12. Since Parsons' commendations of Tolman's work are some of the best evidence of a shift in his evaluation of the merits of behaviorism, it will help forestall misreadings to cite here the epigram with which Edward Chace Tolman opened his *Purposive Behavior in Animals and Men*, New York: Century, 1932:

The motives which lead to the assertion of a behaviorism are simple. All that can ever be actually observed in fellow human beings and in lower organisms is behavior. Another organism's private mind, if he have any, can never be got at. And even the supposed ease and obviousness of "looking within" and observing one's own mental processes, directly and at first hand, have proved, when subjected to laboratory control, in large part chimerical: the dictates of "introspection" have proved over and over again to be artifacts of the particular laboratory in which they were obtained.

Now in "A Short Account of My Intellectual Development," *Alpha Kappa Deltan*, 29 (1959), p. 8, Parsons claims that in his earlier years he took heart from Tolman because "[Tolman] did not swallow the behaviorist position."

These remarks were taken from a tape recording of a talk by Parsons and as such might have been unguarded. Parsons testifies again, however, to Tolman's early influence on him in his long and important statement of the action scheme in his essay of 1956 "An Approach to Psychological Theory in Terms of the Theory of Action," in Sigmund Koch (Ed.), *Psychology: A Study of A Science*, New York: McGraw-Hill, 1959, p. 620n. and 623n. (Hereafter cited as "Psychological Theory.") The point, of course, is that Tolman always went to great lengths to establish both that he was a behaviorist and that there could be a behavioristic account of purposive conduct. This latter point is precisely what the voluntaristic thesis denied. And since the war Parsons has hailed Tolman as a leader in extending behaviorism to reach the phenomena of action. See Parsons, "Values, Motives, etc.," pp. 64, 234. Yet Tolman made few changes in his methodological position after 1925; Parsons would have gotten the same exposure to Tolman in 1932 as in 1951. See Tolman, *op. cit.*, pp. 84 ff; and the book's glossary; also any of the several methodological papers (antedating *Purposive Behavior*), reprinted in Tolman, *Collected Papers in Psychology*, Berkeley: University of California, 1951. *Structure* contains no reference to Tolman; in fact none of

Parsons' references to him antedate Tolman's post-war visit to Harvard.

13. Although the secondary discussion in *Structure* is notably extensive, that of the emergence of voluntarism in each writer studied is much more brief. Parsons acknowledges that in the case of Pareto, the crucial notion of "effort or will" cannot be found (*op. cit.*, p. 298). It is not so much that Pareto was a voluntarist, as that his social thought contained nothing inconsistent with voluntarism (*ibid.*, p. 300). But it is interesting to speculate whether Pareto, had he in his lifetime been confronted with Parsonian voluntarism, would have assented to the doctrine. Parsons notes that Pareto was not a metaphysical positivist as were Comte and Spencer but a methodological positivist; Pareto "attempted to divest logico-experimental science of all metaphysical elements whatsoever" (*ibid.*, p. 293). Pareto would thus have objected to the metaphysics involved in voluntarism.

14. *Structure*, p. 44.

15. *Loc. cit.*

16. *Op. cit.*, p. 45 (emphasis added). Apparently Parsons means that the normative orientation need not have any particular *content*, since it is clear from other parts of his writing that a normative orientation of a type reducible to "heredity and environment" would be excluded.

17. *Ibid.*, p. 46 (emphasis in the original).

18. *Loc. cit.*

19. The methodological implication of the subjective point of view, especially for the claim that "ego" is spatially non-isolable, is that a technique of *verstehen* is involved; and Parsons acknowledges its use as an adjunct of the subjective point of view. See *ibid.*, p. 764.

It is also worth mentioning that "ego" or "self" need not be non-spatial in order to make possible reference to action where properties of the organism are means. Five years before Parsons argued this could not be done, Tolman made very nearly the same distinctions, without involving inobservables, with his notions of "manipulanda" and "discriminanda" in *Purposive Behavior in Animals and Men.*

20. *Structure*, p. 439.

21. At an informal gathering in 1961, the present writer asked Parsons whether "Ultimate Values" could be read as an introduction to *Structure*. Parsons replied that it could, "essentially," but cautioned that the article was "polemical."

It is fair to note that "Ultimate Values" preceded *Structure* by three years, during which interval Parsons could have reconsidered his position. Then too each text had a different audience; the paper appeared in a philosophical journal, while the book was intended for sociologists. Perhaps these considerations should be kept in mind, because anyone who reads "The Place of Ultimate Values" today will probably be a little surprised by its content. But the book is entirely consistent with the paper: it differs from it only by way of incomplete exposition. Whatever its importance, the paper is unquestionably a document in Parsons' intellectual history: it represents the starting point in his intellectual metamorphosis from an early philosophical idealism and uncritical acceptance of a *Natur-u-Geisteswissenschaft* distinction (though not, to be sure, the most

extreme form of that distinction) to the present *prima facie* naturalism.

22. "Ultimate Values," p. 282.

23. *Ibid.*, p. 286.

24. *Ibid.*, p. 287 (emphasis added).

25. *Loc. cit.*

26. *Ibid.*, p. 289. Parsons' usage with respect to the synonymy suggested among the terms "science," "natural science," "empirical science" and "positive science" is not consistent. The last term is the only one he defines, yet often he writes as if the defects of "positive science" (because of its metaphysical materialism) are found in all science. The present concern, however, is not to show that Parsons' critique of "positive science" is hard to pin down, but to show that voluntarism involves premises of metaphysical idealism parallel to the premises of metaphysical materialism that he finds in "positivism."

27. *Ibid.*, p. 290.

28. In view of the present emphasis on the action scheme's involvement with idealism, it should be iterated that Parsons (at least in his published work) was not a radical idealist. He criticized the tradition of *Geisteswissenschaft* (*Structure*, pp. 476 ff., 581 ff., and 683–684) both for its antitheoretical "particularism" and its monistic depreciation of the role of the natural conditions of action. Parsons' position derived from Weber's: action does indeed have an ideal element, but it has non-ideal elements as well. Thus Parsons can say of Durkheim: "in escaping from the toils of positivism [he] has overshot the mark and gone clean over to idealism." (*Structure*, p. 445; on idealism in Durkheim, see pp. 441 ff.)

Structure's sustained polemic is against "positivism," but it also contains many unconnected remarks on the defects of monistic idealism; e.g., ". . . an explanatory science must be concerned with events, and events do not occur in the world of eternal objects." *Ibid.*, p. 445.) Writing for an American audience, Parsons directed his polemic against materialism. Had he instead been writing for a German audience, the polemic might have been against idealism.

29. "Ultimate Values," p. 295.

30. More of these techniques, involving Parsons' treatment in *Structure* of the notions of "utilitarianism" and "science"; and the paradox in his idea of a "positivistic theory of action," are reviewed in Scott, "The Impossible Theory of Action," *op. cit.*

31. "Ultimate Values," p. 306; see also the parallel but more cautious discussion in *Structure*, pp. 76–77. "Heredity and environment" are more than omnibus categories of explanation for "positive science." Very few practicing scientists of any kind would ever consider the distinction between them so as not to include, in one or the other, *all possible* explanatory factors that could bear on any organism in any way. Parsons' usage has a special import: it reflects the idealist thesis of a non-natural realm which is causally efficacious in the natural realm.

32. See, e.g., "Ultimate Values," p. 283; *Structure*, p. 117.

33. Parsons acknowledges that his position involves metaphysics. See "Ultimate Values," pp. 285 and 299.

34. The discussion in Roscoe J. Hinkle, Jr.,

"Theories of Social Stratification in Recent American Sociology," unpublished Ph.D. dissertation, University of Wisconsin, 1952, pp. 227–237, also deserves mention. Hinkle studies the dualism in Parsons' early work and shows the parallels between *Structure* and the epistemology of Kant. But he does not refer to "Ultimate Values" nor does he consider the temporal shifts in Parsons' position.

Hinkle also claims that the "voluntaristic-structural-functional theory of social stratification" —he names Parsons and Davis—"ultimately derives from the German idealist tradition" (p. 225). The present writer would not want to go that far.

35. The two principal sources of Tolman's relevant to this section are *Purposive Behavior in Animals and Men* and his monograph, "A Psychological Model," in Parsons and Shils (Eds.), *Toward a General Theory of Action*. Tolman's theories in the field of experimental psychology analyze behavior in terms of means and ends. Ends are inferred from behavior, and while "mental states" are used as intervening variables, there is explicitly no intervention beyond the sphere of the natural. Tolman has said that his position agrees with Parsons' postwar position, and Parsons has strongly suggested the same thing. See Tolman, "A Psychological Model," p. 279n., and Parsons and Shils, "Values, Motives, etc.," pp. 64 and 234.

36. While the two sources used as the basis of the prewar theory and the ones to follow for the postwar theory cover nearly all of the points under discussion, there are other relevant papers of Parsons intermediate between the two periods. Generally, the shift from the prewar involvement with idealism to the programmatic behaviorism of the Parsons and Shils monograph of 1951 is rather abrupt, but there are passages in the intermediate papers suggesting that voluntarism was progressively weakening before that time. Comments on action in "The Present Position and Prospects of Sociological Theory" (first published in 1945; reprinted in Parsons, *Essays in Sociological Theory*, 1st ed., Glencoe: The Free Press, 1949, pp. 17–41) hold pretty much to the prewar position: action is held to be normative, teleological, "or possibly better," Parsons notes, "voluntaristic." But this paper also refers at some length to Freud. Next, in "The position of Sociological Theory," read in 1947 (*op. cit.*, pp. 3–17), the reason why the scheme has to go beyond the data available to behaviorism has changed. Subjectivism is now necessary "in order to make it possible to attain a high degree of articulation with the motivational categories of contemporary [presumably psychodynamic] psychology." Before the war, it will be recalled, psychology in any form was depreciated: e.g., "A psychological explanation of moral obligation really explains away the phenomenon itself" ("Ultimate Values," p. 290). In the introduction to his *Essays, op. cit.*, Parsons summarizes the argument of *Structure* and the idea of convergence among the writers whom the book treats, but he omits any reference to the convergence as being voluntaristic. This is also the case in Parsons' autobiographical remarks in "Psychological Theory," pp. 619 ff. Finally, no mention is made of voluntarism in the preface to the second edition (1949) of *Structure*. There Parsons mentions that the

book would have been better had it taken Freud's work into account. Yet the daring involved in making a voluntarist out of Pareto would be as nothing compared to that involved in making one out of Freud. To say that *Structure* would have been better had it attended to Freud is really to say that it would have been better had it not been voluntaristic at all.

37. Quotations are from "Values, Motives, etc.," p. 53.

38. Parsons *et al.*, "A General Statement," in *Toward a General Theory of Action*, p. 11.

39. "Values, Motives, etc.," p. 59.

40. Not necessarily, however, for by "gratification" Parsons could also mean the psychological state produced by the realization of ends, without raising any question of whether the end has a natural source. It is clearly not possible to follow up every possible line of interpretation of Parsons' postwar theory in a short paper.

41. *Loc. cit.* (emphasis in original).

42. Again, not necessarily; for while "mechanisms" is pretty much a naturally flavored word, the "selective mechanisms" could logically be the "independent" and presumably idealistic factors spoken of before the war.

43. E.g., "The inner sense of freedom of moral choice . . . is just as ultimate a fact of human life as any other" ("Ultimate Values," p. 290). One may, of course, question whether this is really so ultimate a fact. It is in the interpretation of matters such as this that the essential difference between naturalism and idealism is found. To the naturalist the fact that somebody has delivered an introspective report on his sense of freedom of moral choice may be a datum of great import for, e.g., the study of moral responsibility and normative internalization; but the *truth* of that report is at best problematic and at worst the object of meaningless conjecture. To the idealist, introspection—inner sensing—provides an immediately true account; therefore free choice exists.

In his critique of what he called "radical behaviorism" before the war, Parsons contended that it ruled on the subjective element on *a priori* grounds. This might have been true enough for, say, Watson, whose program antedated the epistemological development of behaviorism. The later objection was not *a priori*, but was made because introspection was found wanting when it was put to the test of use as a scientific method. Thus Tolman was able to say in 1931 that ". . . the dictates of introspection have proved over and over again to be artifacts. . . ." (See above, note 12.) Nothing in Parsons' early writing suggests that he was familiar with the long decline and fall of introspective psychology. See Edwin G. Boring, *A History of Experimental Psychology*, 2nd ed., New York: Appleton–Century–Crofts, 1950, chs. 18 and 22, esp. pp. 410–420 on E. B. Titchener. Titchener's was the psychology *par excellence* embodying the subjective element of Parsons' prewar work.

44. "Values, Motives, etc.," p. 63n.

45. *Op. cit.*, p. 63 (emphasis in original).

46. *Ibid.*, p. 64 (emphasis in original).

47. *Loc. cit.*

48. Theodore Abel's critique of *verstehen* is

essentially behavioristic in that it calls attention to the need for intersubjectively verifiable data for confirmation; the use he sees for *verstehen* is heuristic. See his paper, "The Operation Called Verstehen," *American Journal of Sociology*, 54 (1948), pp. 211–218.

How does the interpretation of thought and feeling as "intervening variables" square with the prewar position? This would depend on the role of "inobservables." Kenneth MacCorquodale and Paul H. Meehl, "On a Distinction between Hypothetical Constructs and Intervening Variables," *Psychological Review*, 55 (1948), pp. 95–107, hold intervening variables to be "behavioristically sound" in Tolman's usage. The volitional factors represented in Parsons' prewar papers would become types of hypothetical constructs by this distinction, and they would raise the sort of "further difficulties" that Parsons now claims to avoid.

49. The discussion in the text takes "Values, Motives, etc." and *The Social System* as the sources for the postwar position because they can most readily be compared to the exposition in *Structure*. But Parsons' later essay, "Psychological Theory" (*op. cit.*), is equally relevant; it is not treated at length here only for want of space. A few remarks are thus in order on the relation of "Psychological Theory" to the changes in the action scheme discussed above.

Generally, "Psychological Theory" is even further to the epistemological left than "Values, Motives, etc." The "organism" is added to the previous three levels of "personality," "social system," and "culture," to which the action scheme may be applied ("Psychological Theory," p. 613). Parsons also postulates "a complete continuity between biological systems and system of action; from this point of view action is a specialized aspect of life" (*op. cit.*, p. 616). Such a complete continuity was scarcely implied in, e.g., the critique of the "positivistic theory of action" in *Structure*, or in the many remarks from "Ultimate Theory" already quoted. Then too before the war Parsons stressed the transcendence of action from "heredity and environment; in "Psychological Theory" that transcendence is disarmed by limiting it to "internal mechanisms of the individual organism and the metabolic interchanges with the environment" (*loc. cit.*). The prewar metaphysical base of the non-reducibility of action becomes the "independent significance of action" based on fairly naturalistic criteria for "hierarchies of organization and control" (*ibid.*, pp. 616 and 618). Parsons also now stresses "value" as a relation between actor and (gratificatory or deprivatory) object. He notes that W. I. Thomas placed values in the object, while "Max Weber . . . placed values in the actor, as 'subjective' in that sense (I had tended to follow him in this) . . . neither view seems satisfactory" (*ibid.*, p. 623). Finally, the normative orientation of action is now based on an aspect of communication: "Only by the observance of conventions or rules regarding the "proper" meanings of signs or symbols is effective communication possible" (*ibid.*, p. 630). In the text following Parsons also defends the subjective reference in a related way.

50. Parsons, *The Social System*, Glencoe: The Free Press, 1952, p. 541n.

51. Parsons, *ibid.*, p. 541.

52. *Ibid.*, p. 543. But cf. with Parsons' remark in "The Point of View of the Author" (in Black, *op. cit.*, p. 324): "The famous Weberian subjective point of view . . . has always been essential to the scheme." Presumably this means the scheme in general. Thus Parsons seems still again to have changed his mind. Something of a trend back toward the old position may be noted in those of his most recent writings which are addressed to sociologists. This is discussed below in the text.

53. *The Social System*, p. 544.

54. Tolman's ideas would be applicable formally to "intelligent" machines, i.e., those operating sufficiently on "feedback" controls to meet his criterion of "organism-environment rearrangement." Parsons might grant this to his postwar concept of "action" too, in principle and in its present most general terms.

55. Parsons, *op. cit.*, p. 544.

56. "Values, Motives, etc.," p. 52n.

57. See e.g., Tolman, "A New Formula for Behaviorism," *Psychological Review*, 1922: reprinted in Tolman, *Collected Papers in Psychology*, pp. 1–8.

58. Today the bulk of non-psychoanalytical psychologists reside in the camp of what may be fairly called the "epistemological left." Sociologists, in contrast, sit on the epistemological right. With a few exceptions, the influential writers and teachers reflect little in scientific epistemology since Kant: we are often as much as told that the ghost of *Geisteswissenschaft* still walks.

59. See e.g., "A Behaviorist's Definition of the Emotions," "A Behaviorist's Theory of Ideas," and "A Behaviorist's Definition of Consciousness," from *Psychological Review*, 1923, 1926 and 1927 respectively; reprinted in Tolman, *Collected Papers in Psychology*.

60. See George Herbert Mead, "A Behavioristic Account of the Significant Symbol," *Journal of Philosophy*, 1922, pp. 157–163.

61. Thus Philip Selznick (in his review article on Black's book, "The Social Theories of Talcott Parsons," *American Sociological Review*, 26 [December, 1961, pp. 932–935] sees *Structure* "as above all an exercise in explication" (p. 934). Selznick also appears to commend "the postulate of voluntarism," but it is doubtful that he would agree with Parsons' argument for voluntarism as developed in "Ultimate Values."

62. Hobbes is one exception. But the dispatch of Hobbes to the camp of "utilitarianism" (a type of positivism for Parsons) is done in too much haste. See Scott, *op. cit.*, p. 54.

63. Parsons was not wholly unaware of the epistemological theme; recall he notes that it was this kind of positivism rather than the metaphysical kind to which Pareto subscribed. (See *Structure*, p. 293.) But Parsons did not follow through on the implications of the epistemological position. Except for one reference to Bridgman, no "empiricists" in this methodological sense are cited.

64. A better informed account of the climate of opinion in which *Structure* appeared is given in Robin Williams, *op. cit.*, pp. 64–67.

65. The discussion of *Structure* in Bierstedt, "The Means–Ends Schema in Sociological Theory,"

American Sociological Review, 3 (1938), pp. 665–671, is an interesting variant on this theme. Bierstedt's critique, though timely, was too strident to-be persuasive, but his remarks on the problem of positing an actor ("ego") not to be found in time or space remain pertinent (p. 670). Bierstedt went on, though, to claim that *all* means–ends analysis was scientifically unfit because the immediate need was for a theory of the causes of ends.

66. See e.g., Kingsley Davis, "The Sociology of Prostitution," *American Sociological Review*, 2 (1937), (pp. 744–755), and "Illegitimacy and the Social Structure," *American Journal of Sociology*, 45 (1939), pp. 215–233; Robert K. Merton, "The Unanticipated Consequences of Purposive Social Action," *American Sociological Review*, 1 (1936), pp. 894–904, and "Social Structure and Anomie," *ibid.*, 3 (1938), pp. 672–682.

Davis, in his *Human Society*, New York: Macmillan, 1949, ch. 5, is one of the few writers other than Parsons explicitly to associate voluntarism with the elements of action. Davis respects *Structure*, and commends a "subjective or voluntaristic" point of view, but his defense of it is based on the need of sociologists to attend to actors' motives rather than on the creative independence of the ends of action. Davis also reconstitutes the elements of action so as to omit the necessity of the normative orientation. See Davis, *op. cit.*, pp. 121–122, and 164n.

Parsons and those whom he influenced were not, of course, the only advocates of a means–ends approach in sociology. The idea of purposive calculation can be found, e.g., in Edward A. Ross, *Social Control*, New York: Macmillan, 1901; and throughout the work of G. H. Mead.

67. Thus the three modes or subsystems of the action scheme—personality, social systems, and culture—readily correspond to the concrete disciplines of psychology, sociology, and anthropology. While there may well be substantive reasons for so distinguishing the modes, this interpretation was probably more acceptable within the Department of Social Relations than it would have been had it omitted a category for each discipline.

68. Devereux, *op. cit.*, p. 6.

69. Parsons, "The Point of View of the Author," in Black, *op. cit.*, p. 341.

70. See *Structure*, pp. 90–93.

71. It is one thing to say that there are systems of norms—*Structure* did say this—but another to say that there is consensus on any one system—this is the implication of Parsons' later writings. It is also one thing to say that norms are important, but another to say that norms are consistent, that is, that norms form a system.

72. See e.g., Davis, *op. cit.*, p. 55; and also Moritz Schlick, *Problems of Ethics*, New York: Prentice-Hall, 1939, p. 1.

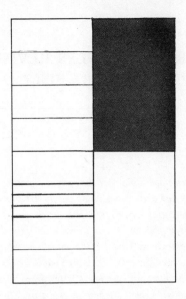

11. FUNCTIONAL IMPERATIVISM

Functional imperativism typically defines the social in terms of subjective behavior relations and seeks to explain it by referring to phenomena imposed on the social through characteristics of the participants' environments and of the participants themselves. The following selection by Parsons deals with the pattern-variables as well as the functional imperatives and discusses some relations between them. (An article by Robert Dubin about Parsons' theories ["Parson's Actor: Continuities in Social Theory," American Sociological Review (August, 1960), 25: 457-466] stimulated this article but it is not necessary to read Dubin's article in order to understand Parsons' main ideas here.)

PATTERN VARIABLES REVISITED:
A RESPONSE TO ROBERT DUBIN

TALCOTT PARSONS

I am grateful to Professor Dubin for the careful attention he has given to the somewhat neglected pattern variables and for his considerable effort in exploring their potential usefulness. His article has led to a serious reconsideration of the problem he has raised—in particular, the relation between what he refers to as Model I (the pattern variables as formulated in Toward a General Theory of Action[1]*) and Model II (the paradigm of four functional problems of systems of action from* Working Papers[2] *and later publications). Dubin suggests that the usefulness of Model II is impaired by too drastic a condensation, and that it cannot be reconciled with Model I. The Editor's invitation to comment on his paper has given me the opportunity to work out an overdue clarification of the ways in which Model II builds on and goes beyond, rather than replaces, Model I.*

Dubin is essentially correct in characterizing the pattern variables as a model that uses the unit act as its building block. The unit act involves the *relationship of an actor to a situation composed of objects*, and it is conceived as a choice (imputed by the theorist to the actor) among alternative ways of defining the situation. The unit act, however, does not occur independently but as one unit in the context of a wider system of actor-situation relationships; this system—including a plurality of acts—is referred to as an *action system*. The unit act is the logically minimal unit of analysis, but as such it can be conceived empirically only as a unit of an action system. Even for analysis of one discrete concrete act, an extended set of similar acts must be postulated as part of

Reprinted from the *American Sociological Review* (August, 1960), pp. 467–483, by permission of the American Sociological Association and the author.

the action system—for example, those comprising a particular role. Figure 1 below is a paradigm for any such action system, not only the unit act.

THE FRAME OF REFERENCE

The pattern variables first emerged as a conceptual scheme for classifying types of roles in social systems, starting with the distinction between professional and business roles. In this sense, the concept "actor" referred to individual human beings as personalities in roles and the analysis—as Dubin puts it—" 'looks' out to the social system from the vantage point of the actor." In *Toward a General Theory*, the scheme was substantially revised and its relevance extended from role-analysis in the social system to the analysis of all types of systems of action.

Action is thus viewed as a process

occurring between two structural parts of a system—actor and situation. In carrying out analysis at any level of the total action system, the concept "actor" is extended to define not only individual personalities in roles but other types of acting units—collectivities, behavioral organisms, and cultural systems. Since the term actor is used here to refer to any such acting unit, I attempt to avoid—except for purposes of analogy or illustration—psychological reference, for example, "motivation," attributed to actors as individuals. Thus "actor" can refer to a business firm in interaction with a household, or, at the cultural level, the implementation of empirical beliefs interacting with the implementation of evaluative beliefs.

Both the pattern variables and the four system-problems are conceptual schemes, or sets of categories, for classifying the components of action. They provide a frame of reference within which such classification can be made. The figures presented below indicate the methods, sets of rules and procedures, that state how these categories may be used analytically; they imply *theorems*—propositions that admit of logical, not empirical, proof—which state a set of determinate relationships among the categories and, in so doing, outline a *theory* of action. The theory, then, is a set of logical relationships among categories used to classify empirical phenomena and, in empirical reference, attempts to account for whatever may be the degree of uniformity and stability of such phenomena.

The pattern variables are a conceptual scheme for classifying the components of an action system—the actor-situation relational system which comprises a plurality of unit acts. Each variable defines one property of a particular class of components. In the first instance, they distinguish between two sets of components, *orientations* and *modalities*. Orientation concerns the actor's relationship *to* the objects in his situation and is conceptual-

ized by the two "attitudinal" variables of diffuseness-specificity and affectivity-neutrality. In psychological terms, orientation refers to the actor's need for relating to the object world, to the basis of his interest in it. For other levels of analysis, of course this psychological reference must be generalized. Modality concerns the meaning *of* the object for the actor and is conceptualized by the two "object-categorization" variables of quality-performance and universalism-particularism. It refers to those aspects of the object that have meaning for the actor, given the situation. The orientation set of pattern variables "views" the relationship of actor to situation from the side of the actor or actors; the modality set views it from the side of the situation as consisting of objects. As Dubin suggests, the pattern variable of self-collectivity orientation does not belong at this level of analysis; it is placed in proper perspective below.

In classifying the components of the actor's relation to a situation, the pattern variables suggest propositions about any particular action system in terms of those components and the type of act their combination defines; thus a particular role can be characterized by the properties of universalism, performance, and so on. An action system, however, is not characterized solely by the actor's orientations and the modalities of objects significant to the actor; it is also a *structured* system with analytically independent aspects which the elementary pattern variable combinations by themselves do not take into account.

In such a structured system both actor and object share institutionalized norms, conformity with which is a condition for stability of the system. The relation between the actor's orientations and the modalities of objects in the situation cannot be random. The *Working Papers* established a non-random relationship between the two sets by matching the functionally corresponding categories on each side—universalism with specificity, particularism with diffuseness, performance with affectivity, and quality with neutrality. This matching yielded Dubin's Model II. It turned out that this arrangement converges with the classification of functional problems of systems that Bales had earlier formulated.[3] This convergence, the main subject of the *Working Papers*, opened up such a fertile range of possibilities that for several years my main attention has been given to their exploration rather than to direct concern with the scheme out of which it grew. However, it is now clear that "Model II" is not a substitute for the earlier version, in the sense that it represents the whole scheme, but rather a formulation of one particularly crucial part of a larger scheme. The following discussion places that part in the context of the larger scheme as the formulation of "integrative standards," those aspects of the action system shared by actor and object and that make the system a stable one.

In analyzing the components of any particular action system, one must also consider the larger system within which that action system is embedded. The action system is related to the "external system" beyond it, which I refer to here as the *environment* of the system, as distinguished from the *situation* of the acting unit. The following analysis treats this relation of action system to environment as mediated mainly through the adaptive subsystem. The combinations of pattern variable components in that subsystem were foreshadowed in the *Working Papers* by the "auxiliary" combinations of neutrality-performance, particularism-specificity, and so on.[4] The present paper, I believe, establishes the analytical independence of *these* combinations from those of the integrative standards in Model II, and goes considerably beyond the *Working Papers* in setting forth their significance for action systems.

Finally, the pattern variables—although they designate the *properties* of actor's orientations and objects' modalities in an action system—do not as such classify *types* of actors and objects. Such a typology cannot be derived from any particular action system, but only from the analysis of a range of such systems. It is this typology of actors and objects with which Dubin's left- and right-hand columns in his Table I (p. 459) is concerned. Figure 2 (below) has incorporated this important aspect of Dubin's problem.

With references to Dubin's Table I, the pattern variables themselves are discussed under what he terms the "actor's evaluation of objects." The column headed "Modalities of Objects" is admittedly redundant, for in addition to the redundancies noted by Dubin, the terms "classificatory" and "relational" are synonymous with "universalism" and "particularism," respectively, as I acknowledged in *The Social System*. In my Figure 2, Dubin's "motivational orientation" towards objects is covered by the pattern-maintenance or orientation subsystem; his "value-orientation" by the adaptive subsystem; and his "action-orientation" is characterized by the types of output of the system as a whole (see p. 274 below).

Thus the conceptual scheme of the four system-problems has added a set of rules and procedures—the basis of theorems—whereby the analysis of components of action in terms of pattern variables can be carried out by "looking down," on them, as Dubin has aptly put it, from the perspective of the action system. The action system is presented in Figure 1 so as to establish the analytical independence of the four subsystems: orientations (pattern-maintenance); modalities (goal-attainment); their combination characterizing the conditions of internal stability of a relational system shared by both actor and object (integration); their combination characterizing the ways in which that system is stably related to the environment (adaptation).

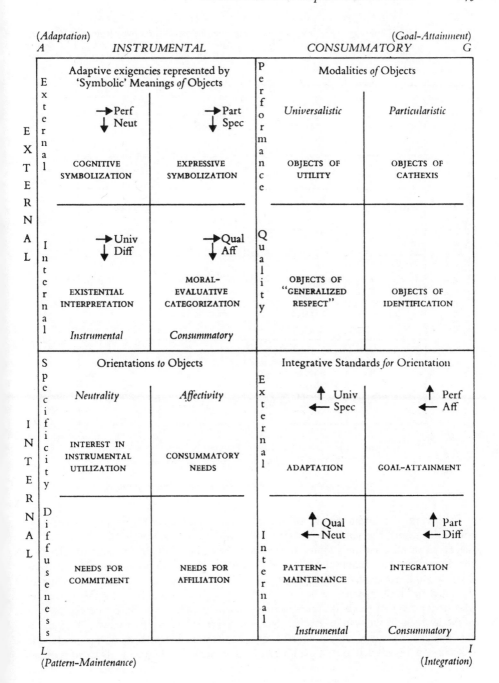

Figure 1. *The Components of Action Systems*

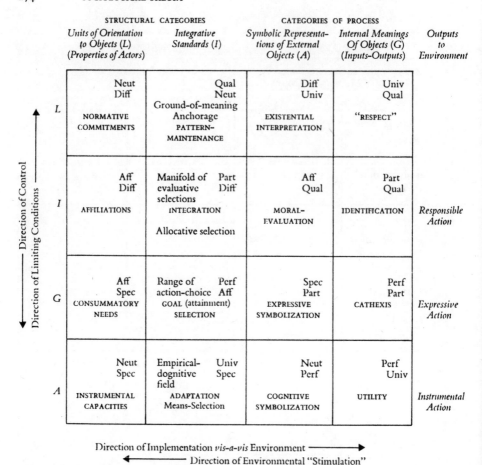

	STRUCTURAL CATEGORIES		CATEGORIES OF PROCESS		
	Units of Orientation to Objects (L) (*Properties of Actors*)	*Integrative Standards (I)*	*Symbolic Representations of External Objects (A)*	*Internal Meanings Of Objects (G)* (*Inputs-Outputs*)	*Outputs to Environment*
L	Neut Diff NORMATIVE COMMITMENTS	Qual Neut Ground-of-meaning Anchorage PATTERN-MAINTENANCE	Diff Univ EXISTENTIAL INTERPRETATION	Univ Qual "RESPECT"	
I	Aff Diff AFFILIATIONS	Manifold of Part evaluative Diff selections INTEGRATION Allocative selection	Aff Qual MORAL-EVALUATION	Part Qual IDENTIFICATION	*Responsible Action*
G	Aff Spec CONSUMMATORY NEEDS	Range of Perf action-choice Aff GOAL (attainment) SELECTION	Spec Part EXPRESSIVE SYMBOLIZATION	Perf Part CATHEXIS	*Expressive Action*
A	Neut Spec INSTRUMENTAL CAPACITIES	Empirical- Univ dognitive Spec field ADAPTATION Means-Selection	Neut Perf COGNITIVE SYMBOLIZATION	Perf Univ UTILITY	*Instrumental Action*

(Left margin, top to bottom): Direction of Control — Direction of Limiting Conditions

Direction of Implementation *vis-a-vis* Environment ———→

←——— Direction of Environmental "Stimulation"

Figure 2. *The Action System in Relation to Its Environment*

Following the presentation of these four subsystems, the *same* information is displayed in tabular form different from the more familiar functional "layout." This second presentation (Figure 2) is designed to "look down" on any particular action system from the perspective of the more inclusive system. At this level, the analysis of types of actors and of objects can be carried out. In addition, Figure 2 highlights the distinction between the *control* of action—that is, the scale of priorities assigned to various ways of regulating action—and the *implementation* of action—the analytical relevance involved in the distinction between structure and process.

This then is the main frame of reference of the paper's approach to the classification and analysis of the components of action. We now turn to the paradigm itself, which is altogether newly formulated from the point of view of the internal relations between its components, and is presented in Figure 1. Its form is essentially that of Dubin's Table 4, which was derived from the *Working Papers.*[5] "Model II" is treated in the paradigm as the integration subsystem of the general system. The pattern variable scheme as formulated in *Toward A General Theory*, that is, the two "attitudinal" and "object-categorization" sets, are incorporated into the "pattern-maintenance" and the "goal-attainment" subsystems, respectively. To avoid terminological confusion we follow Dubin in referring to the two sets of pattern variables as the *orientation* set and the *modality* set. The fourth block of cells, representing the adaptation subsystem, is also entirely new, and is explicated below.

We have noted above that the primary reference of the concept "actor" is to the individual personality, but that in secondary respects, collectivities, behavioral organisms, and cultural systems may be conceived as actors. It is important to remember that our scheme concerns the *generalized* components of action, so that such psychological terms as "cathexis" and "identification" and "need," as used here, stand for more generalized concepts than would be applicable to actors and objects on these other levels; their reference is not confined to the personality level.

THE ORIENTATION SET (PATTERN-MAINTENANCE)[6]

The *orientation base* of a system of action, may be categorized in terms of the two pattern variables, affectivity-neutrality and specificity-diffuseness. The relevant characteristic of the actor in defining his (or "its") orientation to an object or category of objects may be an "interest" in the object as a source of "consummation." This may be defined as an interest in establishing a *relation to* an object, which the actor has no incentive to change. In psychological terms, this may be phrased that the actor has a "need" for such a relationship, which can be "gratified" by its establishment. The alternative to the need for a consummatory relationship is the "need" for *help* toward the attainment of such a relationship to an

object. Therefore, besides the consummatory, there is an instrumental basis of orientation to the object-world. At this point a pattern-variable "dilemma" arises because it is a fundamental assertion of our theory that consummatory and instrumental interests in objects *cannot* be maximized at the same time. The instrumental and consummatory bases are *analytically* independent.

The very discrimination of different bases of orientation of actors to objects implies that actors are conceived as systems; they are never oriented to their situations simply "as a whole," but always through specific modes of organization of independent components. From this point of view, it is always important whether the primary reference is to the *relation* of the acting system to its environment *or* to its own internal properties and equilibrium. The situation, or object-world, is in the nature of the case organized differently from the actor as system. Hence, in orientation *directly* to the situation, the specificities of differentiation among objects and their properties become salient. On the other hand, where internal "needs" of the acting system are paramount, the salience of these specificities recedes, and the orientation to objects becomes more diffuse. This is the setting in which the specificity-diffuseness variable fits. It indicates that where the "interaction surface" between actor and situation is approached, the actor's interests in objects must be more highly specified than where internal states of the acting system itself are in the forefront.

There is a pattern-variable dilemma here as well as in the instrumental-consummatory case. This is to say that the imperatives of specificity and of diffuseness cannot be maximally satisfied at the same time.

The cross-classification of these two orientational pattern-variables yields a four-fold table which is presented as the pattern-maintenance subsystem (L) of

Figure 1. As distinguished from the pattern variables themselves, which are rubrics of classification, this constitutes a classification of *types* of orientation to objects. This distinction has not always been clear, I believe, neither in my own work nor in that of other writers.

It will be seen that the pure type of "consummatory needs" combines affectivity and specificity of interest; it is "pure" because it can focus on the actor's relation to the *specific* discretely differentiated object. But where the basis of interest is diffuse, there must be generalization to a broader *category* of objects, so the basis of the interest is the establishment of a relation between the acting system and a wider sector of the situational object-system. We have called this a "need for affiliation," for example, for a relation of mutual "solidarity" between diffuse sectors of the acting system and the object-system.

On the instrumental side, it is apparent that the same order of distinction applies to specifically differentiated bases of interest in objects and diffuser bases. *Manipulation* of objects in the interest of consummatory gratification or even passive adaptation to them requires concern with the specificities of their properties. Hence the "interest in instrumental utilization," though affectively neutral, is also specific; interest in the *category* is not enough. Where, however, the problem is not utilization, but the place of the orientation in the internal structure of the acting system, this level of the specification of interest not only is unnecessary but, because of the independent variability of the object-situation, becomes positively obstructive. *Commitment* to the specifics of object-situations introduces a rigidity of orientation which can be highly constrictive. Commitment can be and, functionally speaking, is better organized on a diffuser level. We therefore speak of "needs for commitment" as oriented to diffuse categories of objects and their

properties rather than to specific objects and properties, and as engaging more diffuse sectors of the acting system than do "interests in instrumental utilization."

THE MODALITY SET (GOAL-ATTAINMENT)

With reference to the obverse side of the action relationship, that of the modalities of objects, the modality set of pattern variables constitutes the classificatory framework—particularism and universalism, and performance and quality. Particularism in this context means that from the point of view of the action system, the most significant aspect of an object is its relation of particularity to the actor: as compared with other objects which can "intrinsically" be classified as similar to it, the significance of *this* object to the actor lies in its *inclusion* in the same interactive system. In the contrasting case of universalistic modalities, the basis of an object's meaning lies in its universalistically defined properties, hence its inclusion in classes which transcend that particular relational system. For example, when a man falls in love, it is this *particular* woman with whom the love relationship exists. He may, like some other gentlemen, prefer blondes, but he is not in love with the category, but with one particular blonde. Thus the same kind of dilemma exists here as for the two pattern variables described above—it is impossible to maximize the particularistic meaning of objects and their universalistic meaning at the same time. A man sufficiently in love with blondeness as such, who therefore pursues any blonde, cannot establish a very stable love relationship with a particular woman. That there is an important "matching" between consummatory bases of interest and particularistic meaning of objects is clear; its significance is discussed below.

A basic postulate of action theory is that the states of acting systems and those of the situational object-world in which they act are independently variable. At their "interface," then, an especially important property of objects is their probable *performance* in respect to the actors oriented to them. Recall that the prototype of the actor-object relation is social interaction, in which the "object" is also in turn an actor who does something. Thus physical objects, which do not "act," are the limiting case of objects to which the term "performance" is inherently inapplicable.

In contrast with this situation, is the meaning of objects in terms of what they "are," of their qualities defined independently of performances, which are inherently relative to situations. The internal reference of the acting system matches with interest in the qualities of objects rather than their performances, since these are presumptively more independent of direct situational exigencies.

These two classificatory rubrics—performance-quality and universalism-particularism—yield a four-fold typology of objects (or of components), seen from the perspective of their meaning to actors. This is the Goal-Attainment Subsystem (G) in Figure 1. This terminology is also adopted from the prototypical case of interaction of persons. Thus an object whose primary meaning is particularistic and based on its actual and expected performances, following psychoanalytic usage, may be called an "object of cathexis." It is "looked at" in terms of its potentialities for gratifying specific consummatory needs. However, if an object is defined in universalistic terms, but at the same time as a source of performances significant to the actor, it can be said to be an "object of utility," for it is viewed with respect to its potentialities in helping to bring about consummatory states of the acting system.

In contrast with both these types, objects may be treated as "objects of identification" if their meaning is both particularistic and refers essentially to what they "are" rather than what they "do." Here the objects' meaning to actors is not subject to the more detailed fluctuations which go with the meaning of cathexis.

Finally, the universalistic case, the fourth type, is called an "object of generalized respect." Here the object is categorized by the actor in universalistic terms, but also with relation to its qualities. This is the type of object which in a social context Durkheim speaks of as generating attitudes of "moral authority."[7]

PROBLEMS OF INTEGRATION AND ADAPTATION

The argument so far may be summarized: We have outlined, in terms of the present conceptual scheme, the elementary components of action and certain aspects of their interrelations. Essentially these are the components of unit acts but do not yet comprise systems of action.

First, we have assumed that all action involves the *relating* of acting units to objects in their situation. This is the basis for the fundamental distinction between components belonging to the characterization of *orienting* actors and those belonging to the *modalities* of the objects to which they are oriented—that is, between the two "sets" of elementary pattern variables. Second, we have used the elementary variables to classify types of elementary combination. The underlying assumption here is that on this level they are always analytically independent; hence the orientation set (cluster L of Figure 1) and the modality set (cluster G) are treated as mutually exclusive, each type being composed of components drawn only from one of the two sets. Third, each cell within each cluster is composed of *only* two pattern variable designations. Fourth, what elsewhere are defined as "pattern variable opposites" never occur in the same cell. Subject to these rules, the classifications designated by the four cells in each cluster are logically exhaustive of the possibilities. We consider the fourth assumption to be the application of a fundamental theorem concerning the conditions of the stability of orientation, namely, that neither the same orientation nor the same object can be successfully defined, in a particular context or orientation, in terms of *both* alternatives without discrimination, for example, universalistically and particularistically or specifically and diffusely at the same time.

Subject to these constraints, however, we see no reason why the composition of possible types of unit acts do not exhaust the range of logically possible independent variation of the components thus formulated. But such a definition does not tell us anything about the conditions of the existence of a *system* of such unit acts other than that there are such limiting circumstances as physical and biological conditions of survival. In other words, this level of analysis describes a *population* of action-units and certain of the ways in which they are empirically ordered in relation to each other. It cannot provide an analysis of the relations of their *interaction*, which constitute a system subject to mechanisms of equilibration and change as a system through "feedback" processes—in one sense, the *organization* of the system.

To take the step to this organizational level, it is necessary to attempt to conceptualize two basic sets of "functions" which cannot be treated either as the orientations of actors or as the meanings or modalities of the objects to which they are primarily oriented. These are, first, the modes of internal *integration* of the system, that is, of the interrelations of the elementary actor-object units. This means, within our frame of reference, the normative standards on the basis of which such relations can be said to be stable. Second, there are the mechanisms by

which the system as a whole is *adapted to the environment* within which it operates. Since from the point of view of orientation this environment must consist in some sense of objects, the problem is that of conceptualizing the relation between objects internal to the system and those (albeit in some sense meaningful) external to the system.

To repeat, those reviewed above constitute the full complement of elementary components of action systems. Therefore, in dealing with these two additional system functions or subsystem clusters, we do not propose to introduce additional elementary components, but rather to suggest new *combinations* of these components. On this basis the I and A clusters of cells in Figure 1 are constructed on the hypothesis that each cell of the two clusters should be defined by *one* pattern variable component drawn from each of the two elementary subsets. If this policy and the general rules formulated above are followed, the combinations represented in the two clusters will be logically exhaustive of the possibilities.

Within these rules the problem is that of the basis of allocation of the components as between the two clusters, and within each as between the cells. The governing principles for treating this problem are more fully elucidated below, following a review of the allocations themselves and some problems of the system as a whole. Here, suffice it to say, first, that internal integration is dependent on the *matching* of the function of the object for the "needs" of the orienting actor with the functional meaning with which the object is categorized. Thus in some sense the gratification of consummatory needs is dependent on the possibility of categorizing appropriate objects as objects of cathexis, and so on. Why only two of the four components which might define this matching are involved, and which two, are also explained below.

Secondly, the significance of objects

external to the system is not their *actual* meaning *in* the system, but rather their *potential* meaning *for* the system—the ways in which taking cognizance of this meaning or failing to do so *may* affect the functioning of the system. With these preliminaries, we may now review schematically the actual content suggested for the cells.

THE INTEGRATIVE SUBSET

How are the formal characteristics of the I and A cells in Figure 1 to be interpreted? The integrative subset states the primary conditions of internal stability or *order* in an action system. These conditions may be formulated as follows: (1) In so far as the primary functional problem of the system, conceived either in terms of structural differentiation or temporal phases, is *adaptive*, stability is dependent on the *universalistic* categorization of the relevant objects, regardless of whether or not they have certain particularistic meanings, *and* on sufficient *specificity* in the basis of interest in these objects to exclude more diffuse considerations of orientation. (2) In so far as the primary functional problem is the *attainment* of a *goal* for the system, stability is dependent on attention to the potentialities of *performance* of the object in its relation to the actor, *and* on affective engagement of the actor in the establishment of the optimal (consummatory) relation to the object—hence the lifting of "inhibitions" on such engagement. (3) In so far as the primary functional problem is integration of the system, stability is dependent on particularistic categorization of the relevant objects (that is, to the extent that they are also actors, their inclusion in the system), *and* the maintenance of a *diffuse* basis of interest in these objects (that is, one which is not contingent on fluctuations in their specific performances or properties). (4) In so far as the primary functional problem for the system is the *maintenance* of

the *pattern* of its units, stability is dependent on maintaining a categorization of the objects in terms of their *qualities* independently of their specific performances, *and* an affectively *neutral* orientation, one that is not alterable as a function of specific situational rewards.

In terms of the regulation of action, these combinations of pattern variable components define categories of *norms* governing the interaction of units in the system. Norms themselves must be differentiated. It is in the nature of an action system to be subject to a plurality of functional exigencies; no single undifferentiated normative pattern or "value" permits stability over the range of these different exigencies. Hence norms constitute a differentiated and structured subsystem of the larger system. They constitute the structural aspect of the *relational nexus* between actors and objects in their situations.

Precisely because the above propositions state conditions of stable equilibrium involving the *relations between* a plurality of elementary components, I believe that they go beyond description to state, implicitly at least, certain theorems about the consequences of variations in these relations. These theorems are considered following the discussion of the system itself.

THE ADAPTIVE SUBSET

In the adaptive subset, the formal bases of selection of the component combinations as we have noted, are antithetical to those used in the integrative subset. This is to say that they combine both external and internal references, and both instrumental and consummatory references.

We have termed these combinations as defining "mechanisms" for ordering the adaptive relations of a system of action to the environment in which it functions. To clarify this problem an important distinction must be made. When we referred above to the orientation of actors to objects and the related modalities or meanings of objects, we were indicating components *internal* to a system of action. Objects that are *constituents* of the system must, however, be distinguished from objects that are part of the *environment* of the system. The boundary concept which defines this distinction is "particularism;" an object categorized particularistically is defined as belonging to the system. Adaptation concerns the relations of the whole system to objects which, as such, are *not* included in it.

Adaptive mechanisms, then, must be conceived as ways of categorizing the meanings of objects universalistically, that is, independently of their actual or potential inclusion in a given system. These mechanisms are "symbolic" media, including language as the prototype, but also empirical knowledge, money, and so on. Use of the media for referring to objects and categories of objects does not *ipso facto* commit the actor to any particular relation of inclusion or exclusion relative to the objects concerned. By use of the media, however, *meanings* may be treated as *internal* to the system, whereas the objects themselves may or may not remain external. This is the basic difference from modalities, which are meanings wherein the objects themselves are defined as internal.

In this context, the pattern variable combinations of the adaptive subset may be explicated as follows: (1) In order to symbolize the *adaptive* significance of objects in the environment of an action sysetm (for example, to "understand" them cognitively), it is necessary to categorize them in terms of what actually or potentially they "do" (*performance*), *and* to orient to them with affective *neutrality*, that is, independently of their potentialities for gratifying the actor. This "pattern" is defined as a condition for stability of an orientation

to the *external* environment which can maximize "objective" understanding of the objects comprising it; adopting a term from personality analysis we may term .the pattern empirical "cognitive symbolization." (2) In order to symbolize and categorize objects that are external to the system according to their significance for goal-attainment, it is necessary to focus their possible meaning on specific bases of interest or "motivation" (specificity), *and* on their potential "belongingness" in a system of meanings which also defines the system of action (particularism). This we call "expressive symbolization," the generalization of particularistic meanings to a universalistic level of significance. (3) In order to symbolize and categorize the significance of *norms* that are external to the system, it is necessary to treat them as aspects of an objectively "given" state of affairs or "order" (quality), *and* to treat them with affectivity—that is, the actor cannot be emotionally indifferent to whether or not he feels committed to the norms in question. This we name "moral-evaluative categorization." (4) In order to symbolize and categorize the significance of "sources of normative authority," it is necessary to combine a universalistic definition of the object, as having properties not dependent on its inclusion in the system, with a *diffuse* basis of interest, so that the meaning in question cannot be treated as contingent on the fluctuating relations between the orienting actor and the environment. This we call "existential interpretation."

Here another version of the external-internal distinction is important. For the first two of these—the adaptive and goal-attainment categories—refer to objects considered as such, irrespective of whether or not they are included with the acting system within a more comprehensive system. In the latter two cases, however, this question of common membership in a more comprehensive system is central. A norm is binding on a unit only in so far as the unit shares common membership with other units similarly bound. An object is a source of normative authority only so far as its authority extends to other units, defined universalistically as similarly subject to that authority. It is on these grounds that we emphasize "symbolization" in the first two cases and "categorization" in the second two.

Note that the differentiation of symbolic media according to functional significance parallels the differentiation of integrative standards. They too are results of a process of differentiating the components involved in the elementary pattern-variable sets and of integrating the selected components across the orientation-modality line. As distinguished from the *internal* integration of the system, the adaptive subset refers to the system's integration with its environment as part of a more comprehensive system of action.

THE PERSPECTIVE OF THE SYSTEM AS A WHOLE

So far we have considered the elementary components which make up a system of action and two main ways in which they are related across the orientation-modality line. These components and relations, however, constitute a system which in turn functions in relation to what we call an "environment." We now consider a few aspects of the properties of this system in its environmental context. The main reference point for this analysis is a rearrangement or transformation of the items of Figure 1, as presented in Figure 2.

The components in Figure 2 are the same sixteen pattern variable combinations represented in Figure 1. However, there are two new features of the arrangement: First, each of the four major blocks of cells of Figure 1 is set forth as a column of Figure 2. Within each column

the cells in turn are arranged from top to bottom in the order L—I—G—A. This constitutes a cybernetic hierarchy of control,[8] that is, each cell categorizes the necessary but not sufficient conditions for operation of the cell next above it in the column, and in the opposite direction, the categories of each cell control the processes categorized in the one below it. For instance, definition of an end or goal controls the selection of means for its attainment.

The second difference from Figure 1 is the arrangement of the columns from left to right in a serial order which, stated in functional terms, is L—I—A—G. The two left-hand columns designate the structural components of the system. The L column formulates the properties of units conceived as actors; the I column formulates the structural aspect of the relational nexus between units, that is, the norms which function as integrative standards. The two right-hand columns categorize the elements of *process* by which the system operates. The G column shows the modalities of objects from the point of view of *change* of meaning as a process of relating inputs and outputs; it brings *into* the system meaning-categorizations generated by the system. The A column formulates the components involved in the symbolic mechanisms mediating the adaptive aspect of process. Whereas the hierarchy of control places the A subset at the bottom of each column, as a column itself it is placed "inside" the system because it consists of a set of symbolized *meanings* (or "representations") of the environmental object-world outside the system, or the categorization of objects independently of their inclusion in or exclusion from the system. It therefore constitutes the *internal environment* of the system, the environment to which *units* must adapt in their relations to each other, but the actual objects symbolized constitute the external environment to which the *system* as a whole must adapt.

We have suggested that the outputs of action systems *consist in* changes in the meanings of objects. It follows that the inputs also consist in meanings of objects. What the process of action accomplishes, then, is *change* in these meanings. We assume of course that new objects and categories of objects are created in the process; these presumably are themselves action systems and their "cultural" precipitates. The distinction between changing the meaning of an old object and creating a new object thus appears to depend on the point of observation.

The modalities of objects in the G column of Figure 2 therefore may be treated as a classification of the outputs of *internal* action process, in a sense similar to the usage in economics of "value-added."[9] Thus action process, so far as it is effectively *adaptive* internally, may be said to add . utility to objects—for example, utility in the economist's sense, the relevant category for social systems, also is a category of meaning in the present context. Action which is successfully oriented internally to *goal-attainment* leads to the enhanced cathectic value of objects in the system. Action which is successfully *integrative* leads to increased "identification-meaning"—in social systems, to solidarity with and among objects. Finally, processes of "pattern-maintenance" maintain or restore the "respect" in which the relevant system itself is held as an object in the social system; here is Durkheim's "the integrity of moral authority."

The designations to the right of the G column in Figure 2 are the "action-orientations" in the Orientation column of Dubin's Table 1 (p. 459). We suggest that these can be treated as categories of output *to its environment* of the *system as a whole* (as distinguished from the outputs of internal process). Thus instrumental action by a system may be treated as resulting in increase in the instrumental

values to it of objects *within* its environment or more inclusive system. Similarly, expressive action produces enhanced cathectic meaning of objects in the environment; and responsible action increases the integrative identification category of meaning (for example, in the social system, "moral" value). In accord with principles we have used consistently,[10] we suggest that there is no category of output for the L subsystem except in cases of change in the structure of the system.

THE CLASSIFICATION OF OBJECTS

One further set of categories which play a part in Dubin's Table 1 needs to be accounted for—the classification of types of object as physical, social, and cultural. This problem can most conveniently be treated at the environmental level. If a given system is conceived as an actor or an action system, then a system with which it *interacts* is a social object. We have explained why this category should be differentiated into at least two sub-categories: the system organized about the single human individual, namely, personality; and the social system constituted by the interaction of a plurality of individuals. A *physical* object, then, is one with which the system does not in this sense interact, and which, standing below the action system in the hierarchy of control, is conditional to it; a *cultural* object is also one with which it does not interact, but which stands above it in the hierarchy of control, and therefore is a focus of its own control system.

However, a further principle is involved, not developed here, of *inter-penetration* of systems.[11] The crucial case of physical systems with which the personality interpenetrates is the behavioral organism, the physical system which constitutes the fundamental facility-base for the operation of the personality system. At the other extreme, are "acting" cultural systems, implemented through social and personal actions, which constitute the operating normative control systems of social systems. At each "end" of the control series, then, is a set of limiting conceptions of nonaction "reality." At the lower end is "purely physical" reality with which the action system does not interpenetrate, but which is only conditional to it. At the upper end is "nonempirical," perhaps "cosmic," reality with which, similarly, there is no significant interpenetration, and which is thus conceived only as an "existential ground" of operative cultural systems.

A similar classification can be worked out for the alternative case where the system in question is conceived as acting, and not as an object. Here it seems that the parallel to a cultural object is the conception of the "subject" as "knowing, feeling, and willing." At the social level, this is our concept of "actor" in the sense of participation in *interaction*. At the interpenetrating subsocial level, it is the concept of organism, as "functioning" in relation to an environment. Perhaps at a still lower level should be placed the "hereditary constitution" of a species (as distinguished from the particular organism in phylogenetic, not ontogenetic terms).

COMBINATIONS OF THE COMPONENTS

We now return to the question of the bases of combination and allocation of the pattern variable components. A maximum number of types could be generated of course by treating the potential combinations as all those randomly possible. This procedure, however, would mean the sacrifice of connections referred to above as the *organization* of systems of action and the determinate theoretical generalizations associated with them.

We have restricted random combina-

tions, first, by composing two cell clusters (L and G) exclusively from one or the other of the elementary sets; second, by never placing both members of a "dilemma" pair in the same cell; third, by placing only *one* component from each elementary set in each cell of the I and A clusters; and, finally, by drawing these from "functionally cognate" cells of the elementary combination paradigms. (See Figures 1 and 2.) Within these rules of organization we have followed a further policy of selection in the allocations to the I and A clusters. In terms of the "geometry" of Figure 1, this policy involves two procedures: (1) for the I cluster, the distribution of the modality components is derived by keeping the "functionally cognate" reference constant and then rotating clockwise the modality axes one quarter turn, and the distribution of the orientation components is similarly decided by rotating the orientation axes in the counterclockwise direction; (2) for the A cluster, the direction of rotation is the reverse in each case. Thus, in the G cluster the distinction between universalism and particularism defines the *horizontal* axis of the paradigm, in the I cluster it assumes the *diagonal*. Put otherwise: of the *two* occurrences of each component in the G table only *one* of each is included in the I table, and these are placed in a diagonal position. The effect of this is to "shift" the relevant category from one to the other of the two positions in which it could be placed in the elementary set. The procedure never leads to "crossing over" into a "forbidden" cell; for example, universalism and particularism never "changes places."

What is the meaning of these patternings? It is inherent in the organization of Figure 2 that integrative functions stand higher in the order of control than either goal-attainment or adaptive functions, which follow in that order. On grounds that cannot be fully explained here, I suggest that the horizontal and vertical axes of the paradigm state the location of the processes, conceived as interunit interchanges, which, respectively, have primarily internal adaptive significance in providing facilities to the units in question, and internal goal-attainment significance in providing rewards. Thus, the "rotation" brings about an involvement of the pattern variable components in integrative interchanges along the axes of Durkheim's "mechanical" (L—G) and "organic" solidarity (A—I).[12]

The suggestion, then, is that, relative to the elementary clusters, both I and A clusters have integrative significance. The I set states internal integrative *standards*, departure from which is associated with those realistic internal consequences known in interaction theory as "negative sanctions." The A set states standards of *meanings* of external objects ("cultural standards"), departure from which is associated with cultural selectivity and distortion, although not with immediately felt "sanctions."

What of the obverse "directions" of rotation? There is a double incidence of these directionalities. *Within* the clusters the rotations of the axes of the orientations and of the modalities are in opposite directions. The modalities of objects, from the point of view of a system of action, constitute ways of relating not only the acting unit but the system to the environment external to it. Hence it is an imperative of integration that, from the modality side, priority should be enjoyed by the category of meaning of the object (internally, as defining the actor-object relation) which is of primary functional significance *for the system* in the relevant context. From the orientation side, the imperative is that priority goes to the mode of orientation of primary significance to the actor in terms of its "needs." Thus, if the system function in question

is adaptive, universalistic meanings take precedence over particularistic. For the actor, then, the primacy of specificity may be regarded as protecting his interest in *other* contexts of meaning of the same and other objects by limiting his commitments to the more immediately important ones.

These two designations are "functionally cognate" in that they share the characteristics of external orientation and instrumental significance. Here the rotation means that on the A—I axis of the integrative cluster (not of the system as a whole) the modality component in the adaptive cell is related to what in the G cluster is its *consummatory* "partner," whereas the orientation component is related to its *internal* partner. This is simply another way of stating the obverse directions of rotation. Put in general functional terms: the obverse relationship protects the system by giving primacy to instrumental over consummatory considerations in the adaptive context, while it protects the actor by giving primacy to external over internal considerations.

Another example from the adaptive cluster pairs the integrative cell with affectivity. From the viewpoint of the system, the significance of the object as "internalized" or institutionalized must clearly take precedence over its varying performances as oriented to the external situation. For it to serve as a standard of moral-evaluative categorization, however, there must also be affective involvement. The rotation in this case means that categorization in terms of quality is specifically distinguished from the performance component in its application to cognitive symbolization, whereas affectivity is contrasted (and thus integrated) with neutrality in the cognitive context. The formula for evaluative categorization on the modality side therefore designates internal significance, on the orientation side, consummatory significance.

The "diagonal" relations of the pattern variable pairs in the I and A clusters thus formulate the relations of combined discrimination and balance between the modality components and the orientational components. In each case the balance "protects" the categorization from confusion with its pattern variable opposite.

The same essential principles hold when the functioning of the system as a whole is considered. Here rotation in the clockwise direction designates what psychologists often call "performance" process, that is, change in the relations of the system to its environment on the assumption that its internal structure remains unchanged. The primary focus of change in this case lies in the adaptive subsystem. The counterclockwise direction of process designates "learning" processes. Here the primary focus of change centers in the internal structure of the system, in the first instance in the integrative system producing a change in its standards.

TYPES OF ACTION AND THE ORGANIZATION OF COMPONENTS

Another theoretical issue requires brief comment. This concerns the fact that the present analysis is mainly an analytical classification of *components* of *any* system of action, including the "unit act" as the most elementary building block of action systems.[13] Dubin, however, speaks of *types* of act. From the present point of view types must be constructed of varying combinations of components. In addition to *composition*—in terms of the presence or absence of components, or different "weights" assigned to them—there is organization of these components. We interpret the restrictions on random combination, and the clustering of pattern variable combinations in the four functional sets, to be statements of organization. The state of a system is never, in our opinion, adequately des-

cribed by its "composition"—that is, by what components are present in what quantities; the patterns of their relationships are equally essential. These considerations should be taken into account in attempts to develop a typology of acts from a classification of components in the act.

Another relevant point concerns the status of the pattern variable, self *versus* collectivity orientation. My present view is that this was an unduly restricted formulation of an element in the organization of action components at the level next above that designated by the primary pattern variables. In fact, Figure 1, I believe, documents four levels of organization. The first of these is represented by the L and G cells, characterized by pairs of elementary pattern-variable components—resulting in orientations and modalities, respectively. The second level is represented by the cross-combinations of elements from each pattern variable set, as shown in the I and A cells; as noted above, these are necessitated by the exigencies of differentiation and integration of the elementary combinations. The third level is the combination in turn of all of these elements into the four subsystems which have functional significance for the system as a whole, while the fourth is the organization *of* the system as a whole in relation to its environment.

The problem of the self-collectivity variable arises at the point where the I and A cells are organized into their respective subsystems. Subunits are or-organized into higher order "collective" units, the prototype being the organization of "members" into social collectivities. This organization takes place along the axis which distinguishes the "external" and "internal" foci in these cells. The inference is that there is another concept-pair which formulates the other axis of differentiation. In the I and A cells this is termed the "instrumental-consummatory" axis, which should be placed on the same analytical level of generality as the former pattern variable.

The difference, I believe, between the two primary pattern variable sets and this other "secondary" set—internal-external and instrumental-consummatory —is one of level of organization. The secondary set formulates the bases of relationship *across* the two primary sets, as distinguished from relations *within* each.

SOME THEORETICAL PROPOSITIONS

These restrictions on combinatorial randomness logically imply certain general propositions about the modes of interconnecting the components of a system of action. As distinguished from the exposition of a frame of reference, these are *theoretical* propositions or theorems. We are not sure that all propositions which can be derived from the logical structure of the system have been exhaustively worked out, even at this very high level of generality. But the following propositions seem to be the most significant:

1. The nature of the hierarchy of control, running from the cultural reference at the top of Figure 2 to the physical at the bottom, indicates that the *structure* of systems of action is conceived as consisting in *patterns of normative culture*. The ways in which types of action system are differentiated, then, means that these patterns may be conceived as *internalized* in personalities and behavioral organisms, and as *institutionalized* in social and cultural systems.

2. It follows from this first proposition, plus the exposure of any system of action to plural functional exigencies, that the normative culture which constitutes its structure must be *differentiated* relative to these functional exigencies. These differentiated parts must then be integrated according to the four standards formulated in the I cells of Figure 1, and action oriented to the four different standards must be appropriately balanced, if the system is to remain stable. This is to say that process in the system, if it is to be compatible with the conditions of stability, must conform in some degree with the rules of a normative *order*, which is itself both differentiated and integrated.

3. For this "compliance" with the requirements of normative order to take place, the "distance" must not be too great between the structure of the acting unit and the normative requirements of its action necessitated by the functional exigencies of the system. It follows that the structure of acting units (which are objects to each other), as well as of norms, must incorporate appropriate elements of the system of normative culture—involving the internalization of "social object systems" in personalities, and the institutionalization of culturally normative systems in social systems.

4. Coordinate with the importance of order as formulated in the hierarchy of control and the place of normative culture in action systems, is the pattern of *temporal* order imposed by the functional exigencies of systems. Coordinate with the normative priority of ends is the temporal priority of means; only when the prerequisites of a consummatory goal-state have been established in the proper temporal order can the goal-state be realistically achieved. In both Figures 1 and 2 process is thus conceived in temporal terms as moving from left to right, the direction of "implementation."

5. A "law of inertia" may be stated: Change in the rate or direction of process is a consequence of *disturbance in the relations* between an actor or acting system and its situation, or the meanings of objects. If this relational system is completely stable, in this sense there is no process which is problematical for the theory of action. Whatever its source,

such disturbance will always "show up" in the form of "strain" or difficulty in the attainment of valued goal states. From this point of reference may be distinguished two fundamental types of process:

(a) *"Performance" processes:* These are processes by which the disturbance is eliminated or adequately reduced through adaptive mechanisms, leaving the integrative standards—the most directly vulnerable aspect of the structure of the system—unchanged. The process may be adaptive in either the passive or the active sense, that is, through "adjusting to" changes in environmental exigencies or achieving "mastery" over them. The basic paradigm of this type of process is the means-end schema. In Figure 1 the directionality of such process is clockwise relative to the goal-focus, from A to G.

(b) *"Learning" processes* or processes of structural change in the system: Here, whatever its source, the disturbance is propagated to the integrative standards themselves and involves shifts in their symbolization and categorization and in their relative priorities. Whereas in performance processes goals are *given*, in learning processes they must be *redefined*. Relative to the goal-focus, then, the directionality of such process is counterclockwise, from I to G in Figure 1.

6. To be stable in the long run, a system of action must establish a generalized adaptive relation to its environment which is relatively emancipated from the particularities of specific goal-states. To preserve its own normative control in the face of environmental variability, it must be related *selectively* to the environment. There are two primary aspects of this adaptive relationship: (a) the level of generality of symbolic or "linguistic" organization of the orientation to environmental object-systems (the higher the level of generality the more adequate the adaptation); and (b) the ways in which the boundary of the

system is drawn in terms of inclusion-exclusion of objects according to their meanings. The latter is synonymous with the conception of "control" in relevant respects. Control can thus be seen to be the active aspect of the concept of adaptation. The generalization here is that only controllable elements can be included in a system. The criterion for inclusion within an organized action system state is the action theory version of the famous "principle of natural selection." This is a fundamental generalization about all living systems, and particularly important for action systems because they constitute a higher order of such systems.[14]

CONCLUDING REMARKS

The whole of the preceding exposition sets out a conceptual scheme, as frame of reference and as theory. It in no way purports to be an empirical contribution. Dubin, however, speaks of the importance of empirical verification of these concepts, and of their promise in this respect. There is no feature of his discussion with which I more fully agree; but the reader should not be misled to suppose that this presentation contributes to that goal. Certainly a good deal has been accomplished in this direction at various levels in my own work and in that of my collaborators as well as of many others, above all through codification with various bodies of empirical material and the conceptual schemes in terms of which they are analyzed.[15]

It should be kept in mind that the six propositions stated above are couched at a very high level of generality, deliberately designed to cover all classes of action system. Therefore it is unlikely that these propositions as such can be empirically verified at the usual operational levels. Such verification would require *specification* to lower levels, for example, the conditions of small experimental groups as a subtype of social system. Only in so far as codification reveals uniformities in the cognate features of many different types of operationally studied system do the more general theorems have a prospect of approaching rigorous empirical verification.

This specification should not be assumed to be capable of being carried out by simple "common sense;" it requires careful technical analysis through a series of concatenated steps. I believe, however, that the theory of action in its present state provides methods for successfully carrying out this specification, and conversely, generalization as well *from* lower-level uniformities to higher levels. Perhaps the most important key to this possibility is the conception of *all* systems of action as systematically articulated with others along system-subsystem lines. The basic system types designated here as organisms, personalities, social systems, and cultural systems must be regarded as *sub*systems of the general category of action system. Each of these in turn is differentiated into further subsystems at different levels of elaboration. Any subsystem is articulated with other subsystems by definable categories of input-output interchange, the processes, in sufficiently highly differentiated subsystems, being mediated by symbolic-type mechanisms such as those discussed above.

In many respects, this possibility of dealing with *multiple* system references and of keeping straight the distinctions and articulations between them, has turned out to be the greatest enrichment of theoretical analysis developed from Dubin's "Model II." A "flat" conception of a single system reference which must be accepted or rejected on an all-or-none basis for the analysis of complex empirical problems, cannot possibly do justice to the formidable difficulties in the study of human action.

NOTES

* In connection with the complete rewriting of the first draft of this paper, I should like to acknowledge especially important help, both in discussion of its logical problems and the paper's drafting, from Harold Garfinkel, Winston R. White, and Carolyn Cooper.

1. Talcott Parsons and Edward A. Shils, editors, *Toward a General Theory of Action*, Cambridge: Harvard University Press, 1951.

2. Talcott Parsons, Robert F. Bales, and Edward A. Shils, *Working Papers in the Theory of Action*, Glencoe, Ill.: Free Press, 1953.

3. Robert F. Bales, *Interaction Process Analysis*. Cambridge: Addison-Wesley, 1950, Chapter 2.

4. Cf. Parsons, Bales, and Shils, *op. cit.*, Chapter 5, Figure 2, p. 182.

5. *Ibid.*, p. 182.

6. There is a pattern-maintenance subsystem *below* the adaptive subsystem in the hierarchy of control of any system of action and another *above* the integrative subsystem in the series. In Figure 1 we define L as the *lower*-level case, on the basis parallel to the usage employed in relating the household to the firm in Talcott Parsons and Neil J. Smelser, *Economy and Society*, Glencoe, Ill.: Free Press, 1956, Chapter 2.

7. Particularly in *L'Education Morale*, Paris: Alcan, 1925. Cf. Parsons, *The Structure of Social Action*, New York: McGraw-Hill, 1937, Chapter 10. This classification of meanings of objects has been more fully set forth in Talcott Parsons, Edward A. Shils, Kaspar D. Naegele, and Jesse R. Pitts, editors, *Theories of Society*, Glencoe, Ill.: Free Press, forthcoming, Introduction to Part IV.

8. Cf. Parsons *et al.*, editors, *Theories of Society*, *op. cit.*, General Introduction, Part II.

9. See Parsons and Smelser, *op. cit.*, Chapter 4, for a discussion of this concept; it is further developed by Smelser in *Social Change in the Industrial Revolution*, Chicago: University of Chicago Press, 1959.

10. Cf. Parsons and Smelser, *op. cit.*

11. Cf. Talcott Parsons, "An Approach to Psychological Theory in Terms of the Theory of Action," in Sigmund Koch, editor, *Psychology: A Study of a Science*, New York: McGraw-Hill, 1959, Vol. 3.

12. On the general problem of interchanges and their paradigmatic location, see Parsons and Smelser, *op. cit.* On the relation of the integrative interchanges to Durkheim's two types of solidarity, see Talcott Parsons, "Durkheim's Contribution to the Theory of Integration of Social Systems," in Kurt H. Wolff, editor, *Emile Durkheim 1858-1917*, Columbus: Ohio State University Press, 1960.

13. The most important attempt to use essentially this conceptual scheme at the level, as I see it, of the "unit act" of the behavioral organism is James Olds' interpretation of the S-R-S sequence which has figured so prominently in behavior psychology, in action theory terms; see Olds, *The Growth and*

Structure of Motives, Glencoe, Ill.: Free Press, 1956, Chapter 4. Another paradigm which seems to be more generalized, but even more precisely corresponding in logical structure with the unit act, is the TOTE unit presented by George A. Miller, Eugene Galenter, and Karl H. Pribram in *Plans and the Structure of Behavior*, New York: Holt, 1960.

14. These propositions represent a further development of the set of "laws" of action systems tentatively stated by Parsons, Bales, and Shils, *op. cit.*, Chapter 3.

15. For example: Bales' work on small groups; the work on family structure and socialization, including codification with psychoanalytic theory presented in Parsons, Robert F. Bales *et al.*, *Family,* *Socialization and Interaction Process*, Glencoe, Ill.: Free Press, 1955; codification with economic theory in Parsons and Smelser, *op. cit.*; and with certain problems of economic development in Smelser, *op. cit.*; codification with learning theory in Olds, *op. cit.*; the analysis of voting behavior in Parsons, "Voting and the Equilibrium of the American Political System," in Eugene Burdick and Arthur Brodbeck, editors, *American Voting Behavior*, Glencoe, Ill.: Free Press, 1958, pp. 80–120; the relation to various aspects of psychological theory in Koch, *op. cit.*; and the recent essays published in Parsons, *Structure and Process in Modern Societies*, Glencoe, Ill.: Free Press, 1960, the bibliography of which contains further references.

INDEX